Acclaim for John Gimlette's

THEATRE OF FISH

"Gimlette . . . crafts ripe, rich, witty prose and is clearly a natural-born storyteller. . . . A compulsively readable piece of work."
—*San Francisco Chronicle*

"A seamless, witty narrative that often rivals Alice's trip down the rabbit hole for strangeness. . . . Marvelous."   —*The Flint Journal*

"Remarkable. . . . Gimlette will become one of those writers you will search out. You'll wish you could read everything he writes, for he does so with wit, enthusiasm, empathy, an eye to historical accuracy and fairness."   —*The Decatur Daily*

"A . . . comprehensive history of these now marginal lands and the tenacious souls who have peopled them for five hundred years, hanging as if for dear life on barren rocks at the edge of a sea once filled with life-giving fish."   —*Los Angeles Times*

"Witty author Gimlette here does for Newfoundland what he did for Paraguay in *At the Tomb of the Inflatable Pig*. He approaches his topic with a combination of respect and good-natured ribbing, shedding light on a previously obscured land. . . . Another delightful and well-researched book by an entertaining travel writer." —*Library Journal*

"A lovely and affectionate travel book. . . . Gimlette sounds like a warm-hearted man who'd be a delight to travel with."
—*The Globe and Mail* (Toronto)

"A revealing travelogue. . . . John Gimlette fears that Newfoundlanders will mistrust his book. They shouldn't, even though the residents of 'The Rock' think it impossible for any foreigner to portray them accurately."   —*Literary Review* (London)

John Gimlette

THEATRE OF FISH

John Gimlette is a practicing attorney in London, where he lives with his wife. He is a regular contributor of travel articles and photographs to *Condé Nast Traveller* as well as other journals and newspapers in England.

www.johngimlette.com

THEATRE OF FISH

Travels Through Newfoundland and Labrador

JOHN GIMLETTE

VINTAGE DEPARTURES
Vintage Books
A Division of Random House, Inc.
New York

FIRST VINTAGE DEPARTURES EDITION, OCTOBER 2006

Copyright © 2005 by John Gimlette

All rights reserved. Published in the United States by Vintage Books, a division of
Random House, Inc., New York. Originally published in Great Britain by Hutchinson,
London, and subsequently in hardcover in the United States by Alfred A. Knopf,
a division of Random House, Inc., New York, in 2005.

Vintage is a registered trademark and Vintage Departures and colophon
are trademarks of Random House, Inc.

Lines from *The Shipping News* by E. Annie Proulx reprinted with permission of Scribner,
an imprint of Simon & Schuster, and Fourth Estate, an imprint of HarperCollins
Publishers. Copyright © 1993 by E. Annie Proulx.

Portions of this book first appeared in *Condé Nast Traveller.*

The Library of Congress has cataloged the Knopf edition as follows:
Gimlette, John, [date]
Theatre of fish : travels through Newfoundland and Labrador /
John Gimlette.—1st American ed.
p.   cm.
Includes bibliographical references and index.
1. Atlantic Coast (N.L.)—Description and travel.   2. Atlantic Coast (N.L.)—
History, Local.   3. Gimlette, John, [date]—Travel—Newfoundland and Labrador—
Atlantic Coast. I. Title.
F1124.A84G56 2005
917.8—dc22
2005044149

Vintage ISBN-10: 1-4000-7853-9
Vintage ISBN-13: 978-1-4000-7853-0

Author photograph © Michael Trevillion

www.vintagebooks.com

Printed in the United States of America
10   9   8   7   6   5   4   3   2

To my mother, Ruth Gimlette (*née* Curwen)

and to the memory of

my grandfather, E. Cecil Curwen (1895–1967)

and my great-grandfather, Eliot Curwen (1865–1950),
some of whose adventures are described here

Contents

Illustrations

Georgie Sterling
Grenfell poses in the bloodied pelts of his dogs
Trap skiff

Second insert

A curtain call for the cod?
The Narrows
St. John's
Jim Baird
The author, Hermitage
Joey Smallwood (Corbis)
Job Anderson
The MV *Northern Ranger* enters iceberg alley
Attuiock (Courtauld Institute of Art)
Grenfell's House, St. Anthony
Battle Harbour
Battle
The Spearing brothers
Albert Anderson
Labradorean sledge-dog
Chamber Cove
John Kelly
Petites

Illustrations in text

Maps

Unless otherwise attributed, all the illustrations are from the author's collection.

Acknowledgements

I would like to thank the following for their help with this book.

In Newfoundland—John Crosbie (former Minister of Fisheries), Lorraine McGrath, Kathy Crotty, Ian and Margot Reid, Carol Brice-Bennett, Dr. Hans Rollman and Dr. James Hiller at Memorial University, Greg Beaton, Rita Hagan, the Roche family of Branch, Gerald Smith of Dildo, Ron Brown and Martin Hanrahan of the Catalina fishplant, the Upshall family of Placentia, Bill and Iona Norman, Lewis and Margaret King of Change Island, Owen Hewitt and Jane Earle of Fogo, Mick Lane, Dr. John Sheldon, Leo Dubé, Myron Benoit, Mayor Joe Benoit and Leonard Cornect of Cap St. Georges, the Parsons family of Rose Blanche, Gladys and Andrew Strickland of Petites, Ken and Mike Benoit, Mr. and Mrs. Crewe of Sandyville, Eileen Kelly of St. Lawrence, Joshua and Lucy Thornhill of Fortune, and, of course, the heroes of Chamber Cove; John Kelly and Charlotte Kelly. I should also give special mention to Professor Ronald Rompkey; his edited version of my great-grandfather's diary, *Labrador Odyssey*, is rich in fascinating footnotes and proved an invaluable companion as I began my research. But, perhaps above all others, my thanks go to Jim and Angie Baird who, from the start, have made me feel at home, lavishing me with hospitality, friendship and indispensable advice. Any errors in this book are entirely mine and made in spite of their best efforts to educate me in the ways of Newfoundland.

In Labrador—Master Keith Stuckless of the MV *Sir Robert Bond*, the Spearing brothers of Mary's Harbour (Alfred, Levi and Albert), Andrea Cumby, Howard Fequet, Herb Brown, Gilbert Hay, the Rev.

ACKNOWLEDGEMENTS

Sam Propsom, Johnny Neville, Max Blake, Muriel and Claude Queval, Michael Earle, John and Tabea Murphy, Christine Ford, and William Lucy.

In Britain—Dr. Jonathan King at the British Museum, my aunt Elizabeth Savile (*née* Curwen), Yvonne Constantinis for introducing me to Captain Cook's Whitby, Sarah Spankie of *The Traveller*, Martin and Ester Keutner, the staff at the Northcote Library (Wandsworth), my agent Georgina Capel, and Tony Whittome and James Nightingale at Hutchinson. I am also very much indebted to my parents, Dr. and Mrs. T. M. D. Gimlette, for their help and encouragement with this book, and to them and Mark Wordsworth for their invaluable suggestions on the final draft.

Sadly, there are two people whose contributions I am now too late to acknowledge properly. The first, my father-in-law, Jack Bunn, died whilst I was writing this book. He was a constant source of support and enthusiasm, and I shall miss him very much.

The other person is Dr. Grace Sparks, who died in St. John's in early 2003. She had provided me with an invaluable (and often highly amusing) insight into the world of Joey Smallwood, and will be remembered in Newfoundland as an indefatigable opponent of corruption and tyranny. Again, it's a matter of great regret that I couldn't have acknowledged her contribution during her life.

But, as before, this book would have been impossible without the help and support of my wife, Jayne. She has provided a brilliant "first tier" of editing—not to mention inspiration, encouragement and companionship. I've repaid her miserably, with long periods of absence, first in Canada and then in the attic. There's much ground to be made up but I can begin here: without her, I can say there'd have been no supper, not much of a life, and certainly no book. My gratitude therefore comes, as always, with all my love.

Glossary

Banker	A vessel engaged in cod-fishing off Newfoundland
Blocky	Lumpy sea-ice
Brewis	Hard-tack soaked in water and boiled
Callibogus	A drink made of rum or spruce beer and molasses
Caplin	A small fish of the smelt family
Chickadee	North American titmouse
Chinse	To caulk or pack in
Connor	A bottom-feeding inshore fish, the blue perch
Crackie	A small, noisy mongrel dog
Crunnicks	Small trees or roots, used for firewood
Dene	A small valley
Dragger	A large fishing vessel, trawler
Droke	A small passage, cleft or valley
Figgy duff	A dried fruit pudding
Finner	A fin whale
Flat	A rowing boat with a square stern
Floater	A schooner-based Newfoundland fisherman fishing off the shores of Labrador
Flobber	Anything loose and flabby; the soft lap of the sea
Gam	Gossip, chatter
Growler	A piece of floating ice hazardous to shipping
Gurry	The blood, slime and refuse from splitting cod
Hakapik	A spiked pole for killing seals

Jowler	A seal-hunting captain
Jumper	A dolphin or porpoise
Komatik	A sledge (Inuit)
Lassy mogs	Molasses cakes
Linny	A lean-to or shed
Mish	Marsh or heath
Molly fodge	Lichen
Nanuq	A polar bear (Inuit)
Nunny-bag	A knapsack used when seal-hunting
Pip	The entrails of fish and squid
Pothead	A pilot whale
Puddick	The entrails of seals, whales or cod
Quality	The rich or upper echelons
Quar(r)	Quarry ice; a blockage of ice and slush
Redshanks	Over-salted, reddened fish flesh
Scrape	A pathway worn on a hillside
Screech	Cheap, dark Demerara rum bottled in Newfoundland
Scroddy	Small
Scrunker	A foreigner
Sculpin	A scavenger fish
Sculping	Skinning or removing blubber from a seal
Scunner	A schooner
Silapaaq	An Inuit (or Esquimau) smock
Sish	Fine granulated ice floating on the surface of the sea
Slide	A sledge
Slob	Heavy, slushy densely packed sea-ice
Stouts	Gad-flies or deer flies
Swatch	A channel of open water through an ice-field
Swile	A seal
Tickleass	A kittiwake
Tilt	A temporary shelter, tent or hut
Tissy	Angry, irritable
Trap linnet	A net used for cod-traps
Tucks	Tuckamores, scrub

Glossary

Turr	Atlantic common murre
Twack	To look around
Twillock	Fool, idiot
Ulu	Inuit woman's knife: a crescent-shaped blade, mounted on a T-shaped handle
Water pups	Abscesses caused by sea water
Wienies	Wiener sausages, hot dogs
Wincy	"To do one's wincy," to go as fast as possible

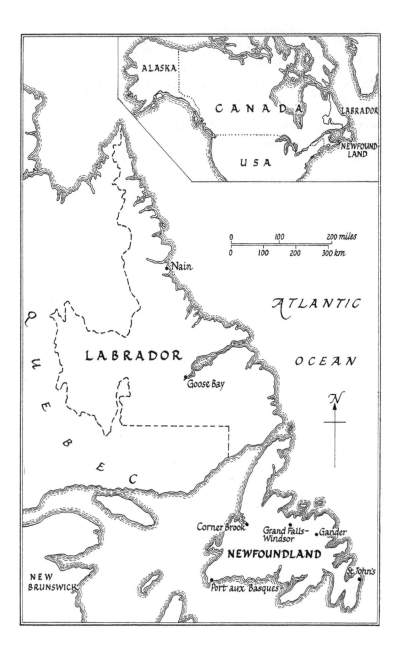

ALASKA

C A N A D A

LABRADOR

NEWFOUND LAND

U S A

200 miles

100

100   200   300 km

Nain

ATLANTIC

LABRADOR

OCEAN

Goose Bay

N

QUEBEC

Corner Brook   Grand Falls-   Gander
                      Windsor

NEWFOUNDLAND

NEW
BRUNSWICK

St. John's

Port aux Basques

Introduction

To those that live there, Newfoundland is, quite simply, "The Rock." This, with admirable economy, expresses almost everything they feel about their island home: a sense of isolation, respect, awe, dread, immutability and an affection that goes geologically deep.

It's different for the rest of the world. Some will be aware of a battered shape lurking on the edge of the North Atlantic. It's hard to place; its capital lies in the ice-lanes, and yet it's more southerly than Paris. The very name, Newfoundland, is redolent of late-medieval promise, but what happened next? Fish, perhaps, but nothing's clear.

If schoolchildren ever learn anything about this far-flung place, it's usually no more than the events on Signal Hill. From this ordinary square-mile of granite, the modern world seemed to launch itself. First, Guglielmo Marconi clambered up there in 1901, and received the first radio-waves skittering over the ocean. Then came Alcock and Brown in their preposterous aeroplane, and Charles Lindbergh, en route from New York. But this isn't Newfoundland's story, more the history of passers-by. As to what happened in the other 41,999 square miles of Newfoundland, or in Labrador, this is a blank that most children will carry into adulthood.

My own childhood was the exception. Labrador has been with me almost as long as I can remember. The reasons for this were partly ancestral and partly the result of my colourful schooling. From an early age, I'd been vaguely aware of a relative who'd sailed off into the ice, although when, where or why was unclear. Then, gradually, a picture emerged. The voyager was my great-grandfather, Dr. Eliot Curwen. In 1893, he'd set off for Newfoundland and Labrador, lands generally supposed to have been gnawed away by poverty and cold. With him—or rather leading him—was the irrepressible Dr. Wilfred Grenfell, or "Grenfell of Labrador."

I might have thought nothing more about this little adventure, but for my school. Mostyn House was still owned by the Grenfell family, and the headmaster was Wilfred's great-nephew. Almost everything about this school was unforgettable, especially Wilfred. He loomed so large that—for a long time—I thought he might still be alive and that one day he'd pitch up again, covered in snowflakes and fur. It came as something of a disappointment to discover that he was long-dead, and that his heroism was peculiarly Victorian—a heady mix of grandiose altruism, Christian athleticism and *Boy's Own* adventure. Whatever else I'd make of Grenfell in the years to come, he would not be ignored.

In Labrador and Newfoundland, Grenfell had found a corner of the British Empire where white Christians lived in conditions little better than savagery. It was a place ripe—some would say desperate—for his brand of Grenfellism. What started, in 1892, as a little light teeth-pulling and evangelism became, in the course of his involvement, an ambitious programme of social reform and medical imperialism. It wasn't long before money began gushing into his schemes, provided by a discipleship that stretched from the London docks to the New York Waldorf. Newfoundlanders, whether they liked him or not, would never forget him either; he was all over their stamps and their banknotes, and in their street-names. He would become an enduring symbol of salvation or—more dangerously—reproach.

Outside Newfoundland, the adoration was always less restrained. People were simply unable to erase from their minds the image of a wiry little doctor battling across the ice to save another wretched, lung-minced consumptive. The plaudits were unending. There were to be at least twelve biographies of Grenfell. He would even appear in fiction, leaping off the pages of H. G. Wells, Rudyard Kipling and Saul Bellow. He would be depicted in the Physicians' window of Washington Cathedral and would be granted the most exorbitant honours of academia; rectorates, honorary degrees, doctorates from Oxford, Harvard and Princeton, and the fellowship of the Royal College of Surgeons. The King summoned him to Buckingham Palace and knighted him, and more gongs followed; a gold from the National

Institute for Social Sciences, the Livingstone Medal and others besides. Even Lloyd-George found it in his chilly heart to honour Grenfell. He sent him two prize pigs.

My great-grandfather, Curwen, never went back after 1893 and became insignificant in Grenfell's greater perspective. But, in his diaries, there are glimpses of the Grenfell to come, and, better still, some unnerving descriptions of life on this coast. It's a sober portrait of an old colony—England's oldest, as it happens—but one still teetering on the brink of juvenile delinquency. To him, the colony's future seemed perilously uncertain but he never allowed himself to finish the story.

Curious about this half-saga and buoyed by my own well-Grenfelled childhood, I set off after them, over a century later, in March 2002.

The "fish" in this book's title need little introduction. Fish have defined and dramatised this coast from the very beginning (and by "fish," Newfoundlanders mean cod. Nothing else counts).

Poetically, if not geographically, the province owes its existence to fish. Newfoundland made its first appearance on European maps in 1436, as the lyrical "Land of Stockfish." Half-mythical, half-piscatorial, it remained a trade secret for the next sixty-one years. Then, in 1497, Cabot made his historic, political "discovery," and after that, the fish-rush was on. It's been a bloody struggle. Fish has been the prize (if not the catalyst) in some nine wars around Newfoundland and Labrador: six with France, two with America and one with the Netherlands. Generally speaking, it was the British who emerged with the fish.

Alive or dead, fresh, green, salted or cured, fish would determine the colony's destiny. Cod was, literally, king, often to the exclusion of everyone else. From 1633 to 1811—almost half the colony's history—settlement was either banned or severely curtailed, in favour of fish. This makes the modern Newfoundlander at least partly the heir to defiance, born of fish-thieves and outlaws. Even as late as 1817, the colony's owners—the great "Fishocracy"—were advocating that the entire population be deported and dumped in Jamaica.

Fish has always been at the heart of politics, the ruling genius. During the years of exclusion, the colony was governed by fishmongers, through their "fishing-admirals." Even after that, it was invariably the men with the fish who held the power. The island was divided up into six fish-districts, and ruled from London and Poole. Newfoundland didn't get its own assembly until 1834, and was an unenthusiastic democracy ("We do not suppose," said the island's newspaper, of its representatives, "that a greater set of low-life and lawless scoundrels can be found under the canopy of heaven"). Women, Labradorians and those on the west coast were excluded altogether, and would be for years to come (this was one of the last countries in the British Empire to offer universal suffrage). Nor would immigrants enjoy a share of the fish; a law in 1932 banned all immigration except from the best, fish-importing countries. Even Jewish refugees were turned away.

Fish paid for everything, and everything was paid for in fish. Even in my great-grandfather's time, it was still the main currency of the colony. Fish was used to pay the first school fees, in 1723, and the first taxes, six years later. A man could be a fish millionaire and not own a penny. For centuries it was an ungainly economy. A good harvest brought wealth for The Quality, and sustenance for the rest, but (as Norman Duncan once noted), the fishery is "a great lottery of hope and fortune." Fish money made in one year could wriggle away in the next. If the harvest failed, many could expect to face ruin and starvation because they had nothing else. Newfoundland's sole contribution to the World Exhibition of 1851 was a single bottle of cod liver oil.

Even today, fish makes a powerful impression on the landscape. Almost every community in Labrador and Newfoundland hangs over the ocean. Although these "outports" are often attractive places, there is invariably an impermanence about them, as if they might be abandoned at any moment, or sailed away. This is odd because many of them appear on maps over three hundred years old. The only new features are the roads that link them. Until relatively recently, many outports had closer ties with Wessex or Ireland than they did with their neighbours. Newfoundland didn't get its first road until 1825, an event that caused outrage amongst the English fish-mongers ("They are making *roads* in Newfoundland!" exclaimed one. "Next thing, they'll be having carriages and driving about!").

Inevitably, changes are coming quickly to the Land of Stockfish. The cod has now all but gone, leaving many the bleak choice of either the lesser species or migration. However, it's also over fifty years since the colony joined Canada (and a vast economy that swims along without the fish). For some, this union was their Declaration of Dependence, but, for others, it's been a liberation. You're as likely now to find a Newfoundlander designing rocket-parts in Toronto, as knitting nets in Bareneed.

Labradorians and Newfoundlanders, if they ever come across this book, are bound to mistrust it. Although throughout my travels I was treated with embarrassing kindness, there was always residual worry. I met few people who thought a foreigner capable of their portrayal. Perhaps that makes Newfoundlanders no different from the rest of us—we all want to be complicated—but for them it was more than this. From the very start they've felt used and mocked, and that the strings are being pulled from elsewhere. Most of the time they've been right. I hope however they'll be indulgent with me, and see this book as a whole. For me, it's the product of real admiration and affection.

Foreigners are perhaps nowhere more adrift than on the question of language. Even the term "Newfoundland" is ambiguous—and replete with tension; it might refer simply to the island, or it might comprise the whole province, including Labrador. There are plenty of traps for the unwary. A "catamaran," for example, is a sledge, a "goat" is a neighbour and even a "trap" is a trick for the cod. The current *Dictionary of Newfoundland English* runs to a bewildering 700 pages, and is a pound or two heavier than my English *English*. But, in a sense, the entire history of Newfoundland is there: you can find Old English, Middle English, bad English, both classical and bog Irish, Portuguese, Micmac, Basque, Breton and babble. If nothing else, the *Dictionary* illustrates that Newfoundland is neither truly North American nor quite European, but enjoys the rough waters between.

Whilst I've done what I can in these semantic swells, some explanation is needed. In general, the meaning of local words will be clear from their context but I've included a glossary should obscurity persist. I've used the government place-names, which may be disappointing to some (like those in "St. Brides" who prefer "Distress"). I've also avoided abbreviations, as Newfoundlanders generally do (they like a mouthful, and one should never say "Newfie"). Where I've referred to aboriginal people in a modern context, I used the names they use themselves. Thus, the group formerly known as the Naskaupi or Montagnais are the *Innu* (or *Innut*, singular), and the Eskimos are the *Inuit* (or *Inuk*, singular). To avoid confusion, I've referred to them as the Innu and Inuit respectively.

Where, however, the Inuit are referred to in a historical context, I've avoided a clash with my sources (including my great-grandfather) and have referred to them as the *Esquimaux*. Such spelling also serves as a reminder that the term is now painfully archaic.

John Gimlette
London 2004

Prologue

John is not yet firing on all six cylinders.
                              —The author's school report,
                                    Mostyn House, 1972

O flesh, flesh, how art thou fishified!
            —William Shakespeare, *Romeo and Juliet*

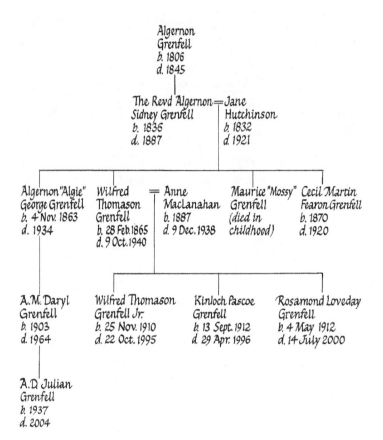

Algernon
Grenfell
b. 1806
d. 1845

The Revd Algernon = Jane
Sidney Grenfell   Hutchinson
b. 1836   b. 1832
d. 1887   d. 1921

Algernon "Algie"   Wilfred   = Anne   Maurice "Mossy"   Cecil Martin
George Grenfell   Thomason   Maclanahan   Grenfell   Fearon Grenfell
b. 4 Nov. 1863   Grenfell   b. 1887   (died in   b. 1870
d. 1934   b. 28 Feb. 1865 d. 9 Dec. 1938 childhood)   d. 1920
                    d. 9 Oct. 1940

A.M. Daryl   Wilfred Thomason   Kinloch Pascoe   Rosamond Loveday
Grenfell   Grenfell Jr.   Grenfell   Grenfell
b. 1903   b. 25 Nov. 1910   b. 13 Sept. 1912   b. 4 May 1912
d. 1964   d. 22 Oct. 1995   d. 29 Apr. 1996   d. 14 July 2000

A.D Julian
Grenfell
b. 1937
d. 2004

This story begins with a girl stripping down to her cooking-foil knickers.

"Jesus, Mary and Joseph . . . !"

She is dancing now, slowly, studying the front row through the glossy architecture of her limbs. Written across baseball caps is the story of mucky jobs snatched between the freeze and thaw; crab-packing, Kelly's gas pumps, the chip trucks. She oils her metallic knickers and offers herself up like a stand of silvery apples.

"Holy *Mother* . . . !"

A strange silence seeps among us like gas. Such nudity would be distracting anywhere, but here it's arresting. This is easy to understand. Follow these men out through the bar, across frosty Water Street and you'll come to the harbour. Feel the air, splintery in nostrils and lungs, like icy seawater. Look out across this great gulp of black, frozen, broken glass where the wind sharpens itself in the stays of old drag-gers. That thin channel through the rock they call "The Narrows" and—if you were to sail through there—you'd find yourself among icebergs, clunking and groaning in Freshwater Bay. Beyond that, there's nothing. Nothing until Ireland, several thousand miles to the east. Nothing, that is, except the sish and sea-lop of the Atlantic. No, Newfoundland has never regarded the removal of clothes as a matter of indifference.

More drinks arrive. "Six double Screech Coke!"

The stripper finishes her act by sliding down a pole, upside down.

"Tell her, Jimmy, *tell* her . . . !"

Down in one with a double Screech Coke.

"God love ya, me old trout!"

So it is that love—or lust—finds expression, safely packaged in fish and God. This no longer surprises me; beyond St. John's, sex hardly finds any expression at all. It is merely one of the complications that follows the removal of clothes. For many, it's still called "grassing," a hangover from the days when Newfoundlanders were packed four-teen to a saltbox, and a dry tussock in the barrens was the most exotic a girl could expect.

Our hostess is now in a mermaid's gown of silver scales. She moves into the audience, paddling in admiration. There are only eight of us and one is asleep, a packet of dog biscuits in his lap. I'm Australian, says the mermaid, on the road since 2001 and stripping my way home.

"Backpack and full frontal all the way!" she giggles.

A poor sense of geography seems to be drawing her into the Arctic. "But that's cool," she says. "St. John's is just *classic*."

She's happy at "Billy's Show Bar" and adores her regulars. And who are they?

"Fishermen," she purrs. "Sweet fishermen."

2

This journey began in childhood.

I can still picture myself as I was then, a scowling ten-year-old in a green school blazer, a slick of ketchup from cuff to elbow. In fact, all other memories of what people wore in the early 1970s have been overwhelmed by these blazers. Even now, I tend to see those years only as a period of pond-green and condiment. Mostyn House blazers could also pack some astonishing luggage and, in the photographs that have survived, I'm grotesquely deformed by wads of letters, Biros, calendars, plasters, Curly-Wurlys, yo-yos, soldiers and biscuits. I even carried a dead mouse around for a while but, before I could stuff it, decay set in, demanding urgent extraction.

Across the breast pocket of the blazers, we wore the heraldry of the school's proprietors, the Grenfells. No one could agree what the shield depicted. Three bagpipes? Three pigs' bladders? Three quivers? As the Grenfells were known to have made their fortune through well-channelled violence, most agreed that these were organs of warfare. After all, warrior Grenfells had popped up everywhere; they'd fought for the liberation of Chile in 1819; they'd gone on to serve the Emperor of Brazil; there were forty-eight Grenfell cousins at the First Delhi Durbar. But the most ambitious of these fighters was an early Elizabethan prototype, Sir Richard Grenville. So ambitious was he that he was almost bound to be slashed to bits by the Spanish, which is exactly what happened to him on a visit to the Azores in 1591.

A hint of military grandiosity had survived in the blazers. As we climbed upwards through the hierarchy of Mostyn House, badges of rank were stitched into the greenery; naval hoops for prefectural powers; crossed muskets for marksmanship; crowns for captains. Every morning we were formed up on parade, badges clinking, matron barking like a seal. A casual observer might have thought the Grenfells were on the march again, working up a little army in the marshes of the Dee. They were wrong only in one respect; the pageant had never really ceased.

This pageant was never more spectacular than in the school chapel. It wasn't a chapel in the ordinary sense, with priests or parsons getting a foot round the door—but every day was like a coronation. Every Sunday was a Durbar. Stained-glass light was filtered through glorious Grenfells, including Sir Richard (restored and whole). There were trumpets, halberds, pikes, more shields, organ voluntaries and candles as thick as your arm. A huge crimson-cassocked choir blasted anthems at the Welsh across the water, an attack sustained by a carillon of forty-eight church bells. There were scarlet gowns for the prefects (the admirals now little Lord Chamberlains), and black and rabbit fur for the masters. At the very crescendo of this spectacle came the entrance of the headmaster, Mr. Julian Grenfell, moving at a fascinatingly slow and stately pace, much as Sir Richard must have done in his slashed doublet and velvet bonnet. Naturally, throughout his entire progress, no one breathed.

Sitting there, looking as stupefied then as I feel now, is probably how I remember myself best at Mostyn House. I've hardly ever been back, not because I was unhappy but because I would prefer to keep the memories as they are.

Some of the detail is startling even today. In particular, I remember the plaque above my head in the chapel. "To the Memory of Three Noble Dogs, Moody, Watch and Spy." Behind this intriguing Grenfell curio lies a gruesome tale. A man takes his three dogs, animals he's had since they were puppies, and stabs them with a bone-handled knife. They fight him as they die and soon his hands are purple and meaty with bites. But, one by one, they are overwhelmed, the knife driven through the ribs, into the viscera, slicing through the hot chambers of the heart. Their master then peels off the dogs' skins and makes himself a jacket. Finally, he takes up the knife again and strips out their bones. Now, he says, I have a flagpole. It is a defining moment in the lives of all those concerned. Moody and friends will be remembered forever in brass. For the man, he was about to become one of the greatest heroes of his age: Dr. Wilfred Grenfell.

In this horrid story, there was hardly a calling, but something was there. The dogs had become part of my imaginative process. I had no idea that, one day, it would all lead to Newfoundland. Besides, back then, there were more pressing concerns; I, and the young Wilfred, had yet to survive Mostyn House.

3

Victorian Mostyn House offered little boys a stark choice: grow up or die. Surprisingly, few perished; Little "Mossy" Grenfell gave in to meningitis; there was one drowning and the usual deadly coughs. However, Wilfred's survival into the 1870s was truly remarkable—even more remarkable perhaps than the school's survival into the 1970s.

There were risks everywhere but the most obvious was the River Dee, which leaked past the school at the bottom of a vast sandstone sea-wall. In Georgian times the river had been a healthy torrent, flushing out the estuary and carrying ships off to Ireland. Parkgate became a breezy little passenger port, and the Mostyn Arms was the most ostentatious sign of its prosperity. But then the channels started to shrink away from the wall, seeking out the lush flanks of Wales, five miles to the west. This left Parkgate with nothing but a horizon of glutinous sludge, swamped twice a day by the discharge from Liverpool Bay. In time, even these tides became less and less urgent and the glue was colonised by wildfowl and sedges. By 1970, high-tides were so infrequent that even the marsh rats were taken by surprise and, for the sake of dry feet, they'd seek out Parkgate in their thousands.

We were never allowed on the marsh, a rule invigorated by terrible tales of quicksands, shrimpers sucked to their deaths, and rats the size of spaniels. Wilfred was under no such injunction and was always out there, blasting away at the curlews with a stolen muzzle-loader, pinching gunpowder from the coastguards and throwing himself in the currents. His parents, the Reverend and Mrs. Algernon Sidney Grenfell, seem to have been indifferent to the fact that their son was semi-feral, and actively encouraged his taxidermy. A century on, Wilfred's cases of stuffed wildfowl were still haunting the juniors.

In truth, Wilfred's parents represented the greatest possible threat to his survival. It wasn't so much his mother, but his father was a rapidly deconstructing neurotic. Although poor brilliant Algernon was an academic by inclination, even the experience of Balliol was enough to topple his wobbly mind. He was fortunate in finding a sensible wife in Jane Hutchinson, an older woman he'd pursued across the country, throwing stones at her window until she agreed to marry him. In 1863, they took a position at Mostyn House School, a decision that Jane regretted from the moment she arrived. Algernon's charges, she realised, were filthy, staring louts in moustaches and waistcoats. They knew far too much about guns because fighting was one of the few items left on the curriculum.

Wilfred was born two years later, in the chaos that followed.

Obviously, things had not gone well for Parkgate since being abandoned by the sea. In 1855, the landlady of the Mostyn Arms saw the last guests out and then hanged herself from the kitchen pump. The school moved in but did nothing to restore the village's dignity. Dressed in old army tunics, the boys fought each other all day with soot bombs and lime. Eventually, the proprietor sold the whole thing to the bewildered Grenfells and fled to Maidenhead. Poor Algernon—the effort of bringing his vile school under control unravelled him even more. Over his twenty years, the school numbers constantly dwindled, bringing on attacks of virulent piety followed by bouts of wallowing humanism. Confronted by relentless disorder, he and Mrs. Grenfell began to spend more and more of their time in the relative safety of France. This left Wilfred to fend as best he could with his surviving brothers, Algie and Cecil.

There were occasional visits from Algernon's cousin, the novelist Charles Kingsley, who was then Canon of Chester Cathedral. Kingsley was deeply impressed by the stories of drowning children, and even managed to churn them into novels. It's possible that some of his Christian Socialism rubbed off on Wilfred but I think it's unlikely; Wilfred—barefoot, armed and predatory—was beyond the reach of dogma.

Naturally, there were accidents. Wilfred blew himself up at least once. But it was worse for Cecil. He took a croquet mallet on the head, rendering him permanently unfit for anything except service with the Royal Marines.

The school that I knew was the product of Algie's genius for survival.

Algie took over Mostyn House after his father's occasional absences turned into a full-throttled flight from reality. Events had taken a turn for the worse when "Guv," as his sons called him, set off for Whitechapel, with a view to saving the East End from drink, syphilis and other evils. It was a crusade that ended much where poor Algernon had started out, in the lunatic asylum. On 18 August 1887, he wrote to Mrs. Grenfell from a nursing home on the Welsh coast, "My darling wife, I send you my tenderest love. I humbly entreat you to remove me from Dr. Tuke's. . . ." He didn't wait for a reply. That afternoon, he strung himself up from the bedpost and Mostyn House passed to Algie.

At first, Algie tried to sell it but couldn't find anyone fool enough to throw so much as a farthing at this madhouse. To stay afloat, Algie had to paddle and—in time—he and his school began to look impressively buoyant. The bandit children were drilled into cadets. The rotten parts were hacked away and the yard mucked out. There were even moves to attract the children of the gentry: a dining room, classrooms and running water. Gradually, Parkgate began to see the eerie shoots of prosperity. By 1900, whether it liked it or not, it was sharing a Grenfell vision.

Even by the time I got to Mostyn House, Algie's vision was still hard to ignore. His school had become Fort Grenfell, a huge mock-Tudor pile of crenellations, bell-towers, gantries, look-outs and last resorts. It even had its own water supply, pumping the stuff out of the Grenfells' own special rock. Inside, there was the parade-ground, called "Covered" (the last place one could still legally draw blood), and shops, workshops, garages, bakeries and darkrooms, all finished in a special Grenfell livery; pond-green and duck-egg. If it wasn't painted, it was monogrammed. Loyalty covered everything from the velvet plush of the theatre all the way down to our socks.

For the most part, events unfolded around me quite happily. Everything was announced in bells and polished in wax. There were huge silver trophies, the size of the World Cup, for relatively innocuous deeds like fielding and good handwriting. We got clean shirts twice a week and slept twenty to a room on horsehair cots. Not only did every day begin with a parade but, for those convicted in the morning courts, the day ended in a march against litter, called Parade Scavenging. Fighting was encouraged but not toys, money, knives or telephone calls. Surprisingly, this was all reasonably enjoyable. In the names of my friends are all the traces of a good adventure; Woody, Ratty, Wigs, Bert and Pickles. My memory of the adults, on the other hand, is less three-dimensional. Time has left them strangely caricatured; a triptych of walrus-heads, monocles, matron smoking her pipe and a grown man dressed as Rupert Bear. The masters even drove story-book cars—all back-firing and gig-lamps—and gave each other elaborate mock-titles like "The Colonel" and "Sir John." In retrospect, they were of course simply the courtiers of Castle Grenfell. Even at the time, I remember thinking that there was much to look forward to in the silliness of adult life to come.

It was hard however to love a school that treated food as merely fuel. I still can't think of what we ate in terms of its taste. There were simply different textures; slop, slab, stringy and paste. I realise now that indifference to food was not a weakness but a Grenfell strength. It enabled Wilfred not just to endure Labrador but to love it.

It was obvious even then that Wilfred had adored Mostyn House. It was the only home he'd ever have in England and he was a frequent visitor. He seldom arrived alone. Algie always had to pick him up with the latest, outlandish trophy—native weapons, perhaps, or some huge stuffed beast. These were the most grotesque aspects of my childhood—matty bears in the billiard-room, spears around the swimming-pool and herds of dusty moose-heads watching me force down my slop. It was not Labrador at its most inviting, and must have delayed my departure for years.

On rare occasions, we were loaded into old Morrises, and ferried into Wales, to Algie's old retreat at Nant-y-Garth. It was a little old lady of a place, tucked into the middle of a dark, chintzy forest. Algie's daughter-in-law, "Mrs. Daryl" Grenfell, who was by now as pale as lace, presided over a tea of uncharacteristic delicacy. Then, with the last crumbs gone, Algie's grandson, our headmaster ("Mr. Julian"), released us—screaming—into the forest.

It was on one of these delirious, semi-wild outings that we scrambled to the top of a grassy crest. There, to our surprise, we found Algie himself, buried under a wedge of Welsh slate. By 1934, his vision and rare genius had expired and, pinched with grief, his loyal staff had borne him up to Nant-y-Garth.

I have always felt that I'd have liked Algie. In his portrait, which hung in the tea-room at Mostyn House, he looked like my great-grandfather, Eliot Curwen, in his later years; warm, avuncular and thoughtful. Both he and Curwen had inquiring, challenging minds and both kept diaries. Algie's thoughts, however, were often so wickedly disparaging that he had to set them out furtively, in Spanish. Wilfred's wife, for example, would be remembered as a "miserable tart."

Unlike Curwen, Algie was doggedly sceptical. He declared that he'd been a devout atheist since the age of ten. There was no life after death, and piety was pointless. He believed that children, given the right intellectual and moral discipline, would find happiness in the world without the wizardry of priests. Fort Grenfell would be there to see them on their way. The school chapel was very much part of his design, which explains why my earliest experiences of religion were so curiously lacking in spiritual content.

If Algie had inherited the humanist side of his father's split personality, whatever became of the evangelist? For a while, nothing happened. Then, to Algie's disgust, it re-surfaced in Wilfred, about half-way down the Mile End Road.

4

The horrors of Whitechapel in the late 1880s affected its inhabitants in different ways.

Poor Algernon's nervous breakdown had been an unusual reaction, a little bourgeois. For the great, stinking, itching crush of poor it was more common to find their exit in gin. London was in the advanced stages of an alcoholic madness; 20,000 wretches a year were being arrested for their stupors whilst nearly a quarter of a million starved. Many just swallowed their bewilderment straight and then died of the shakes. Others embellished their drinking with spectacular violence, and every night the surgeons charted the vividness of their brutality; gun-shot wounds, a nose sliced off, a tankard buried in brains, a girl roasted in paraffin. Somebody was even chopping his way through the neighbourhood's whores, taunting the police with a catchy name: Jack the Ripper.

Wilfred's reaction to all of this—a blinding flash of religious zeal—was modest in comparison.

It was a variant of evangelism that brought Eliot Curwen to Whitechapel in 1887, although his beliefs were never in danger of flaring uncontrollably.

Although only twenty-two—born just a few weeks after Grenfell—Curwen was already a person of great precision. He was never someone to rush things, but always weighed up the opportunities and toured the alternatives. He liked to see his life mapped out before him, to follow the route he'd planned; from the family home in Clapton, on to Mill Hill School, a science degree at Cambridge and then into medicine. In the practice of medicine, he could see all the different strands of his vocation coming together: the commitment to public service; the life of muscular Christianity; the curiosity for science. There was also, some way off, the prospect of visiting China.

Rather different impulses had driven Grenfell into medicine. At Marlborough, he'd been "The Beast," a boisterous sportsman and an unpredictable classmate. Much of the educational eccentricity of Mostyn House had been thrashed out of him but he still wanted to be a big-game hunter. Then (as he always told people later) the local doctor showed him a human brain in a jar, and Grenfell was instantly transformed. At the age of eighteen, he pitched up at the London Hospital Medical College, demanding to be a surgeon.

Grenfell and Curwen—arriving four years apart—found teaching at the London Hospital in a state of transition. Until then, it had been a haphazard affair (only thirty years earlier, doctors hadn't required any instruction at all). The key to diagnosis had lain in the condition of the pus, whether sanious, laudable or ichorous. Treatment, on the other hand, owed more to theatricality than hygiene. Gradually, things were changing. The great surgeons in their blood-caked velvet coats were not long in retirement when Dr. Frederick Treves arrived promoting the novel idea that, from now on, surgery was to be conducted with science and carbolic acid—and rather more regard for the patient's survival.

Treves was a salty and courageous pioneer. In later life, he'd earn the nation's admiration for his service in the Boer War (and would be knighted for excavating the Prince of Wales's appendix, on the eve of his coronation). In the meantime, he had to grind his pupils into shape. Curwen was easy enough; Treves thought him "painstaking, conscientious and careful . . . a good surgeon." Grenfell, on the other hand, was "lamentable." He seemed to belong to the pre-education era and, in his first year, he attended only four of his sixty lectures. He tried his hand at Oxford for a while but came away with nothing but blues—for rugby, boxing and athletics. Within two terms, he was back at The London with Curwen and Treves.

There was plenty of work, plenty of horror. These were long days of gin and mutilation. Then, each evening, one or other of the students would visit "The Elephant Man," Treves's most celebrated patient. Ruthless neurofibromatosis was causing John Merrick to erupt in massive, foul-smelling cauliflowers of tissue. "He used to talk freely," Grenfell recalled, "of how he would look in a huge bottle of alcohol—an end to which in his imagination he was fated to come."

Despite Grenfell's indifference as a student, Treves liked him. Perhaps he saw in him something missing in other students like Curwen—a certain fearlessness, confidence perhaps, or just the magnificence of his intentions. These were all qualities useful to a surgeon but when Grenfell suddenly embraced a brand of breezy, outdoor evangelism not unlike his own, Treves saw possibilities. Here was a promising Christian adventurer. Already, Grenfell was flexing his muscular beliefs around the boxing clubs, and invigorating the poor with week-ends of icy water and camping. Now, Treves enticed him into his own favoured charity, the Mission for Deep Sea Fishermen. Curwen followed, some distance behind.

For Curwen, shared beliefs didn't necessarily give him much in common with Grenfell. His beliefs had travelled along the road with him from childhood, from the Clapton Congregationalists. For him, Christianity was a hereditary commitment. For Grenfell, it was a conflagration. He would often talk of his enlightenment, more an explosion than a dawning. He'd describe how he stumbled upon the powerful American evangelist, Dwight Moody, at a meeting in Shadwell and how his life was incandescent from that moment on.

Certainly, he never forgot Moody—and even named a favourite dog after him (which was unfortunate, given the fate of the dog).

Then, in 1892, Grenfell got his calling. It was a desperate cry for help, from Newfoundland. He jumped aboard the *Albert* and headed for The Narrows.

Act I: St. John's

In one respect the chief town of Newfoundland has, I believe, no rival; we may therefore call it the fishiest of modern capitals.

—G. D. Warburton, *Hochelaga, or England in the New World*, 1846

The settlement that has been variously described as the fifth province of Ireland, or less lovingly, a slum on the hill.

—Michael Harris, *Unholy Orders*

St. Johnsmen seriously believe that they are several cuts above just about anyone else, and that they can lick the world single-handed.

—Harold Horwood, *Newfoundland*

Beneath the charm there lies a bitterness. St. John's is full of disappointment, and is an exposed and isolated place in more senses than one.

—Jan Morris, *Locations*

5

I've suddenly realised that every one of my visits to St. John's began and ended with The Narrows.

This channel, no wider than a shout, linked the harbour to the sea. The gap through which it passed was like a crack in a sky full of granite. As fissures go, it was simply mesmerising. The whole city faced it, as if watching a door ajar. Out there was the weather, the Old World, shades of darkness and ice. In here, life had a more turquoise texture, and smelt of potatoes and fresh-cut pine. As a natural portal, it had defined the beginning and end of journeys for centuries. These were the most easterly rocks of the Americas and the beginning—or end—of the New World. The French, when Newfoundland was briefly theirs, had called it *Le Goulet*—The Throat— a name that was nicely sinister and functionally perfect. From its place in the hills, St. John's watched, waiting to see who'd sail in next.

I often found myself plodding round the harbour, responding to some primordial urge to be uphill, up in the rocks. First, I would climb through The Batteries, several layers of Victorian artillery; Inner, Outer, Middle, Upper, Lower. These old dug-outs had long been colonised by eccentrics, people living in driftwood cottages and flotsam. I always imagined that their proximity to the wild, gnashing sea had left them a little distracted. Their homes dangled over the black froth and they themselves were given to some curly pronouncements: "Inteligence not Educasion!" said a sign, or

"CANADA = NEWFOUNDLAND'S NEWEST COLONY"

Every now and then—and most dramatically in 1959—the walls above The Narrows crumbled, crushed these dwellings and swept them out to sea. When that happened, the Battery people reacted as all Newfoundlanders did in times of wrecked homes; they simply went out into the woods and cut themselves new ones.

As I climbed higher, the broader picture emerged. St. John's just about filled the foreground. Although I would become very fond of this city of planks and ship's paint, it told terrible lies about its age and size. It was not, as it claimed, the oldest city in North America (for that was to overlook—among others—Mexico City) nor had its population ever reached much beyond 100,000. But it behaved like a capital and, from up here, I could see two cathedrals, a Supreme Court and a miniature government.

Beyond St. John's, I fancied that I could see into the heart of the island. This was, of course, an absurd thought; Newfoundland is the size of Ohio or England. All I was looking at were the soggy hinterlands—the barrens—where Johnsmen went on week-ends for boilups, gunning and perhaps a little grassing.

If I turned and faced the other way, up the great gulley, I could see the draggers running for home, each beneath a helix of seabirds. At the end of winter, the horizon would be speckled with ice and, in summer, a crease of brilliant blue. Had I been here on 9 July 1892— on the cusp of Spring—I might have spotted the *Albert*, picking her way through the last knobs of ice, Grenfell on the fore-deck, troubled by the smell of burning.

Up until then, Grenfell was pleased with the course his adventure was taking.

He was relieved to be away from the North Sea and all the rotten teeth and dirty pictures. His mission work had been surprisingly unrewarding; four years of crushed fingers, casual drownings and ungrateful Norfolk fishermen. They hated his jokes and his insistence on washing and, whenever they saw him, they affected what he described as "a superficial deadening gloss." His attempts to shut down the drinking in Gorleston ended in failure—and contempt—and so Grenfell cast around for another crisis, one more to his liking. When news came through of trouble on the Labrador station, of famine and white slavery, he was intrigued. He volunteered to take the *Albert*, a hefty old smack equipped as a clinic, and run an exploratory mission. Treves agreed.

The *Albert* was re-fitted, with ice-chocks and a sheath of oak around the hull. A crew was selected but Curwen would not be among them. He was still trying to get to China, urging his talents on the shipping lines. The *Albert* set sail without him, in a glorious display of bunting, rockets and matching Mission guernseys.

Eighteen days later, Grenfell realised that there was a new crisis ahead, but not the one he'd bargained for.

St. John's had just burnt to the ground.

6

The city, I soon realised, was used to being burnt down.

The place was built on its own ash, its history one of ever more industrious arson. Three times St. John's had been torched by the French, once by the Dutch and once by its own Royal Navy. Even when the fighting stopped, the fires didn't. The great fires of the nineteenth century consumed five brand-new cities, one after the other.

Johnsmen seem to have borne these disasters with surprising equanimity. They even joked that the only thing that made them anxious was the long pauses between the fires. With each aftermath of dying embers, their response was the same; they were out in the woods, cutting sticks and rebuilding their city, as inflammable as ever.

This little, obstinate wooden city, sprawling before me, was built on the charred fish-sheds of 1892. Of course, some buildings had survived the inferno—buildings made of bricks and stones like the cathedrals, the forts and the governor's house. These places ought to have given some clue of the city to come but the Johnsmen wouldn't have it; they wanted their houses clinker-built and slapped in colour, like the boats they'd arrived in. So, that—broadly speaking—is how I found it: a fishing-fleet anchored to a hill.

Grenfell wasn't going to let the Johnsmens' fire distract him from his own.

Although two thousand homes had been burnt and twelve thousand souls left homeless, there was little he could do. Casualties had been light (three dead and a few scorched) and, besides, the Johnsmen had their own way of tackling the crisis, often disconcertingly venal. Even at the height of the fire, when burning shingles were floating over the city, off to ignite the unaffected, business was booming; salvagers, dousers and heirloom-rescuers. It was a catastrophe Grenfell could well do without. He wriggled into his "tight-fitting tweed hunting suit" and went off fishing.

A week later, the Labrador Sea had thawed enough to let the *Albert* through. Grenfell was up in Labrador ("Down north," in local jive) for two months. What he saw convinced him of his calling. Here was suffering commensurate with his enthusiasm—five thousand thready settlers, supplemented every fishing season by thirty thousand equally thready Newfoundlanders. These were the very people that needed him; hungry, loosely Christian and grateful.

Grenfell absorbed the possibilities. Although technically Newfoundland's domain, Labrador was not represented in St. John's and bore all the marks of abandonment. There were no roads, no doctors, no governors and little justice. A fishery maid could be violated without the intervention of the law and could die without the intervention of a midwife. In times of hunger, it was easier to kill a child than feed it. Relief was delivered with an axe.

In his imagination, an enormous Grenfell scheme took shape. At last, the ambitions that had run wild all his life had become an enterprise. The MDSF might take some convincing but, back in St. John's, the merchants were with him. Healthy fishermen meant more fish. Besides, Grenfell was bizarre enough to do what he said he'd do.

There was patriotism too. Grenfell would sail home and rally his fellow Englishmen. The mother country was coming to the rescue.

7

If the great navigators had ever heard England described as "the mother country," they'd have been in titters.

Everybody knew that there were all manner of sailors in at the conception: Spaniards, Normans, Portuguese, Genoese and of course the crafty Basques. Some even thought that the first to paddle over here was an Irishman—St. Brendan, in his upturned shed. For those who insist on comparing discovery with parentage, Newfoundland is colourfully illegitimate.

Politically, credit for finding Newfoundland goes to Giovanni Caboto (even though everyone else had been hauling cod out of its waters for years). It's a neat solution because it gives everyone a share of the glory. Born in Genoa, raised in Venice, enriched in Spain and contracted to England, "Cabot" was prematurely pan-European. Even the Channel Islanders claim him as theirs.

Beyond that, I couldn't make much sense of the voyage of 1497.

Cabot, it seems, had been looking for a short-cut to Cipango (Japan) or Cham (China). He expected a long voyage and took his barber with him. The *Matthew* was at sea for thirty-five days and then, on the Feast of St. John, land appeared. Troubled by the prospect of being eaten, Cabot dashed ashore, planted his banners and rushed for home. Although it wasn't exactly Cipango, King Henry VII was much amused by this excursion and gave Cabot £10 ("to him that found the New Isle").

Fame went to Cabot's head. On rather slender evidence, he was convinced he'd found the edge of "the land of Khan." He appointed himself Grand Count of the new territories, and made gifts of land to all his friends, with bishoprics for the friars. Watch me, he said, I'll bring back spices and gold. He also decided that, on his next voyage, he would be a little bolder with the savages (if there were any). The following year, he set off—this time with gifts of "coarse cloth hats and laces." He was never seen again.

It was left to his son, Sebastian, to finish this saga. Although he was generally an enthusiastic fibber, his voyages to "the newe founde Island" make skinny reading (his last trip ends in another attack of nerves, a "want of stomacke" among his crew). However, in 1501, Sebastian did at least come back with three savages, who "were clothed in beastes skinnes and ate raw flesh, and spake such speeche that no man could understand." He presented them to the king at Westminster Palace, who kept them for a while, as pets. When, two years later, they started to dress like Englishmen, even their appeal began to pale.

The Cabots' adventures are hard to enjoy. Newfoundland's grittiest historian, Judge D. W. Prouse, declared that the whole story was "as dull as the log of a dredge-boat." Others were frustrated by the fact that there was no certainty as to where they landed (or whether they hit the island at all). Occasionally, this caused lapses of realism—as it did for the Mayor of St. John's one day in 1930.

"Cabot landed right *here*!" he roared. "Right here in this bloody harbour!"

I wandered down there, to see what had prompted his conviction.

8

The Johnsmen were fond of their harbour—even though there was less drama now than there had been.

"I remember this place was *blocked* . . ." they'd say.

"Ye couldn't scarcely move . . ."

". . . every snot from here to zed . . ."

There were still a few crabbers, of course, and the draggers, hauled along by their seagulls. There were occasional warships, too, and oil-tankers and survey-boats, sniffing around for work. But the ships at the wharf had a weary, end-of-season look about them, that yearning for a long, rusty snooze. Even their names had an old, pantomime feel; *Northern Princess*, the *Funk Island Banker* or twanky little *Sibyl*. Every now and then a big-shot would slip in among them, a liner from New York, perhaps, or a show-boat from Miami. For a few days the whole skyline would be fabulously transformed by funnels and palm courts and then, its curiosity sated, the visitor would gather up its pac-a-macs and ease out—stage right—through The Narrows.

The city had done its best to fill the empty stage. Someone had put a train-carriage on the wharf, and a jaunty English telephone box. The old fish premises, the "rooms," had taken new roles with furriers and fancy catering, but on damp days—it's said—they still wept cod. Along the waterfront, history-boards described the shows that no longer ran; sealers by the thousand, on a berth to the ice; dreadnoughts on Coronation Days; troopships heading for hell-knows-what; freighters limping off the ocean, and colliers in a smudge of muck. Two streets up, these were memories to the older drinkers, their faces polished in wind and salt.

"All the best lies in the world," they'd say, "were told down here."

From the harbour, the town sprawled up the rock.

"It's like an auditorium . . . ," I suggested.

"That's it," said one of the old boys. "The greatest show there is—for free!"

His friend ("laughs like a seagull, thirst like a whale") began to hoot. "Yer freckin' twillock! Why then you're livin' in the cheap seats up at the top!"

"Aw, fuck ye, Tommy Doyle, yer shit-bag!"

Tommy the Seagull was right. The best spots were always at the bottom, near the fish. Water Street even showed signs of brickwork and department stores ("the oldest commercial street in the Americas," ran another fib). It had always been the preserve of The Quality, although nowadays they had to jostle with the riff-raff brought in by the sea—Black Rose Tattoos and the tarot-card lady (not to mention Billy's Show Bar). Gentility, however, had survived.

"Welcome," said the signs, "to the Canadian Deaf Festival."

One up, on Duckworth Street, were the slightly lower forms of life, the tropical tanning shops, the lawyers and the Indian restaurant. I spent hours rummaging around up here. The antique shops told the history of Newfoundland in biscuit tins and Jubilee milk-bottles. The best was "The Curiosity Shop," a name which—far from hubris—was pure understatement. Never had so much of the Soviet navy been assembled in so small a space; flags, bearings, wrenches, ribbons, white duck and gimbals. The owner didn't really want to see it all go.

"They were lovely boys," she said, a mouth of broken pottery. "They just stripped their boats down for me. I loved them *all*."

As I climbed higher, the colour intensified. Up here, both the poor and those a little richer enjoyed extravagant harmony: they all lived in outrageous stage-sets of magenta, raspberry, banana and turquoise. Upper St. John's, it seemed, was built for showing off—but not for ever. Nothing seemed very permanent. Every now and then, I'd heard, the garrison church had simply left its moorings and flapped around for a while, until the wind dropped it back into place. Everyone else just creaked and yawed. For those who could afford them, there were gables and fretwork and curly mansions called "Southcotts." For the poor, there was Rabbittown, which says it all.

Criss-crossing these strangely alluring human strata were the chutes. Despite all their tarmac and dinky handrails, the chutes were what they'd always been: lanes dropping straight down into the coves. In good ice, I'd be back on the wharf in flash.

What, then, might link all this with Cabot? Not much, I decided, except a huge swig of ebullience. The Mayor was simply exercising his right to be theatrical.

On my first visit to St. John's, in winter, a Portuguese trawler tied up at the wharf. Her crew were well-barrelled men who spent Holy Week visiting the Basilica and playing football on the dock. Watching them take delivery of trucks of wine and fresh rocket, they seemed thrillingly exotic, even in a town like this.

"St. John's is home-from-home for the Portuguese," they told me at the Duke of Duckworth. "They been coming here for years . . ."

". . . five *hundred* years!"

Everybody nodded as if they remembered how events had unfolded.

"Scattered times there was trouble . . ."

". . . but they never moidered us and we never moidered them!"

This was much as I thought. The Portuguese had never attacked Newfoundland—but had been the first to describe it. Whilst the English dithered over their "new founde Islande," Gaspar Corte Real was already on land in 1501, sizing up the trees and assessing the fish. Even his slavery was more ambitious than the Cabots'. He sent fifty-seven well-proportioned, green-eyed savages back to Portugal and then sailed off in the other direction and drowned. It was good enough for Lisbon. By the next year, *Terra Nova do Bacalhau* (The New Land of Salt-fish) was appearing on maps as part of the Portuguese estate. According to Mark Kurlansky's brilliantly-fishy history, *Cod*, the sixteenth century opened like a gold rush for Portuguese Newfoundland.

The aspirations of the Portuguese were, I realised, still scattered across the map. To the extreme west was *Cà nada*—the Land of Zilch—literally, "Nothing here" to its earliest visitors. But in Newfoundland there was hope, fortune, codfish and virgins; *Cabo de Espera* (now Cape Spear), *Fortuna* (Fortune), *Bacalhau* (Baccalieu) and *Virgems* (Burgeo). Vianna and Aveiro alone sent nearly three hundred vessels a year, scooping up the cod.

"They found us all right, and all the freckin' fish!"

Then, on 3 August 1583—just when Newfoundland's story was assuming a decidedly Portuguese flavour—who should sail through The Narrows but England's most princely buffoon. It was Sir Humfrey Gilbert, accompanied by a troupe of minstrels, a dozen Morris dancers and a Hungarian poet called Stephanus Parmenius.

9

Parmenius' tale is the story of a great poem that was never written, and an Argosy doomed from the start.

"Although I was born in the servitude and barbarism of the Turkish empire," he wrote, "my parents were, by the grace of God, Christians."

In 1579, at around twenty-five, Stephanus left the decomposing Pashalik of Buda, to investigate the Renaissance. Calvinism, he'd decided, was the shape of things to come. He went on a grand university tour, soaking up Zwingli in Zürich, law in Bologna and beauty in Florence. Then, in the summer of 1581, he was invited to Oxford, to study at Christ Church.

It was obvious that Parmenius was destined for greater glories. Despite his peculiar accent, he soon found himself amongst those that mattered most; the humanists, the brilliant refugees and the heretics on the run. At Oxford, he was—quite literally—in the thick of wisdom. He even shared a bed with a genius—Richard Hakluyt, leading light in the "literature of geographical speculation." At the time, Hakluyt was finishing his masterpiece, *Divers Voyages touching the Discoverie of America,* and, as the price of hospitality, Parmenius helped him round it off. The work was exhilarating.

"No situation, no people, no state have pleased me so much," he thrilled, "as your country of Britain."

All he needed now was a vessel for his obvious talents, an enterprise of appropriate worth. At that moment he was introduced to Sir Humfrey Gilbert, who—coincidentally—was looking for a poet to accompany him on his conquest of the New World. He had in mind an epic, something in Latin perhaps, to cast him in the same light as Jason or Ulysses. Parmenius seemed equal to the task.

Parmenius was flattered and signed up, a big mistake.

Although Sir Humfrey was not exactly witless, his enterprises had a tendency to end in farce. He was brave, and impressive in his ruffs and doublets, but he lacked the ability to see much beyond the first surge of glory. Too often he was guided by bizarre family mottoes about the virtues of death over flexibility. Whilst this lent a certain inevitability to his failures, it was terrifying for those around him, whether sailors, courtiers or creditors. The extraordinary thing about his life is that nobody spotted that he was "prodigall, impatient and enfeebled of abilitie and credit" until it was far too late. Parmenius was no exception.

Only Sir Humfrey's queen, Elizabeth I, saw trouble coming. She'd been aware of Sir Humfrey making rather a meal of the last decade. Although he was foppishly charming (and she occasionally threw him a bauble), he was also uncannily accident-prone. He'd lost all his wife's money in alchemy, and in matters of the sea, Elizabeth observed, he was "a man noted of no good hap." He'd enjoyed even less hap in his talks with the Irish chieftains, declaring his "dogges ears too goode to heare the speeche of the greateste noble man amongst them." After a while, he abandoned diplomacy, cut their heads off and mounted them about his tent. It was a flourish Elizabeth could have done without.

But it was in exploration that Sir Humfrey was so worrying. The fact that his ventures were backed by Sir Richard Grenville—Wilfred's ancestor—was an ominous sign. Prudence, from now on, was continually struggling with pride. Things went wrong from the start. Sir Humfrey's first foray, in 1578, set out to crack a few Spanish heads and claim America but ended up, adrift, in the Cape Verde Islands. Sir Humfrey thought hard about this failure and decided it was due to understatement. His next voyage would therefore be an odyssey of superlative dimensions.

Parmenius was on hand to turn the preparations into verse. *De Navigatione* tells of a Golden Knight, bringing light and order to the savage New World. Naturally, Sir Humfrey paid for its publication. It was about all he paid for. He was, he complained, deep in the red, "subjecte to dayle arestes, executions and owtlawreis; yea, and forside to gadge and sell my wyffes clothes from her back." In order to fund his venture, Sir Humfrey had to sell off America before he'd actually conquered it. Sir Philip Sydney was assigned three million acres and Dr. Dee got Labrador.

Somehow, the troupe took shape. There were five ships, 260 men (mostly pirates) and a German miner to winkle out the gold. The minstrels were hired to provide "musicke in good variety" and a pleasing accompaniment to the trials ahead. As an afterthought, Sir Humfrey also brought along the Morris dancers—together with a hobby horse and other "maylike conceits"—"to delight the savage people, whom we intended to winne by all fair means possible." On 11 June 1583, the flotilla set out, sailing first for Newfoundland to capture it with entertainment. They'd left a little sooner than expected because the crews had already eaten half the stores.

Parmenius puts a brave face on his Atlantic crossing. A voyage that should have taken thirty days took fifty. On the second day, one of the ships turned back with a bad case of "the fluxe," or team diarrhoea. His own ship, the *Swallow*, got separated in the Newfoundland fog, and the crew, now starving, reverted to a little therapeutic piracy and captured some wine. After several days of uncomfortable merriment, Parmenius was pleased to be reunited with the rest of the tootling fleet. Together they headed for The Narrows.

To his disappointment, Parmenius noticed that the harbour was already packed with fishermen, none too pleased by the arrival of a pageant. Some were English, others French or Portuguese. None were impressed by the conquest. The Golden Knight's triumphant entrance had begun well enough but then the *Delight* had snagged itself on Pancake Rock. The fishermen had had to haul it off, leaving Sir Humfrey somewhat short of dignity. If it hadn't been for his guns, he might then have been booed all the way back to Plymouth (abandoning America to an unthinkable fate). Instead, he clambered ashore and began to stamp his authority.

Sir Humfrey was as unlucky in government as he had been in alchemy.

His first difficulty was simply one of disappointment; Arcadia was proving rather less heavenly than he'd expected ("hideous rockes and

QVID NON:

VIRGINIA

Sr Humphry Gilbert knight
Heere may yee see the pourtraict of his face
Who for his countries honour oft did trace
Along the deepe, and made a noble way
vnto our growing fame Virginia
The picture of his minde if yee do craue it
Looke vpon vertues picture and yee haue it

mountaines, bare of trees"). His men weren't much impressed either and began to abandon him. The pirates stole a ship and tried to break for home. Others ran off into the barrens. A few simply lay down and let the fluxe overwhelm them. Even Parmenius began to feel a certain emptiness.

"What shall I say, my good Hakluyt," he wrote, "when I see nothing but a very wildernesse?"

Sir Humfrey's second problem was emptiness of another sort; his expedition was starving to death. He had no alternative other than to sell the colony, bit by bit. With so many guns, finding purchasers was easy. St. John's was sold off to the fishermen for marmalade and pots of olive oil.

On the third day, America's latest laws were tootled across the harbour. "If any person should utter words to the dishonour of her majestie," proclaimed Sir Humfrey, "he should lose his eares."

No one argued. They must have known this circus would soon move on.

They were right. The Golden Knight and his troubadour only stayed for seventeen days. There was little to excite them but fish; *"Piscium inexhausta copia,"* wrote Parmenius—"Fish without end." Most of what they learnt came from the fishermen; the white bears in winter and the mountains of ice. The Saxon refiner had no better luck; he found some shiny grit but no gold. Sir Humfrey decided to move south and conquer somewhere warmer.

This time, there weren't enough men to fill the *Swallow* and so they left her behind. Parmenius now rode in the *Delight*, along with the minstrels and the bits of grit. As they sailed south, they began to hear weird voices in the mist, and saw spectres that "scared some from the helm." Perhaps it was all that marmalade. Or perhaps these really were ghosts, an escort to lead them from the New World to the After.

The next day, the *Delight* impacted with the south coast.

The musicians played on till the end, "like the swanne that singeth before her death." As the *Delight* was prised apart by the sea, there was one last, great refrain of trumpets, drums, fifes and cornets, until eventually all that was left of their "jolitie" was "the ringing of doleful knels." Only sixteen men survived the wreck. Almost eighty drowned, among them Parmenius.

Although Newfoundland got her first dead poet, everyone else was the poorer. Hungary was deprived of her Camões, England lost an epic and Sir Humfrey lost the dirt that would make him rich. He spent the next day beating his cabin-boy "in great rage," and then sailed for home. It is a measure of his greatness that, even at such a time, he allowed his pride the upper hand. When he heard a rumour that he was scared of the sea, he decided to ride back in the *Squirrel*, "a miserable bark of ten tons." To his peers, this was vintage stupidity, preferring "the wind of a vaine report to the weight of his own life." It was also his undoing.

A few days later, the *Squirrel* took a sip of the sea and foundered. Sir Humfrey, now thoroughly demented, was seen in the stern, a book in his hands. His last words were his best, a fine end to the unsung saga.

"Courage, my lads!" he howled. "We are as near to Heaven by sea as by land!"

With that, the Prince of Fish slid beneath the bubbles.

10

I walked out to Cape Spear, the most easterly tip of the Americas, and tried to imagine the voyage home.

The mist was haunting. I took a track that lurched blindly along the coast, through a wintry tangle of claws and purple ponds. There was still snow in the hollows, helpless flobs of slush shrinking under the whip of March. Occasionally, way below me, I caught glimpses of the ocean, a rinse of grey, deaf with fog.

To early sailors, these fogs were all that remained of Noah's flood, the vapours of a vast rotting forest, deep in the interior. Some thought that the only solution was to set fire to Newfoundland and to rid the Atlantic of this rot. The fog worried them. It gave the sea its own scream, and was white darkness for the weird things that inhabited it. Occasionally, these creatures were seducers, like the half-fish, half-woman that went for Richard Whitbourne, a captain in St. John's, in 1610. She "seemed to be so beautifull, and in those parts so well-proportioned, having round about the head many blue streakes resembling haire." Fortunately, Whitbourne's curiosity got no further. His servant stepped in, cracked the thing over the head with an oar, and it swam off.

"Whether it were a maremaid or no," writes a rueful Whitbourne, "I leave it for others to judge."

Fog seduced, maddened and wrecked. In the three miles between here and St. John's, there were over a hundred ships de-boned across the seabed. Worse, the fogs could sometimes muffle the shore for months. "Down the coast," they said, "it's mauzy almost half the year. Some days, ye don't even get to see yer feet."

At Cape Spear, I stood next to a lighthouse made in Scotland and admired the blur. The edge of the world had washed itself of form; land, wan and shapeless; the horizon rubbed out; the air blank, howling colourless streaks, sparkling with cold. It was strange to think that, every day, America's first dawn had to struggle out of these smudges on its way to New York, 1,200 miles to the rear. Cape Spear seemed so much more an end than a beginning.

I crabbed my way upwards, fingers finding the pinky-black rock. At the top, at the cracked rim of the cape, I peered down. It hadn't taken the sailors long to realise that the fog was nothing to do with rot. The answer was in this sleepless, crumpled sea—the sea now boiling, pale and furious, several hundred feet below me. Freezing water, they realised, loaded with ice, was streaming down from the Arctic, turning to vapour as it embroiled the warmer oceans of the south. This strange phenomenon, known as the Labrador Current, had a curiously distorting effect: it brought "white beares" and "mountaines of yce" all the way down to St. John's—a city, as it happens, at the same latitude as Paris.

Ice and bears weren't all it brought. It also explained the fish: sequinned whirls of cod fattening themselves in the rich, black cold. Soon, the Atlantic voyage wasn't so much about reaching Cipango or the Seven Golden Cities—or anywhere in particular. It was about hauling Neptune's Sheep. Sebastian Cabot promised England the greatest fish pastures in the world, seas so stiff with fish they'd slowed his ship. They were easy to catch: huge, lugubrious creatures, too greedy to think or dive. Just throw out a basket, thrills Cabot, and haul in the wealth. Unsurprisingly, the English were soon pouring after the Portuguese.

Fish was not uppermost in Grenfell's mind the day he threw the *Albert* back into the blur. Nor, I suspect, were the next two weeks, heaving home through the November seas. The Mission had just spent £2,000 on his 1892 expedition—the equivalent of 166 little motor boats. Grenfell now had to persuade the MDSF to return him across the

Atlantic with more doctors, more medicine, and his own peculiar brand of Christian anger.

Surprisingly, the Mission was won over with ease. So too were the doctors.

Six months later, my great-grandfather, Dr. Eliot Curwen, was standing on Paddington Station. He had with him twenty-seven pieces of luggage, and was bound for Labrador.

I I

Curwen's photographs of his journey have fascinated me for much of my life.

Their survival is almost as eerie as the pictures themselves. They've emerged from a century of near-disasters: bombing raids, moths, puppies and three generations of jammy-fingered children. The latest outrage was pig slurry, a tidal wave of muck that engulfed my parents' village on an otherwise unexceptional day in 1999. Curwen's *Labrador, 1893* missed this fiery, acid stink by inches.

Although the red calf covers are now soft and felty, like a powdery face, the images inside are startlingly fresh. I don't know how many times I've been on this journey, on rainy days, half-terms and wet week-ends. I notice new detail every time; the fish-boys in St. John's, cocky and barefoot; a clock in a house made of turf; hands tattooed with lamp-black and herring; Esquimaux faces, as dark and shiny as chestnuts; a fancy waistcoat, on a man who'd killed his wives; a brass band in seal-skin boots.

The sequence begins with good-byes. Here are the Curwens at home, bonnets and smiles, nine in all. Mother appears frail; her illness worried Eliot and discouraged him from China. In Labrador, he'd be nearer home. He'd lessen the gap still further by writing to his family every day in the form of journals. "Goodnight, all . . . ," he'd write, as he packed off the instalments, along with drawings and sprigs of caribou moss. These too have survived the slurry and war, the writing furry now on thin, translucent sheets.

The next pictures are of the *Albert*. Curwen joins her at Bristol; her mahogany gleaming, books fenced in, swing-cots and an operating table, a plate of biscuits on an oilskin cloth. She sails to Swansea, streaming ribbons and bunting from her cross-trees. She never moved quietly from place to place. Every arrival and every departure was announced in rockets and flares and huge blasts of gunpowder. Like Grenfell, she was seldom unobtrusive.

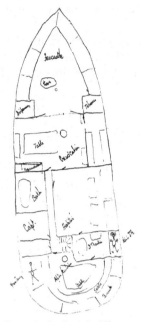

Curwen's sketch of the Albert

The Superintendent joins them, in seaman's jersey and Oxford blues, gazing distractedly beyond the camera. Grenfell looks tired. It had been a busy six months, touring the country, lecturing, selling Inuit curios on Yarmouth pier—anything to raise funds for his Labrador venture. Mostyn House donated a bed.

Then a group photograph; Curwen, Grenfell, an Australian doctor called Bobardt, "Piecrust" the cook, "Sails" the bosun, a handful of God-fearing seamen and the captain, Joseph Trezise. Here is a face that hates the sea. Once, Trezise had loved the ocean, had done no good and smuggled rum. Then he'd lost his nerve in the Newfoundland ice, three days adrift in a lifeboat of frozen corpses. Now he is endlessly sea-sick, his eyes sunken and his joints knobbed. He has only God and hard work left. Grenfell despised him—"An awful duffer," he wrote, "constantly afraid."

It's hard to know what Curwen made of them all. He was a man whose opinion of others tended to emerge as a series of clues rather than outright judgements. This was partly a matter of upbringing: reserve was valued way above appraisal. It was partly too a facet of personality, a need to understand his surroundings rather than re-shape them. This applied to people as much as to places, a quality that often drew him into the confidence of men less cautious than himself. Curwen was hermetically discreet. My mother, who remembers her grandfather well, says his true feelings were often only apparent in tiny modulations of gesture—a slight eyebrow, perhaps, or a sniff—punctuation that's not survived.

There is a pause in Swansea. Grenfell buys an unsuitable river launch and Curwen buys a revolver. Luggage was so much more impressive then than it is now. I had a few clothes, tent, air-mattress, camera, bottle of Scotch and several kilos of books. Curwen had sea-boots, an ulster, a leather coat (soon trimmed with muskrat), waistcoats, formal wear, nightshirts, knickerbockers "for scrambling overland," his medicine chest, a huge photographic apparatus (with everything necessary for developing plates), a tweed hat, a rifle and a box of "exploding bullets."

"2 June 1893—set sail."

There are snapshots of the next three weeks; harpooning porpoises, and games of cricket; Grenfell throwing himself overboard to fetch the ball; Trezise, furious, busying himself in knots and midday observations; "Piecrust" ringing the dinner bell (corned beef and relish); pickling a specimen of puffin; quoits and the ship's band. Then there was fog and ice, and the mood changed. Trezise refused to leave the wheel. An iceberg looms out of the mist, filling the shot with mountainous flanks of crusted sepia.

They edged forward—Cape Spear somewhere to the left—and then, suddenly, the fog cleared and they were in The Narrows.

The last frame of this journey is St. John's. The city is smeared across the hillside, lanes cut through the sludge of oily, black ash. All that remains of the houses are their chimney stacks, a forest of charred stumps. I can just make out the Basilica and the Anglican cathedral, its transepts gaping upwards through blackened ribs. Nor had the burning stopped; now the barrens were ablaze, and a vaporous, coppery sky was crumbling onto the city.

"St. John's," wrote Curwen, "looks like a town recovering from a bombardment."

The *Albert* moors between HMS *Blake* and HMS *Cleopatra* ("giant man-killing machines") and—from nowhere—the Johnsmen appear, thousands of them. Up until then, the sight of a city in cinders had been mildly disconcerting. Curwen now faces an even more alarming prospect; the survivors. Even at the best of times, the citizens of St. John's have proved cheerfully unpredictable.

To the crackle of rockets, he steps ashore.

12

On my first visit, at Easter, I stayed in a house a few streets above the landing stages. Curwen would have known this area as a field of soot but the following year, 1894, Gower Street made its sudden and exuberant appearance. The houses looked much like those I was used to in London, except that they were built entirely from pine, clouts and tarpaper, and painted like boats. Each had a very small, dark forest to the rear, territory bitterly contested by various carnivores long in fur and red in claw.

Some of these houses rented out rooms. The grander ones even called themselves "hospitality homes" (which always makes Europeans snigger) and had given much thought to their alluring names. Some were cuddly ("The Fireside Guesthouse"), others were slightly desperate ("Oh! What a View"). I opted for the "At Wit's Inn," not so much because its name offered the prospect of some amusing catastrophe, but because it was startlingly Victorian. There were runners in the hall, leather armchairs, bevelled mirrors, and a cream-jug on the table. I could picture Curwen here, unloading his exploding bullets in the hall and hanging his knickerbockers in the wardrobe.

It wasn't just the house that was poised for drama. So too was my landlady, Bambi, an attractive woman dressed in Lacroix commando fatigues. When she heard that I was on Grenfell's trail she sprang at the bookcase, frisking it for family history.

"My aunt," she explained, "was a nurse with the Grenfell Mission."

The pleasure of finding myself among such wholesome Grenfellians was, however, short-lived. Moments later, Bambi leapt into the street and shot off on an errand. It was an errand that must have lasted at least three days because I never saw her again. In fact, I never saw anyone "At Wit's Inn" after that. Apart from the bloodshed in the backyard, I was all alone.

This loneliness extended much of the way down Gower Street. For the first two days, I didn't come across anybody on the street at all. This may have been unusual for St. John's, but it served as a warning for the days ahead; there were times when it seemed that the human colonisation of Newfoundland was faltering. The pronouncements from Bambi's radio only encouraged this illusion; coyotes were making their way across the ice from mainland Canada ("Our children are at risk"); moose were eating their way into the city from the west.

"There are already beavers back in our ponds."

Whilst the animals kept up their siege, I kept up my hunt for neighbours.

Eventually I found one, laid out on his doorstep in an oblong of frozen sunlight. He turned out to be a mime-artist, thawing himself out for a little summer work.

"Yes, boy, I thought today would be snowly but it's alright."

I asked him about our other neighbours.

"That one there's an archaeologist (digs up rocks all day long). People next to him belong to Pouch Cove. . . ."

A long purple finger was singling out their homes. ". . . Over there, he's sick with the schizophrenia—in and out the Mental all the time (gets right tissy if he don't know yer. Some pitiful he is). That one's a cop. That one's never worked and that one's a shit-head."

I was struggling to keep up with the actor's door-to-door raids.

"Next door, she never eats nothing—so freckin' skinny ye could smell the piss through her. The one after that's got eight kids—and there's *none* of them that looks no more like her feller than I does . . ."

The pace got even quicker.

". . . Dead. Bald. Hospitality home. That one's after falling down the stairs . . ."

The finger had almost reached the end of the street.

". . . The purple door had a girl in Bay Bulls—told his wife he had a dragger . . ."

This was obviously a favourite. ". . . Now I says ye can't have your Kate and Edith. But the feller on the other side was even worse . . ."

I could see that the gossip was about to reach the end of the road.

"You seem to know a lot of stories," I tried.

"Everyone likes to gam, don't they?"

"But you know *everything* about *everybody*?"

He smiled wearily. "Yes, boy. There are no back doors in St. John's."

13

It no longer surprises me that the first of my new-found neighbours was so doggedly thespian. Since then, I've often thought of St. John's as a theatre overrun by its audience.

Everybody had a speech or a song or a little act. A few took their repertory to the pubs and chip shops, lacquering the walls with gluey warnings of the shows to come: *Getaway, Molotov Smile, Not Quite Sonic* or *Queen Sized SHAG*. But, for most, expressing themselves loudly and expansively was just a matter of instinct and, as an outsider, I wasn't so much a curiosity as a spectator. Dramas simply tumbled out of people, complete with prologues, heckling, applause and curtain-calls. I couldn't even get through Customs without a ballad of Trepassey Lighthouse, performed with all the gasps and roars of the sea. Teenagers dressed as gargoyles, and taxi-drivers harangued the ocean for being empty of fish. Even my bank-teller had tales of giant dogs and snowdrifts as high as your house.

"And if you want know what *really* goes on around here," she added, "ask the old mayor. He knows where all the bodies are buried."

There was no escape from these histrionic torrents. The great, wise Jan Morris thought that the personality of St. John's hit you like a smack in the face with a fish. She was lucky that it was only one smack. For me, the assault came in shoals. Stories seemed to follow me around and then, just as I survived one, I'd be enveloped in another. Most people talked about themselves, very quickly, very amusingly and without any apparent need for breath. St. John's was a city of show-offs, in a state of terminal loquacity.

For those who couldn't find me or anyone else to perform to, there were radio chat shows. Every morning, Bambi's machine sounded like a box of Atlantic seals fighting in Irish. VOCM ("The Voice of the Common Man") produced sounds quite unlike anything beamed in from mainland Canada—voices unrestrained, barking, anecdotal, extreme and often brilliant. All the best scandals broke on *Open Line*, although believing the stories wasn't half as important as the way they were told. The regular pundits were performers of mythical reputa-tion—people like "Captain Corruption," "the Million Dollar Man" or the fearsome, ferrety Marj (who worked a check-out till in Rabbit-town). Most people rang in about cod, the stupidity of government or the Prime Minister's Italian shoes. Occasionally, however, there was the unmistakable tinkle of surrealism.

"I'm just ringin' in," said one woman, "to say I've not been murdered as many people seems to think."

The Johnsmen, I realised, had inherited all the ebullience of the conquering Morris dancers. There seemed no end to their demand for attention. Small wonder that one of the most powerful *matadoras* of the 1960s Mexican bullfight was a woman of St. John's. Carolyn Hayward's greatest talent, perhaps, was in finding an audience that appreciated her for the qualities she'd considered only natural; brawn, blatancy and flourish. How many others, I wondered, saw themselves in a suit of lights, swaggering around to adoring applause?

Even the town's beggars would not be out-performed. Some danced, some sang. One had a vast hunchback of luggage at the top of which sat a chihuahua, barking directions like a mahout. Perhaps best of all was the Brown Paper Pope, with his brown paper mitre and his brown paper robes.

"Don't mess with me, Boy," he'd mutter. "I'm the fuckin' Pope."

In Curwen's time, theatricality was still in the hands of professionals.

Even now, people still remember the greatest of the troubadours. There was Johnny Burke with his bowler hat and pamphlets and his characters like Flipper Smith who ate seals and prowled the streets, streaming ribbons. And who could forget Professor Danielle, "Costu-mier and Dancing Master"? Whilst Grenfell and Curwen were enticing the half-starved, half-frozen Johnsmen into prayer-meetings, this "Prince of the Orient" was playing to packed halls, in his woolly tights and Graecian helmets. There was no question of *him* living in pine and tarpaper. He built himself Octagon Castle, a palace of tinsel, sea shells and satin. The Johnsmen were dazzled and, when he died in 1902, thousands lined the route to watch his stately "Egyptian" sarcoph-agus slide imperceptibly down to the Forest Road cemetery.

But the fire had seen the beginnings of change. None of the theatres had survived. From now on, congregation would be largely a matter of religious devotion. The only new playhouse to emerge in the years to come was the hall of the stevedores' union, the LSPU. I once tried to get tickets there, for *Twelfth Night*. "No, my darling," they told me. "We're booked." Booked now, as I remember, and for ever and ever.

This of course left St. John's with almost nothing by way of drama. Except, of course, just over 100,000 actors.

14

Whilst I was getting a rather eccentric reception up on Gower Street, Curwen was enjoying ringside hospitality two blocks down, in Devon Row.

This part of the harbour still bears the marks of spectacular destruction: ghostly, burnt-out plots of cinder, unfilled gaps and grassy hummocks of old masonry. By some miracle, Devon Row had survived the fire-storm. I found Number 3 much as Curwen had: red bricks, a brown front door and lacy curtains. Perhaps it had simply gone unnoticed by the conflagration.

It was a different story for its owner—although he owed his fame more to monsters than to miracles. Dr. Moses Harvey's life hadn't taken quite the course he'd intended. He'd arrived in Newfoundland forty years earlier, bringing his own stiff brand of Scottish Presbyterianism to an island already splintered by dogma and schism. Fortunately, his limitless curiosity—for everything from protozoa to "Atlantic Ooze"—saved him from a fate worse than bigotry. He became a Fisheries Commissioner, a Reuters agent, a correspondent to the *Montreal Gazette* and the author of over nine hundred articles. Then, in 1873, the waters of Trinity Bay parted and up popped Harvey's monster, twenty-seven feet long and with a mouth like a parrot.

Curwen got every tentacle and sucker of the story. For years, the Esquimaux of Labrador had warned of a terrible creature—the *Kraaken*—with countless arms and a voice like low thunder. No one believed them. No one, that is, until Theophilus Picco found one wrapping itself around his skiff one fine October morning. It was his son who saved the day. "The men were paralysed with fear as they saw their boat being drawn under the water but the boy of 10 yrs. cut off first one arm & then the other with his knife and the enormous squid disappeared in a cloud of sepia." With these two twenty-foot arms, the world had suddenly become a little weirder. The first arm went to the Piccos' dogs, the second went to Dr. Harvey.

The timing couldn't have been better. That same year, Jules Verne had published the English edition of his *Twenty Thousand Leagues Under the Sea*. The public badly needed a giant squid and Dr. Harvey had one—or much of one—in his bath at Devon Row. The sensation lasted for years and—to some extent—it still goes on: Harvey's monster is now and forever *Architeuthis Harveyi*.

Curwen could not have wished for a more congenial host. At the time, Harvey was writing the island's first guidebook, which became *Newfoundland As It Is in 1894: A Handbook and Tourist's Guide*. It's hard to see what there was for tourists in burnt-out St. John's—but forty years in the city had left Dr. Harvey nothing if not flamboyant. There is a whole chapter on the weather. The island, he promised, is covered in "ice jewellery" and "each tree has the appearance of a great chandelier of crystal."

Meanwhile, Curwen was struggling with the reality. St. John's was deeply mired in catastrophe. The luckier ones, he found, were living in flimsy "matchboxes," robbed daily by builders and carpenters. The rest were still camped out in Bannerman Park. There was only one hospital, a large grey slab built by the army, but without any nurses or operating facilities. Matron had died seven months before and had not been replaced. I went up there one day to find that the old hospital had only recently closed. Someone had painted "HELL" on the wall, a hundred years too late.

Worse, Curwen found himself overwhelmed by mud and ash. This was no ordinary sludge, as the naturalist Sir Joseph Banks had discovered in 1766:

> For dirt and filth of all kinds St. John's may, in my opinion, reign unrivalled ... Offals of fish of all kinds are strewed about. The remains of the Irishmen's chowder, who you see making it, skinning and gutting fish in every corner.
>
> As everything here smells of fish, so you cannot get anything that does not taste of it. Hogs can scarce be kept from it by any care, and when they have got it are by far the filthiest meat I have ever met with. Poultry of all kinds, ducks, geese, fowls and turkies, infinitely more fishy than the worst tame duck that ever was sold for a wild one in Lincolnshire. The very cows eat the fish offal and thus milk is fishy ...

Curwen was grateful for some new waders. I enjoyed the thought of him squelching round St. John's in his banker boots, and set off after him. He joined the Commercial Club and the Piscatorial Society, caught a trout and shot a duck on Murray's Pond. It was not tourism that was easy to repeat.

One day, however, he hauled his giant camera up to the cathedral. It had been designed by Sir Gilbert Scott but had always looked more like a cave turned inside out. Instead of bats, it was decorated with local politicians, all spouting rainwater in times of civic urgency. Six previous churches had stood on the site and the graveyard had been filled so many times that it now rose like an eerie soufflé. Anglicanism had never impressed Curwen. Grenfell thought it "highly ritualistic" and declared that The Church was dead.

The only photograph of that day shows furniture heaped up in the chancel. The Anglicans had believed the cathedral would protect their worldly goods but the fire was an undiscriminating leveller and soon everything was evenly charred. There was then the question of repairs. Scott's Gothic creation had absorbed almost all the 1846 Fire Relief Fund. Was the 1893 fund going to be lavished on its Gothic reconstruction? Grenfell had launched a wild protest, felling friends and rallying enemies. At the end of that summer, he'd survey the Episcopal battlefield with some surprise. "The Church of England," he noted, "is our most bitter antagonist. Alas. Alas."

As I walked through the Cathedral, I realised that Grenfell had been ignored. Splendour had triumphed. The walls had been scrubbed of soot and the choirs re-lined in English oak. New windows had been shipped out from Exeter, along with fourteen sparkling panels of C. E. Kempe's stained-glass. Only one of the original windows had survived. It depicted the Virgin Mary, a tear of molten lead running down her cheek.

A little further up the hill stood the Basilica, separated from the Cathedral by a little patch of wilderness and carnivores. It was just as imposing, giant towers instead of a stalagmite. The site had been cleared in 1839 by seal hunters, on their way to the killing grounds. The spoil, they say, had been carried away by fishwives, in their aprons. These weren't exactly tempting stories although, there was always some truth here: whatever the Anglicans had achieved with money, the Catholics had to earn by the sheer force of muscle.

· · ·

If the trees in *Newfoundland As It Is* had seemed a little twinkly, its inhabitants were flattered out of all recognition. Dr. Harvey seems to have mislaid himself in some mythical Arcadia: "Quiet, orderly, church-going," he wrote, "the people live peaceably among themselves." Perhaps it was an aspiration. Perhaps he'd hoped that Newfoundland would become the island of his guide-book, rather as Jules Verne's fantasy had turned into a real squid. Although Curwen was receptive to most things, it was not an impression he'd be taking home with him.

So how did the Johnsmen see themselves?

Most people happily believed they defied description. Others told me to go and see Bernadette McFie.

15

I first met Bernadette in her office downtown, a room immediately diminished by her formidable appearance.

Bernadette, like Dr. Harvey, had spent almost fifty years writing about St. John's. But whereas he busied himself with its tentacles and protozoa, Bernadette was a reporter of wider perspective. The entire tragi-comedy of the city had unravelled before her; the years of dicta-torship and the corruption that fed it, the Cocomalt and head-lice, the ships lost and the cars wrecked, Dr. Farrell in his underpants leaping from his burning apartment (and the libel suit that followed), the honey-wagons and the day the cod ended. They were experiences that seemed to have left her curiously expressionless. Everything else about her suggested armour; the black suits, the blackened, helmeted hair, the slow cantilevered movements.

I was determined not to be over-awed by the sheer scale and improbability of Bernadette and so I decided to greet her with a polite kiss. This, as it turned out, was a miscalculation because, as I craned forwards, pursed and blind, she did something I hadn't thought her capable of: she ducked, and her sudden disappearance almost over-balanced me. It was an imbalance that our relationship never truly recovered from. Although I would come to very much like Bernadette, there was an uneven quality about her that often troubled me.

This always seemed worse when we were driving around.

"I'm the best of old St. John's," she'd rumble. "Irish and working class!"

It was the fact that this was only half-true that worried me. What was she trying to say? When Bernadette told me that her father had died of tuberculosis during the last years of British administration, in 1946, I thought I felt a draught of chilly rebuke. Perhaps I was being over-sensitive, ill-attuned to a remarkable woman who believed her life had been one long fight.

Besides, in all other respects, she was right. She *was* the best of old St. John's; she enjoyed gossip and cod's tongues, flipper pie and pints of stout; she described her city as "ugly" and "grimy" when what she meant was lovable; she called her island "The Rock" but would have lashed out at anyone daring to suggest it was barren; she hated the winter ice—"as hard as the hobnails of hell"—but would have been miserable anywhere else. It was impossible not to share her enthusiasm even if, sometimes, it emerged as raw and bloody as a parcel of flippers.

I was relieved that whenever we went out, Bernadette brought along her friends: Doreen, Noreen, Janice and Roxanne. Like her, they were all in black and made much the same impression on the landscape. Unlike her, they tended to be more enveloping than awesome and so I found myself, quite literally, in the crush of overwhelming friendship. Together, we made slow progress from bar to bar like a small migration of ruminants.

To start with, everyone—except Roxanne—wanted to tell me how different they were from the rest of the world. Roxanne, who was twenty years younger than the others, was more worried about her wedding. She'd spend the evening in a lively parallel conversation, a light turbulence of cakes and invitations.

"There's no one like us . . . ," promised Noreen.

"We're not even the same time-zone as Canada . . ."

"If the world ends at midnight, we'll still be here at half-past . . ."

"Chocolate piping!" sang Roxanne. "Chocolate piping everywhere!"

Everyone agreed that at the core of every Newfoundlander was genius.

"We've got the highest proportion of MENSA folk in all of Canada . . ."

". . . we write more books than in any other part of the country . . ."

". . . the best music, the best singing, more bars than anywhere else in America . . ."

"And a white stallion!" bellowed Roxanne. "That's what I need. And some fancy white knickers from Toronto!"

More drinks arrived. Some sailors started dancing.

"Jasus, look at him! Doin' his wincy!"

". . . so freckin' loud in here I can't hear me ears . . ."

". . . that feller's looking for a knee in the cheeses . . ."

Janice was now next to me. She hated it when people mistook her for a Canadian.

"But you *are* Canadian?" I protested.

"Newfoundlander first!" she roared. "Then Irish! Then Canadian!"

"But what's *wrong* with being Canadian?"

I soon realised that, for most Newfoundlanders, the answer to this question was rather unspecific—and mattered only to an older generation. For the younger ones, like Roxanne, there was more to Canada than just fancy knickers. They felt Canadian, spoke Canadian and had a clear view of themselves living in mainland homes, earning mainland money.

Older people had found it harder to become Canadian. Some remembered the island as a British colony—even though fifty years had passed since confederation, and flying the Union Jack was now more a matter of mild rebellion than loyalty. Others remembered the hungry 1950s and '60s, arriving skinny and illiterate in Ontario, begging for the dirtiest work, mocked for their clothes and their outlandish accents. They remembered too the decades of "Newfie" jokes that followed, Canadian audiences yelping themselves hoarse at the witless, snaggle-toothed oafs inhabiting their unspeakable outer margins. For them, relations with Canada had settled down to low-grade resentment, kindled every now and then by a belief that the Canadians had eaten all their fish.

"And they come here expecting to find *Indians!*" added Bernadette.

Whether this was true or not, Canadian visitors were in for a surprise. I had often seen them lurking around the tourist areas, trying hard to feel at home. "What do people do here?" they asked. "Do you have television?" They found it difficult to believe that they were still in the same country they'd left five hours ago. This was more like Europe or some other crazy place, shockingly uninhibited and always on the brink of something unpredictable. For people brought up with such a strong sense of proportion, the drama of St. John's was unnecessary—and unnerving.

Not that they dared complain.

Or patronise. St. John's was a city of Bernadettes and Doreens, all ready to flare at the least whiff of condescension. "People need to know," said Doreen, "that we're not quaint, we're not cute and we're not feckin' pixies."

Everybody, it seemed, felt the same. When, a few days later, the mainland's *Globe & Mail* ran a tiny piece suggesting that Newfoundland was otherworldly, the response from St. John's was cyclonic; it took four days to print out all the anger.

> "St. John's," wrote one man, "is actually a key transatlantic point in the world. We thusly [sic] are not 'in the middle of nowhere' but a prime cross-roads of the world, connecting Europe to North America and vice-versa . . ."

Even the city's historians were at its defences, blasting away at the outside world. Writers like Judge Prowse—normally boisterous, chatty and happily irreverent—had been vicious in his defence of Newfoundland. Not much had changed in a hundred years. Nowadays, one Kevin Major delights readers with the darts he scatters among his Newfoundlanders (venal politicians, idiotic architects and indifferent writers), but at the first sight of foreign snipers, his tone turns savage. Suddenly, all guns are on the "patronising drivel of the English upper crust."

"We're not good," warned Bernadette, "with people from aways tellin' us how things are."

"You will be nice about us?" said Noreen sweetly. "Won't you?"

Roxanne rose from among the ribbons and lists.

"And perhaps we'll even see you on the big day?"

16

There are few statues in St. John's because the Johnsmen have never been able to agree who is the greatest of them all.

Like the rock it sat on, the city was riven with faults and fissures. For centuries, Catholics and Protestants had ground against each other, forging heat and occasionally sparks. There were also the rifts between the English and the Irish, the Irish and the Scots, confederates and patriots, and the Liberals and the Tories. Then, criss-crossing these fragmented strata, was a general contempt for anybody from the hinterlands—the Baymen. Not long ago, any hick showing up at the university found himself in elocution classes, whether he wanted refining or not. Johnsmen tended to think of beyond the barrens as beyond the pale.

Bernadette was no exception. She could still recall the slap of seal-skin boots on cobbles. "We called them the Skinny Wops. It was a name that stuck for years."

Unsurprisingly, there were new cracks appearing all the time, like the hairline fracture between the generations. But the oldest and most persistent of the flaws was the most intriguing of all. It was a subject that made Bernadette shudder as if she'd been caught in an un-expected squall. This happened every time we drove along Circular Road.

"See these houses?" she growled. "These people think they shit Dixie Cups. Have you ever seen such pretension?"

The houses were Victorian, a little curlier, the paint fresher perhaps. Some had gingerbread gables, and I might have caught a glimpse of tiny chandeliers. But it was hardly extravagance.

"Every one of these houses was made in England," she continued. "Dismantled, numbered, shipped over here—and reassembled for the merchants!"

I tried to sound impressed, as if I believed this.

"I used to come up here as a child," she said absently, "and steal their apples."

But Bernadette's grudge extended well beyond her childhood. She was digging away at a seam of discontent that stretched back to the origins of the colony. The rich had even retained their Shakespearean tag—The Merchants—a sure sign of the mythology at large. For many Newfoundlanders, the merchant was a sort of a sub-Arctic Shylock, draining honest fishermen of their credit and their health. This merci-less oligarchy now lived in giant doll's-houses on the hill, a life of ungodly extravagance.

The difficulty for outsiders was that there was never much evidence of wealth. Even now there were few home-grown millionaires. In Curwen's time the merchants were never more than middle-class, one eye on their social standing, the other on the price of fish. Their power frightened no one. People called them "The Fishocracy."

Grenfell was disappointed. How could social injustice be so paro-chial? "It is most odd," he wrote, "to go and look for the Prime Minister behind a grocer's counter, or a Colonial Secretary selling boots but such is the case & one learns to be surprised at nothing."

Surprising or not, things seemed much the same a century on. It was still possible to bump into politicians just by wandering around. In time, I'd meet the Premier, half a dozen ministers and the Attorney-General. Even odder, all the old fishocratic families were still out there, somewhere near the helm; the Hickmans, Ayres, Bairds, Bowrings and Crosbies. To Bernadette, this was simply the tail-end of the same old junta.

"Look at our Court of Appeal," she said. "It's just a golf club."

Such deeply faulted rock makes for poor statues.

As I made my way around the city, I counted only three. Perhaps they represented the only points on which the Johnsmen could agree.

There was gratitude to Corte Real for leaving them alone.

Then there was "The Fighting Newfoundlander," which was how everyone felt.

Finally, there was Peter Pan.

Time may be moving on, he seemed to say, but we haven't changed an inch.

17

At the heart of the world's only fishocracy was a palace as purple and black as a month of storms. It was the only palace the island had ever had, hewn from its own rock, hated, loved, mocked and occasionally pelted. People liked to imagine that Government House had been a mistake from the start, that it had been intended for Bermuda and that the moat around it was a trap for snakes. The idea of government was always faintly amusing and now here was a building that looked much as the governors had: alone, awkward and besieged. Any remaining dignity had been despatched with an artful swipe from old Judge Prowse.

"Government House," he declared, "is a huge pile of unredeemed ugliness."

I walked up there one day, following the ghostly, ancestral squelch of waders.

The palace was set in a large well-trained shrubbery that would have reminded the governors of England. They'd even cultivated home-sickness in their choice of trees—oaks, elms, hawthorns and horse-chestnuts—twice as many species here as in the rest of the island put together. To me, it felt almost like home but with more light, more rock, more of everything. Every summer, I'd read, the great and good were paraded into this little forest, thanked, flattered and plumped up on lemonade, ham, tea, eggs and cakes. Medals were given out and The Boys' Bands played. Six thousand biscuits later, everyone sang *God Save the Queen* and *Ode to Newfoundland* before wandering back down the hill. With tea parties like this, republicanism hadn't stood a chance.

There was once a time when the chances of survival hadn't looked so good for the governors themselves. The first of them had been admirals who'd stayed on their ships, reluctant to put so much as a toe in this stinking midden heap. In 1817 a residence was found, but it proved murderously damp. Half-way through that long mildewed winter, the governor simply coughed himself to pieces and had to be scooped into a puncheon of rum. It took his funeral ship three weeks to hack its way out of the iced-up harbour.

Before there could be any more pickling, a solution had to be found. It was a Grenfell moment, a point in Newfoundland history so desperate that wild extravagance seemed suddenly sensible. This time the saviour was Captain Sir Thomas Cochrane. Descended from Scottish pirates, Cochranes had cropped up wherever there was fighting, from Yorktown to Chile. Sir Thomas was congenitally irrepressible and now threatened to take Newfoundland by the scruff—as long as he could have his palace.

When it came to lavish gestures, he disappointed no one. He imported twenty-five carpenters and twenty-eight masons from Scotland, and had all the quoins, jambs and lintels finished in Portland stone. Then, in case anybody thought they'd sighted completion, he'd turn his plans inside out, tear out the chimney-stacks and punch new doors through the dining-room. Sky-lights came and went, and a new wing erupted on one side. When he'd used up his budget of £9,000, Cochrane used it up again—and again and again. The house was finally completed in 1831, a year after the White House, Washington, and at four times the cost. Completion, however, was not the end. Soon afterwards, the roof blew off and the roofers were back again, enjoying another budget.

Although Cochrane would leave Newfoundland under a hail of Catholic rocks and mud, his rule is generally reckoned to have been a triumph. Perhaps he simply compared well with the dross that followed. One of his successors had a son who was shot whilst out on a burglary. Another had been such a busy-body that he'd even come out to supervise the burning of his own effigy. Worse still was Sir Anthony Musgrave. For five years, Government House became a bawdy house of "licentious revels" until, in 1869, the unbuckling governor was hauled back home.

For a moment, my visit looked as if it might turn into a sex tour of nineteenth-century royalty.

My guide was a wiry lady from the historical society. Curwen had enjoyed the company of the governor himself, but this was now harder to arrange. The present incumbent—called the Lieutenant-Governor these days—was a neurologist. He was always busy, seeing patients, touring the province, pinning medals—and cancelling our meetings. Eventually, he handed me over to the steely Miss Storey.

As it turned out, Miss Storey was only momentarily terrifying. A slightly ferocious look had served her well during her years as Director of Nursing, and now she wore it with lipstick. The terror was mostly illusory and I soon found myself drawn into a sort of conspiracy, as if neither of us should have been there. This was partly because Miss Storey was disconcertingly irreverent. She knew much about the house and everything about who'd slept there. I'd been quite wrong to hear only imperialism in her vowels; she was thrillingly democratic.

"Take all the photographs you want!" she told me. "This is public property."

We started in the hall. If Cochrane's palace had looked a bit lumpy on the outside, inside it was exorbitantly fancy. There were skylights and fanlights, flying staircases, battle-ragged flags, columns, frescoes, acres of well-groomed scarlet and a stand of silver caribou. It was a house designed by an adventurer for gentlemen. Through colossal doorways, I could make out a series of interconnecting reception rooms, all looped and swagged and silkily papered. In one of them, a piano-tuner was teasing harmonies out of the grandest of grands.

Above us, along the walls, hung a collection of Miss Storey's Great Philanderers.

"This is George IV," she said, "who was with Mrs. Fitzherbert."

There were tuts of pleasure and disapproval.

Miss Storey then rounded on William IV. "Know him? The Sailor King?"

"Well, yes . . ."

"Another scamp. He had ten illegitimate children in London and still got up to no good with our girls . . ."

More tutting and we found ourselves before a full-length Edward VII.

"Him too," said Miss Storey. "Fathered a few in Newfoundland."

There was even scandal in the ceiling. The frescoes had been painted by a Polish convict, convicted of forgery. In 1880, he'd agreed to commute his time in the St. John's Penitentiary in return for some artwork. Creativity had also provided a welcome opportunity for a little seduction. Or perhaps the scurrility of Government House had simply got to him. Either way, the housemaid in question still peers out of the acanthus leaves, as naïve now as she was then.

From the hall, we descended into the basement. Down there, we found the kitchens, half a dozen housemaids and a stuffed tiger.

The place is haunted, said the maids.

"I've seen all sorts funny in the last thirty years," reported the eldest. "Gongs ringing . . ."

". . . a lady on the flying staircase . . ."

Another had seen one of the old boys, on his way to an assignation in the scullery. Even the ghosts of Government House, it seemed, were maddened by the itch.

None of this impressed itself on Curwen. He often came down here to develop photographs with the governor, Sir Terence O'Brien. Although, in describing O'Brien, Curwen was typically oblique ("hearty, blunt but very friendly and portly"), the two men found friendship of sorts in their photography. Together they spent hours in the darkroom, Curwen absorbing the gossip, almost without realising what he had. "It must be very dull, poor man, for very little goes on here and he has no hobby but photography."

But, for O'Brien, the darkroom was more than a hobby. His stories were suffused with despair. He was in a state of advanced political collapse. The darkness was a comfort to him, a retreat.

"The people here," he told Curwen, "think of nothing but fish."

18

I sat in the dining room and considered the Governor's fear of fish.

Curwen had often sat here, through lunches that sometimes roamed into the early evening. Had O'Brien's darkroom talk ever resurfaced here, in a crueller light? Probably not, although here was a room with a strategic air, worthy of the island's catastrophes. Most of the furnishings had been salvaged from warships. Even the wine-coolers had giant brass eyes so they could be lashed down in times of trouble. There was privacy too; vast mahogany doors, double-layered, to shut out the inquisitive.

Curwen describes the Governor's torment with Boswellian detachment. Part of the problem was that, as a veteran of India, O'Brien was outraged by the insolence of the Atlantic. "The question does not rest on the governor's individual judgement," he once snapped at his superiors. "It is one dependent on the conditions of the ice."

It wasn't just the weather that made him feel powerless. He was commander-in-chief of an army of nothing, the last soldier having left twenty years before. With half the population sympathetic to the Irish rebels and the other half sliding into bankruptcy, O'Brien had every reason to feel edgy. He told Curwen he was constantly haunted by the prospect of an uprising—a miniature war to be fought with fire, hooks and sculping knives.

Even without insurrection, Newfoundland was ungovernable. Its obstinate, unfathomable people were strung out over six thousand miles of coastline, in hundreds of outports. For most of the winter they were unreachable, and they fed their fears with rumours and speculation. Not that newspapers would have helped. "Here, the press is at its lowest ebb," lamented O'Brien, "and is used mainly as the vehicle of personal abuse, or of vindictive political recriminations."

It was hard, however, to know which was the more vindictive: the churches or the politicians. "Sectarianism," noted Curwen, "seems to be the root of the miserable want of honesty and all the quarrels & bitterness here." Every outport, it appeared, was torn three ways, between Catholics, Anglicans and Wesleyans. Each faith had its own church, its own school and its own firebrand. If one had wanted to find the equivalent religious turmoil in Europe, said one commentator, one would have had to travel all the way back to the twelfth century.

But O'Brien reserved special contempt for the politicians. They'd scattered public money not where there was necessity but where they'd needed favours. Pointless roads led to pointless piers. Every tiny community squawked for its own steamer service and, in the scramble for votes, often got it. Rampant jobbery had created a ghostly economy.

"In politics," said O'Brien, "corruption and sharp practice are studied as fine arts. No one hides it! For what's the good—if everyone *knows* it?"

The politicians fought hard for the scraps. Judge Prowse would describe the election of 1893 as an "indecent carnival of scurrility. There was not even a stray gleam of coarse humour to paliate the nauseous dose."

Curwen, too, was finding that the squalor got everywhere. "Polling day," reads his diary, "much mud thrown about & much underfoot, both very adhesive."

There was no question of the Governor favouring one politician above another: he was disgusted with all of them, even those who'd sat around this table. Curwen was himself particularly suspicious of the Prime Minister, a little weasel from Devon called Sir William Whiteway. He was right to be wary. The following year, Whiteway and seventeen other Liberals were charged with corruption. Unable to think of a convincing defence, they turned on the Tory leader, accusing him of indecently accosting ladies on Rennies Mill Road. In the meantime, Whiteway made his escape. He shrugged off the charges and launched himself back into the mud.

All this left Curwen not a little bemused. He turned to his friend, Dr. Harvey. Why hadn't *he* ever stood for the House of Assembly?

"Sir," he replied. "Am I a dog that I should do this thing?"

19

O'Brien's career had merely turned into a nightmare. His lawyers, on the other hand, were struggling with a deadly riddle: when is a fish not a fish?

For as long as anyone could remember, there were only two issues in Newfoundland politics; the first, union with Canada, was intractable; the second, the French Shore, was rich in surrealism. The French story is odd because it begins with a loser winning a prize, and ends in lobsters.

The loser was France, defeated in war. Her reward, in 1713, was the fishing rights to the whole of western Newfoundland. She took the same prize in the next two wars, which she also lost. Although the "French Shore" included nearly a quarter of the island's coastline, the French were never happy. They were always nibbling back the treaty boundaries and distorting their entitlement, which was the right "to fish and to dry fish" on the shore. The British Navy defended their rights—and their distortions—to the exclusion of all others, as the price of peace. None of this made any sense to the Newfoundlanders.

Nor did it really matter—until the French developed a taste for canned lobster. When they built a lobster factory on the west coast, even the British were roused. By 1857, the two countries were almost at each other again. It would have been the first war ever fought over the meaning of fish.

But, eventually, diplomacy made "fish" of lobsters, and war was averted. Now the Newfoundlanders were angry. Union Jacks flew at half-mast around the island. The anger fizzled on for decades until a whiskery Johnsman decided to test the boundaries himself. He set up his own factory on the French Shore, and when the Navy swooped on his pots, the merchant sued. He was victorious in both Newfoundland and in the Privy Council. English constitutional law would never look quite the same again, the doctrine of "Act of State" being forever weakened. Although none of this made him a lobster millionaire, the rebel's name would be forever set in precedent: James Baird.

Poor O'Brien—this was almost a fish too many. In his unhappiness, he planned his escape, green fields and resignation.

There'd been no such easy options for the James Bairds, and—a century on—our paths were about to intertwine again.

20

The Bairds now had a bookshop on Duckworth Street.

The present James Baird was the third of that name since Lobster Baird but, with each generation, the legacy had lightened. First, the family whiskers had gone, then the English education and finally the money itself. In fact, like all the other merchants, the Bairds had spent much of the twentieth century on the hop, financial ruin snapping at their ankles. They'd sold anything and everything just to keep running—lobsters, groceries, insurance—but all that had happened was that they'd got faster and fitter. At some stage, the latest of the line had even stripped down his name, surviving on a simple utilitarian "Jim."

His bookshop was, however, far from utilitarian. As Jim insisted that nobody in St. John's ever freckin' well read a book, his sprawling labyrinth of words was gloriously surplus to requirement. It was—quite literally—a warren of 100,000 books, tunnels burrowing through literature and dross, up through Science, Pet Care and Politics and then down, deep into the Humanities. I often found myself sneaking in there, out of the wind, nesting down in the History section or in Sexology and Beauty. No one seemed to mind. Jim had found helpers who liked the troglodytic existence, and who wore black costumes and jewellery made out of barbed wire, ring-pulls and other bits of magpie booty. Joe had claws and teeth exactly like a cat, and Dina told me that she never slept, not a wink.

In this enchanted semi-subterranean world, Jim was a sort of beardless, magicless Merlin. Because he also wore black, he would appear out of the fug, Yorick-like, a bony head chattering with wisdom. He loved books and—because he couldn't bear to see books and purchasers mismatched—he often immersed himself in the rituals of selection. When we first met, he regarded my armful of books with priestly scepticism.

"Leave these outport memoirs. Outporters churn them out, just a lot of freckin' moanin'. You need Prowse's *History of Newfoundland*. Horwood was our home-grown leftie, but never as sharp as this one: Farley Mowat. He's pretty astute about life in the bays, even though they hate the Jesus guts of him now. Do you need this life of Grenfell? What for? It's just a hagiography, doubtful scholarship. I'd dump it. What d'you like reading? Then you'll need *The Colony of Unrequited Dreams . . .*"

The rituals—and the battles—continued most of the afternoon. This, I realised, was why people came to "Wordplay," to buy books that they not only liked but which fitted them like handmade shoes. It also meant that, unwittingly, Jim had collected people, his eerie bookshop wired to all corners of the world. Some of those he collected were well-known writers, like E. Annie Proulx and David MacFarlane, whilst others were just curious or admiring. That afternoon I felt myself drawn into Jim's collection—or perhaps I threw myself into it. By the evening, I was round at his house, smashing eggs with his wife, Angie, and throwing back the brandy.

The other curious feature of the bookshop was that it ended in a shaft of sunlight and a staircase. Up the steps was a dazzling white space that bore no relation to the Middle Earth below, or to anywhere for that matter. It was just a dazzling white space where the Sorcerer hung pictures of his wild, wind-whipped world. They weren't literal images, of course, but Newfoundland in the grip of expressionism and genius. Sometimes, I thought I saw motifs I recognised: the purple ice; the barrens crushed beneath the sky; a bouquet of frozen salt.

But where were the tigers from, eating lobsters? Or the tartan sea and the tangerine beaches? And whenever was life just green?

Jim's gallery was popular with the Johnsmen, probably the most fantastic they'd ever had. I often found people up there, wandering around in a daze, overwhelmed by the sheer splendour of unreality.

Jim lived in a world of abstraction, as if in one of the paintings. He was an industrious talker, filling his canvas with splashes and indignation, colour, contradiction, momentary absurdity and brushstrokes of rich, thick brilliance. It was impossible not to like him and, even now, I count him amongst my most exotic friends. But as he stood there, slapping the words about, it was sometimes hard to tell where conviction ended and entertainment began. Then suddenly he'd stop, minutely responsive to a tiny inflection in mood, like one of those inspection machines that hurtles through the railway system, sensitive to the tiniest of cracks.

"You're smiling?" he'd say, when I'd hoped I wasn't.

Then he'd be off again, piling on the scarlet and blasphemy. Occasionally, the words would vanish altogether, leaving us bounding after them in a split-second of silence. Then some distant latch would click and the riot was on again. I'd catch glimpses of a past tumbling along in fragments: boarding-school in Ontario and a life dangerously in awe of beautiful women; a political career exploded, live on radio; the days of dark rum, drinking it like beer; three bright daughters, all too far away; the insolvency and the icy water pouring through the ceiling. And now the fear of pointlessness. He was forty-eight and had yet to make the sort of gesture that Bairds expected of themselves.

"I have no friends," he'd declare.

This wasn't true at all but it said much about how he felt. He wanted his friendships in vermilion, cobalt and magenta but was constantly disappointed by the tawdriness of human interaction. He expected warmth and loyalty and wanted to gather people up, to rally them, to talk till the brandy was gone and the eggs done, and to despise nothing but stupidity and Ottawa. Sometimes I felt the inadequacy of my own friendship but Jim was far too generous to show it. Besides, Mankind in general had been slow to respond and the Johnsmen in particular. Jim felt his idealism ebbing away.

"There is more joy on Water Street for one failure," he often told me, "than for a hundred successes."

Jim's need for magnificence was understandable—he was a

Johnsman—but his deeply ingrained disappointment was harder to explain. Of course, it was in part self-inflicted (no player can enjoy such drama without stumbling occasionally into the pit) but it was more than this. A sense of hereditary failure seemed to stalk the city. Jan Morris had warned that, beneath the charm, there was bitterness, and others spoke of the backlash of humiliation. I was often told that people in St. John's no longer dreamed. There was little sense of destiny, just relief that they'd survived this far. Perhaps this was the legacy of all fishermen, the belief that fate was weather-borne and beyond the scope of human mastery.

"We've been ruled by King Cod and the ocean," shrugged Jim.

Such fatalism gave politics a peculiar lack of poignancy. Even the best of the island's political memoirs were sludged in futility. Jim picked out a handful for me but the tenor was always the same: books of recrimination and excuses, never a moment of vision. In the nineteenth century this inertia had appalled outsiders. "They are easily led," wrote an English traveller, J. B. Jukes, in 1842, "and always ready to look for guidance, being ready to follow anyone who will take the trouble of thinking and deciding for them." A Nova Scotian politician at the end of the century was rather less charitable: Newfoundlanders, he said, were "too green to burn."

If politics was just idle necromancy, politicians were the worst of charlatans. Jim believed that almost all local government in his lifetime had been simply a matter of "graft." Like every Johnsman, he had praise for no one. His cynicism made me feel much as Curwen had done, listening to O'Brien. Jim, however—unlike the good Dr. Harvey—had run for office. Why, I asked.

"Boredom," he said, embarrassed perhaps at his youthful idealism. He sensed my disbelief.

"I thought I could make a difference," he confessed.

But it wasn't to be and Jim fell, in the early brawling. Nowadays, he brushed this off as an escape from a worse fate. "I'd have been in the cabinet for the past decade, and would have been an entirely larger arsehole than my current manifestation."

As I got to know Jim, I soon found myself among his local collection, the friends he said he didn't have.

For the most part, this social life unfolded like a harlequinade. There seemed to be endless characters rushing into our evenings with a little piece of farce, looking at their watches, screaming and rushing out again. Angie eased this fantasy along by giving everyone pantomime names. There was Turkish Delight, Cinderella, The Great Dane, Don Quixote, Porn Star and Pistol. Perhaps my favourite was Cherry, who seemed to have jumped out of a cartoon. He wore a spaceman's jacket and was never less than a blur of arms and legs. "I must go and groom," he'd say and then re-emerge with his hair like a garden exploding. Like the rest of the collection, he was brilliant, marginal and thrillingly weird. Once, we went to his house and I was surprised to find it a gallery of priapic art, with etchings by Picasso, Henry Moore and Hockney. I have never seen so many erections in one log cabin, or anywhere come to that.

For Jim, the best of his troupe were the abstract expressionists. Perhaps in their zany untrammelled imaginations he saw the broad liberated landscape of the future. It was not a vision I was able to share. Most of the artists were from the mainland, big sticky painters all eager to throw off their inhibitions. In a place so obviously lacking in inhibition, this seemed rather forced. One of them said he was an Afghan gun-runner and burst into tears at the mention of Racine. After he'd recovered and started issuing warnings of a North Korean invasion, I began to think that zaniness was nothing more than wearying.

"And I'll tell you something else," added my tormentor, "the next fuckin' Newfie that calls me Boy, I'm goin' to knock the shit out of him."

Fortunately, this wasn't going to happen in the sort of places Jim took us to. There were only one or two bars purple enough for his exquisite entourage. The first was a cocktail bar called something like Grobbles, where the money-men went to irrigate their floozies. Everything was black and chrome and we sipped dry Martinis. This would have been perfectly normal but for the fact that there were still bergy bits in the bay, and harps to be clubbed. "It's *so* fuckin' Newfie . . . ," declared the gun-runner, who then lit a joint and passed out.

The other place was Bianca's. Now we were in the Mediterranean, sprawling in leather, cork and ochre. It was just another tantalising illusion, because Bianca's was far more Bohemian than anyone would have dared to imagine: the owners were Bulgarians, relics of the Cold War. In 1990, they'd been on a plane to Cuba and had stopped in Newfoundland to refuel. Although capitalism must have looked a little scrawny in Gander, it was good enough for them, and they'd defected.

They weren't alone. Bulgarians made up the only significant group of immigrants to have arrived in Newfoundland in living memory.

One night, Jim urged us upstairs to a party for the film festival. All the other guests seemed to be women—divorcees, with the chocolatey boots and chocolatey faces of Florida.

"God knows why I came back," sniffed one. "There's eight women here to every man."

"I just watch the sex channel all day," said another, "to see what I'm missing."

Now I could feel her lazy eyes on me, and was glad when Jim reappeared.

"John, there's someone I should like you to meet."

I recognised him. He was the only Newfoundlander to take a lead role in the island's big moment, *The Shipping News*. Gordon Pinsent, said Jim. Then I ruined his introduction by doing what I always do in the face of anyone remotely famous; I became incomprehensible.

"*Gotsh fantashto . . .*"

Pinsent frowned.

Fortunately, he spoke my shredded language. "*Who shay ye are?*"

I got something out, and we stood there blinking and swaying until he'd formed another question. What was I doing in this ugly little place?

"I'm off. *Shoon*," I promised. "Driving away. Over the barrens. To the capes."

I didn't catch his response. At that moment, he was swept away in a surge of chocolate and fur. I did, however, get a glimpse of his expression.

Like a man falling headlong into icy water.

21

I had another premonition of life in the bays—it was Angie.

Angie distrusted Jim's redefinition of St. John's. She came from Fogo Island, two hundred and sixty fog-drenched, sea-splintered miles to the north. "I was born in Fogo, Fogo," she told me, "a house of thirteen and a puncheon of molasses. When we were children, we shot ice-birds, clipped their feet off and roasted them on a blaze of crunnicks. Good meat," she said, "and sweet." To Angie, St. John's was a Promised Land, the end of a journey, not a renaissance.

She'd arrived twenty-six years ago, a pretty Catholic girl who'd never seen a comic. She took a job in a bank and caught her eye on a wizardly young man, from a long line of merchants. Within four days she and Jim were engaged.

"My parents never forgave me," she recalled. "Marrying a Presbyterian! We didn't speak for the next five years."

After that, she saw no need to change anything. Life continued much as it had around the puncheon, a life in parallel to Jim's. She frowned on intellect as unnecessary ostentation and was suspicious of all forms of seriousness. The pantomime names were typical of Angie and I became "King John." The abstract expressionism she tolerated, although bemused by all the tangerine and tigers. She was less sure about the artists, and valued breathing-space way above intimacy. I noticed that she was never tactile and shrank from the touch of others. Whenever people left her, she would stand back and wave at them like parting ships.

I adored Angie but I understood Jim better. Angie seemed so self-contained, like a conspiracy of one. She was still as pretty and fair as the day she'd arrived, but her smile was her own, a private affair. Perhaps she just lived with an unruly imagination. She once told me that she got up in the middle of the night and laid the table. "I could have sworn there were ten for dinner," she said.

She hated the cocktail bars but never let this spoil a good night out. On the nights when I wasn't out with Jim, I was out with Angie. We often took one of the divorcees with us, called Heather. She didn't like any bars much but she came along all the same, just to feel hot hands again on her fleshy hips. Unlike Angie, she was terrified of loneliness and, when she saw files of women trudging round the dance-floor, waiting to be picked, she seemed relieved. At last, women more desperate than herself.

Angie always took us to George Street, to The Earl of Water, Fat Cat and O'Reilly's. This is how she liked it—sweltering, roaring and uncomplicated by conversation. There were occasional fights, never more than a flurry of fists, but mostly people sang. Angie knew all the words. The boy was always a fishermen. Sometimes he got his girl but, usually, he drowned. For some reason, everyone found this funny and we all laughed although we couldn't think why.

At around three, the hot-dog men were on the street and then came the Mounties, to herd us all home.

. . .

It was time to leave St. John's. Apart from anything else, the endless, sleepless cycle of Martini, stout and fiddles had given all my thoughts the texture of a thin reedy scream. Or perhaps I'd overstayed, and too much of St. John's always felt like this? Whatever it was, I managed to get myself to a garage, where I hired a Grand Am. It had a luminous release handle in the boot.

"What's this for?" I asked.

"Jasus, I don't know," said the salesman. "In case you're kidnapped, I guess."

"Will I need it, here?"

He looked doubtful.

"Or maybe it's in case you fall," he tried, "and lock yourself in."

This was possible. I hate cars and cars hate me. I can easily imagine being swallowed by one. I'd have been happy never to sit in one again but, right then, with 42,000 square miles of island spread out ahead of me, I was dependent on a car. I'd even asked at the tourist office about hitching. Their answer was intriguing.

"No," they'd said. "You might do something, sexually assault someone . . ."

I must have looked surprised.

"Or they might sexually assault *you*."

Jim was more practical. "You might not see another car for hours."

There was, it seemed, no choice other than to hire the Grand Am. The controls looked horribly unfamiliar, just a lot of things for holding coffee-mugs. I decided to practise and did a few slushy circuits of the garage, in reverse. The salesman was still panting at the window.

"Watch out for blizzards on the barrens. And the fish trucks are stopping for nobody . . . And you want to be right leery in the dark. There's moose everywhere . . ."

I was sorry to be moving on but not sorry for a moment of reflection. My great-grandfather had felt almost exactly the same. "We had a very good time in St. John's," wrote Curwen, "but have been oppressed by the kindness, generosity & extreme hospitality of the people; we have had *no* time to ourselves and are wanting a little quiet."

I released the hand-brake, and prayed for the Grand Am's compliance. Very slowly and with almost no dignity at all, we bunny-hopped out of the garage, up Mount Pearl and into the barrens.

Act II: Planting Avalon (and Reaping the Storm)

The fisheries of Newfoundland are inexhaustible and are of more value to the empire than all the silver mines of Peru.

—Francis Bacon (1561–1626)

Terra Nova, of the codfish, is a cold place.

—Ptolemy's World Atlas,
published by Mattioli, 1547

A Country, where people are seldome pinched with want and where they liue fat and as healthy, as in any other part of the world, the Countrey being full of Hawkes, Partriges, Thrushes, and other fowles, hunting deere, and other beasts, with delicate Fruits which are there in great abundance.

—Richard Whitbourne, *A Discourse and Discovery of New-Found-Land,* 1620

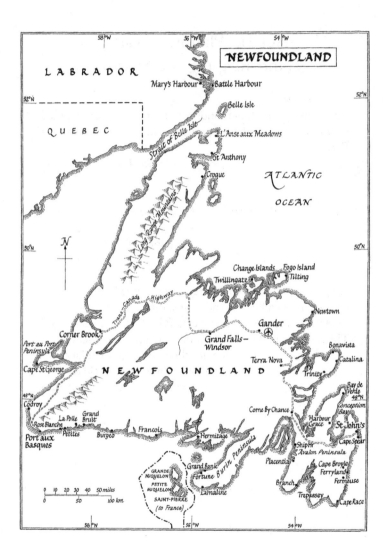

NEWFOUNDLAND

LABRADOR

QUEBEC

Mary's Harbour • • Battle Harbour

Belle Isle

Strait of Belle Isle

L'Anse aux Meadows

St. Anthony

Croque

ATLANTIC

OCEAN

Long Range Mountains

N

Change Islands   Fogo Island

Twillingate   Tilting

Trans-Canada   Highway

Newtown

Corner Brook

Gander

Port au Port
Peninsula

Grand Falls—
Windsor

Bonavista

Cape St. George

Terra Nova

Catalina

NEWFOUNDLAND

Trinity

Bay de
Verde

Codroy

Come By Chance

Conception
Bay

La Poile   Grand
Bruit

Rose Blanche
Petites

Harbour
Grace

St. John's

Port aux
Basques

Burgeo

Francois

Hermitage

Ship H'r

Cape Spear

Avalon Peninsula

0 10 20 30 40 50 miles

0   50   100 km.

GRANDE
MIQUELON

PETITE
MIQUELON

SAINT-PIERRE
(to France)

Grand Bank

Fortune

Burin Peninsula

Lamaline

Placentia

Cape Broyle
Ferryland
Fermeuse

Branch

Trepassey

Cape Race

22

The Bog of Avalon is another case of good intentions cluttering the road to Hell.

Once, it had formed part of a colony of fanciful hopes. In 1616, the land had been sold by the Company of Adventurers and Planters to three well-ruffed idealists. They'd decided that all a fresh start needed was a good name, and had called it Avalon. It would be a delightful utopia, far from injustice. Things had not worked out as they'd planned.

I studied their failure on the map. The Avalon Peninsula was a knobbly parson's nose of land, blue-pocked and threaded with bogs. Giant forces had scraped it of hills and had hacked its shores to tatters. It was said to be the most southerly "Arctic" region in the world, the interior a featureless, untitled blank. On the north coast I could make out the scribbly banter of pirates: Heart's Desire, Turk's Cove, Dildo and Blow Me Down. In the south, the bog spirits had been at work, with wicked taunts: Bald Head, Mistaken Point, Maggotty Point and Cape Dog. Elsewhere, the landscape was just vaguely impish, a place of reaches, rattles, arms, guts and tickles. It was hardly inviting.

Nor was there much encouragement from the early sailors. Most saw little point in wandering inland. "The Earth is hid from the Eye of Man," wrote one Aaron Thomas in 1794, "being cover'd with snow and bounded down by a strong cement." Almost everything living in this sorry glue, he said, had the appearance of "heaviness of mind and the gait of sour sullenness." Fifty years later, an American Missionary, R. T. S. Lowell, was sludging his way through the wilderness. "A monstrous mass of rock and gravel," he shuddered, "almost without soil, like a strange thing from the bottom of the great deep, lifted up suddenly, into the sunshine and storm, but belonging to the watery darkness out of which it has been reared."

Now I was wheeling through the same great deep. The reverend was right; the world was inside-out. Here was the land, as black and fierce as fire, and the sky like liquefied rock. The bones of a glacier were scattered through the vapours, picked apart by talons of juniper. This is how I imagined the Earth had looked in the beginning, or how it would look at the end. I stopped once, and listened to the clank of rusting birds. Then I was off again, rolling between lakes of smoke and nursery-blue ice.

The road splashed over the barrens and then, at the first sign of settlement, it swooped on the shore. These were the only settlements the Bog of Avalon had ever known, a tidemark of clinker and skiffs, between one wilderness and another. Life was still just a mooring. There were no gardens or barns and nobody built out of stone. It was almost as if, at a given signal, everyone would up-anchor and sail away, leaving it all behind—the fish-stages lashed out of sticks, the green smoke, the fresh-cut spruce and the moose-head nailed to the gate. Even in their names, the coves were just a phase: Petty Harbour, Witless Bay, Mobile.

In one place, I stood on the stage with a fisherman, scunning for whales. Most days, he told me, a beluga came. They could never wait for summer. It was the same every year.

I asked him if he'd always lived here.

"Always," he said. "We've been here four hundred years."

The first settlers were called "planters" even though the soil was thin and sick, and their seeds rotted in the ground. A few had arrived with the utopians but most saw life for what it was. Up on the northern coasts there were Englishmen, scraping out a new existence, but down here they were Irish, fine men who knew how to starve.

In fact, Irishmen had been living on these rocks ever since Sir Humfrey's musical conquest. By 1670, there were 1,700 planters scattered along the coast. Some were sea-robbers and some were deserters. But most were just running from peonage and destitution, working wherever they could. They were called the Irish Youngsters as if their whole world stretched before them, which in a sense it did; there was nothing but the sea ahead of them, their backs to the land. The barrens were exactly what they said they were, best left to pestilence, the "muscetos and garnippers." The Youngsters would be slap up, next to the waves. They even called their new home *Talamh An Eisc*, the Land of Fish. It may have been hell but at least it wasn't England.

But their numbers soon began to worry the English. Every year, the West Country merchants encountered more and more of these wailing, gingery mystics. Worse, they were littered across English "rooms," the cobbles where the summer catch was dried. Irishness was stifled. For a while, it was illegal to build a permanent home, to keep an Irish woman or to say the holy Mass. Resentment flourished but still the Irish came. Immigration was at its wildest in Napoleonic times, as the price of saltfish soared. It was a time of madness, brigs packed to the gunnels. In 1811, the *Fanny* sailed in with two hundred more, a fifth of them already dead.

After that, the torrent became a trickle. For those peeling themselves away, there was an Irish future further west, in America. For those already in Newfoundland, there was only a past. Their Irishness had ground to a halt by 1850, pre-Fenian, pre-Joyce, pre-Troubles. All they had left was their voices—the sounds of Waterford and Cork—and a handful of words. An oaf was still an *omadhaun*, and pigs' feet were always *crubeens*. The road was theirs too, this drunken switchback—they called it the Irish Loop.

I paused at Cape Broyle, a filling-station and a scattering of cabins. This was as far south as Curwen had got, "the fog so thick that we could see very little." He was on a hunting expedition with the Mission's agent and Edgar Bowring, the merchant who gave St. John's its Peter Pan. At every outport they were besieged by the sick, and in Cape Broyle their tent collapsed under relentless rain. They ended up in the house of the Liberal candidate, Michael Cachin. Sir Michael—as he became—was the head of a political dynasty that's bubbled and hissed ever since. Cachins had been in the thick of all the great punch-ups of the twentieth century: Catholic champions, stalwarts against Union, defenders of the fish. Their house had proved less enduring.

"Rotted away," said the pump attendant. "Not a stick left."

After this, Curwen headed back to St. John's. I continued south, towards Ferryland, the capital of forgotten dreams.

23

Ferryland stood under a dog's head of rock, scabbed in the last of the snow.

An isthmus curled into the sea. It was called The Dunes, a wistful name for a spindle of crumbling shale. There was nothing there any more, just the shadow of old tracks and the seething of wintry straw. Beyond The Dunes, the bay was toothed in black, snagged here and there with boat-meat, boilers and flaps of rust. Deep within this ring of shoals was a circle—greasy-calm—which they called The Pool. It was one of the first harbours of the New World.

In 1620, an advance party of utopians had landed here. They'd been sent by Sir George Calvert, Secretary of State, a man of steady gaze but variable conviction. By then, he was beginning to wonder if he wasn't a Catholic after all, and was dreaming up a refuge in *The Newfoundland*. He wasn't the first idealist to sink his hopes in this bog but his failure was easily the most impressive. Two old Oxford friends were already well on the way to disaster. Both had set up colonies a little to the south. The first, Viscount Falkland, had sponsored a Little Ireland, trying to grow tobacco in the snow. The other, Sir William Vaughan, had come unstuck with his vision of Wales, called Cambriol. It was a project he'd owed the world ever since being saved by angels after falling off a ship. Unfortunately, he'd selected his Welshmen carelessly, "idle fellowes" who'd never left their fish sheds, and the project foundered. Vaughan had, however, managed to snatch something back from failure. He'd flogged his colony to Calvert—and his story to the public; *The Golden Fleece* was widely enjoyed, and *The Newlander's Cure* was probably the first medical textbook to emerge from the New World.

Initial reports from Ferryland were suspiciously encouraging. Calvert's colonists told him that they'd built a manor house and established a "Kitchin-Garden." It was said that the grass was "fat and unctuous" and that they'd grown a radish as big as the captain's arm. In their requests, there was no sign of the trouble to come; they asked for a tailor, a couple of strong maids, some coarse-knit hose, ratsbane, a plough and a glazier. All seemed well. Within two years the colony had a hundred planters, and a Royal charter. Although he'd never actually seen Avalon, Calvert was now charged with making its laws, appointing ministers and providing a white horse for every Royal visit. His Ferryland would be the first stepping-stone in a missionary trail leading all the way to China.

Modest though this might have seemed, Calvert now had more clout in Avalon than he had in England. His drift into Catholicism hadn't been popular. In 1624, the King conferred on him the title of Lord Baltimore, a clear hint that he was no longer wanted. He resigned. Four years later, he was in a 24-gun ship, off to see what had become of Avalon, his earthly dream.

I walked out across The Dunes, through the old courtier's "plantation." Here were the forge and the saltworks, the captain's manor house and a closet flushed by the tide. They were merely outlines now, a rocky sketch doodled in the straw. Here too was the "Kitchin-Garden," mistaken for wealth. It produced roots alright—turnips, coleworts and carrots—but never enough. That winter, the planters were rotten with scurvy. At any one time half of them were unfit for work, and the harvest collapsed. Food became so scarce that the Privy Council was forced to send them relief. It was too late for some; one in ten died.

Baltimore was shrewd enough to recognise defeat. He petitioned Charles I for a colony in Virginia. It would be another haven for Catholics, this time called Maryland. Whilst the people of Ferryland would often remind themselves that their little outport was a template for the great city of Baltimore, it was also a reminder of failure.

Fate had been no kinder to those who'd seized on Baltimore's absence. Sir David Kirke was a brawny little oaf, who'd got where he was by forgetting to pay for what he'd had. He held most things in contempt, especially the weather. Perhaps this made him a survivor, at least in the short-term. "The Ayre of Newfoundland," he declared, "agrees perfectly well with all God's creatures except Jesuits and schismaticks." He might even have thrived, had he not misjudged the outcome of the English Civil War. On a visit to London, he was banged up in The Clink, where he died in 1654. His family struggled on but ruin was inevitable. Ferryland was first sacked by the Dutch, and then torched by the French. David Kirke II died much as his grandfather had, in a dungeon.

All that the Kirkes had left Newfoundland was a coat-of-arms, a curious fantasy of lions, unicorns and armoured Indians. All that they'd left Ferryland was now scattered at my feet, ankle-high—a hearth of blackened stones.

24

There was nowhere to stay in Ferryland and so I stayed on the barrens, in a house of congenial ghosts.

All the best people in Mrs. Duggan's life had lived here at one stage or another. It was a simple place, boots in the hall, Christ in every bedroom and the lingering murmur of family life. Among the snapshots on the dresser, I counted three mortar-boarded daughters, all gone now to Calgary and Edmonton. There'd been one other child, Finn, but he'd passed on, too young even for his photograph.

I also spotted a picture of Mr. Duggan, his dory bobbing in the limitless blue. There was a jig playing through his fingers and his eyes said "I've never been so happy." He was wreathed in smiles now but soon he'd be wreathed in lilies. It was twenty years since the tragedy of Paddy Duggan but I had the feeling he was always there, Poor Paddy, easing off his sea-boots, muffled feet on immaculate linoleum.

With the girls gone and Poor Paddy in his grave, Mrs. Duggan had taken in travellers. Most were on their way to Ferryland. Once, a famous photographer stopped by, seeking shelter from a blizzard; he was Mr. Karsh of Ottawa. At other times, her visitors were Japanese, fish-mongers who'd come to buy tomcods and caplin, which they'd called *sushi*. They'd given her bottles of Cherry Tree whisky that she'd never drunk but which she treasured like a little orchard on a shelf. Then there were the fishing crews, like the boys from the *Johnny and Sisters II;* they'd come every season, with never an oath or a speck of ash. For Mrs. Duggan, they were like the sons she'd never had—until Christmas 1989 when their dragger flipped over in the sish, and sank like a rock. All ten drowned, none of them a day over forty.

"It took time to get over that," she told me. "For years I was all mops and brooms. What was happening to everyone around me?"

But providence hadn't left her entirely alone. She still had her uncle and aunt and, in winter, they came to live with her. They were the sweetest ghosts of them all, even though they still had time to run. It wasn't simply the transparency of old age; they just lived in different worlds. In her dreams, Aunt was back in St. John's, the maid-servant she'd been all her life. Uncle Charlie was in the forest, with his chain-saw and a pocketful of fish. Nowadays hammer-toes lolled at the windows cut in his slippers but the sound of my voice caused his mind to slip backwards, into the past, to a time sixty years before.

"We sailed to England to cut trees for the King. Three hundred of us from the Newfoundland Forestry Unit . . . there was a war, ye know, but England was the grandest place I'd ever seen. All those fields and roads and houses like ye never saw. And Capstans too! And girls as fat as butter! Is it still like that, is it? How much do ye pay for Wood-bines now?"

For a moment the cabin was almost a family again. Aunt warmed the teapot and Uncle Charlie fell into a foresty doze. I left a trail of guilty snowflakes across the hall, and a cat appeared like a tiny polar bear, whiskers wet and red. From her galley, Mrs. Duggan hauled a spread of ancestral treats—tea-buns, tinned milk, a waxy ship's sausage called Bologna, and a "Shipwreck dinner," which was everything thrown together. At breakfast, there was a cauldron of "fish and brewis," an oily mulch of salt-cod, onions, hard tack and scrunchions of fat-back pork. It was the sort of thing that Curwen would have enjoyed after twelve hours in a storm, or a swim across the bay. Three generations on, I was only able to endure it.

"Take your time," said Mrs. Duggan, as I shovelled it away. "God made time and he made plenty of it."

It was hard to know what Mrs. Duggan made of the deathly attrition of her life. She said she was terrified of the sea but, in every other sense, there was now a calmness about her as if tragedy was just a phase like middle age or bad weather. Every day she went to Renews to pray at the Grotto of the Virgin. It had always been a secretive place, where Irishmen had once mumbled through Mass, well out of English earshot. I sometimes wondered who Mrs. Duggan spoke to in her prayers. Was it God? Or was it Finn and Paddy? Or the boys from *Johnny and Sisters II*?

It wasn't so much that I'd caught a whiff of heresy about Mrs. Duggan, but that Catholicism here seemed so spiritually infested. On the outside, the Newfoundland church was the same fortress that it was elsewhere; 99 per cent of this shore was Catholic; abortion was an abomination; divorce too might have looked exotic if St. John's hadn't opened up the possibilities, in 1968. But inside the bastion, it was a different story; there, the spirits were running free. Even in St. John's, I'd heard earnest talk of fairies. These weren't pretty little fairies either but revolting creatures that mocked the unwary, tipped them over cliffs and drowned them in ponds. Mrs. Duggan said that, as a child, she wasn't allowed on the barrens without bread to buy off these goblins. Others had their own stories. Aunt left water out for the Lost Souls on All Souls Night, and Uncle Charlie heard the "Old Hollies," the men who'd drowned and who found their voices again in dirty weather.

In Ferryland, they'd never hoped for much but they did ask for miracles. In October 1926, they'd made a novena, prayers for a heavenly interruption to their hunger. On the last day of the novena, the SS *Torhamvan* had hurled itself into the bay, ripped its hull off on the shoals and spewed three statues onto the beach: Christ, Peter and Paul. Then came a wave of macaroni, hundreds of tons of pasta washed up on the shore. For Ferryland, it was salvation of sorts, though not quite as they'd imagined.

The *Torhamvan* Christ still stood at the door of the church. One day, I asked Mrs. Duggan if she'd take me with her, to my first-ever Mass. Although she called it an "old time" place, it wasn't somewhere she held in much affection.

"This place," she said, "would freeze your feet to the floor."

We sat down among the salty coats and hair-oil. Most of the pews were empty. "It was *blocked* once," whispered Mrs. Duggan. "Blocked with everyone."

"There don't seem to be many young people," I said. "Don't they come any more?"

Mrs. Duggan seemed to sag.

"Oh, blessed Virgin that's dead. No, they don't come any more." She hesitated. "Not since Father Hickey."

It seems I'd stumbled on the latest of Ferryland's great disappointments.

Father Hickey was an outport hero even though he was born in St. John's. In fact, being almost perfect was as much as most people could remember of him. He was a small man with an engulfing personality, and a nose like Mr. Punch. For many years it was only his illegitimacy that kept him from the priesthood but then, in 1970, at the age of thirty-seven, charm won and he was ordained.

As a priest he was—more than ever—nearly perfect. He came to be regarded as a champion, a voice of youth, the scourge of drugs and "filthy magazines." He was around wherever there was greatness, at the side of royal visitors or at the heel of the Pope. In fact, he seemed to be everywhere, often all at once. He even had time for his parishes, like Ferryland, and for baptising babies, like the Bairds'. Everyone was spell-bound, even Angie.

"He could charm the cats off a fish truck," she'd say.

The Hickey charisma began to flare, with rallies and camps and a magazine called *The Monitor*. In a place where many still thought that insulting the priest was the cause of deformity, here was power indeed. Father Hickey even bought a car commensurate with his saintliness— a Cadillac—and a silver-plated revolver. It was a warning that was ignored; so often there is more hobgoblin to perfection than first meets the eye.

Hickey's sexual abuse of children makes for a grim footnote in the history of Ferryland. It was the worst of abuse, beginning with trust and then exploiting guilt. The victims were altar-boys and truants, impressed by a flash car and the dollars left around for them to steal. Once he'd had their guilt, the priest took their innocence; licking eyes, a man's hand in a child's lap, French massage, This Won't Hurt. No one knows how many boys he spread out in his cabin on the barrens. There were many he could rely on to stay silent forever. He even officiated at their weddings, or oversaw their depression and the long bouts of self-loathing.

There was little joy in Ferryland when, in 1988, Hickey pleaded guilty to thirty-two charges of abuse. Nor was there much joy when, two years later, his cold heart ruptured and sprawled him across his cell. By some miracle of morality, Mr. Punch had managed to recast himself as the victim in all of this. Anger turned on the Catholic Church.

"There is something loose somewhere in the structure of the Church . . . ," admitted Archbishop Penney, but it was more than that; the whole edifice was tottering.

For Ferryland, the experience of Father Hickey was as bleak as anything before and, for its young, it was the end of faith. But, for Newfoundland generally, it was a dress rehearsal for a much greater calamity, known simply as Mount Cashel. People say that life was different after Mount Cashel, as if at last they were suddenly wise.

Poor Paddy Duggan would know none of this. The evil unleashed at Mount Cashel killed him long before it reached the light of day.

25

Sonny Maher, they say, was taken by the wind.

"After Finn died," said Mrs. Duggan, "we adopted Sonny. He was God's own child but, you know, the world can be a cruel place. The Mahers, they belonged to a place near here, just down the road, but the father was always away, fishing down on the Labrador. When Sonny's mother dropped dead on Ascension Day, the father said that's it, I can't look after the boy no more. He'll need a new home—and so he sent him to St. John's."

She paused, her fingers finding the edge of the table.

"Don't worry, he said, they'll be other lads like you. You'll be happy there."

For a while he might have been. It was a grand house with a carpet room and minced-beef suppers. There was a television too—still a miracle for an outport boy in 1972—and all the dorms were named after saints; St. Al's, St. Pat's, St. Pius' and St. Joe's. A ten-year-old could hardly wish for more.

It was true, there were other lads like Sonny, "saved" as the Brothers would say "from the terrible disease of being unwanted." Most had been pulled from lives on fire, from the casual violence of drinkers, from bereavement or the lash of ill-defined psychosis. Some brought the fire with them, the screams and the tantrums. They're just retards, said the Brothers, don't worry about them.

The Brothers themselves were harder to forget. They weren't like other men Sonny had known. Some were big and powerful, but given to bewildering tenderness like mothers. Others were just imponderable and had nicknames like Radar and Bugs Bunny, and carried sticks called Mr. Ouch. Childhood might have ticked away like this, a sort of strange, over-blown caricature—except that, at every moment, there was terror.

To the Christian Brothers of Mount Cashel, beating a child was a useful prelude to complete violation. If the boy could keep it to himself, he could bear much more, and—even better—he was enjoyably compliant. The assault on childhood became almost a matter of curriculum—beaten for bed-wetting, beaten at breakfast and beaten through the day. Each of the Brothers had his own style. Brother English liked to gouge his anger deep into young flesh with a buckle. Brother Burke just lashed out with his great red fists. Even the superintendent, Brother Kenny, took time for a little savagery.

But savagery is not savagery without a bit of ritual. Just as my own school, Mostyn House, was made a pageant of the Grenfells, so Mount Cashel made a pageant of its cruelty. There were mock-expulsions and parades, all performed with lavish humiliation. A seven-year-old was once made to tour the home with his suitcase, saying good-bye to the only family he'd ever known. For Brother Ralph, the best bit of this was that the child was completely naked and had no idea that it was all a joke.

But there was no joke about the atrocities that followed. Whatever Father Hickey had taken by guile, the Christian Brothers seized upon with force. Their greed for boys was insatiable. Well over a dozen Brothers were involved, in the buggery, the outrage, the "hauling" and fellatio—the list is merciless. For children like Sonny, having their sleep and their bodies invaded would never be normal but it did become routine. Perhaps normality had long gone, taking with it the prospect of ever being happy. At Mount Cashel, the novelty in the cornflakes packet became a reward for masturbation, and the carpet room was not a place to play. Brother English was always in there, working up a new nickname, bleaker than any before—the Jigger.

The worst feature of Mount Cashel was not that it happened but that those who had the power to prevent it seemed to collapse under their own indifference. By December 1975, the evidence was all over St. John's, on the right desks, stapled to confessions. Later, it was reckoned that some eighty-seven officials had had the full facts before them. The three Brothers accused hadn't even contested the charges but had turned up at their interviews with their bags packed, expecting nothing worse than exile. They were right to feel safe. What happened next was a struggle to do nothing.

These were the most shameful moments in Newfoundland's story, a time of inexcusable paralysis. The Social Services didn't think they had the power to visit Mount Cashel, even though it was a home where they placed their wards (they were, in the words of one commentator, "stupefied by the deadly opiates of job description and the policy manual"). Meanwhile, the police did nothing because the Chief was deeply embedded in the Christian Brother hierarchy, and was even planning their Centenary. He simply ordered his detectives to call off the chase and rewrite their reports, omitting any reference to sexual abuse.

Even the media stifled the facts. "The story could do more harm than good," shrugged one of the editors later. "We could undo the good that the Brothers had done for eighty or ninety or a hundred years . . ."

But it was in the Ministry of Justice that the truth petered out. The Deputy Minister, Vincent McCarthy, had no stomach for a fight with his church, and sought a secret deal. No more would be said if the three Brothers left Newfoundland forever. Within three months, they were on the mainland and—after a spell of light therapy—back among children. McCarthy's papers were filed, as a dead letter.

It was another fourteen years before the truth emerged.

Whether justice in 1975 would have saved Sonny from himself is anyone's guess. There were plenty of boys whose lives were already in fragments—alcoholics, depressives, prostitutes, the restlessly criminal and the hopelessly lost. Some hadn't even moved far from Mount Cashel but lived rough in the woods behind. Others had taken a longer journey, blown apart with a stolen gun or broken across the rocks.

"Sonny had never been right," said Mrs. Duggan. "But after Mount Cashel he was took by the wind . . ."

He came to live with the Duggans but there was nothing that could calm him. His anger was nomadic, simultaneously seeking both solitude and destination. Eventually, fury settled on his father, the man who'd promised him a childhood, but he was nowhere to be found.

I had no idea what was coming next. Mrs. Duggan's face was clouded with pain.

"When he killed my husband, Paddy," she said, "he was killing his father."

For many Newfoundlanders this tragedy doesn't have an end.

Uprooting the institution of Mount Cashel was, in a sense, the easy part. The scandal finally broke on the radio, on *Open Line*, in February 1989. Within months, the province found itself facing claims of over $18 million, and the rounding-up of the Brothers began. By the end, fourteen were arrested, including Radar, Bugs Bunny and the malevolent superintendent. They were tried and convicted, on the basis of some eighty-nine sample charges. It was not a blow Mount Cashel could survive; that autumn, the Christian Brothers abandoned it and, the following year, the doors were nailed up, and it was closed forever.

For the powers that had slumbered through the crisis, the agony was more protracted. What had seemed at first like a tiny nick soon had the government disembowelled. The anger was everywhere—in the papers and in the police, on *The Oprah Winfrey Show* and in every outport. At first, the Ministry of Justice bridled at the thought of an inquiry, but the press smelt blood.

"Even for a Minister who acts as though she is a permanent resident of Disneyland," ran one editorial, "a more complete abdication of responsibility to government could not be imagined."

The inquiry that followed was not the catharsis that it ought to have been. One of those who watched was a young journalist called Michael Harris. His book, *Unholy Orders*, is an extraordinary record of death by tribunal. Everybody blamed the minister, McCarthy—principally because he was dead. The evidence of the police chief, says Harris, was "the intellectual equivalent of a few revolutions of the family dryer: disorientating, nonsensical and hard on the head." As for the Social Services ministers, they emerged as "The Three Blind Mice."

Torpid though it may have seemed, the evidence eventually proved fatal. The children, wrote Harris, had been "the victims of a stunning moral entropy that had immobilised the entire system and allowed the authorities of the day to sleepwalk through the sordid affair as though it were a dream." That same year the provincial government fell and Archbishop Penney resigned. Within a decade, Mount Cashel itself had been bulldozed and church education had gone. The denominational system—which my great-grandfather had considered to be at "the root of all evil" on the island—was finally abolished. The Church, perhaps more than anyone else, had been guilty of dreaming.

There were plenty of people for whom the dream was still a nightmare. In the travels which followed, I'd meet several men whose lives had foundered at Mount Cashel. Like veterans of a dirty war, they wanted me to know they'd been there but not the detail. For many others, Mount Cashel opened old wounds: sectarianism, a mercantile judiciary and a belief that there was still a privileged class, above the law. Some even saw Mount Cashel as a condemnation of themselves. Were Newfoundlanders uniquely perverted? These were the people that hated *The Shipping News* because child abuse re-emerges, in a Newfoundland story.

"Let's not talk about Mount Cashel," a man once snapped at me at dinner. "I don't want to hear it again. The whole freckin' business makes me sick."

Meanwhile, I wondered what had happened to Sonny.

"He'll be out soon," said Mrs. Duggan. "I seem to have spent half my life campaigning for his release. After all, it wasn't his fault, was it?"

26

A short distance out of Ferryland, idealism had died altogether.

I was back in the wilderness, the great lifeless anarchy of bog and ice. It was impossible to imagine ownership here, or even hope and failure. I put my foot down and soared through the emptiness, alone for the rest of the day.

Once, a band of angry men had made a kingdom of this dystopia.

As I drove south I caught a glimpse of their brutal Shangri-La, a knob of purple rock they'd called the Butterpot. It was a pretty name for men who'd wanted nothingness. They were angry men, after the lives they'd fled; men press-ganged into the navy, indentured fish slaves and Irish serfs. By 1750, they had a leader, Peter Kerrivan, a callow youth who brought cunning to their rage. Up until then, he'd only known the discipline of the yardarm and the lash. From now on, there'd be no rules at all. He called his outlaws The Society of Masterless Men.

Rules, I realised, were not all that was missing. There was no contour, no feature, no words and no belief. Kerrivan had conquered the void, an anti-society in an anti-state. The desolation of it all was oddly satisfying. Throughout that day, I only came across one sign, an incongruous yellow moose, blown to bits by wind and shot.

Just as there were no boundaries to their land, so there was no end to the Masterless Men. For generations they enjoyed the squalor of the Butterpot, and the steamy meat of caribou. Occasionally, they emerged from their wasteland, out for chicken and women and bits of clothes. Later, people would allow themselves to forget this robbery; there's something of the Masterless Man about every outporter, a brilliant rogue on the run from reality. Being elusive is just the price of survival.

The Royal Navy were less indulgent, and sent marines to hunt The Society. It was a forlorn task. Every path seemed to end in a watery blank, and toes began to rot. They burnt the tilts on the Butterpot but it made no difference; the Masterless Men had already wafted away like rumours. Only once did they capture outlaws—four boys—horrible, blackened bog-creatures that they strung up like crows. After this, the Society became more elusive than ever, moving deeper and deeper inland until, eventually, it slipped into folklore. Peter Kerrivan was never found but his name has survived in the long lists of Kerrivans who've inhabited this shore.

As for his kingdom of nothingness, it's never been replaced.

27

I passed through Fermeuse, where the madness of the barrens became a religion.

It all began with the visions of Richard Brothers, "Prince of Hebrews, Lion of the Tribe of Judah." He was the son of a soldier, born during the peculiar war of the Masterless Men. It was a peculiarity that never deserted him. In 1770, at the age of thirteen, he became a midshipman and, by the age of thirty-seven, he was a prophet. He moved to London, where he discovered that he was descended from James, brother of Jesus, and that—better still—he was the Nephew of God.

He inhabited a curious world—the barrens but in a state of biblical riot. There was the emptiness, of course, and the lightning and destruction, and plenty of wind. London would be swamped with brimstone and replaced with a New Jerusalem—a city of Masterless Men perhaps, or at least Anglo-Saxons. It was a thrilling vision and—when London wasn't swamped—Brothers could claim the gift of salvation. Hundreds were entranced, including scholars and MPs. Together, they threw their money into an outlandish scheme to occupy Palestine. The Anglo-Israelite movement was on its feet.

Not everybody was enraptured. King George III was less than enthusiastic about giving up his throne for some freak from Newfoundland. In 1795, Brothers was committed to London's Canonbury Tower as a criminal lunatic and, just in case he recovered his wits, there was a charge of treason left on file. He was there for the next eleven years, and never recovered. He died, still babbling, in 1824.

The movement born on this crack-headed coast didn't quite end there. In years to come, Brothers's visions would re-surface, as a bulwark of white supremacy. In the meantime, his followers sought another prophet. Some went to Mother Buchan, a Scot, who told them to starve themselves for forty days and shave all their hair off except for a top-knot. On the appointed day, she declared, angels would haul them into heaven by their knots. When the angels failed to appear, Mother Buchan's emaciates began to drift away.

For the rest, there was Joanna Southcott, on the frothy end of British Methodism. She promised her disciples that she was pregnant with Shiloh, son of the Holy Ghost. Even after she died, they awaited a miracle from her putrefying corpse. It was several years before a physician was allowed to do his post-mortem; there was no Shiloh, the Southcott movement was at an end.

Joanna Southcott was buried in St. John's Wood. At least in death she found a form of reunion. A few rows away, across the cemetery, lies the man whose madness kindled her own: the Prophet of Fermeuse.

28

Eighty miles south of St. John's, the Bog of Avalon threw itself into a boil of turquoise surf, and disappeared.

I stopped the car on a bluff, some distance from the shore. According to the Grand Am, the temperature in the wind was minus seven, although the sky was diamond-blue and feathered in plumes of frozen white. Even from up here, I could hear the languorous suck and heave of the sea as it beat itself to vapours on the shore. Elsewhere, nothing moved—just the sunlight flaring and cooling in the sedge. Newfoundlanders called days like this weather-breeders, merely moments of gestation for the cruelty ahead.

Then I noticed a tiny settlement in the foaming landwash. It looked like a dusting of crumbs in the corner of an angry shout. The thought occurred to me that—if this was real—its inhabitants weren't merely living with the weather, but living right inside it. Great squalls of spray swirled across the village, everything soaked in salt. On the map it was called Portugal Cove South, and so I drove down there, to re-assure myself that it was all a trick of light.

Half the houses weren't houses at all but fishing boats, dragged up into the streets. There was no one around, just the roar, and the flotsam of essential lives: white-washed planks, skidoos, lobster-pots and bedrooms in the eaves. These were not lives that I readily under-stood. Even the signs were strangely oblique. "CHICKEN THIGHS CLEAN OUTS," said one, and on the shop was another: "NO PETS TOPS AND FOOTWEAR MUST BE WORN." It was, I suppose, a reminder that people would eventually emerge, some months from now, and that winter was not without end.

The wind tore at my coat like hunger. In my own life, the weather is almost incidental to my day—water on the pavement, a cold draught, a cat curled up in the sun. These are details that can easily be missed. Not so here. To Newfoundlanders, the weather gives the day its personality, a system of emotions that has earned its own language: mauzy, civil, scuddy, dirty, duckish. The best weather for fishing is caplin weather and the rest "you can leave to the birds." Mostly, the weather has to be defied, like living with blindness or a crazy dog. No one knows this better than the people of Portugal Cove South. Unof-ficially, they endure more foggy days in a row than anywhere else in the world.

Occasionally, the Newfoundland weather is so fantastically brutal that it becomes a perfect storm. This happens perhaps once every hundred years, most memorably in 1775, when violence converged on the island from every side. Seven hundred ships were lost and 1,400 people killed. It happened again just before Curwen arrived—eighty schooners smashed to pulp, and another 300 drowned. No one knew when it would happen again, nor which outports it would smash and sweep away. Most people hardly gave it a thought; it was just another, bigger crazier dog that had to be endured.

A few miles to the east was a lighthouse, to warn the Atlantic of the madness ahead. I'd already passed the turning for Cape Race as I'd come off the barrens. A thin, knobbly spine of grit twisted away, deep into the muskeg. I'd not been tempted to take it. Perhaps I should have done; Cape Race had also been a radio relay-station and its name was once a by-word for the hottest transatlantic news. "Via Cape Race," said news reports, a mark of their immediacy.

On 14 April 1912, a great ship was passing by, tapping signals into the Cape. They were messages to New York from rich people paying a dollar a word with no idea they were about to die.

Then came a message from the SS *Californian:* ice ahead.

"Keep out!" replied the liner. "Shut up! You're jamming my signal! I am working Cape Race."

It was one of the last messages RMS *Titanic* sent before she hit a lump of frozen weather, burst open and sank into the frenzy.

Half-frozen myself, I climbed back in the car and drove on, to an inlet known to the Basques as the Place of the Dead.

29

A gloomy name and a life at the edge of the froth had rendered the inhabitants of Trepassey irrepressibly quaint.

At the mouth of the inlet stood a lighthouse, Tom Corrigan and a dog the size of a grizzly. Mr. Corrigan said he'd been on this cliff for forty-six years, the most enduring lighthouse-keeper in the whole of Canada, and probably the world.

"How's it been?" I asked.

"Notbadconsiderin."

"Have you had any wrecks?"

"Nothinheresinceboutsixtyfive."

This was about as much as Mr. Corrigan and I ever clearly understood of each other. We were competing with a foghorn, a force four, forty-six years of gales and five generations of Irishness. Still, we were happy for each other's company and sat in the lamp-room all afternoon, trying to make sense of it all.

Trying to make sense of Mr. Corrigan's life was easier than I'd imagined. It was like a life from a nursery rhyme. Mr. and Mrs. Corrigan had known no other home but their place in the sky. They'd had nine children and lived in a cabin as dry as a boot. Sometimes the waves came right up the cliffs, and burst over their roof. Every winter, Mr. Corrigan took his gun to the big woods for partridges and moose. Once, there was fish too. Every summer, he'd put to sea in a homemade skiff. When the fishing was over, he'd haul his boat up the rock. Now it stood at the summit, like the Ark, except that it was a home for battered chickens.

As we talked, Sailor the dog ran up and down the cliffs as if she had sticky feet like a fly. This was the only landscape big enough to contain her. She was a delightful monster—a Newfoundland—part-bear, part-pony, web-toed and with a tail like an otter. It was strange to see such a lot of dog, running almost upside-down across the view. Mr. Corrigan said she was even better in the water, and could catch her own fish. She'd not, after all, got as big as she was by sitting around looking monstrous. Eating a lot was a matter of inbuilt emergency. Someone once told me that if a Newfoundland and a human baby were born on the same day and grew at the rate of the Newfoundland, the human would weigh ten stone by the end of its first year.

The odd thing about Sailor is that her ancestors probably weren't sea-dogs at all, but came from the Pyrenees. Perhaps being half-Basque and half-everything-else made her more Newfoundlandish than anything. She even had the islanders' generosity and, as I left, she gave me a lick. It almost knocked me over, like a slap with a bundle of fish.

On the way back to Trepassey, I noticed a house that was such an unlikely pea-green that I had to stop and stare. At first, I thought it stood by itself, on its own vast scrape of bay and cobbles. Then I heard a cackle in the grass.

"There's nobody home but the cat—and she's gone!"

There was another rattle of laughter, and I suddenly realised that the pea-green house wasn't alone after all. A little further up the beach was another saltbox, half-buried in cobbles and droppings. It had also been a pretty place—sash-windows, clapboard and cables to hold it all down. Now the wind had stripped it to the driftwood, and there were sheep in the hall. The owner was sitting out in the molly fodge in an armchair spangled with frost. He wore a pointed hat and raised his hand, as if about to tell a story.

"I'm sorry," I said. "I was just looking at the house . . ."

My apologies were torn away by the wind, and the story began. It was not a story with a beginning or an end, but more like a book falling open on a favourite page. I caught snatches of the 1880s, of a grandfather and a rascal called Charlie Fox-Bennett. At one point, the narrator's name even appeared, in the undergrowth of words; he was Billy-Joe Kennedy, born in Trepassey and hoped to die here.

". . . Fox-Bennett toured the island in a schooner," roared Billy-Joe, "with one message to the Irish: Keep Newfoundland out of Canada! Vote for Confederation, he warned, and they'll make Presbyterians of ye and cannon wads of yer children. Yer bones will bleach in the desert wastes of Canada . . ."

I listened until dusk. Then, just as grandfather was about to buy Charlie's pea-green house, the story turned to sheep.

"We got fifteen of them," said Billy-Joe. "All pets. We never eat them. Meat is a terrible crime, ye know. We all eat seaweed, straight off the ocean!"

"And the sheep all live with you? In the house?"

"Well, they got the kitchen and parlour. We got the upstairs."

Billy-Joe and his wife hadn't always lived on the brink. He'd done a spell in Nova Scotia but there was no contentment like the life they'd had here. Mrs. Kennedy hardly ever came downstairs any more but watched the tides as they came and went, through skeins of dust and wool. Billy-Joe brought her lipsticks, they said, and pieces of kelp on a plate. God bless you, Billy-Joe, she'd say, and all my friends, the sheep.

I stayed in a little hotel of fairy lights and hot-buttered toast. As almost everyone in the town was called Pennell, it was easier to think of my hosts as the Christmases. Perhaps they even made toys. They did everything else. Apart from his hotel, Harold Pennell ran the dump, drove trucks, delivered telephone books and served the town's writs.

Poor Trepassey, Place of the Dead, these were the last jobs left. On 1 July 1992, the Minister of Fish had news for the town. The time of plenty is over, he'd said. The Ocean's empty.

30

I met the Minister of Fish once, back in St. John's. The day that John Crosbie had closed down the sea had been the greatest moment of his political career, and also his worst.

Although he was now almost retired, Crosbie had kept his office over the harbour. We met there one Saturday, me slightly in awe and he in his Saturday shirt. I don't know what I'd expected. At one stage, they said, Crosbie had almost been Prime Minister of Canada. He studied me momentarily and then never looked at me again. I studied him for rather longer—frayed pockets, a tendency to jowliness, and a magnificent stoop. A life, perhaps, spent enduring little people.

Now he was squinting at a tiny shred of numbers, and punching at some "fucking combinations." After a few false clicks, we were in a boardroom that smelt of cigars and a week of law. It was insufferably hot and all the chairs squeaked as we talked. Crosbie wafted me into a slug of leather and found one for himself. Then he settled down among the squeaks, shut his eyes for an hour and began to talk about fish.

"My job at the Ministry," he said, "was to control a disaster."

It was, I suppose, a hereditary role.

The Crosbies had been stifling disasters ever since they'd fled the Scottish cholera in 1843. Like the Bairds, they'd enjoyed moments of prosperity but, even at the best of times, they'd drunk themselves to death. If John Crosbie had been able to peer upwards into his family tree, all he'd have seen would be the marinated victims of disaster. The Crosbies of St. John's were—as everyone knew—cursed, and always died at fifty-five. The young John had even tried to stifle congenital disaster by fleeing to London in 1956. It was a hopeless ruse. He flunked out of LSE and spent his time watching trials. His most vivid memories of London would be of a sodomy trial, and a claim by a circus midget squashed in a stampede of elephants. The next year, he was back in St. John's.

Nowadays, the most remarkable aspect of his life was that he was still alive, sober and seventy-one. It occurred to me that, deep down, there was euphoria, a sense that as these were years he'd stolen from disaster—he could say what he liked. But when I read his lumpy memoirs, *No Holds Barred*, I realised that John Crosbie had been saying what he liked all his life. To his enemies, he was the "Crosbiesaurus." To his friends, he was "The Codfather," a man who'd always done the right thing but said the wrong one. After forty years in politics, most Newfoundlanders held him in awe. He'd fought their corner in Ottawa, often at the expense of dignity—dressing up in sealskin and roaring at "the effete elites, the snobs, the literati" and the "global village idiots." For many, this made him a champion.

It was only when they remembered their fishing that they still felt their anger.

The end of fishing was caused by its own success. By the 1960s the process of scraping the ocean of all living creatures had become industrial. Men were floating factories out to sea, and hauling up the seabed and sifting the currents. The Atlantic had become a city of abattoirs, working all night and working through the ice. There were no quotas, no limits, no restraint. In 1968, fish were being gathered up at almost three times the rate at which they could replace themselves. Over 810,000 tonnes were caught that year, enough fish to stretch nose-to-tail three times round the world. Still the slaughter continued. The ocean was to be scoured of life, thrashed into a watery desert.

No one saw the future, empty ahead. In 1976, Canada imposed a 200-mile fishing limit, but then filled the empty space with its own expanding fishery. Even when the harvest faltered, the Newfoundlanders weren't worried. The cod had wandered off before—in 1857, 1874 and 1890—but they'd always returned. When it happened again, there was first panic and then a collective failure of logic. The seals had eaten an ocean of fish—or was it Ottawa? Newfoundlanders simply refused to accept that they'd played any part in the plunder. Nor was anyone about to teach them conservation.

"There was a tendency among politicians of all stripes," said Crosbie dryly, "to put the interests of the fishermen—who were voters—above the interests of the cod, who weren't."

Didn't anybody want to save the harvest?

"There's a great myth in Newfoundland about the fisherman. He's a folk hero and can do no wrong. In fact, he's just as much a scoundrel as fishermen anywhere. They throw away the small fish or the species they don't want. They use the wrong kinds of gear. They pay lip-service to conservation but the name of the game is to blame everyone else . . ."

So it wasn't Ottawa's fault?

There were squeaks of irritation as Crosbie shifted in his chair.

"No, that's bullshit. If we'd had control of the fishery the codfish would have disappeared twenty years sooner."

The problem, it seemed, was one of wiring. Newfoundland's fiscal system had been wired by amateurs, or rather fishermen. It was probably the only place in the world where fishermen were paid unemployment insurance. Nor was it just fishermen—UI paid for fish-wives too, and processors, freezers, canners and baggers, anyone in fish. They called the system "10-42" because ten weeks' work bought forty-two weeks of pay-outs. It was a simple system but the effect was spectacular: the economy arced and glowed with mainland money; everybody wanted ten weeks' work; every outport got its fish-plant. It was a tangle that even Ottawa couldn't unravel. Crosbie had fought off reform—and won. With UI, he'd argued, outporters at last had a half-decent life.

But what was good for Newfoundland wasn't good for the fish. Hundreds of tiny fish-plants were screaming out for their catch. Money and fish were crackling round the grid in a frenzy of over-supply. The state was paying men for something it didn't want in order to keep them out of work. It was a short-circuit that couldn't last. The only question was: which would go first—the economy or the fish?

The fish lost. In 1992, scarcity became catastrophe. John Crosbie had only been at the Ministry for a year but at least his options were stark. There was no question of one quota for the whole province. The southern shore would have met the quota before the northern fishery had even begun.

"Well, that would have been bloodshed, right?"

For the Minister of Fish there was only one solution, and it still made him gasp. "Imagine! Me, a Crosbie and a Newfoundlander, shuttin' down the industry that had made the settlement of this island possible, and which had enabled us to survive for centuries . . ."

He took the news first to his constituents on the Irish Shore. He hadn't expected much warmth, and even now the anger still simmers.

One in five Newfoundlanders was already unemployed. "The idea of another 26,000 out of work was more than most could stomach."

There was some consolation in the benefits that followed. Crosbie worked hard to squeeze the government of welfare, and secured a package worth over $4 billion. There was money for those who'd abandon fishing and money for those who'd re-train. A fisherman could thrive, just by throwing it all in and learning to read. Within eight months, over 80 per cent of outporters were dependent on benefits and over 10,000 of them had left the fishery for good.

It wasn't what anybody wanted. Almost five hundred years after Cabot had announced its wealth of fish, people began to wonder if Newfoundland was needed any more. Self-esteem tumbled, and the exodus began. Outports closed, and the stragglers drifted off to the cities. In the next decade, over 50,000 people left the island and the birthrate, once the highest in Canada, shrivelled to the lowest. To those who witnessed this period, it was like packing up a show at the end of a weary run.

"I remember the silence," said Billy-Joe Kennedy. "For the first time ever, there was silence."

31

That night I ate deep-fried fish nuggets at the First Venture.

"We were the first business to open after the fish plant closed," said a voice at the hatch. There were no other customers, and the nuggets were probably Russian.

At least it had survived. Over five hundred people had lost their jobs when the plant closed. In a town that was now less than nine hundred strong, it had been a bewildering blow. Going to work each day was now something that most people could only imagine. Few businesses had ventured down to this end of the bog. I'd noticed a place making ships' lights, and another assembling false teeth. But they were merely workshops, employing no more than a dozen at the most.

For everybody else there was the UI.

Making an adventure out of welfare was nothing new to Trepassey. They'd been "hobbling," or stacking up the claims, since the game began. They'd even developed a fruity reputation for persuasion and smoking out informers. But the scam was the same as anywhere else.

Once a man had earned his UI stamps, he started fishing in his wife's name, and she became entitled. Then the rest of the family was out, floating around in a fantasy of fishing.

Crosbie told me the whole system was ripe with deception and fraud.

"In Newfoundland," he said, "no one thinks there's anything wrong with robbing the welfare. They figure the government makes the rules and—if the rules are stupid—it's the government's fault."

Even officials were at it, cheating officialdom.

"I had one of my supporters appointed to the Board of UI appeals. She turned out as bad as anyone—claiming fisherman's UI on the very same day she was hearing appeals! She'd not spent a day on the water in her life . . ."

There'd been no resentment in his voice. He talked of "a lawless tradition," as if Newfoundland were a nation of Masterless Men. I suspect that, if he'd ever opened his eyes, I might even have seen a gleam of admiration.

"Some families can clear up to $20,000 a year. With no mortgage and plenty of berries and moose, that's alright." He hesitated. "Yes, boy, a good life."

No one, I realised, wanted to believe this more than the Minister of Fish.

32

Eighty-two miles down the coast, I met a truck-driver who told me that whisky was the Devil's work, and so was the Internet. Vincent Roche saw the hand of God in most aspects of his life and the rest he left to chance.

Even the way we met had a certain haphazardness about it. One minute I was sloshing through the ice and the next he was calling me in for tea. I don't think even he knew where the idea of tea had come from—especially as there wasn't any. Vincent's bungalow had been stripped of everything except two chairs, a kettle and a note pinned to the plaster. WANTED, it read, ONE WOMAN. MUST HAVE BODY HEAT AND OWN TEETH.

"Jingling Joe . . . ," he cursed.

A promising cup of tea turned into a tour of Branch.

Vincent was forty-two and believed that any day now his luck would change. Up until then, he said, his life had been dismally Canadian—an unspecific spell with the army, trucks in Alberta and the loneliness of a place so flat you could see for weeks ahead.

"Jeepers, I hates Canada. I missed this place like an arm."

Things would be different from now. He was back in Branch forever, and with a plot of land up on the barrens. For no particular reason, he was sure it straddled a seam of gold. The thought of all that wealth filled his head with bells and, as we walked, they tinkled and chimed.

"Ring a ding ding," sang Vincent, "ring a ding ding."

Branch was a village of Vincents, charming, embattled and in defiance of the odds. It had been tucked into the haunches of its own little estuary, a few flecks of tin and paint against the great restless night of smoky black brine. Vincent said it was not the place it was; about thirty saltboxes had rotted away in his lifetime alone.

"And then they just pull the whole jingling thing down and chuck it on the fire."

The outport that survived had faced destruction with extravagance. Up each alley, we clambered into new layers of colour—lilac, iceberg, Arctic yellows, and barns in wintry pink. One house was decorated with a shoal of fish-knives, and another was overwhelmed in Virgin Marys. There was a vast biblical ladder propped up against every chimney, and the village horse was called Prince.

"We used to have a bar too, called The Shamrock. Or was it The Hog and Slug? 'Twas a great place for fighting. Most of the time we just called it The Bucket of Blood . . ."

Fighting was about all that Vincent could remember of the bar. These were simple contests, one-to-one, and no gloating over a victory. Nor was there much chance of a good punch-up being spoilt by the police. The nearest Mounties were forty miles away.

"My father and I were down there all the time. There was a fight every night, as sure as there's shit in a cat. The only thing we liked more than a fight was two fights . . ."

At the store we met Henry Power, an old crab-man, the best fighter of all.

"Remember the fights, Henry?" said Vincent. "If you got a hold of someone, it would have taken a *torch* to cut him free!"

I didn't catch the reply. It sounded like Irish rinsed in shingle.

"They thought he'd had a heart attack," whispered Vincent, as soon as Henry was out of reach, "but it was just an *ingrown muscle*!"

Nowadays things were quieter. There were only two brawls in the calendar. The first was the Garden Party, a little summer carnage for the children, and the other—which happened to be that evening— was the Fire Truck Social. Vincent said I should come along.

"Will there be any fighting?"

"Not much," shrugged Vincent. "Just the women."

There was another problem; I had nowhere to stay.

"Ye can stay with my parents, out on the farm."

Mr. Dermot Roche built his saltbox in 1958. The following year, he decided he'd had enough of Branch, and so he and Mrs. Roche had lifted their house onto a raft of tree-trunks and cod blubber, and rolled it into the barrens. Everyone in Branch had taken a hand at the ropes.

"We couldn't give them nothing for their trouble, we'd nothing to give."

For the Roches, it had been a happy mooring, and they'd had eight children. From the swelter of their stove, they could peer out across the estuary into the hunting grounds beyond. The smudges of grey out there were companies of caribou, part of a herd of 5,500 chewing their way across Avalon. There were partridges too, and rabbits, said Mr. Roche ("although you'd call them ptarmigans and Arctic hares"). Better still, he said, was the stupidest bird in the world: the spruce partridge.

"So stunned, it won't move!" said Vincent.

"Ye can save a bullet," said his father, "and pick it up with a noose."

Every winter, Mr. Roche and his boys would set out for the woods with a pony and slide. The business of gathering firewood was so instinctive that it even had its own vocabulary, and five different words for logs; junks, billets, bavins, crunnicks and splits. In every other respect, life on the estuary had seemed beautifully simple. It might even have been perfect if Vincent's older brother hadn't drowned on a hunting trip in 1986. His picture hung in the parlour alongside the rifle and Our Lady of Guadaloupe.

"Everybody came to the wake. This place was blocked."

It was obvious Mrs. Roche had given a lot of thought to where the path led next. "I'd like to be waked here, in the parlour," she said, "but Dermot wants to be waked in the church."

A trail of bleeding hearts and printed agony led upstairs, to the upper deck. There were only two bedrooms, both fitted with pink carpet, or "canvas" as Mrs. Roche called it. My room was barely big enough for me to stand in. Eight children once slept in here. "We used to heat up rocks in the furnace," said Mrs. Roche fondly, "and pop them in their beds, wrapped in an old sock."

In the corner was a small shelf of books (including some alarming works on home surgery) and a Virgin Mary plugged into the mains. Whenever I woke at night, I found myself at my own wake, the Virgin glowing green with what I hoped was pity.

"And if ye need the bathroom," said Mr. Roche, "it's at the stern, in the linny."

I followed his directions, into the lean-to. To my surprise, the bath itself was swagged in huge red curtains. It looked like a Jacobean four-poster—except, of course, that it was plumbed in to hot- and cold-running peat.

Back in the parlour, Mrs. Roche was laying out supper: salmon fish-cakes, pickle, home-made bread, figgy buns and damper dogs cooked on a skillet. I don't know what the Roches made of their guest, but I felt a sudden surge of affection. Mr. Roche saw it all as an excuse for partridgeberry wine.

"The people here got backbone . . . ," he began.

It was the signal for a torrent of family pride.

"Branch sent out more volunteers to the war," said Vincent, "than anywhere else in Newfoundland . . ."

Mrs. Roche nodded. "The priest was pulling them out of the recruiting booth to go and make the hay . . ."

". . . and one of our lads was a journalist at the liberation of Auschwitz . . ."

". . . and the first three nurses at the Twin Towers disaster . . ."

". . . and there's Carl English, who plays for the Hawaii Warriors . . ."

"That," said Mrs. Roche, suddenly sombre, "was such courage—especially after his *tragedy*. They pulled him from a fire about fifteen years ago—the same one that killed his Mam and Dad."

There was a moment of solemnity and then another rush of blood.

"Never," said Mr. Roche, "was a people so proud of a rock!"

When the wine was done, there were hot screech toddies, made with Big Dipper, and a fiery nudge-nudge spirit, known only as "the white stuff." At some stage we watched an ancient video, made in

Ireland. It had been played so many times that the picture was now soupy but I could still hear the voice, aghast. "The Irish Shore," it said, "is the nineteenth century fossilised . . ."

Then Mrs. Roche had a premonition of Christ, emerging from the sunbeams. It would happen at dawn the next day. "I'll wake us all up," said Vincent, "and we'll get him on film."

I don't remember much of the Fire Truck Social, filtered as it was through a haze of toddies and the nudge-nudge grog. In the smears of memory that remain, there are accordions and drums, and huge, meaty people dancing the Lancers and the Square Step. I had a long conversation with a man called Snitty, who'd had cancer all his life. Vincent said it wasn't cancer at all but just a life of welfare. Not even the women fought—or not much. I walked back to the farm behind a big damp girl who was throwing punches at a prickly head. At the end of the village, they teetered theatrically for a moment, and then fell into a saltbox.

No one got up to see Christ in his ascension. Vincent would admit that he had slept through yet another miracle.

"All my life," he said, "I've had the luck of a shithouse rat."

33

I said good-bye to the Roches, and took the road out to Distress, or St. Brides as they now insisted.

"We built the road to Distress when I was mayor," said Mr. Roche, "as part of a work programme. There were only twelve jobs for fifty-nine hungry men."

Outports had never had to face such choices before. After that, there was not much fighting in Branch. Too many men hated each other for real.

34

I drove all day, to the northern shore, where my great-grandfather had once preached to English settlers, more receptive to his version of God.

It was a curious journey. I spent the morning muffled in fog as I edged my way across the northern bog. Then the fog rolled away and I found myself among the brittle, charcoal lines of Conception Bay. Here, the ragged edge of the island was defined in great frosted headlands, buttresses and capes of beautiful wind-whipped gloom. I found myself both in admiration, and then shrinking away at the coldness of its splendour.

I imagined that the outporters along this shore had felt much the same. There was no sense of permanence about their settlements; no stone, no square, no public trough or market. It was as if they were still the fishing camps they'd started out as—places of planks, jig's dinners and flotsam. Deaths were announced in garage windows, and the tombstones of the living were lined up in the undertakers', only the date of departure incomplete. Did I know the Slades in England, people asked me, as if they hadn't been away for centuries. *No Loitering*, said signs, *No Roaming Animals*. Who was doing all this loitering? Sometimes I didn't see anyone at all.

There were few clues as to the lives lived on the bay. Occasionally I came across an asbestos dance-hall, anchored out in the barrens, offering a Hawaiian Theme Nite or just quietly unbuckling itself in the breeze. Most of the time I found myself thinking about the details that seemed to be missing: bars, playing fields or a walk in the woods. Even new videos were announced at the store with an intriguing dearth of letters—*Shipingnew*, perhaps, or *Lordofring*.

I stopped to eat wherever I could, but these were monosyllabic encounters, a simple exchange of gravy and dollars. Even Newfoundland's most effusive patriot, Harold Horwood, had warned about the roadside "diners" in 1969. The only thing he was wrong about was that the gruelling food ("badly prepared by people who can't cook") would get any better. If anything, it was worse. It wasn't so much that it tasted bad, it just didn't taste of anything—whether it was feathery bread rolls, gluey meat or hopelessly optimistic "Chicken Delite." The only way that Newfoundlanders could punish these places was by not going to them. I always found myself eating alone, sometimes with the uneasy feeling that I was the first victim of the season.

Perhaps I was just missing Mrs. Roche's cooking, or the Irishness of the Southern Shore. Up here, it seemed, the English were at their most Calvinist and battened-down. The sight of doorways in the turf didn't cheer me much. They were root cellars, I was told, where people stashed away turnips and wurzels for the long winter. It was not an uplifting thought.

· · ·

I was surprised to discover that Eliot Curwen was not the first of my ancestors to visit this coast. The other was from the Gimlette side of the family, a tangle of West Country merchants and Huguenots in the seventeenth century. He was Robert Hayman, sometime law student, dilettante, bon viveur and layabout. By the time of his forty-third birthday in 1618, he'd had virtually nothing to show for his life except some excruciating doggerel. Here is his *Antidote for Drunkards:*

> If that your head would ake before you drinke
> As afterwards, you'd ne'r be drunke, I think.

Such foolery might even have carried him harmlessly into old age if his brother-in-law hadn't been the Master of the Merchant Venturers. That year, he offered Hayman the governorship of a colony on Conception Bay. It was not an offer a man of poetic vision could refuse. After all, the Merchant Venturers had already established a colony on that shore with the delightful name of Cupids.

That afternoon, I drove over to Cupids, with the uneasy feeling that it was not going to be quite as cosy as it sounded.

35

I didn't stay long. Although Cupids was crouched at the end of a deep inlet of splintered shale, the wind was as vicious now as it had been four hundred years ago. Great blasts of icy pins were ripping up the water, lashing at the straw and scrub, and prising the old net sheds apart. I watched in fascination as a raven flew over to investigate the carnage and was caught in a hail of frozen noise and tossed back into the barrens.

To Canadians, this was their first-ever English settlement, in 1610. Some might even see it as a tiny mangled prototype of the British Empire to come. For the forty planters who settled here, the experiment can't have ended soon enough. It was the same story as Ferryland, ten years later: scurvy; rotting livestock, rotting seeds and rotting morale. There was only a brief moment of joy when a child was born—the first Englishman born in the Americas—but death was more ambitious. As in Ferryland, that first winter one in ten of the planters rotted away, and were buried in the scree.

As if it wasn't hard enough surviving the winter, the summer brought

hatred. England's fishermen were disgusted by the idea of colonisation (the planters ate all the best seabirds, and took the best "rooms").
Piracy erupted and the sawmill was torched. The colony, or "plantation," began to fall apart. It's hard now to see why my forebear, Robert
Hayman, had ever agreed to hitch his fortunes to such a calamity.
Either he wasn't in full command of the facts, or he'd lost his grip
on reality.

I prefer to think that he was just a little giddy, his reason distorted
by a peculiar story. You will be the ruler of a strange red people, they
told him, who dance and squawk like gulls, and dress in feathers.

The planters of Cupids had just had their first, charming encounter
with the natives. Sadly, it would also be their last.

36

If it hadn't been for what happened later, the meeting at Bull Arm
might have been seen as one of history's great little picnics.

To begin with, both sides were cautious, and waved at each other
in white—a flag for the colonists, a wolfskin for the "saviges." Nearly
a century of suspicion lay between them. Up until then, Europeans
had tended to regard the natives as souvenirs, to be taken home and
sported. The natives, for their part, had responded with stealth and
petty theft. Now the Merchant Venturers sought a fresh start. Make
their acquaintance, they ordered, and "with their good likinge and
consent" seek to retain one so that we might learn the savages' language.
This was coupled with a strict injunction; "we wish you herein to
followe our advice and otherwise not to meddle with them."

For a moment the two parties stared at each other in utter astonishment—the Jacobeans in their boots and doublets, and the savages
drenched in paint and feathers. The report that the colonists sent
home is breathless with excitement:

> Their faces flat & broad, red with okir, as all their apparell is, & the
> rest of their body. They are broad-breasted & bould, & stand very
> upright . . .

It was a powerful image—so powerful that, even though these were
the only savages on the Atlantic seaboard using ochre, the term "Red

Indian" would soon apply generically to all native Americans across the continent.

The two parties moved together. Then, suddenly, they found themselves tangled up in each other, laughing and hooting and slapping each other's chests. As the hilarity subsided, there was an exchange of gifts. In this, as in most things, the Merchant Venturers showed themselves to be determinedly genteel; in exchange for an arrow and a few feathers, they gave the savages two fresh table-napkins and a hand-towel. The savages were delighted, and broke into a fresh round of singing and slapping.

One can only imagine what they made of each other's food. The planters chewed through some dried caribou, and the savages put away a tub of butter and raisins. They liked it well enough but the beer was more to their taste. And then the aquavitae. The afternoon ended with one of the Indians producing farting noises out of the empty aqua-vitae bottle, a jape which (noted our chronicler), "they fell all into laughture at."

It would be nice to assume that the relationship between the Red Men and the Europeans continued like this, a simple exchange of farts and slaps and bits of tableware. But the next stages were harder. The Merchant Venturers never got to learn the savages' language—and nor did anyone else. Even two centuries later, no one had any idea what the Indians called themselves. Unsurprisingly, they also thought of themselves as "the Red Men"—they were the *Beothuks*.

The following year, 1613, the planters and the Red Men both turned up at the same beach to develop their acquaintance. Unfortunately, the assembled Indians were spotted by a French fishing crew, who mistook them for a riot and "let fly their shott." The Indians scattered, running deep into the woods. From now on, there would be no more picnics and no more jollity. The Beothuks took to a life in the shadows, slinking round the fish-stages at night, scavenging for nails and rags and then fleeing, as quiet as moonlight. The planters never saw them again.

By the time Robert Hayman arrived in Harbour Grace, five years later, the Beothuks were little more than a rumour.

37

Harbour Grace had never recovered from its failure to become the metropolis that Hayman envisaged.

But it hadn't stopped trying. Like St. John's, it was all wildly grandiose—except that everything had been miniaturised or made out of odds and ends. The streets were marked out in old ships' cannons, and there was a whole parade of mansions built—they say—out of English ballast, and with English soil in the rose-beds. There was also a tiny aeroplane decorating the waterfront, and an old sealing ship in the cove—the SS *Kyle*, still painted-up as if ready for the ice. As to the rest of the town, it was all mullioned and corbelled and dripping with peppermint and verdigris. I even found a sign that promised Piano and Organ Repairs, although the shop had long since rotted away.

I was also surprised to find them still building bankers in the harbour. Although the cod moratorium hadn't lasted forever, fishing was now a matter of regulation and niggardly small print. But there was nothing abstemious about these hulks, draggers big enough to suck up a hundred tonnes of fish—or a mansion come to that. One of the carpenters hauled me up the side, and into the hull. "We got videos," he said, "fitted kitchens, showers and microwaves. Ye'd hardly know ye was away from home."

He was right. It was like a show-house squashed into a helmet.

"Will there be any fish left," I asked, "by the time it's finished?"

"The fish will be back, my son, any time now."

In his optimism, I thought I heard the sound of Dorset or Devon. He was soon probing for news. "What's happened to Hampton Court?" he asked. "My great-grandfather once owned it, ye know. But he lost it in a game of cards."

Meanwhile, my own distant—and somewhat distracted—ancestor was working up a fantasy of his own.

Hayman was enchanted by Newfoundland and had even given it a flashy new name, *Britaniola*. Quite how this court poodle survived his tenure is a mystery but—remarkably—he was happy. Perhaps being a poet gave him an edge over the idealists. He simply couldn't understand why his old Oxford friends, Viscount Falkland and Sir William Vaughan, were making such a mess of things down south—and he told them as much, in verses dedicated to Vaughan's wife. Although the occasional references to the "scurvy deaths" can't exactly have cheered her, he spoke of his island in delightful terms. All that was needed to settle Newfoundland, it seemed, was an unusual imagination.

Even more remarkable is that the Merchant Venturers continued to subsidise this poetry. The historian Prowse thought that Hayman was nothing more than "a rhyming simpleton" and yet, during his ten years, his colony met with "good and hopeful success." Hayman even stayed for a winter, and oversaw the move from Cupids to the altogether more elegant Harbour Grace.

Not that he got his ruffs dirty. If gentlemen were to dabble in plantations, it should be done with dignity. "Hauing onely had the ouerseeing others hard labour" to trouble him, Hayman allowed his mind to wander, onto a higher plane. Initially, he spent his time translating Rabelais ("that excellently wittie Doctor"), but then he began work on his own, rather curious, oeuvre: *Quodlibets, lately come over from New Britaniola, Old Newfound-Land. Epigrams and other fmall parcels, both Morall and Diuine.* In the first English rhymes ever to emerge from the Americas, the island appears as gentle and tame—and deliciously clunky:

> The Aire in Newfound-Land is wholesome, good:
> The Fire, as sweet as any made of wood:
> The Waters, very rich, both salt and fresh:
> The Earth more rich, you know it no lesse.
> Where are all good, Fire, Water, Earth and Aire,
> What man made of these four would not live there?

Poor Hayman, his fantasies got curlier and curlier. By 1628, he was sending messages to King Charles I, via a lush mutual acquaintance, the Duke of Buckingham. Send me a million men, he urged, to make a city out of Harbour Grace. It will be a city named in honour of a great king, Carolinople.

When, in August 1628, Buckingham was sliced open by an assassin, the scheme began to fall apart. With it went Hayman's interest in Harbour Grace. Two months later, he was embarking on another adventure: the conquest of Guiana. It was to be his last.

A year later, he boiled to death in his own "burning fever," drifting, somewhere up the Amazon.

38

Curwen arrived in Harbour Grace in November 1893 to find it in a fever of its own. If he'd assumed—as I had—that this northern shore was wholly and doggedly Protestant, he was wrong. Harbour Grace had—and still has—three churches, all vying for its citizens' souls. In 1893, the evangelism was simmering away, at just below boiling point.

I walked up to the church hall, where Curwen and Grenfell were to lecture. It was a lumpy, defensive building—one of the few made of granite—just behind the church. "1835" said the date-plaque, the same year that insults turned to mutilation. The first victim was the editor of *The Public Ledger*, Henry Winton, who'd been enraging Catholics with his poisonous, intemperate editorials. His description of the Catholics' temporal leader as a "subject fit for the lunatic asylum" was too much for some. He was ambushed a little way up the road from here, beaten unconscious and had his ears stuffed with gravel. Then, as a reminder that the sword still had distinct advantages over the pen, one ear was notched and the other sliced off. It didn't stop him ranting but it meant that, for the rest of his life, he had to do it beneath a large pair of splendid velvet ears.

If only the rest of the century had been so velvety. There was a war declared in education, and every school became a skirmish, and then divided into three: Anglican, Catholic and Methodist. Arch-deacons slept with pistols under their pillows, and Harbour Grace threw a riot, its first, in 1860. It was worse in 1883. This time, hundreds of Catholics and Orangemen went head-to-head, with sealing-guns and rum and axes. There were more ears lost, and teeth and hands, and five ordinary lives. In the rush to calm the situation, every one of the nineteen men arrested was acquitted. Harbour Grace—poor Hayman's city for gentlemen—now glowed with rage.

Almost exactly ten years later, Curwen and his friends were chuntering up the branch line, wondering what to expect.

They arrived in the miniature metropolis on a miniature train (that's survived only as a roundabout, out in Grand Falls).

To everyone's surprise, it was a day without trouble. Even Grenfell was discreet in the face of riot. "If I had said a word about religion," he once wrote, of one of his lectures, "the whole pack would have been at each other's throat in a twinkling."

Despite the calm, Curwen was horrified by the war of the churches. Each of them had contrived to make a wasteland of whatever public assets were available. Either there had to be three of everything, or important posts had to be shared in rotation. "The result," he wrote, "is that promotion by merit is unknown . . . [and that] a village is either without a school altogether or has to have three—three bad ones with teachers who scarcely know more than ABC . . ."

Oddly enough, he disagreed with his new friend, Dr. Moses Harvey, about sectarianism. Dr. Harvey, who'd been so wise about the giant squid, was rather less impressive on this issue. "Denominational zeal," he wrote, "perhaps furnishes a stimulus to educational effort . . ."

Whoever was right, it would take another hundred years and the atrocities of Mount Cashel to dampen down the zeal. These days, although the churches had retained a vague hold over the Sabbath, the old fire was now just scattered embers. Whenever the question of religion was raised, it always struck me that—for most Newfoundlanders—observance was more a matter of niceties than salvation.

"Going to church," as one man put it, "is just something to do on a Sunday."

I booked into the hotel across the road from Curwen's church hall. It had replaced the old Archibald's Hotel and was an ugly, unapologetic lump of bricks the colour of Bologna sausage. There was more Bologna for breakfast, and the unmistakable spectre of Bologna lingering in every room. Next to my bed was an evangelical work and a note, which suggested that the fight was not yet over. "For more info about the Book of Mormon," it read, "or about the Purpose of Life, call Carbonear 596-1008."

That evening, I whittled away my loneliness in the bar with the Book of Mormon and a glass of sausagey wine. Nobody else spoke or drank or took their coats off. With so much welfare trickling into the poker machines, it was rather difficult to follow the Mormons' thread, and in the end I gave up. Looking back on it, this was a low point in my travels; the combination of evangelism (which I've always found incomprehensible) and despair (which was all too stark) had got to me. I wondered if it had got to Curwen too. After Newfoundland and Labrador, his evangelism—although it had never exactly blazed—became measured and controlled. He would make no wild assumptions about the benefits of proselytising, and sought to relieve suffering primarily through medicine and his sense of order. Perhaps we would both have envied Hayman; through all the layers of poetry, he was unable to see any suffering at all.

I couldn't even finish the wine. Sausaginess, too, had taken its toll. Had I been sitting here, in the old Archibald's, on 20 May 1932, the ambience would have been different, not sausage but chicken soup. Nor would I have been struggling with Mormonism. Instead, my attention would have been torn away by the sight of a beautiful American woman: auburn, gamine and forthright. She would have been dressed for flying, and pouring her soup into a Thermos flask. She was already famous.

Her name was Miss Amelia Earhart, and she was about to change the way Americans felt about aeroplanes and the Atlantic and—most of all—their women.

39

Miss Earhart's story has no easy place in the history of this island, despite what everyone says. She didn't come to Newfoundland because it was at the centre of anything but, rather, because it was at the edge of the world. It just happened to be the last lump of the Americas before the great nothingness that presaged the first lumps of Europe. She didn't tour it, or eat cod's tongues or dance The Lancers. She couldn't even remember much about the place in her memoirs. It was just something firm, a perch from which she and her Lockheed Vega could hurl themselves. She left nothing behind—not so much as a goggle or a toothpick—and the field she flew from is still just a strip of flattish bog. She didn't even take anything away, except of course the chicken soup.

But, as it turned out, this liquefied chicken's adventure was one of the most enjoyable in aviation history. It was hardly surprising that the rest of Newfoundland wanted a part in it.

Miss Earhart blasted off from their island just after breakfast, with a magnificent promise: "You'll hear from me in less than 15 hours." She was out by four minutes—although she'd landed not in Paris, as she'd hoped, but in a bog not unlike the one she'd emerged from. It was a spectacular arrival, flames pouring from the manifold, and the little aviatrix soaked in aero-fuel. Unfortunately, the only person to witness this celestial splashdown was an Irish cowherd.

"Where am I?" she asked him.

"In Gallagher's pasture," he told her.

Her flight from Ulster to London was more triumphant. Hanworth Aerodome was packed. Miss Earhart had been the first woman to fly the Atlantic alone and the first person of either sex to have flown it twice (she'd flown as a passenger from Trepassey four years earlier). To cap it all, she'd broken the speed record. The newspapers adored her. "HEROINE OF THE AIR," proclaimed the *Daily Sketch*. Within five days of her return, Walter Sickert had painted his haunted cinematic masterpiece, *Miss Earhart's Arrival*. In all the blues and greys and splashes of London rain, Harbour Grace was forgotten.

Although this was never really Newfoundland's story, it has a Harbour Grace ending. There was a moment of sublimity and perfection, and then all was lost in uncertainty and doubt. For the next five years, Miss Earhart was the embodiment of almost everyone's ideal, whether they saw beauty in women or merely injustice. She was sporting and modern, an American, a mistress of powerful machines, and desired by both men and women alike. Then, in 1937, she simply disappeared, somewhere over the Pacific.

The U.S. government spent $4 million searching for her, and then the rumour mill began to churn; she'd survived, said one, and was living on an atoll; she'd been captured by the Japanese, went another, and cruelly interned. Even now the search goes on but there's nothing much there.

Just as she had left Harbour Grace, Miss Earhart had left the world without a trace.

40

I continued north, on a peninsula of scattered Dorsetmen.

Although the coast was black and cracked and speckled with ice and crippled shrub, I sensed a change of mood. Perhaps it was just the first rays of spring. There was now meltwater bubbling out of the barrens, and the straw was slowly unslathering itself from the frozen gravel. Or perhaps I now saw defiance where previously I'd only seen despair. The same grim determination that had survived the voyages from Wareham and Poole had survived in the outports' names: Job's Cove, Bareneed and Breakheart Point. The diners were decorated with hunting rifles, and the tombstones with magnificent trawlers (the same boats that had taken their owners to their deaths). Best of all were the cars with their ludicrous chrome and smoky windows and cartoon flames pouring off the wheels. It was as if the only way of surviving this struggle was to be Batman or The Incredible Hulk.

Whenever I came upon an outport, tucked in its cove, I bought an ice-cream. It was just an excuse to explore the stores. These were like the old supply-boats that had called in from England, packed with fish-hooks and molasses bread, Christmas lights and dickie birds (which were just another form of sausage). The traders were from much the same families as three or four centuries before: the Blundens and Pyes and the Taverners.

The peninsula ended in a beautiful outport and a sign: "Extremely dangerous beyond this Point." After that, there was nothing but vapours and a grinding sound, which I assumed to be the sea, somewhere way below. The makers of Disneyworld had thought that Bay de Verde was so improbable that they'd copied it for their World in Miniature, the archetypal outport. It was like a shelf of curly coloured hats, sloping gently into its own tiny cove. Millinery might have seemed a strange response to such extremity but in Bay de Verde they'd been quietly prospering for centuries, in the harvest of seals.

I clambered down among the narrow lanes and curly mansards of the outport. The last of the sealers was pulling out of the harbour, loaded with guns and hakapiks, and flats for getting in among the harps. It was the Basques who'd started this ice-hunting long before Cupids and *Quodlibets*. For them, there was profit: six gallons of seal-oil to be boiled out of every harp. For the Dorsetmen who followed them, there was merely survival. Eating seals was the only way of getting through the hungry spring, the months before the cod-grounds thawed. They called the killing *swiling* and, in time, their foraging became an industry. By 1857, there were 13,000 going to The Front, in over 400 ships. Over half a million seals were going for lamp oil, and Bay de Verde got its curly roofs.

I watched the last boat leave, from up on the hill, with two old swilers. They had eyes like gulls', hunting backwards and forwards through the water, and faces cured in salt and thawed in the gale. A parchment hand pointed out the old pelt-stores and boiling pots but, when I asked about the seals themselves, I found myself snarled up in ancient jargon. Depends what you mean, they said; we got white-coats and bedlamers, dotards, jars, nog-heads, turners and raggedy jacks.

"And dog hoods that could rip ye open. Even a scroddy one . . ."

"Took two of we to kill 'em—with *good* hakapiks."

I asked them if there was still any money in ice-hunting.

"Yes, boy," said the younger of the two. "It's $60 a pelt up in Catalina."

"But as we all knows," said the other, "seal money's got flippers of its own."

Even for Bay de Verde the money had eventually flipped away. It wasn't just that no one used seal oil any more. The world simply didn't understand the killing. Even Newfoundland's own Harold Horwood thought it was "a barbarous trade," that made men like savages, wallowing in filth and blood. When pictures of the gory open-air slaughter were shown across the globe, outsiders began to question the hunt. Then, in 1977, Brigitte Bardot turned up in Newfoundland, looking both dewy-eyed and dangerous. When she accused the sealers of being "ignorant, primitive, stupid, cold-blooded people," there were plenty inclined to agree. London joined the ban on seal prod-ucts, and—at a stroke—alienated thousands of Newfoundlanders whose loyalty to Britain had been unconditional for centuries. For the first time, they turned to Canada for help. But Ottawa reacted instinc-tively and, in a flurry of liberality, hunting was banned in 1987.

It wasn't, said the Minister of Fish, a ban that could last.

"Seal hunting," he told me, "has an honoured place in the history of this island."

In the end, the fish lobby prevailed, and Ottawa was persuaded that it was seals that had dredged the Atlantic. The ban was lifted in 1995 but the swiling was never the same again. From now on, it would be conducted furtively and guiltily. The swilers employed PR men and then closed off their work to the cameras. For my part, I was never allowed to see inside a seal plant, let alone aboard a sealer. I regretted that, because I didn't feel it was necessarily a simple matter of condem-nation.

Anyway, whatever the rights and wrongs, the sealers had become fugitives.

Oddly enough, it was as fugitives that their Dorset ancestors had started out.

By 1630, "Britain's first colony" was looking neither British nor particularly colonial. Instead, it was part of an English anti-empire, a determined attempt to ensure that the world's seventeenth largest island would be forever uninhabited. Just a vast, barren rock.

41

After the failure of the early plantations, the fish took control of the law.

Ferryland and Hayman and all his silly doggerel had demonstrated that the only thing that mattered about Newfoundland was cod. It didn't just matter, it was vital. Sir Francis Bacon thought that Newfoundland cod was bringing in more wealth than all the silver of Perú. By 1593, it was the mainstay of the West Country economy, and was keeping the navy fed. It was of such strategic importance that the fish merchants were even forbidden from letting it fall into the hands of potential enemies. Other than that, they could do what they liked—which is what they did.

In the years that followed, the Court of Star Chamber was persuaded to pass some of the most ludicrous laws that England has ever known. The idea was to empty Newfoundland of all life and all competition, to sweep out the Irish, and to ensure that the merchants got fish and the planters got nothing. To begin with, a law was passed in 1630, vesting control of each bay in a "Fishing Admiral," who was simply the first fisherman to get there that season. He was to be given his exalted powers regardless of whether he was a drunk or a pimp or a lunatic. According to Prowse's *History*, he was often all three.

The Crown had no role in this fishy jurisdiction, and it wasn't long before Newfoundland became a sort of sub-Arctic Gomorrah. The settlers were sharing women as if they were boats and, by 1670, some 3,000 islanders were landing 280,000 pints of liquor a year. One might have assumed that such a stupefied populace was no threat to the West Countrymen but they thought differently. That year, the fish merchants campaigned for every single planter to be plucked off the island and dumped in Jamaica. Remarkably, the Court of Star Chamber went some way to accommodate this madness. All settlement within six miles of the shore was banned; planters could not repossess their stages until the migratory boats had arrived; no one was to visit Newfoundland except as a fisherman (and their captains had to sign a hefty bond for their return). With the Rule of Fish established, almost every planter became an outlaw. A wintry silence descended on the island.

It was almost ten years before the full stupidity of this anti-colony was realised: if neither Dorsetmen nor Irishmen could have Newfoundland, then surely the French would take it. They were already in Placentia, digging in for trouble.

I turned the car round and headed west, to see what they'd been up to.

42

It wasn't hard to see why the French had called their town Plaisance. Only later did the English give it its more obstetric name, although there was something in that too. If ever a place could be geologically womb-like, it was Placentia—hidden, protected and muffled in the deep, soft flanks of the west. The sky was now harmlessly out of the way, somewhere way above the forest, and the ocean was no longer a roar but a gentle lop. Like me, the early French pioneers had been enchanted, and, in 1650, they'd set up their colony on a rump of scarlet shells and silvery cobbles.

I walked out along the beach, out past the crumbly skiffs and the heaps of old nets and whale harpoons. It was these cobbles that had first attracted the fishermen of Saint-Malo, the perfect place to dry their *morue*. The cod here, they said, was the best anywhere, "plus délicat et exquis qu'en aucun autre endroit." They were less impressed when France sent them a fancy governor in 1662, and when he failed to relieve the famine of that year, they took to him with axes. In the early negotiations for a royal *Terre Neuffve*, he and his servants were brutally chunked and filleted, and their corpses ground into the cobbles. After that, Louis XIV decided that his colony needed taking in hand.

I didn't expect to find much left of old Plaisance, despite the grandeur of Louis's enterprise. There'd been shipyards and ironworks, churches, hospitals and a monastery—but it had all gone. Over 15,000 people had lived here in the summer, including English and Irish planters who'd been outlawed by their own King. But, in the wars to come, they'd all be wiped out or evicted, so that all that remained of the old French capital were the cobbles and a stubborn strain of Catholicism. Of all the dandy wooden cabins of the town, the largest was still a Catholic church, Our Lady of Angels, with its peachy carpets and a silver dome. Other than that, there was just the debris of war, cannons in churchyards, redoubts and smashed revetments.

War wasn't long in coming. By 1680, the English had woken up to the folly of their wilderness laws and reclaimed the north. Nine years later, they decided it was time to clip back Louis's imperialism, before the whole world was coiffed in French. They wanted Newfoundland back, and said as much in their declaration of war. It would be a magnificent adventure, one of the first wars fought across the world: the War of the Grand Alliance. In Plaisance, the colonists and their Irish *engagés* rushed to fortify the gorge.

I climbed up into the walls of the inlet, to Le Gaillardin, the greatest of their forts. By the time I got there it was in cloud, and the cannons were aiming their blasts into the void. Although I hadn't expected Gettysburg or Corfu, I was surprised by how small it was, a reminder that in the 1690s warfare was still a relatively intimate matter, and that the future of the world was being decided in a series of sporting encounters, albeit a little bloodier. However, although it may have looked stunted, the fort had served its purpose. In the three wars that followed, it had never been captured. It had been beyond the range of naval cannon and, if any marines had managed to cut their way up here through the pine needles, they'd have found themselves in a maze of sharpened stakes and redans. The walls were as thick as two troopers laid end-to-end, a grim thought in the face of lacerating enfilades of shot.

But, however it had sounded in the declaration, there was nothing magnificent about the war itself. In Newfoundland, it was a filthy, savage rout that decided nothing. The French found their champion in a Canadian, Pierre le Moine d'Ibberville. Harmless though he may have looked in all his lace and curly wigs, d'Ibberville was steeped in hatred and Indian warfare. In November 1696, he set out from Plaisance to destroy Newfoundland with just 124 men. Among them were his Abenaki Indians, some ruthless *coureurs de bois* and a Récollet priest, to record it all for posterity. Within nine days, they'd snowshoed across the barrens to Ferryland, sacked it and eaten all its horses. D'Ibberville then turned, to smoke the English out of the north.

But one man's hero is another's monster. Lacking a garrison to retain his conquests, d'Ibberville simply looted them, then set them on fire. He killed any farm animals and left them to bloat and pop in the pastures. St. John's was charred, then Harbour Grace, then every other settlement on the north coast. If anyone resisted him, there was some crude and terrifying diplomacy. D'Ibberville considered scalping to be just part of the ritual of persuasion. One William Drew, for example, was returned to the obstinate fishermen defending St. John's with a simple message carved in his head; the skin had been sliced all the way round—just above the ear—and the scalp ripped away, from the forehead right back to the crown. If that's what the Johnsmen wanted, there were enough Abenaki to tonsure the lot of them like this.

To everyone's relief, a halt was called to the war in Europe, and— after nine months of terror—d'Ibberville swaggered home. It was not, however, the end of the burning. War re-started within the year and continued through until 1713. Nothing was ever resolved. It was just stalemate and fire. St. John's was defended by a British commandant best known as "a great promoter of whoring and Adultery." The French attack so took him by surprise that he fought the last battle in his dressing gown. The city was sacked and then abandoned.

All the modest achievements of the last century were now just dirt and ash. Only Plaisance had survived intact but its future was to be determined by victories on the other side of the world. Under the Treaty of Utrecht, France surrendered *Terre Neuffve*, and the little town of Pleasure passed to the English.

I walked back down, through the drip and creak of trees, to the harbour.

There was no one around except a crow-like character, staring into the water. His coat-tails were flapping around behind him like broken wings.

The English had never loved Placentia like the French. They'd even renamed its harbour "the Gut," an unlovable name for such a pretty slash of cold green water. After twenty-four years of war, there wasn't much about Newfoundland they'd loved—except the fish. The rest was a smouldering, unnecessary excrescence. Settlement remained illegal—although no one enforced it—and authority passed back to the Fishing Admirals. But real power was vested in the pirates, men like John Phillips, who was the scourge of New England (until his pickled head turned up in Boston). Even more enduring were Eric and Maria Cobham, who enjoyed twenty years of killing, poisoning crews, using captives for target practice or just sewing them up in sacks and dumping them in the sea. In the end, Eric bought himself into the French aristocracy and became a rural judge, but the madness was too much for Maria; after a hefty slug of grog, she climbed up into the cliffs and threw herself off like a seagull.

Newfoundlanders were outlaws again. More Irish Youngsters appeared, along with a flotsam of criminals, no-hopers and dreamers. All babies were "merry begots," their parents consumptives and sots. Drink, said one missionary, was now a necessity of life. There were no rules and—until 1729—no government, and St. John's was just a stink of drinking-holes and offal. Newfoundlanders, said the new governor of 1764, were "mere savages."

The figure on the dock came flapping towards me.

He had long, black, feathery side-boards, and thin, crinkly fingers that gripped my arm as he spoke. Soon he was cawing and cackling with history.

"This is where the French was, and this is where we put our house, when we floated her over from the islands in sixty-six. This is where Captain Cook came sailin' in, and this is where I built me boats, right *here* on these cobbles! I'm too old for real boats now—but do ye want to see the little ones I make?"

I said I'd like to, and with that I found myself drawn into a peculiar, forgotten world. Together we set off towards the old man's house on the Gut.

"Why did you live on islands?" I asked. "Were your ancestors French?"

"God, no, Sir," he said. "We're Upshalls, all rogues and runaways!"

43

Freeman Upshall was born in 1920, and had spent the first half of his life hidden away on an island and the other half in his shack, at the end of the Gut.

Scattered around this little wooden home were the components of his life—flats and bits of draggers, lobster pots, crates and the outlines of a whale-gun. It was the same story inside, except that everything was in miniature: shrunken bankers and skiffs, draggers made out of dowel and old earrings, and a fish-box schooner. There was no other decoration, except a photograph of a ferry, and some new carpet speeding greenly from the parlour out to the two rooms in the back.

Mrs. Upshall was spooning meat from a barrel. Although she seemed happy in the extravagant greenness of her old age, a stroke had left her with a look of permanent astonishment. This, I imagined, was much how she felt about life on the mainland, about televisions and cars and Placentia. The second move in three centuries had been a move too many.

"We were from Devonshire . . . ," said Freeman, as if he remembered the day they'd all run away. He was thrilled that, after so long, an Englishman had at last come to visit them. Stay and eat with us, he said, my sons would like to meet you. Andy's a fisherman, and Eugene's got a nice-looking wife and a job in Planning. "So there's more in his head than nits and lice."

It was a curious lunch, disconcerting and nostalgic and yet full of affection. Freeman gripped onto my shoulder throughout the stories, and we ate much the same food as the outlaw Upshalls had eaten all those years ago: salt beef, pease pudding, hard tack and figgy duff. Everyone had their own memories of Long Island, and the house at Kingswell.

"There was a pretty little church, with a steeple to guide the boats in . . ."

". . . and a store for molasses and flour . . ."

"But everything else we grew . . ."

". . . and we made our own shirts out of the flour sacks . . ."

". . . and kept all the chickens' feathers for our pillows . . ."

"There were caribou too, which we hunted in the winter . . ."

"It was the best life. Just ten families for three *hundred* years . . ."

". . . and we all sang *The Jolly Poker* as we hauled the boats in . . ."

Freeman was now swinging around at my shoulder hooting with song, ". . . and *Gully Rock* and *The Squid Jiggin' Ground* . . ."

". . . and the kids all caught connors off the stage . . ."

There was a pause.

"But nowadays," said Andy, "you'd need a licence even for *that.*"

There was anger in his voice, the deeply ingrained Newfoundland anger that came of centuries of respecting authority but never trusting it. In the end, it was the government who'd enticed the islanders back to the mainland. They'd never forgiven themselves for going.

"We loaded the house with oil drums and floated it over the ocean . . ."

There was silence as the Upshalls contemplated their departure.

"The last thing we did was to burn the church down."

"Why?" I asked.

"We didn't want people going there," said Freeman, "and showing disrespect."

No one had much to say about life after 1966.

Eugene's wife didn't say anything at all. She just sat there wreathed in serenity and a pile of mending. Eugene told me that she was Russian, an Internet bride from St. Petersburg. Like the Devonshire Upshalls, she'd simply walked out on a life of European poverty, setting out for an uncertain future on The Rock. She'd arrived in Placentia with just her darning needles and not a word of English. But, like Eugene's mother, she seemed quietly happy—bemused by the way her life had lurched from the present into the eighteenth century. If she'd ever understood the word "Newfoundland," it would have puzzled her; there was nothing new-found about this land, it was old and delightfully lost.

44

I discovered from the Upshalls that the outlaws had enjoyed theatre of sorts, called mummering.

"We had them every Christmas," said Freeman. "Knockin' at the door. Any mummers 'llowed in? they'd say. Any Christmas here? They was all dressed up in their old duds—night shirts, dresses, waders, veils and old brin bags over their heads. And they breathed inwards as they talked—so couldn't tell who they were . . ."

". . . and if ye were stunned, you'd let 'em in," said Eugene.

". . . and then they'd be all over your house, doing the mummers' walk and bargin', and jostlin', and bein' all lewd and singin' . . ."

Freeman remembered their tune, *The Terra Novan Exile's Song*, and began to croak:

> How oft some of us here tonight
> Have seen the "Mummers out"
> As through the fields by pale moonlight
> They came with merry shout
> In costumes quaint with mask or paint . . .

There were spoons and drums and the fearful drawl of accordions. But most alarming of all was the hobby-horse. Sometimes "Horse-chops" was a real horse's head on a stick; at other times it was wooden, with a snapping jaw and teeth made of nails.

There were characters too, among all the paganism and drink.

"We had the cunning Turkish knight," recalled Freeman.

". . . and Good King George with a bladder of dried peas on a stick . . ."

". . . and the general officer and his lady . . ."

". . . and Champion, the Blackie and wise Father Christmas . . ."

No one knew much about how this Saturnalia had begun, except that it was medieval and that it had come on the boats. Freeman was astonished that there were no mummers or jannies in the West Country any more.

Eugene was less surprised. Even in Newfoundland there were those who despised this fishermen's pantomime. For The Quality, mummering had always been repulsive. For others, it had been lethal. In the sectarian years, the carnival of masks had provided a useful opportunity to crack a few Catholic skulls, or to slot an Orangeman. There were plenty who'd taken a beating at the hands of Old King Cole, or Humpty Dumpty and his mermaids. Some didn't even know that anyone hated them until the mummering. One such man was poor Isaac Mercer of Bay Bulls, during Christmas 1860. According to his obituary, he didn't think he had any enemies, and had no idea that he was being murdered until the party was well under way. The St. John's police reacted with determined plod; mummering was banned along with its "disgusting attendants—rioting, drunkenness and profane swearing."

Then, the year before my great-grandfather's visit, these piscatorial operas were banned across the island. Governor O'Brien's legislature passed a law as baroque as anything that had ever fallen from Star Chamber. "Any person," it stated, "who shall be found at any Season of the Year, in any Town or Settlement in this Colony, without a written Licence from a Magistrate, dressed as a Mummer, masked, or otherwise disguised, shall be deemed guilty of a Public nuisance." Generally, the outporters ignored this ban. It was like telling them they couldn't be themselves. The outlaws' theatre moved underground.

I asked the Upshalls if mummering still went on.

"There's some, in the outports," said Eugene. "But the Mounties don't like it." He shrugged. "They say it's dangerous, lettin' people in ye don't know who they are. Make sure ye know at least one of them, they say."

But this wasn't mummering as the Upshalls had known it, and so they'd left it in Kingswell, along with their past.

"Andy's the only one who goes out to Long Island any more," said Freeman.

"Nothing but seals there now," said Andy gloomily, "eatin' all the fish."

45

Freeman took me to see his church, the relic of a womaniser and a century of naval brutality. "We're outnumbered here," he clacked merrily. "There's only twelve Anglican families left."

He was still clacking as he pranced through the thick wintry weeds of the graveyard. Somewhere, deep among the stalks, was Placentia church, like a little white boat with gothic windows and a bell-tower. The navy's great pitted, bellied guns were gathered up around it like a last stand, and so too were the best of the garrison, now safely scrolled and skulled in stone. Freeman hopped from slab to slab, chattering out the inscriptions. Here's Sir Joseph Blackburn, who died in 1709, and the Bradshaw boys who all went down with their schooner. And here's the surgeon's little five-year-old, Marmaduke Bradshaw, "who by falling into a pot of boiling water was too dreadfully scalded but he survived the accident but a few hours." Freeman tutted sadly as he read off the last lichenous words, and then chattered off, into the church.

Inside, the air smelt of boots and old wool and tallow. It was a simple military place of straight lines and wardroom greys. High up on the wall was the coat-of-arms of the greatest king the Placentia garrison had ever had, George III.

"Good King George," said Freeman fondly.

Not that he'd been good to the Upshalls, and nor had the navy. By 1790, the settlers were still outlaws, neglected fish-serfs that one missionary society described as "a barbarous, perfidious and cruel people." The Royal Navy had persecuted them mercilessly throughout the century, particularly over Labrador. If any settler put so much as one stinking toe in Labrador, he was liable to be flogged and to lose all his gear. As far as the Navy was concerned, there was only one lot worse than the Newfoundlanders—and that was the Americans. Captain Palliser, the new governor in 1764, referred to them as the "very scum of the colonies," and found himself stirring up some dangerous passions. For the time being, the Americans were merely chased away. It was another twelve years before they returned fire.

Men like Freeman Upshall could forgive George and the Navy for all of this. In all other respects it had been a glorious century. The Navy had snatched back a little jurisdiction from those drunks, "the Fishing Admirals," and—when the French invaded again in 1762—the Navy had seen them off with great economy and flourish. The last-ever battle on Newfoundland soil was fought like a carnival above the Narrows, a swift rout that cost the British only sixteen lives. It was another deadly blow for France. King George III was now—it was thought—king of most of the world.

"And it was he," said Freeman, "who gave us this church."

The building was started by George's third son, Prince William, who happened to be bobbing around Placentia for a year in 1786. It was not a year that people were ever likely to forget. Prince William— later William IV, "the Sailor King"—was a young man of rosy good looks and insatiable intentions (I remembered his portrait in Government House—and the warnings). He was probably safest when he was drunk, being tossed in a blanket by his fellow-officers on HMS *Pegasus*. Sober, he was unstoppable. He was particularly inflamed by Placentia's Catholics and took some pleasure in bawling at them and giving them ridiculous punishments. When the bishop raised this with the Prince, William hurled a horse-file at him, forcing the old man to dive for cover and hide for a week.

In all other respects, the inflammation was amorous. William seems to have been determined to have every maiden and every fish-wife in the town, and, in this, he was horribly fertile. In addition to all the actresses' children that he'd father in London, there was another litter in Placentia. The tragedy of the Prince's fecundity is that, by the time he'd hitched his fortune to some poodly European princess, it had deserted him. All they managed to produce was a clutch of sickly runts and so, when he died, the throne passed to his rather less inflammable niece, Princess Victoria.

Placentia enjoyed the rumours of royal blood.

"There's plenty of princes and princesses here . . . ," cackled Freeman.

Some say that William found commissions for all his merry-begot boys in the Navy. It was probably the best thing he ever did for Placentia. Except building the church, of course.

46

Sex was a rather less prominent feature of James Cook's week in Placentia in 1762. Although he was only thirty-four and still unattached, he was keener to impress himself on his seniors than on the wenches. Placentia was simply part of his ambitious plan. Instead of putting his feet up after three foul years of Canadian warfare, Cook spent his time making a chart of the Gut.

I remember seeing this chart once, in Whitby, where his adventures began. Cook's escape from this fishy Georgian slum is almost as remarkable as his three great Pacific voyages. He simply shrugged off poverty and a dull life as a shop assistant, and took off with the Whitby "cats," taking coal to London. His first post was on the *Freelove*, which is ironic because throughout his life Cook was tempted by nothing but glory and self-improvement. It's now thought that his austerity and sense of justice were his undoing. Seventeen years after Placentia, the natives of Kealakekua Beach in Hawaii mistook it all for weakness, and had him skewered and jointed.

I walked around the Gut. Cook had reduced this great broody, green chasm to immaculate copperplate and ox-blood browns and—in doing so—had won over the Admiralty. The Seven Years' War had left Britain with vast tracts of new uncharted territory and here was a man of "Genius and Capacity" who'd turn it all into maps. He was completely self-taught, having learnt the principles of Euclid and mathematics on the Québec campaign (whilst those around him were rotting away with cold and scurvy). Even better, he was inflexibly serious and disconcertingly sober. The Admiralty commissioned him to survey the Newfoundland coasts every year from 1763 to 1767, on a princely ten shillings a day.

Every spring, Cook left his new wife behind—pregnant—and every autumn he returned to a new little Cook. That was as much intimacy as he ever had the time or inclination for. Even on the Pacific voyages, when everybody else was coiling themselves up with the unblushing Polynesians, Cook remained aloof. Although naval discipline revolted him, he despised human weakness even more. In Newfoundland he had his men flogged for brewing spruce beer, and made his trusty Senior Hand run the gauntlet for being "drunk and mutinous." But there was never mutiny in earnest. Although Cook was hard to get close to, he was a reassuring leader: in all his five Newfoundland expeditions, only one man died. That was remarkable, given the weather, the weevils, the absence of any surgeon and the fact that—by the end of each voyage—their little survey schooner was "very much eat with worms."

The Gut and the Whitby map were probably as close as I'd ever get to Cook in Newfoundland. Apart from the odd cairn, he'd left nothing behind but names. In fact, the entire coastline was scattered with Cook's labels, mostly rather prosaic and formal and only very occasionally lacking in decorum. One rather voluptuous pair of mounds, for example, he'd named "Our Ladies Bubies"—until his prudery got the better of him. They're now "The Twin Islands."

Otherwise, the Newfoundland coast rings with Cook's nostalgia and ambition. Some features he'd named after places at home (the River Thames, the Humber and the Medway), whilst others had a more flattering objective. All the most important figures at the Admiralty were honoured (Grave's Island, Parker's River, Hawke's Bay, Port Saunders and Keppel Harbour) and when he'd worked through them Cook started flattering their boats (Pearl, Tweed and Guernsey). It was clearly a ruse that worked; the year after Newfoundland, the Navy stumped up for an expedition to measure the dimensions of the world, to sail round it and to investigate the rumours of Australia.

There was something else that Cook almost left in Newfoundland and that was his thumb. It was all but blown off when a powder-horn exploded in his hand in 1766. Fortunately, it was lashed back together by a passing French surgeon, but the scar remained for the rest of Cook's life. It even played a role in his death. After the Hawaiians had hacked him up, they returned his components to the expedition under threat of bombardment. There wasn't much left—the scalp, a jawless skull, some long bones and the hands. All the bones had been scraped clean and seared, except the hands which had been stuffed with salt. Only when they saw the Newfoundland scar did his men know they'd got their hero back, or at least parts of him. The rest, it is said, were worshipped all over Hawaii until idolatry was finally abolished in 1819.

Captain Cook's maps were revered for even longer. Over fifty have survived, the largest over ten feet long. Many Newfoundlanders were still reliant on them when Grenfell and Curwen sailed by, well over a century later.

47

By a curious coincidence, the rollicking naturalist of Cook's later Pacific adventures was also in Newfoundland in 1766.

Although he too was a northerner, Joe—later Sir Joseph—Banks couldn't have been more different from Cook if he'd tried. For a start, he was loud and blunt and recklessly wealthy, preferring to travel around in turbans and fancy jackets decorated with gold lace or silver frogs. He paid his own way on the first round-the-world expedition, and brought with him two servants from his Lincolnshire estate, two Negroes, several clerks and two greyhounds.

He was also formally educated—not that it did him much good. He went to both Harrow and Eton (Harrow was thought to be making him a little feral) and then on to Christ Church, Oxford. There, he discovered that the Chair of Botany was held by an old twig who'd only given one lecture in thirty-five years and who had no intention of giving another. Unwilling to fritter away his passion for the natural world, Banks borrowed a horse and rode to Cambridge to hire a new tutor. His attempts to educate himself were always slightly alarming. On another occasion, he and his wild friend, Lord Sandwich, planned to drain the Serpentine in Hyde Park, to see what fish it contained. It didn't seem to bother them that they didn't have permission for this scheme (or that they were very unlikely to get it). Science would not be hindered, and nor would Banks. In 1766, his brilliance was noticed and he was nominated for the Royal Society, at the age of twenty-three.

Oxford also brought out another difference between Banks and Cook. Wherever there were women, Banks was always ready with his spark. "Oxford," wrote one gossip, years later, "echoed with his amours, and the bed-makers of . . . college have given the world some testimonials of his vigour." Unwisely, Banks himself provided yet more vigorous testimonials after the Cook Expeditions. His canoodlings in Tahiti would revisit him in incessant mockery throughout his forty-one-year presidency of the Royal Society. There was, however, little that Banks's detractors could say about Newfoundland. It was never going to be a vigorous adventure, as Banks discovered in St. John's, on the sixth anniversary of Good King George's accession:

> We were all invited to a ball given by Mr. Governer, where the want of ladies was so great that my washerwoman and her sister were there by formal invitation. But what surprised me the most was that after dancing we were conducted to a really elegant supper set out with all kinds of wines and Italian liqueurs, to the great emolument of the ladies who ate and drank to some purpose. Dancing it seems agreed with them by getting them into such excellent stomachs.

Even if a couple of dyspeptic old scrubbers failed to excite Banks, Newfoundland was in every other sense much to his liking. His family had tried to persuade him to go somewhere genteel, like Italy, but Joe wouldn't have it.

"Every blockhead does that!" he roared. "My grand tour shall be one round the whole globe!"

Newfoundland proved to be a grand start. Banks hitched a lift on a warship and travelled all the way up to Labrador. He identified over 340 plants and 91 birds and countless fish. He painted an Eskimo Curlew and then contributed to its extinction by eating it ("most excellent"). There was no shortage of exotica to thrill him; he wrote about spruce beer and seal hunts, brewis, and walrus slaughters. He went polar bear hunting, acquired a porcupine and caught a halibut that was only 14 lb. lighter than the ship's ox. His was the first survey of Newfoundland's wildlife, and the most exhaustive—and exhausting—for years to come. By the end, Banks was ordering specimens from his bed.

Nobody knows if he met Cook. As far as I can tell they were only in St. John's together for a day. Perhaps Cook wouldn't have been ready for him yet; Banks was ten years his junior and still alarmingly frisky. Yet, somehow, Cook sailed home with Banks's samples lashed to his deck, including a Beothuk canoe. Sadly, they were all lost in the mouth of the Thames, where—after four years of Newfoundland's threats—Cook now found himself bashing his way through a storm. Although his partnership with Banks would become one of the most well-laurelled in exploration history, it was an inauspicious start.

I had rather imagined that the departure of Cook and Banks had brought to an end the best of the Royal Navy's days in Newfoundland. I was pleased to discover that I was wrong and that the best pageant was yet to come, a great meeting of warriors like the Field of the Cloth of Gold, except saltier and damper. It took place twenty miles down the road from Placentia, during the murkiest days of the Second World War.

"Just keep going through the forest," said Freeman, "till ye gets to Ship Harbour."

48

I followed his instructions and took a narrow track out through the spruce.

First the houses fell away, then the Tarmac stopped, and then everything faded into a frosty blur. I slowed to a growl, uncertain whether the car was moving at all. It was only when I saw things looming at me—alder, tree-trunks and boulders—that I realised that I was still making progress, north along the shore. Occasionally, I stopped and turned the engine off, anxious to hear the sea. Mostly there was just silence, the woolly silence peculiar to fog. At other times I heard screams, which I convinced myself were eagles rather than excruciating agony. I have never liked forests much and this one was more fingery and gnarled than most.

I was relieved when, after what seemed like hours, the windscreen was filled with great rusty thighs. They were part of an anchor, I discovered, a German submarine's anchor, placed in Ship Harbour to give it a sense of naval history. There wasn't a sense of much else, just turnips and peeling paint. If Ship's Harbour hadn't witnessed what it had, I suspect that it might long ago have been forgotten or picked apart by the forest.

I followed the gravel out to the headland, and back into fog. Surprisingly, it was the fog that had made this place so perfect in August 1941; the Luftwaffe will never find us here, said the Admirals. But they were wrong about the Newfoundland weather, of course. On the day the battleship *Prince of Wales* sailed in here, with her American friends, the sky was as clean as a knife.

In the madness of the fog, I half-imagined that they were all still out there—a brand-new British ship, four American men-of-war (including the battleship *Arkansas*), Sir Winston Churchill in his yachting blazer, and the President of the United States, Franklin D. Roosevelt, in a Palm Beach suit. They stayed for three days, the great men eating Scottish grouse and turtle soup from Fortnum & Mason. But, although this might have looked like Newfoundland's greatest-ever beach party, there was an urgency about the encounter. The two statesmen were here to discuss the war—which America had not yet joined—and what would happen afterwards. The principles that they agreed would eventually become the basis of the United Nations Charter, still some years off.

Getting here had been easier for the Americans than for the British. FDR simply told his nation that he was off fishing, which was a bit unlikely with Libya in flames and Germans gushing into the Ukraine. Nor was anyone fooled; before he'd even arrived, German Radio in Cincinnati told its 100,000 listeners that FDR was off to meet Churchill in the Atlantic.

This made the British secrecy somewhat futile. No one had been allowed to know anything. Whitehall wouldn't even allow journalists to accompany the voyage, but then relented and allowed two well-known authors along: the travel writer H. V. Morton, and the novelist Howard Spring *(Fame Is the Spur* and *My Son, My Son)*. Morton had no idea what to wear for such a momentous event and so he turned up in his Home Guard outfit. Spring looked even stranger; he'd lost all his clothes and had just had his teeth removed. "I am," he lamented, "just a clotheless, toothless literary stowaway."

With their cover blown and the Atlantic now a thickening soup of U-boats, the *Prince of Wales* made a dash for it. She'd already been mangled in her duel with the *Bismarck* three months earlier, and her paintwork was matted with camouflage and her crew well-blooded. Captain Leach spent the entire voyage on the bridge, and his officers wore Mae Wests under their dinner jackets. Everybody was fond of the ship—she was modern enough to bake 1,500 fresh loaves a day, and yet emboldened by traditions that went back way beyond Cook. Each morning, the sailors tumbled from their hammocks to cries of "Stand to!" and "Heave-Ho! Heave-Ho! Lash and stow!" Every day was a ritual of strange customs, like "Up spirits!" and "Permission to Grow"—all to do with rum and beards—and any man who caught a rat was given an extra half-day's shore leave. This still left plenty of work for Blackie and the junior ship's cats, who were inspected every morning by the guard.

Winston loved it, and declared that it was the first holiday he'd had since the war began. He zipped himself into his siren suit, moved his bed up to the bridge and presented the wardroom with a box of movies. Together they watched *The Devil and Miss Jones, High Sierra* and *Lady Hamilton*, which made Winston weep, even though he'd seen it four times before. Between films, he led them through a few deafening blasts of *Mad Dogs and Englishmen*, and the war was temporarily forgotten.

There was more joy in Placentia Bay. Although he was momentarily disappointed not to find himself in New York, H. V. Morton was delighted by Newfoundland. He thought it looked like Red Indian country, and imagined trappers and canoes and fiery Fenimore Cooper characters. But for the ranks there was better still: the Americans gave every British sailor an orange, an apple, 200 cigarettes and half a pound of cheese. After two years of rationing, this was wealth indeed. That night, the *Prince of Wales* flung off her blackout and, for the first and last time in her life, floated around in a blaze of colours.

In the morning, the two navies moved together for John Hampden's hymn, and the Prayer for the Victory of Right. There were more tears from Churchill, perhaps for the good intentions of men, or perhaps for the tragedy that was yet to come.

"On this lovely day," he told his sailors, "the sun shining as it is on this beautiful harbour, surrounded as we are by American men-of-war, it is difficult to believe that we are fighting for our very lives."

With the Atlantic Charter all but signed, Churchill took the American advisers for a walk on the shore.

I slid down onto the shingle, still blinded in mist.

Churchill had clambered along here with some of the great architects of the American years ahead: Stark of Allied Command, Marshall of the European aid plan and Harriman of the Vietnamese peace. He'd picked a bunch of pink flowers, as if to commemorate the day, and I suddenly felt the urge to repeat his gesture. Being winter, there was nothing but icicles and crushed sea-urchins, and the plastic curios thrown up by the currents. I settled on a fir cone, which I decided I'd take home and grow into my own United Nations tree. Churchill's United Nations fared better; mine was eaten by squirrels, American greys as it happens.

Placentia Sound was almost silent now, just the faint hiss of surf out in the vapours. On the fourth day, the great ships had departed. Although the Britons were sorry that America was not yet joining them in war, they repaid her generosity. Grog was forbidden on "Yankee" boats and so the *Prince of Wales* hosted a party unlike anything the Sound had ever known before. There were anthems and port and plenty of "ragging." A piper played, and all the furniture was piled up in the wardroom so that the officers could charge over it like monkeys in a steeple-chase.

"I guess you boys take this war very lightly," remarked one American.

If only the war had always been like Newfoundland. Four months later, American sailors were gasping for their lives at Pearl Harbor, and the *Prince of Wales* was under attack. She and the *Repulse* were ambushed by fifty-two Japanese bombers as they steamed off Malaya. In the maelstrom that followed, 840 men were burnt or drowned, and the *Prince* was holed and sent to the bottom. Captain Leach went down with her, along with all the dinner jackets and bagpipes, the three cats and the portraits of Winston Churchill, happy in Placentia Sound.

49

It was time too for me to leave Avalon.

It had been a curious spring. I sometimes felt that I'd learnt more about the late-medieval world that the Newfoundlanders had left than the place they'd ended up in. Many, I realised, felt the same, and that their ties to Britain were still umbilical. They remembered how their exam papers had been sent back to England for marking, and how the Queen's picture had once hung in every saltbox. Newfoundland had produced the biggest-ever Union flag and there were still plenty who celebrated royal birthdays and Guy Fawkes Night. There was even a Monarchist League, still alive and curtseying. "Newfoundland," said its founder, Lady Barlow, "is as nice as England used to be."

Others were less sure that England had ever been very nice. When I'd asked the Roches of Branch what they'd felt about the Queen Mother's death, they didn't hesitate to be honest.

"We don't care," they said. "We're Irish."

I was surprised that there weren't others more resentful. Britain had made fish-serfs of the planters, and outlaws of the mummers. Even as late as 1789, London was refusing Newfoundland any colonial status, and didn't abolish the last laws against settlement until 1811. It was, wrote one Imperial historian, "Britain's greatest experiment in retarded colonisation." Even when colonisation got under way, it was hardly embracing.

Old Billy-Joe Kennedy remembered the unrelieved hunger.

"There were plenty of days," he told me, "when we never had a mouthful."

As I wriggled back along the coast, I began to see the pattern of the anti-colony. There was no scheme to the settlements, and hardly any link between them. Each outport was simply its own little colony, with its own accent, its own words and its own names. Somebody had once worked out that there were sixty-six different dialects in Newfoundland, and there might have been more. Every outport had its own life, its own cove and its own fish. They hadn't even spoken to each other until the age of Tarmac and the bulldozer.

What if anyone needed a doctor, I'd asked.

"Ye took a horse and slide, over the barrens," said Mrs. Duggan. "Or ye died."

By the time I got back to St. John's, I had some idea of the task confronting Curwen. If Avalon was the heart and soul of the old colony, what would he find up north? Or in Labrador? It was too early yet to follow him up there. The Labrador Sea was still stiff with ice.

I returned to England, to await the thaw.

Dr. Eliot Curwen, 1893. My great-grandfather set off for Labrador with twenty-seven pieces of luggage including a rifle, knickerbockers and a box of "exploding bullets."

St. John's, 1610. All sorts of creatures were creeping out of the fog, including this mermaid. "So beautiful," panted Captain Whitbourne, "so well-proportioned" (until his boatmen cracked it over the head).

A Beothuk princess, Demasduit (c. 1800–1820). Within years of her capture, her race was extinct.

Whilst most Georgian sailors made a rollicking time of Newfoundland, Captain Cook gave it sensible place-names, and almost left it his thumb.

Above left Dr. Wilfred Grenfell, 1893. Feted, honoured, knighted and occasionally loathed, his sermons included "Sleep as the Urging of the Devil."

Above right Cecil, Algie and Wilfred Grenfell, 1905. They'd enjoyed a childhood of extraordinary violence.

Right Wilfred's father, the Rev. Algernon Grenfell, whose wild school drove him over the edge

Below Mostyn House School, Parkgate, Cheshire. By 1900, Algie had wrestled it under control, and "Fort Grenfell" emerged.

The *Albert*'s complement. She was unequal to the Labrador Sea, and Captain Trezise (standing, left) had already spent three days adrift in a lifeboat of frozen corpses.

Left The *Albert* in St. John's, 1893. The city had been reduced to ash the year before.

Sexual adventurer and Arctic explorer Robert E. Peary. In the end, even the missionaries mocked him.

Labrador's livyers, 1893.
Clothes were so scarce they were stripped off the dead, even the drowned.

The Hopedale Mission as it looked then (and now).
At the age of six, Moravian children were sent to Europe, and never returned.

A Labrador tilt, made of turf and wrecks.
Grenfell shamed the colony with his taunts of slavery.

Left The "Esquimaux" of Hopedale. Until the Moravians arrived, in 1765,
few Europeans had survived an encounter. *Right* Hannah Michelin, aged eighty-two.
Her mother escaped mutilation in 1792, and married a stowaway.

The killer Tom Brown (right),
with Benjamin and his son, soon to die.
For the Inuit, murder was a matter
of great complexity.

The son of the Mission's agent, in Battle.
People here, noted Curwen, think of
nothing but fish, fish, fish.

April 1908: Grenfell poses
in the bloodied pelts of his dogs.
It was an image the world would
find hard to forget.

Newfoundland's diva,
Georgie Stirling. Born among fish, she
sang at La Scala and died under curse.

A trap skiff, 1893.
Cod was still the currency of the colony. No one saw trouble looming ahead.

Act III: North with the Floaters

A watery place. And Quoyle feared water.
>   —E. Annie Proulx, *The Shipping News*

Codfish, alive or dead, wet or dry, have exercised an all-pervading influence over the destiny of Newfoundland.
>   —J. D. Rogers, *Historical Geography of Newfoundland*

The woodsmen and the fishermen . . . are in fact serfs. For 300 years . . . the major part of their earnings has gone to create about 300 wealthy families. And that system of sweating still exists.
>   —John Hope Simpson (British Commissioner), 1934

This was death's kingdom. This was a dangerous place. Nothing lived here . . .
>   —David Macfarlane, *Come from Away*

On a foundation of sterility and desolation the men and women of the coves built their small strong worlds.
>   —Farley Mowat, *This Rock Within the Sea*

50

By July, St. John's was bursting out of its summer.

I'd arrived at a moment of transformation, the point at which Nature, sensing the first strong rays of sun, is thrown into panic at the prospect of winter only three months ahead. This left barely enough time for the cycles of life, and so the revolutions came faster and bigger and ever more florid. There were sycamores exploding all over the city, and suckers, clingers, thorns and purples billowing out of the rocks. Great clouds of greenery were rising out of yards and parks, huge gassy clumps of ash and willow pouring up the hills and frothing into the gullies. Cow vetch was rampant and coltsfoot on the move. There were reports of unruly slender willow, and of innocent gardens smothered in pearly everlasting. The city—so often overwhelmed by its actors—was now being choked by the set.

Such fecundity had not gone unnoticed by the city caterpillars, who hung in the maples like grapes. When every leaf had been stripped down to the purely diagrammatic, they allowed their fat, sappy bodies to plop into the streets. Every night the Johnsmen had to pad home through this slick of grubs and half-digested pulp, but they didn't mind. Like the trees themselves, they were in a state of summer euphoria; more Guinness, out all night and enough fiddle music to make your ears sing. Many of the men over fifty, I noticed, now wore black shirts, all ready for the season of love (or grassing, at least).

There were only two other changes since the winter. Billy's Show Bar was now called "SIRENS. The Finest in Exotic Entertainment." Such an obvious upturn in its fortunes had produced a rash of imitations. Several bars now offered nudity with their pies and beers, although finding locals willing to strip hadn't been easy. "Exotic dancers wanted," said one desperate notice. "No experience required. Training provided."

The other change was to the skyline. St. John's was digging up part of its old fortifications to build a cultural centre. Down at the bookshop, Jim Baird was incensed. He said the cultural department were always pissing into the wind.

"And if you don't believe me, go and see their gallery . . ."

I decided I would, and went to an exhibition of litter and paper petals.

"See what I mean?" said Jim, wearily. "Fatuous."

The new place was called The Rooms, and was as pretty as a fish shed. It was also a mast higher than the Basilica.

"Funny, isn't it," said Jim, "how the new religions are superseding the old ones?"

This time I stayed with the Bairds, on Rennie's Mill Road.

It had once been known as Horse Gully, until the Rennie brothers had brought it a biscuit factory and a little gentility. The Newfoundlanders had never been able to afford their biscuits but the gentility had survived, with all its gingerbread houses and politicians, homes for the second-tier merchants, and Himalayan shrubs. This is where the Minister of Fish had lived—and old Dr. Cluny Macpherson, who'd served with Grenfell before the Great War, and who'd invented the gas mask just in time.

Nature was as rampant as ever up here, trees erupting deliciously and woodpeckers in a frenzy of drilling. The Bairds lived at the top of a lawn of great green breakers, which threw themselves at the house in swish after swish of drunken ecstasy. Twice a week a gardener appeared—like Canute—to talk it all back into place. But the grass would not be deterred, and nor would the elements. There was damp blooming across the drawing-room, and on my second night Hurricane Arthur broke the front door down and sent Jim's paintings flapping round the house like chickens.

"That was some gale," I remarked, over the debris of a chocolate cake breakfast.

"Gale?" said Angie, genuinely puzzled. "*That* was just a little blow."

Peace was never truly restored. Apart from the pantomime friends who would burst in through one door and hurl themselves out through another, there were the fighting cats. Angie said she had three of them, with names like Brown and Cream and Terror. To me, they were just a ball of claws and fur but occasionally their fights rolled indoors, and bounced around my room for a while before tumbling harmlessly out of the window.

"Just ignore them," said Angie impossibly. "They get a bit loppy about now."

Then there were the paintings themselves. These were the last things I saw as I drowned in sleep each night, after four Baird gins and a spit of tonic. Here was Newfoundland expressed in dreams. Red-hot icebergs, and cardinals dressed as babies. Paint applied like barnacles, thick enough to keel-haul a sailor.

51

As before, I walked out to the Narrows and out along the cliffs. This time, however, the sea was writhing with muscles and flukes and teeth. The krill were in the bay, and pouring themselves between the shoals were the enormous, liquid shadows of the whales.

I watched, fascinated, the sea tufted with little trees of exploding water. I tried to count the spouts at first but the sea would not be tallied. This was the largest population of humpbacks in the world, and that was that. It wasn't just humpbacks either. There were minkes and fin whales too, and a tiny monster—only the size of a skiff—called *Globicephalia melaena*. In the local mockery, he was just the pothead.

Sometimes it wasn't just a spout that broke the surface but the whole finner gushing up from the deep, ninety viscous tons of glossy black flesh. In less than a second, it could blast away its spent breath, reverse the forces and implode another truck of air. Then it would curl itself back into the darkness, hover—flukes aloft—for a moment, and plunge back into the krill.

Who, I wondered, had ever wanted—or dared—to kill such a thing?

The Johnsmen swooned in denial.

"Lord livin' Jasus, don't ask me," said a taxi-driver. "I didn't even know we had those things out there."

Eventually, people told me about an old whaler, Gerald Smith.

"He's forty-five minutes round the bay. Out in Dildo."

Some people think that the Basques had intended to call their whaling station Bilbao. Others say the name was a punishment for all the slaughter.

"And we're not after changin' it now," said Mr. Smith. "Men has died trying to get back to Dildo, in the wars and in the boats. So the name stays."

Gerald Smith had spent twenty-five years of his life killing whales, and the next thirty wishing he hadn't. Now his hair was white and fluffy, and he lived among the debris of the killing years. There was a crumbling wreck of fin whale up behind his stage, and his shed was like a mythical armoury in a war against giants. It was stacked with vast harpoons and outlandish helmets, scabbards and axes, sea-chests from Poole, and the spades they'd used for digging through blubber. Dildo was the best, he said, the centre of the kill.

We walked down to the shingle shore.

"It all started here," he said. "They'd chase the potheads in, with muskets and shoutin', and then they'd club them on the beach . . ."

After that, the slaughter turned into factories. By 1900, Newfoundland was processing 1,200 finners a year. Declaring war on whales was easy; they ate fish. The Canadian Air Force even bombed them for a while, and—in the Cold War—they were "enemy subs" and things to be zapped. But mostly they were processed. Even in the last ten years, to 1972, nearly 3,000 finners were pulled to bits in Dildo alone. They used to call it "Newfoundland Beef," but only the Japanese would touch it, and the dog food people.

"I was trained by the Japs," said Mr. Smith fondly, "in 1947."

This was the best bit: money in a time of TB. A monthly wage and $3 a whale.

". . . and steady work from June right through to *November!*"

But there was no affection for the work itself, for the dog watches of four-hours-on and four-off, for the slub of rancid fats and coal-dust, and for the shout that dragged men from sleep to icy decks: "There she blows!"

"The Old Man was always the gunner. A pound of explosive for every minke."

He dropped an iron pineapple into my hand, sharpened to a cone—the harpoon head. "Ye had to get her right in the head, or there'd be shrapnel cuttin' up the ship. And if she wasn't killed outright, she'd take off on a length of rope. There'd be two hundred fathoms payin' out in a blaze of flakes and smoke . . ." He paused. "A young lad once got his foot caught in a clit of that rope. It dragged his leg through a hole the size of a saucer. He was screeching like a lamb till the whole leg came away . . ."

There were other dangers as the whale was winched up the gump.

"If the cables went, they'd whip yer face off. But ye couldn't leave her over the side. There'd be fifteen orcas on ye—killer whales, sure—all tearing at the tongue . . ."

Mr. Smith took me back to his cabin for a mug-up and a snig of cake.

He was relieved when the slaughter finished. Looking back, even the killing of a single whale seemed strangely unreal—to say nothing of the filth and the slime, and the lifeboats rusted to the deck. Nowadays, Mr. Smith just watched the whales, and took trippers out in his boat. He even had an old whaling song for them, which he now sang through a mouthful of crumbs and molasses.

It was a curiously happy song: Jack is swallowed by a whale and thrown up in Baffin Bay. No one's hurt and no one ends up in the dogfood.

52

Several doors up from the Bairds lived the Reids, who'd played a part in Curwen's adventures in 1893. One Sunday morning, I swam out through the grass to visit them.

Everything about my visit was a delicate pink. The Reids' bungalow was pink and so was much of the furniture. Mrs. Reid was pink from gardening, and Ian Reid was in the pink of his retirement.

"Dr. Curwen met Sir Robert at dinner," I explained, "at Government House."

There was surprise. Although Ian looked something like the sepias of his great-grandfather—a dome of concentration, a face more determined than strong—the look of surprise was entirely his own. Robert Gillespie Reid was a man of limitless horizons, who was surprised at nothing. He'd left his native Perthshire as a stone-mason, cut a railway across Canada, hacked out its parliament and, by 1893, he was in St. John's with an outrageous scheme.

"What did Dr. Curwen think of him?" said Mrs. Reid. She'd now trained her magnificent orb of hair back into shape, and was sitting between us with a tray of sherry flutes.

"He was very discreet," I replied. "He just says Mr. Reid had a railway."

Newfoundland had been waiting for a man with a railway for nearly thirty years. Some saw such a project as the only way to make a nation of Newfoundland, to link up the thousands of outports and open up the interior. Curwen's friend, Dr. Harvey, was sure there were gold fields in there, ranches, prairies and "hives of industry." Others saw it as a way for Newfoundland to assert itself over the west coast, where the French were still squatting. That was the problem: Britain had no intention of aggravating Paris over "The French Shore," and wasn't going to fund any railway invasion.

"St. John's," said Ian, "would have to find the money itself."

There was never enough. By 1893, the track had barely covered the first stages (the equivalent of a few days' walk), and the money was gone.

"That's when my great-grandfather came up with his plan," said Ian.

It's an intriguing thought that, whilst my own great-grandfather was working his way through a few plates of mutton and figgy duff, Robert Reid was formulating his conquest. The terms he demanded were shameless; he'd complete the railway across Newfoundland in return for its surrender. He wanted a million acres of land, a monopoly of all communications, a tax exemption, a whopping steamship subsidy and a nice $15,000 a mile towards construction. At the end of that, he'd buy it all back for a song. In London, the Colonial secretary, Joseph Chamberlain, watched in horror as St. John's placed the "future of the colony...entirely in the hands of the contractor." The deal was done.

"It wasn't such a bad deal for Newfoundland," said Ian. "She got a railway..."

"...and there was no way she'd have got it otherwise," said his wife.

Nor was there anyone who could have built it, except Reid.

The task was formidable. The new railway had to curl through the north of the island and up into the Long Range mountains, into a trackless wilderness and through snow drifts up to twenty feet deep. A chain of tarpaper huts sustained the men as they hacked and blasted their way through rock and forest. It was an unforgiving 540-mile slog, from one end of the island to the other, and yet Reid completed the task within five years.

No sooner had he done so than St. John's revised the agreement and wiped out his profit. This was still a great joke to many Newfoundlanders, the idea that a cunning outsider should get a ducking and go home with no jam. It didn't matter that they didn't have much of a doughnut either, or that they had a railway they probably didn't need and that they'd spent six times as much on it as they had on education. At least they'd not been humiliated. Besides, there was loot for those near the wreckage. "It is," ran a Colonial office memo in 1898, "a quaint recurrence that all parties in Newfoundland can join hands when they think these hands can be dipped in Imperial pockets."

Robert Reid didn't stay but left his sons to run what remained of his railway. St. John's arranged a knighthood for him, as Second Prize, but it was of little comfort. He died of disappointment a few years later, at the disagreeable age of sixty-six.

"My grandfather, Harry, and my great-uncles then spent their lives squabbling in the courts," said Ian, "and the money soon ran out."

Mrs. Reid produced a photograph of Harry taken in 1908, the year Sir Robert died. He was sitting in a Rolls-Royce ("Newfoundland's first car," she said) above the Narrows. At his side was his German chauffeur, Otto Oppenfeldt, a huge man with a face of ham and brushes. Not only could he bring terror with his ten-miles-an-hour of brass and plush, Otto was also a professional wrestler, known as "Young Hackenschmidt." He was champion of St. John's for a moment but, as the Reid fortunes trickled away, he lumbered off back to Germany. It is said that he joined the navy and returned to Newfoundland in a U-boat, bringing saboteurs and terror back to his old home.

Mrs. Reid wrinkled her nose in disgust. "What a horrible business."

Worse, the horrible business of the railway would strip the Reids of everything but gentility. By 1923, they'd admitted exhaustion, and handed the whole system over to the Government of Newfoundland.

"And that," said Ian, "was the end of the family's railway."

My own great-grandfather's role in the Reids' adventure was refreshingly trivial. After a good figgy-duffing, the old railwayman gave Curwen a free pass to Terra Nova. Not only was Curwen pleased to be heading to the northern coasts, he was delighted to have saved $8 on a ticket. Taking such pleasure in small economies was, I realised gloomily, an ancestral vice.

In every other respect, following in his footsteps would prove harder. On 7 November 1893, Curwen set off for the station with his rifle, a fowling piece and a box of exploding bullets.

53

Curwen and I would have very different experiences of the northern coast—differences born in the upheavals of the century.

For a start, there was no longer a railway looping up through the bays. The St. John's railyards had long been embalmed in asphalt, and the old terminus building was now whiskery with sawdust and cobwebs. The tracks had been sliced up by a snarl of flyovers, and those that managed to escape into the barrens had long ago been ripped up, and the sleepers shipped abroad for furniture and fancy garden borders.

In winter, the ghost of the railway was a snowmobile track but, in summer, it was just a streak of gravel wandering off into the hills. Whole areas of their island once familiar to Newfoundlanders—like Topsails and Misery Hill—were now lost again. In 1988, after sixty years of snowdrifts and carriages lost for weeks, of trains blown over, of money gushing away and of forests blackened and stumped by engine-sparks, the system was shut forever.

Another difference between our travels was that—for me—the northern coast was the route to Labrador, whereas for Curwen it was merely an excursion. In 1893, there were plenty of craft working between St. John's and Labrador, whether a hospital ship like the *Albert* or ferries and schooners. Nowadays virtually nothing went that way, and when I asked people about boats to Labrador, they looked at me as if I was haunted.

"There's nothing like that for years . . ."

"Ye got to traipse up to Lewisporte to get the ferry . . ."

When I rang Lewisporte, they said there was still too much ice.

"Try again mid-July."

This gave me three weeks to traipse across the map, along a coast-line of broken plates and shattered lakes. What strange lives they must lead, I decided, on Random Sound, and in Goobies and Gambo, and up on New World Island. There was only one road north, the TCH or Trans-Canada Highway, branching off from time to time to feed the outports.

Out here, of course, were the greatest changes of all, and it all came down to the same thing: fish. Although there was no longer any fishing "down on Labrador," it was different in Curwen's day. Captain Palliser's attempts to keep Newfoundlanders from Labrador had spectacularly fizzled. By 1850, over 400 ships a year were setting out from the north coast, to sieve the Labrador Sea of its cod. By the end of the century, there were nearly 1,400 schooners involved. The scale of this annual migration is almost unimaginable; every year, some 30,000 fishing serfs—men, women and scrags—set out to make their living in the offal and freezing brine of Labrador. With ten per cent of the entire colony's population at sea, summers on the northern coast must have seemed almost as eerie as the winters, if that were possible.

And what of Curwen's patients now? He'd never visited them on their own coast: Newfoundland was not part of the Mission's remit. The crisis, they thought, was down in Labrador.

54

I took a bus to the Bonavista peninsula, despite the advice of my friends. To them, bus travel was something primordial, as if the failure to own a car was a failure to evolve. I imagined that most Newfoundlanders felt like this, dreading any slide back into the past, the wet feet and the slog.

"You'll meet all kinds o' snots and losers on the coach," said one.

I suppose some of my fellow-passengers might have been snots, and certainly most were on the losing side. Almost everyone was slabbed in poverty, and many were tufted in unlikely blondes and oranges, or streaked in purple. Peering along the line of headrests, it was like an outing of Muppets but there was no Muppetting in the sounds around me—just the slurp and cud of sugary drinks and Cheez Whiz. At my shoulder was a stubbly head and an ear so loathingly pierced that it could probably be unzipped in times of trouble and stashed away until things improved.

No one spoke. I ventured some remark about the weather.

"A jacket colder than yesterday," said the stubble.

It was a statement full-stopped with a burp, and so there was no more conversation until the stubble had sluiced away two Molsons. Then he asked me about my boots, and I asked him where he was going. In all the froth and slur it sounded like Horse's Arm or Nora's Arse.

"What happens there?" I asked.

"We're all on the public tit."

Although our exchanges never got more lively than this, they were never as desolate as the world outside. It only took me an hour to develop a life-long hatred for the Trans-Canada Highway. It was just an endless, featureless black runway driven deep into a forest, and our bus took it like a fledgling bomber. At times, I caught glimpses of the old railway as it ran alongside, and I thought of Curwen eating his poached salmon off Newfoundland Railways china. Nowadays, it took fourteen hours to blast oneself from one corner of the island to another. It took Curwen as long to cover a third of that distance, albeit well-coddled in velvet and plate. There was even a meat wagon for gentlemen returning with their game.

I was wrong to say the road was featureless. There were features but they were often bleaker than the empty forest itself. I remember the chip trucks and a lake of lonely seaplanes, and the filling-stations where the coffee tasted of mayonnaise, the smears of mist and the hares spewed across the Tarmac. "Why burn?" said a sign. "God made heaven for holy people."

"There's only one way to do this trip," said my stubbled companion, "and that's totally freckin' corned."

I was pleased when this journey ended. By the time we got to the peninsula, the sixth Molson can was being concertina'd into the floor, and my neighbour was slavering like a wolf. I was pleased, too, to be breathing fresh sea-breeze again instead of cheese, and to see the forest broken open by rocks and shingle and a gorgeous sliver of blue. I hired a car and headed for the bays. The road, they say, was built not only to bring baymen to the railway but to provide work in times of hunger.

It was called a relief road, which matched my mood precisely.

55

The summer that had so aroused St. John's was now inflaming the Bonavista Peninsula.

Everything seemed to have compacted itself into the short burst of warmth and light. Even the colours seemed concentrated; the blood-reds of the twine sheds and net lofts, the purple cliffs, the slash of golden marsh, the brilliant damasks of the woods and the blinding indigos of water. It was as if I'd emerged from the shadowy interior into two brand-new summers rolled into one. The celebrations seemed endless and reckless. The verges had erupted in violet pom-poms, and the sky was spinning with kittiwakes and turrs. There was strong rum for sale at every garage, and live worms and oranges as big as your head. Everybody, it seemed, was flying the old Newfoundland tricolour: pink for screech, white for ice and green for the morning after.

"Just look out for the moose," the hire-car agent had said. "They're also on the road. They likes to be out of the crunnicks and in the air, and gettin' a proper lick o' salt . . . I lost three cars last week, and two the week before."

The wreckage of these collisions was lying all around us—wind-screens vaporised, roofs torn away, engines flapping loose like offal.

"What happens to the moose?" I'd asked.

"Sometimes she hardly notices, and just slews off into the woods.

Other times, you get all seven hundred pounds comin' aboard through your window, four big feet and two yards of antlers." He pointed a toe at one of the metal bundles. "This driver here got his head took off, and what was left of the moose came flyin' out the back window . . ."

I wasn't going to let decapitation spoil a good summer, and crawled up the peninsula at moose-speed. I saw them occasionally, knee-deep in ponds or lying in the juniper—and in ambush. Perhaps they knew that one day Newfoundland would be theirs. They'd only arrived in 1878 but now there were 120,000 of them, all hurling themselves at the traffic.

"And you only got to turn your back," the agent had said, "and they're in your garden eatin' everythin' you got."

Nature was never more wild or exuberant than the day I arrived at the tip of the peninsula. Gannets and guillemots were wheeling giddily around the stripy lighthouse as if it were a maypole. Puffins were bursting from their burrows and then flopping madly across the blue like rabbits. The birds weren't calling but screaming like bombs and ripping up the air with their swoops and cuts. Beyond them, I could see cod, swelling out of the shallows and flashing their fat bellies at the sun. Further out still were the whales, tossing their heads and thrashing the sea with their flukes.

"What's the matter?" I asked. "Why's everything gone crazy?"

"The caplin's in," said the lighthouse-keeper. "Out in Dungeon Cove."

I followed a line of trucks and fishermen out to the cove. This was the highpoint of the peninsula's natural festival, sometimes known as the Miracle of the Caplin, or otherwise the caplin scull.

Gathered around the cove was a furious congregation of men, whales, birds, dolphins and cod. Then, into the arena poured a long liquorice curl of fish, perhaps half a mile long. There was hooting and gnashings of approval as the turquoise turned to black, and the water began to boil. Each component of this bubbling school was a slip of biological insanity, programmed to a moment of ecstasy and then immediate, violent death.

The caplin swirled for a second and then surged at the cobbles in their millions, males dragging females, clouding the water with their milt and spawn. They were already drowning as they copulated, it's said, and then the audience were upon them. Now the caplin were reaped in their thousands, gathered up in cast-nets and buckets, in teeth and beaks and talons, colanders, pots and tiny children's hands. Women had stripped down to wade into the icy water, and men were filling their cars with fish. They're smaller than ever this year, they cried, as they hauled away their barrels. But there were still more fish than they could carry. After a life so black and dark, the caplin now plated the beach in silver.

"What will you *do* with so many fish?" I asked.

"We'll salt a barrel for us, and a barrel for the dogs," said one.

Others said they'd corn them or freeze them, or smoke them in the chimney.

"or use 'em for bait."

". . . or rot 'em down with peat and straw and dig 'em into the taties."

"I just grills 'em over a few splits, and takes 'em with a good horn of rum."

There were murmurs of approval. "Better than sex," they agreed.

I stayed that night in the drowsy wooden town of Bonavista, where the air was green and fat with fish-smoke. I took a room in the house of an old fisherman who lived alone with a stuffed seal and some portraits of his grandparents. "This is the bed where I was born," he said, as he showed me up to the attic. It was an unwelcome thought after such a day, and brought on a night of slithery, wriggling dreams.

By the morning, there was no sign of the carnage of the day before. Dungeon Cove had been picked clean—by foxes perhaps, or crabs and gulls—and then rinsed by the tide. The remnants of the caplin slick had long gone, rolling themselves up and flowing back into the deep, lost for another year.

56

I ought to have liked Trinity more than I did.

Like Bonavista, it was a town dreamt up in the eighteenth-century rush for fish. Although people had been scrobbing and clawing a life on these rocks ever since the finding of New-found Land, it took fine Dorsetmen like the Lesters to make a virtue of it all. To begin with, they were reluctant to spend the whole year on such a mad-dog coast (in Maggotty Cove or on Calf's Nose or Naked Man) but, as the cod-money thickened their purses, they brought their mansions over, brick by yellow brick. I was surprised to find that Benjamin Lester's pile had survived—or parts of it—along with a Sheraton bureau, and a table so radically weevilled that it looked as if it'd once been colonised by rabbits. I was also surprised to learn that the house was a replica of another of the Lesters' mansions, in Lytchett Minster. They weren't the only West Countrymen enjoying such symmetry; all over Dorset there were opulent mantelpieces adorned with leaping cod, and in Poole, eighty per cent of the population were drawing their wealth from the Labrador Sea.

A little of this extravagance had rubbed off on Trinity, which was why Newfoundlanders loved it. There were three churches like schooner hulls, onion cupolas and marble tombs, a High Street, a Water Street and a Fish Street. We had the first smallpox inoculations in North America, said the outporters, and we got the first jail, the first court and the first fire-engine. I imagined that this was all true, although the fire-engine was an unconvincing contraption dated "Black-friars Bridge, 1811." But by then, the town was more than merely combustible, it was roaring. There were now 2,500 Trinitarians, and for the merchants there were tennis clubs and cricket. However, like all sub-Arctic opulence, it was totally dependent on the fish, and when they swam off, so did the Dorsetmen and all the money. Trinity was now a tenth of its former self.

The extravagance still haunted it, although not like before. The old fish-lanes now swaggered around herbaceously, and every plank and picket had been spruced up in taupe and Evening Yellows. Even the fish store had turned mauve although, in the absence of cod, it'd become a theatre. Trinity was now pretty in a way that visitors readily understood. There was no train-oil in the shops any more, or cricket bats and scroopy boots, but for anyone wanting a sealskin bow-tie, cloudberry jam or scented candles, there were hours of browsing. The Newfoundlanders loved it all so much that they'd left me nowhere to stay. Trinity was all sold-out until the ice.

In the end, I camped in an old turnip patch on Glen Cove.

"There's no one trouble ye there," promised the farmer, "and not a wag of sea."

He was right; it was almost silent out there except for the dog-whistle of an eagle and the slap of waves in the wash-bottle rocks.

Every morning, I had breakfast with the old farmer in his tiny, creaking parlour. It was stacked from canvas to rafters with books on war; Nazis, confederates, Kursk, Vietcong, smallarms, anything. Each morning the farmer would muddle up the worries of the day before, just as he muddled his battles. "Did the moose find ye? Did she?" he'd say. "I worried she'd trample your tent."

Each day I woke untrampled, and every evening I went to the theatre. These evenings began with long trestle tables of chops and mash, and some raucous vaudeville. There always seemed to be more actors than visitors at these jamborees but perhaps it was just a matter of volume. The Ontarians and Albertans would shrink in terror as the mummers descended on them, jabbering in Dorset and walrus, or howling along to a fiddle and an old sieve.

"Look at her!" the actors whinnied. "I seen more meat onna Good Friday . . ."

". . . Would *someone* haul the battery cables outta him!"

Then the tables and mash and funny noses would be swept away for an "outport drama." This time the players would be brilliant, always digging away at the interstices between Newfoundland's pride and its self-loathing. These plays were too raw to be truly funny and too unassuming to be tragic. The anxieties of the outporters might be momentarily trivial—a craving for a ten-egg cake perhaps—but would become a longing, an urge for Spain or nudity and matadors. I'd often return to my turnip patch feeling as if I'd already been trampled.

With such an abundance of actors and cuteness, it was inevitable that the movie-makers would find their way to Trinity. They were still filming *Random Passage* in some fantasy hovels on the edge of town, and there were plenty of script-writers and paint people who'd slipped in among the Trinitarians. Almost everybody had been an extra at some stage but their big break came with the arrival of *The Shipping News* crew, in March 2001. These were still the best stories in the town's bar, an old Legion hut called Rocky's Place.

"They were here eight weeks, in the snowliest winter for one hundred and twenty years . . ."

"Sixty of us was taken on to shift the snow—and then, when it looked just *too* like Newfoundland, we had to shift it all back again."

"Joe lent 'em a punt for two hundred dollars and it didn't even have oars . . ."

There were crackles of weaselly laughter.

". . . and Kevin Spacey—a proper gentleman—turned up with five body-guards, took one look at this place and sent 'em all home."

"A fine gentleman indeed, in here every night, shootin' pool and throwin' darts."

At the hub of these stories was Rocky himself, a crumpled paper cowboy in stetson and Cuban heels. In the pictures around the bar, he was a Jacobean snot and a passable rogue. He insisted that his shed was the heart and soul of the movie even though there was nothing to eat but Hot Wings, and nothing to look at but faded boobs.

"There was never any disrespect," he drawled. "They loved it in Trinity. Judi Dench learnt to bake, and there were three of 'em bought houses and stayed."

The reports coming back from the crew hadn't always been so frothy. There was cappuccino deprivation at first, and then panic at the thought of so much minimalism between here and a good lettuce. Even for a Welsh actor, this was sobering. "I didn't know," said Rhys Ifans, "that God had made so much nothing."

Others remembered the cold and the boatloads of clammy cod.

"Never," said Spacey, "act with children or fish."

57

I began to realise that it was this surfeit of make-believe that troubled me most about Trinity. It called itself a "heritage site" but was the past ever really like *this?* Guides in period costumes have never been more than shrivellingly embarrassing for me, but when I saw three sets of village stocks, it struck me this was two stocks too many. Perhaps Trinity was now just a back-drop for some wishful thinking. Even the theatre was a fantasy to people who'd spent almost half the last millennium in a state of outlawed drama. I couldn't resent anyone for making money out of not-very-much but I had an uneasy feeling that history was being scrambled, like the battles in the old farmer's mind; Red Indians at Stalingrad or fishermen in freshly laundered gingham, it was all the same.

I wasn't the only one having doubts. Later, Jim Baird told me that he loathed the re-hashed Trinity, and that it was "Newfoundland Disneyfied." Others had more general warnings about "Interpretation Centres" (lots of writing, nothing to see) and "Fun Parks" (what's fun about a stuffed moose and a broken swing?). Trinity, I noticed, had both.

It was also hard to reconcile all this with the horrors dropping from the pages of my great-grandfather's journals.

Curwen realised that there were two types of fishermen sailing off to Labrador, but that the slavery was the same for each. First, there were *floaters*, who hoped to fill their schooners with fish, salt it and bring it back still "green." Then there were *stationers*, who'd land in Labrador, fish from the shore and dry their catch on the rocks. They'd be away all summer, returning with stacks of fish as dry as toast.

It was slavery because of what was known as the Truck System. The idea was simple: the merchant sold the fishermen goods "on tick"—whether nets, string, boots, lamp glasses, flannel, buttons or rice—all to be paid for in fish. "Cod is the coin of the country," explained Curwen. "Money is scarcely known and no other medium of exchange is used ... All live on goods advanced on credit, to be paid for by their catch of cod."

Here lay the problem; the merchant fixed both the price of goods he sold, and the price of the fish he bought. In other words, he had the fishermen in his thrall. "The men," says Curwen, "became absolutely dependent on the charity of their merchants and in many cases from year to year did not know how much they owed ... The spirit of pauperism was directly fostered."

As usual, Grenfell was even more florid than Curwen on this iniquitous system. He told a Royal Commission that it was "subtle because it impoverishes and enslaves the victims and makes them love their chains ..."

For some, this was just Grenfell whipping up charity. Even now, there were those still defending the Truck; there was no alternative, they said, in a wilderness without money, and it was better than England—at least people had land. Others, like the Minister of Fish, rallied behind their ancestors.

"In our mythology, we're always critical of the merchants," he'd told me, "but they provided all the credit and kept the whole thing going ..."

Perhaps so, but for the people of Trinity—and all along this coast—they'd been bonded into poverty. In fact, they were the poorest and most illiterate people in the Americas. They couldn't argue or study—

or even move away. Cloudberries there may have been but never scented candles. "Many fishermen," wrote another missionary, "never saw the colour of the dollar, and remained in debt to the merchant from the cradle to the grave." What's so extraordinary about all this is not that the Truck existed but that it survived for almost two centuries. Despite Grenfell, there was no law requiring wages to be paid in cash until the mid-1940s, long after his death.

"The colony lives by the codfish caught," concluded Curwen, "but in no wise recognises that the codfish-catchers are human."

Which all left me wondering what a Victorian outport might have looked like before all the paint and jollity. Then I spotted one on the map, a few miles up the coast: "Kerleys Harbour, Resettled 1963."

58

It was another day as blue as cornflowers. I took the path out from New Bonaventure.

"Just follow this scrape," said an old woman selling jam and quilts by the road. "Ye'll find yourself in a hat of woods. Keep goin' till ye comes to a thingummy like a droke. Go through and there's more hills—nothing big, just nuddicks. Keep on straight, through the trees, and Kerleys Harbour is there at the bottom of the dene..."

"Is there anything left?"

She shrugged. "I haven't been back there since we left. It's unlucky."

I asked her what her name was.

"Melba," she said. "After the boat that brought our supplies, the SS *Melba.*"

I followed Melba's medieval instructions up into the green, well-eagled canopy, along a chain of rum-coloured ponds, through a portal of hot silvery rock, and down into an empty cove. It took my eyes a moment to get used to the wreckage. The cove wasn't empty at all but scattered with Victorian lives—iron beds crumbling away in the grass, barrel-hoops, a broken fruit bowl, cracked stoves and boots abandoned to the ants. Root cellars had burst open like some strange old fruits-of-the-turf, and the boat winches had buckled over in the wind. It felt like a world in cross-section, the structures there but the lives all gone.

Melba told me a hundred people had lived here, defining themselves, I suspected, by what they didn't have. Apart from the sea and the scrape, there was no contact with the other world, and no mail, no gas, no electricity and no running water. When Kerleys Harbour died, families like Melba's had simply thrown their possessions into a saltbox and floated it away. Only a few houses had remained, on a bluff overlooking the tickle. Nowadays, they were bony structures of black skin and clouts, gradually flopping themselves apart.

Below them was the shadow of a fish-stage. It was only a stump now, but this is where the schooners had called, seeking crews for the Labrador Sea.

Curwen often met these schooners as they plunged their way north.

"I had heard something of the want of comfort & misery endured during the passage to Labrador," he wrote, "but had formed no idea of the terrible hardships and discomforts that have to be put up with."

It wasn't long before he had the picture. For a start, a large proportion of the schooners were "utterly unseaworthy." Nobody knows how many perished in these boats because there was never a list of passengers kept. Ice-damage was simply patched up with tin or felt, and many captains were barely competent to get their craft out of the harbour let alone along the most dangerous coasts in the world. They had no use for compasses or lead-lines, and as for the law limiting them to one passenger per registered ton, it might as well have been written in Inuktitut.

The over-crowding was spectacular. The outporters called it "chinsing," the same word that describes the packing of a draughty crack with bits of moss and dirt. Typically, a fifty-six-ton boat might be carrying ninety passengers. This would have been bad enough for a ferry but these schooners were also loaded up for the summer: salt for the floaters, cod-traps, and window-frames for the stationers. The passengers would have to insert themselves into the two-foot gap between the freight and the deck above—along with their crockery, straw mattresses, barrels of molasses, chickens and goats. If Curwen wanted to visit a patient in this stinking hold, he had to crawl on his side "in a manner not unlike the sidestroke in swimming." Once, he visited a woman who'd given birth in the salt. She was unable to sit up and had to hand her baby out sideways, as if it were a parcel.

"I am not surprised," comments Curwen, "that the owners & skippers try to keep us from visiting these places where the people are stowed."

Women weren't allowed on deck, and had to be grateful for the rain that poured through the hatches. One skipper told Curwen that "if he was caught in a severe storm, and had to batten down the hatches many of the people would be suffocated." Never mind, this rancid voyage would only last a week (although it might be three). The journey home would be much the same, except that then of course they'd be bedded down on fish.

There was a special place for women in this misery. They were recruited because they were cheaper and better at splitting cod, but many men assumed they had a more carnal function. Whether the woman herself wanted a roll in the fish was often academic. "If the crew are decent men," one girl told Grenfell, "we are alright. But if they aren't, there's nothing we can do." Those who took up prostitution were just as helpless, desperate to pay off a bad season's debts. Decency—as one old sage put it—was impossible, and vice was flagrant.

Curwen was horrified, more strident on this issue than any other. "Women certainly ought not to be allowed to travel in this way; in England they would not be allowed!" But it wasn't just prudery. In such filth, pregnancies could easily be lethal. Even Grenfell managed to avoid being censorious on these occasions—or almost. On his 1892 mission, he'd given the last rites to an unmarried mother, but had been unable to resist a lofty epitaph: "Neither do I condemn thee."

Of course, there were plenty of others who perished. Usually, if they were on a schooner, they'd be "salted away" in the hold. Then, some months later, they'd make their sad return—to Kerleys Harbour, perhaps—as white and brittle as fish.

59

Thirty miles up the coast was a memorial to a revolution that never happened.

It was a vast cemetery for heroes but only one man is buried there, and a handful of his lieutenants. How do I describe the style? Stalinist? Muscular Socialism? Newfoundland Realism? There were elements of all these things in the tomb of William Coaker, even though they'd eluded him in life.

The trouble all started in 1908, when Catalina's fishermen set out to rescue some drunks from the courthouse, and to pull it down with a cable. Such lusty action was mistaken for the first signs of change, and a movement began. At its head was Coaker, an ex–fish handler who said he'd make the grass grow again on Water Street. He collected thousands of fisherman's subscriptions, and dressed his rebels in matching roll-neck guernseys. They marched under the banner of a leaping cod and an inauspicious motto—"To each his own." We need a fishermen's city, they decided, and so they came here, to this little hill on the edge of a wide, honest bay. They called it Port Union.

As I wandered through their empty, nailed-up soviet, I had to admire their audacity. The Fisherman's Protective Union had built rows of terraced saltboxes for the workers, a hotel, shops, bakeries, a temperance bar and a fish plant. They'd even had their own Pravda, called *The Fisherman's Advocate*, although the presses were furry now with droppings and age. Perhaps most Stalinesque of all was Coaker's memorial to his dog, or his huge green bungalow—the first electrified house in Newfoundland—which glowed like a cheese.

It couldn't last, even though there were moments of insurrection and power. The high point came in 1919, when the Prime Minister, Sir Michael Cashin (who'd sheltered Curwen back in Cape Broyle), sent a gunboat against the bootleggers on Flat Rock Island. By the time HMS *Cornwall* arrived, the rebels had gone fishing in Labrador, and there was no evidence against those that remained. In the farce that followed, Cashin resigned and Coaker found himself in government.

Power showed up the real weakness of the FPU, which was the absence of any dogma other than fish. The Catholics didn't even think it had that, and suspected that the Union was just a bunch of Orangemen in new jumpers. Coaker was forced into bed with the same merchants he'd threatened to grass over—and became inexplicably rich. The final ignominy was a knighthood, and then a long holiday in Jamaica which lasted until his death in 1938. Without its rudder, the FPU drifted on until 1960, when it finally went under.

Their old premises were now run by a trust, determined to restore a little glory.

What did they think of Coaker, I asked. It caused a scurry of excuses.

"Don't ask me, I'm only new here."

"You'd have to ask the manager, and he's out in the bay."

"We still got a fish-plant, would ye like to see that?"

I said I would, and I did. It was a surprisingly enjoyable afternoon, watching the best part of 40,000 lbs of shrimps chugging through their stages: shelling, grading, boiling, frosting and then speeding off in sandwich boxes. Britain, I learnt, is the "biggest consumer of shrimps in the world," and today's lot were bound for Marks and Spencer. Coaker would have liked all this, the work, the fish and the cash. Oddly, no one mentioned him again.

His story had fizzled out, like his revolution.

60

I returned to the Trans-Canada, and the dreaded forest.

The density of trees was stultifying. It was as if the whole land-scape had been smothered in perpetual night-time—a damp, prickly night without orientation or end. I was glad it wasn't just me that was appalled by the Newfoundland forests. For the South African painter, Peter Bell, they brought on a rash of enmity. "I hate this place," he once said. "Look at the vegetation. All those acres and acres of endless balsam firs and nasty, spiky trees . . . There is no stature about the forest at all, and it is monotonously boring."

Originally, I'd planned to stop in the forest of Terra Nova and plod around as Curwen had. He and the Australian doctor, Bobardt, had spent six days hunting up here, along with two "packers" and a trapper. It was a magnificent adventure. They survived on pork and pea-meal, and slept under a tarpaulin "tilt." Over the week, they'd covered almost a hundred miles—"thirteen miles further than any sportsmen"—and had named their discoveries the Doctors' Commons and the Doctors' Hills. Initially, all that Curwen caught was a moth, but soon the packs began to bulge.

Most magnificent of all was the trapper, who hunted with a six-foot muzzle-loader, slept outside and woke every morning with his beard frozen stiff. He could shoot in the dark and was a legendary tracker. Even Curwen managed to put an explosive bullet in a caribou, and there were gifts for everyone—venison for Captain Trezise and the Governor, and a few chops for Dr. Harvey.

Peering over the steering wheel, I shuddered at the thought of tramping after them. It wasn't just the fear of monotony; Curwen's diaries were infested with snarly beasts. There was talk of the Newfoundland wolf although—after the Museum had acquired itself a lanky specimen in 1894—these were soon extinct. Far worse were the lynx (which people said liked to follow you around for fun) and the bears. How would I manage without a trapper? Besides, I was bound to get lost. The newspapers were full of Hansel-and-Gretel stories of children being lost (or found) in the woods, and I wouldn't be any better. Although sorry not to see the only bit of this planet named after an ancestor, I wasn't going to stop the car for anything.

I touched the accelerator, and shot off for the Straight Shore.

<h1 style="text-align:center">61</h1>

It took me almost a week to crawl up this shore, which wasn't straight at all. To a seagull, the southern end must have looked as if it had been attacked with an axe but, when I stopped in Dover, I discovered that (as is so often the case with geology) there was more to it than that.

Instead of a single maniac, Dover had been rammed by an entire continent. About 490 million years ago, Gondwana (Europe and Africa) had ground its way over and smashed into Laurentia. For a few million years the two were welded together, here in Dover, but then Gondwana broke away, and creaked back again across the Iapetus Ocean. As it departed, however, it left its nose behind, still welded to Laurentia. This was the chunk of rock that I'd already covered (known to geologists as Avalonia). Before moving on to the next chunk, I decided I'd camp in the weld. It was a narrow gully of silt that ended in beach—and that happened to be owned by an unruly clan called the Hounsells.

I shall never forget the generosity of the Hounsells, nor their irreverence. They couldn't care less about Gondwana and the Ordovician chaos. It was bad enough being a family of twelve without worrying about plate tectonics. Although it vaguely amused them that the rocks on one side of their plot were bluer and slimier than those on the other, they had a party to get to. "We're havin' a time for Father," they said, "and yer welcome to come."

I pitched my tent next to a cormorant and went to buy some beer. I was already fond of Dover. In order to squeeze itself into its fault, it had become a toy, with tiny cherry trees, and hay-fields that you could almost harvest from the gate. The Hounsells lived in a mobile home, buried in diggers and bits of Christmas. By the time I got there, the party appeared to be in its third day, and father was as pink as a sausage. There were little trails of grand-children and turkey over every surface.

"Shaun! Would ya get yer bobbin' skirly arse out of my dinner!"

"And Mickey ya can quit mangin' that cat!"

Eventually we were forced out into the mosquitoes, where I found myself next to a fisherwoman called Nicey. She had purple hair and wore "piss-quicks"—or slippers cut from old rubber waders.

"We're trailer trash," she said apologetically. "Never been anywhere, never will."

Not that they wanted to know about England. The Hounsells had all they needed from *Coronation Street,* which had somehow leaked into the wrong continent. Instead, Nicey sang, and everybody gossiped about Jimmy so-and-so and the moose he poached.

"And there's plenty folk could name a proper place for the likes of he . . ."

The party rumbled on all night, much as the continents had done beneath us. I was back in my tent by dawn, just in time to hear Nicey's trap-skiff purring into the bay. In the new way of things, she was allowed to take 7,000 pounds of cod a year although—she said—it was easy to lose count with numbers like that.

What about this summer's catch?

"Well, there's a good sign o' fish," she said, "but nothing you'd call a price."

She also said that if I wanted to know about the Labrador fishery, I should go and see her uncle. He was seventy-six and had seen it through.

62

Jim Rogers described the end of the migrations in a strange, Wessex brogue of lost consonants and stowaway Hs.

"We don't belong ere but come from the h'islands sure. From there, I got a berth on a schooner h'every year from the h'age of h'eleven till the war. We was floaters I'd say, took the fish green. We was h'about a month fillin' the boat with fish and then we'd aul em down to St. John's . . ."

The fishing was much as Curwen had described. The cod were herded into huge rooms made of twine where, unable to find their way out, they soon drowned. Jim thought it was a lazy death but the work was hard. The food gave him the scudders, he said, and his hands were always rotten with the water-pups. But there were moments that amazed him even now. "Those h'Eskimos! They could smell their way up the coast in the dark."

He didn't go again after the war. The Labrador fishery had collapsed. "That's when we floated this ouse back over the h'ocean."

Nowadays, only his son still fished, gathering sea urchins for the Japanese.

"That's not a *proper* fish," said Mr. Rogers, "it's just a whore's h'egg."

63

Eventually, the shore began to straighten out for the spindly sealing ports of the north: Wesleyville, Greenspond and Musgrave Harbour.

It was a long, empty coast, the land merely sediment at the bottom of a great wash of sky. There were no trees; the old "corduroy" road had eaten the last of the forest and corrugated itself with logs. Nor was there anything to stop the weather rolling up the rocks, and smashing all to chips. People had learnt to live with that, and built their stages from twigs and stilts—not for durability but for the ease of re-assembly. It was a life wrought between the shingle and the froth. At Cape Freels, I found them growing rhubarb in rowing boats, and out in Ladle Cove I met a Mrs. Whelan, taking her cat for a walk among the rock-pools. Did other people find these things peculiar? Or even funny? Probably not, I thought, when I spotted a macabre sign in Deadman's Bay: "The Turning Point Drop-In Centre."

Occasionally, I thought I saw the little wooden mansions of the jowlers, the generals of this coast, who'd led the sealers to the Front. These were vicious, freezing wars. Of the fifty great sealing steamers, forty-one were crushed and swallowed by the ice. The jowlers were entitled to their greatness and their seats in the Assembly, and could be forgiven for a little eccentricity. Curwen knew the curliest of them all, from his time in St. John's. Captain Samuel Blandford wore seal-skin waistcoats with his morning coat, and thought of nothing but pelts. He fought his war with carrier-pigeons and other gimmicks, and spent twenty-one springs in the ice. By the end, he'd hauled half-a-million pelts home from the Front.

Jim Rogers gave me this account of life at the Front, which I've trans-lated into something more twenty-first-century:

I went every March from 1948. We took a dog-slide down to the railway and then rode nine hours to St. John's. We stood around freezing on the harbour for hours, 'til we was selected for a berth to the ice: about fifty or sixty to a ship. First, you got your crop— about $9—to buy the outfit: rope, sculping knife, boots, nunny-bag and club. Some years, I sailed with the *Kyle*. You said you saw her, didn't you? In Harbour Grace? Them days she was black with all the coal and fat.

Everyone came to see us sail. Bloody decks! they shouted. Bloody decks and safe return. And then we was banging through the ice, let me tell. Get stuck in that and you're there 'til the summer! Scattered times, we used powder to blast our way. I was usually barrelman, up the mast scunning for seals, and swatches through the ice.

By and by we was at the Front. If it was good whelping ice, we was in the fat, sure. Everybody over the side, said the Old Man, and then we was copying over the ice-pans using our hakapiks. Oftentimes we had a cruel lot of walking to do, ten mile or more, but we usually had some tea and a bit of bread and butter. Then we was in the herd, and the ice was red with blood. You sculped your swile there and then, and heaped up the pelts to be collected later. You also took a little snig o' tail to prove it was yours (if you didn't kill enough swiles, there was no berth next year). Later, the foxes and polar bears came to eat up all the bits we'd left.

We got to our bunks about midnight, after shovelling coal and stacking up the pelts. There was usually a bit o' lobscouse for supper (What's that? Like a brew of oats and flippers). That was it for the day, and then we was up again at five. There was no washing. We just dumped our duds at the end: you could never wear them again for all the filth.

Yes, boy, it was good work. We took about 40–60,000 pelts a season, and the money was good too. By 1960, I was making $250 a trip, and that's a pretty sum, ain't it?

64

Sailing through the nightmares of every old Newfoundlander are two sealing ships, owned by Curwen's shooting friend, Sir Edgar Bowring. Like all Sir Edgar's boats, they were named after Shakespearean characters, always a temptation for drama. In the case of the *Florizel* and *Stephano*, it would be tragedy.

By 1914, the *Stephano* was under the command of the greatest jowler of them all, Captain Abram Kean. He was great because he'd killed a million seals but in all other respects he was a hapless, lumpen man with a foul mouth and a weakness for disaster. At the age of ten he'd killed his nephew, fumbling with a gun, and seven years later he married his nanny. She bore him two sealing captains and then seized up like a winch, and never moved again.

On the 31 March that year, all three skippers were hunting together, about a hundred miles to the north. Joe was in command of the *Florizel,* and "Captain Wes" was on another sealer, the *Newfoundland,* out of Wesleyville. When the *Newfoundland* became caught in the ice, Wes decided to send a watch of 114 men over the side, and five miles across the ice to the *Stephano.* There, he hoped his father would feed his men, find them seals and keep them overnight. But he'd over-estimated his father's generosity, and the old jowler simply ordered them back to the *Newfoundland.* Now, neither ship expected the men that night, and in the blizzard that followed, there were no guns or flares to guide them home.

There's no subtlety in the plot from here. The storm screamed across the ice for two and a half days. Some men died in their soliloquies, others in a chorus of tears. Some tried to dance to keep warm, and were caught forever in a grisly sealer's waltz. Others just lay down and let the howls freeze on their lips. Seventy-seven men perished. There was no sky in this final scene, no breath or blood or flailing limbs, just the patter of snow on marble faces. When the blizzard stopped and the curtain drifted away, there was hardly a voice left among the knots and gnarls of the watch.

Joe carried the dead back to St. John's on the deck of the *Florizel,* still tangled together like trees. Ten thousand people came out to watch, as they sailed in, and there'd be poems and paintings all abounding in black. The photographs of this day still haunt the Newfoundlanders—frozen men stacked like logs. People assumed this was the end of tragedy and that life could get no worse than this.

But they were wrong, of course. A few months later, the *Florizel* was carrying the first Newfoundlanders off to a devastating war, and then the *Stephano* was torpedoed off Nantucket. The *Florizel* soon followed. In 1918, she was smashed to bits on Cape Race, along with poor Captain Joe. His funeral was the biggest that Newfoundland has ever known.

65

The *Florizel*'s bell had been returned to the sealers' coast, and is kept in Newtown, "the Venice of the north."

Newtown is a "Venice" because it is an archipelago of islands stitched together by eleven bridges. I camped on a tiny triangle of grass belonging to old Billy Norman. His island hardly broke the surface of the ocean, which was why Billy liked it.

"There's no forest fires 'ere, or black-fly, and the snow don't settle but blows straight through."

It was a "new town" because—until the Labrador fishery ended—there'd been no town at all. Men like Billy lived even further out, among the crumbs of the horizon.

"There was h'only the Barbours 'ere, in the merchants' premises."

The Barbours were the Doges of this Venice. I remembered having seen Barbours once, in my West Country ancestry, and wondered if this was a branch that had broken away, to come and build themselves a palace in the cove. It was a barn of a place, hardly Venetian, but fanciful enough with all its pine turrets and coloured glass. It was now open to visitors, and I wandered around trying to feel ancestral. Part of the complex was a house built like a mirror: two front-doors, two staircases, two of everything. It was once the home of three brothers—Leslie, Job and Carl—who'd never seen the need for a wall between their lives, and so their house remained a mirror. Such happiness might have continued forever, if Leslie hadn't caught a bullet in the throat at Passchendaele. His room was much as he'd left it—hook-mats and piety—except that on his desk was a tin of Passchendaele soil.

Only Carl's wife Dorothy had survived the century. I often saw her on the balcony, in a sun-bonnet, gazing out over ninety years of the sea. This is where Job wrote his book, she told me, about how they were all lost, and drifted off to the other side of the world.

Billy remembered the day the *Neptune II* set out: 7 November 1929.

"I was h'eight years old, and my father worked for Job Barbour, in the galley."

We were sitting in Billy's parlour, which slewed and yawed in the breeze. Mrs. Norman—who I was asked to think of as "Aunt"—was cooking navy beans and onions for dinner. "You're kindly welcome," she said. "We'll storm the kettle and have a little time."

"*Neptune* was some schooner," continued Billy, "but she 'ad no charts, no sextant and none of 'em could swim."

There were eleven on the return leg from St. John's, including Job and "One-eyed Johnny" Norman. They were on the last run before Christmas, loaded with apples and salt pork, and 300 pounds of gunpowder.

"It was only undred miles to Newtown, but they ran into dirty weather . . ."

The hurricane stripped the *Neptune* down. The wheelhouse and booms were torn away, the life-boats wrecked and bulwarks smashed. Although the mate was up and down the mast like a wood cat, there was no saving the sails. Then came the ice, clogging the rigging and threatening to drag them over.

"The h'Old Man knew he 'ad to drift south, into warmer waters . . ."

They drifted like that for forty-eight days. There was no fresh water except what they could lick off the sails. It was too rough to open the hatches to get at the provisions, and so they had to tunnel through the bulkheads, half-expecting the powder to blow at any moment. The pork was "as salt as Lot's wife" and so there was nothing for it but seven weeks of biscuits and rotten apples. Old Aunt Esther almost died of the damp, and bosun threatened to follow her into The Deep. They drew straws as to who'd shoot who, and then threw the accordion out because it was making them mad. Some wondered if they'd ever see land again.

". . . or if a h'earthquake 'ad swallowed it all . . ."

Then they shot a tickleass, and felt the bottom of the ocean on a line. Land! But who would find them? Would it be savages? Hunger was edged aside by a fear of being eaten. The mate started blasting away at the shore with his musket, to scare off any pirates. The noise attracted a little gunboat. This is Scotland, said the coastguard, and just who are you? News of the Newfoundlanders' deliverance rippled up the coast. In Oban, the whole town turned out to greet them from the rooftops.

On 16 January, Job cabled home with the news ("It's still a flag day in Newtown," said Billy). The following month the crew were home. Only Job lingered in Britain. Much of his book—which he wrote for

Newfoundlanders—is about the wonders he found there; crowds of 60,000, musical beggars, elevators and people travelling underground in trains. His last service was to visit Leslie's grave at Ypres, and to scoop up a toffee tin of Passchendaele soil.

I visited the tombs of almost all the survivors of this curious adventure. Blind Johnny and the mate were buried shoulder to shoulder, and bosun a short way off. Aunt Esther had grown vegetables for a while and then died the way she'd always wanted to, in a good dry bed. The only one who was missing was Uncle Job, who at the age of thirty-seven said he'd had enough of sailing and went off to St. John's to sell engines, and never came home.

And what about *Neptune II*?

"She was sold," said Billy. "And sank off h'Oporto just short o' the war."

All that remained of her was the smashed wheel, and the musket. These were Venetian treasures now, along with the *Florizel*'s bell.

66

Some say that the islanders who live off the north shoulder of Newfoundland are the last of the old Elizabethans.

Even before I'd got to the Change Islands, I realised that its people spoke with the voice of the Old World. There were only a handful of passengers on the ferry—a gold-miner going home, a strawberry merchant, five pensioners and a poacher—but they were all vociferously archaic. There were the rogue Hs, of course, and I was still disentangling Hireland and Hindians from their stories, and hold songs and what haunt used to say. But the words too had a certain patina; a man might have *clomb* a hill here, and his daughters were still his *maidens*. We spent much of the voyage misunderstanding each other; I thought their politicians seized power in a *boil action;* they were puzzled that I was a lawyer. To the poacher, this seemed unnecessarily frank.

"A *liar?*" he kept saying. "Well, that's something, a *liar*."

As we eased our way between the rocks and tickles, I began to appreciate why their world had remained so old. The Change Islanders had had no ferry until 1962, just the occasional visit from schooners or the *Kyle*. Even now, the ferries often froze solid in the winter, and the islanders were themselves again, until the ice-breaker called. Such isolation made them resistant to everything, including the eponymous change.

"'Tis a paradise," said the poacher. "No one to trouble ye. And no cops . . ."

"And no work," said the miner, "so we h'all has to go some place h'else."

Once, they told me, there were a thousand islanders, living like lords off the Labrador fishery. Now there were only 250 of them—and nothing but sea-cucumbers, which they collected for the Chinese. These days, they said, there were still four churches—Anglican, Pentecost, Army and United—but hardly a preacher between them.

". . . and we honly gets the doctor once a fortnight."

At the southern end of the islands, the ferry disgorged its strange cavalcade—a few trucks, the strawberry van and a conspicuous Buick for carrying moose. Together, we spluttered through the dust and crunnicks, eleven kilometres to the town. In 1875, Change had burnt to the roots and, even today, the islands tended to look like two bald heads peering inquisitively from the sea. What remained of the town dangled over the causeway between the two.

I was enchanted by Change, and its grim refusal to be modern. Although many of the old fish-lofts had simply ossified and pitched into the cove, others were obstinately bloody-red, in seal-oil and ochre. The stores still called their merchandise "freight," and salt-pork was still ordered by the keg. Even more intriguing were the secret societies—the Royal Black Knights and the Sons of United Fishermen—with their huge clinker-built halls, and all their skull-and-crossboned flummery. "Love the Brotherhood," said their lumpy tracts. "Fear God, Honor the Queen." Anywhere else, such words might have been sinister. Here it was merely the sound of the past, resisting the passage of time.

I camped on a low promontory, which the gulls used as an anvil for smashing crabs. The saltbox next to me had been abandoned so suddenly that the logs still lay in the grass, where they'd fallen from the saw-bench. At first, I thought all the houses in the cove were empty, until I saw an elderly couple sitting in the dark. They weren't going to let a stranger go without breakfast, and so every day began with the Kings, and a mug of berries or creamed wheat, and caplin eaten with jam.

I asked Mrs. King if they'd always lived here, meaning Change.

"No," she said. "We 'auled this hold 'ouse up the droke from Garden Cove."

Mr. King still grew strawberries and carrots among the rocks. Once, we used to grow everything we ever needed, he said, and in winter we knitted trap linnet, to pay the school fees. "And berries h'every-where! Yaffles of 'em! 'Ave ye been h'out to the point?"

One hot afternoon, I took his directions, and fought my way out through the whip and snap and alder. Go past Lord and Lady Gulch, he'd said, to a white rock as big as a lassy puncheon. I did as I was told and, after an hour, was standing, scratched and berried, by the mysterious rock. Ahead of me was nothing but the north, and a horizon chipped with sparks of light. They were icebergs, filing down from Labrador.

In the Kings' parlour was a tract to remind them of the beauty of Change.

"He bringeth them," said the Black Knights, "into their desired heaven."

67

It's often said that half the lies they tell on Fogo are true.

The island has seldom sounded credible. To the Portuguese, it was the Land of Fire, although I remember merely radiant days, toothed with ice. To the Flat Earth Society, it's where the world ends, even though the islanders have never worried about sailing over the edge. Perhaps their continued defiance of the odds had left them congen-itally optimistic. Neither their past nor their future seemed to worry them, whether it was schooldays roasting seagulls, or an iceberg barging into the cove, grinding everything to bits.

I spent a Sunday in an archipelago of reflections and orange rocks, called Barr'd Islands. It was all so luminously pretty that sometimes even the fishermen just stopped, entranced by the detail—punts mirrored in the tickle, stilts and huskies, pigs in the kelp, and the grass lazy with warmth. That afternoon, a group of fishermen asked me to join them, to drink away the illusion with a bottle of rum. It was an afternoon blissfully lost, stretching stories on the stage. Often they conjured with the past, and childhood reappeared—long expeditions in search of birds' nests, berry-picking and lots of guns, and some strange, unruly games like Pedley, Tiddley and Grump. Everyone was amazed at how they'd survived.

When the heat and Old Sam became too much, I slithered off the headrails into the icy cove. Although I was too numb to feel much, I was aware that swimming in the same panorama as an iceberg had a certain Grenfellness about it. Grenfell, on the other hand, would have hated my slither, and would have torn all his clothes off and leapt into the cove as naked as an egg. Would anybody have minded? I doubt it. The icebergs were the greatest joke of all. The fishermen were often chugging out there, to hack bits off for their drinks.

"Listen to the bubbles in that!" they said as they clinked it round their glasses.

"Ten thousand years in the ice! Just smell it!"

We all inhaled the air, and decided that the prehistoric world had smelt of almonds.

More Old Sam, and I found myself in an even deeper seam of improbability. None of the men had ever been to the eastern tip of their island, to Tilting, a few miles up the coast. We were always warned not to go, they said; the place is full of Catholics.

Tilting was merely the other half of all the lies.

Being the Irish extremity of a "Black"—or Protestant—coast, Tilting had made an artform of eccentricity. I arrived to find it in the throes of a festival of the absurd. There was only one artist— "the Amazing A. Frank Willie"—but he could play six instruments at once, and sang like a fish. Not that anyone cared. Today was a day to be "half-in-the-bag," to be half-full of moose, and half-full of truth. I met a great sealer whose cat slept in the oven from Christmas through to Easter, and who believed it was women that made the sea unlucky. Another told me his great-grandfather had once married a Black, triggering a family war that was now in its eightieth year. It was only when people fell into their trucks that they remembered sobriety.

"Just watch for the cops," they slushed. "They're maggotty today . . ."

Tilting was obviously much loved by its old sealers. Although some of the saltboxes were now stuffed with hay, others were still being hauled from cove to cove, dodging the feuds and finding the sun. It's solid in winter, they told me, cold enough to freeze the nuts off a tractor. At least one sealer thought the ice had been good for the Irish settlers—or at least for parts of them.

"We sometimes find 'em in the boneyard with *perfect* teeth," he said, "but they was only youngsters."

That evening, Tilting sunk into a bloodshot snooze. It was too hot for noise, and so the children sought television at Rita's Store, despite her protests and her appeals for air. I took myself off to Sandy Cove, a long luminous sash of white that curled off into the haze. There I slept, wrapped in my tent, until the turrs began to flock, just before dawn.

Sandy Cove hadn't always been so serene. Early on 13 June 1809, two fishermen, Turpin and Murphy, were absently mooching along the beach when—suddenly—they felt wild, scaly hands at their throats and eyes. Murphy wriggled free but Turpin was caught in a rain of heavy stone flakes. At first, the axes found only meat and agony but soon they were in foamy blood, and were splintering home through the bone. Then, Turpin's head was free of his heart (at last), and—in new hands—was held aloft in a long unnatural scream.

The Red Men had returned, this time for revenge.

68

The Beothuk world had fallen apart since John Guy's picnic of October 1612.

For a start, the southern shores of their land were now infested with Micmacs. These savage people had sea-canoes and guns, and not a shard of mercy in their frozen hearts. Nor was there any escape to the north. Beyond the sea there was nothing but the land of the *Ashki-mow*—the "raw meat eaters"—who dressed as seals and fought a brutal war in the water. The Red Man was now a fugitive in the northern heartlands of his island.

Then came the fishermen, with more guns and the smell of the hunted. For a while, the two races studied each other with undisguised suspicion. There were even moments of uncertain civility, like the picnic, but the doubts were always there. For the Beothuks, there was so much about the white men they simply couldn't comprehend: the metals, the booming voices, ownership, leadership and the burning powders. Only one thing was certain; they liked the metals, and every night—as silent as shadows—they crept down to the stages to scavenge for nails and wire and pieces of bucket.

For the fishermen, who were outlaws themselves, such mischief had long since ceased to be endearing. They could see their own bony lives being picked apart by vermin, and responded with swan-shot and grape. Everything about the Beothuks now appalled them—their lives made of birchbark and skin, their stinking wigwams, and the puddings they stuffed into gut: seal fat, rotting livers and sea-birds' eggs. The gunfire was incidental at first but soon it was cleansing. It was no crime to kill a savage and so, by 1640, the two races were caught up in a shadowy war.

It took the Red Men over 150 years to gird themselves against the slaughter. They'd always been skilled archers, able to put five or six arrows in the air at once, each with fearful accuracy. They'd also brought their own signature to the art of scalping, peeling a man's face away, right down to the lips. The problem was that they had no concept of concerted action, of the massed attack, and the campaign ahead. They fought the war as if in denial of the future, or in denial of anything new. Whenever they captured guns, they destroyed them, instead of turning them against the invader.

For the fisherman, it was just a vermin hunt. By the 1730s, the Indians had become no more than occasional, and so tracking them down had become good sport. Sometimes, the Indian-hunters captured these freaks, gave them summery names (like "Tom June" and "John August"), and exhibited them for tuppence a peep at the Poole fair. But most of the time it was butchery. "On the part of the English fishers," says a governor's report of 1768, "it is an inhumanity that sinks them far below the level of the savages." The report is a catalogue of mutilation—of "squaws" hacked down as they bared their breasts in supplication, of children bled to death and of a pregnant woman ripped open out of drunken curiosity. Of this last atrocity, says the author, no one would have believed the hunters' boasts but for the fact that they'd severed the woman's hands, and brought them back as a trophy.

Taking a few heads—like Turpin's—was the nearest the Beothuks would ever get to revenge. By the time of the 1768 report, the white men were in command of the rivers, taking over a million pounds of salmon a year. By the end of a vicious century, there were only a few hundred Beothuks left, and their annual migration to the coast was no more than a scurry. It was a harvest fraught with Christians, and so they gathered up their auks and eggs like ghosts, and fled.

Now came the long trek back to the winter grounds, with Turpin's bean all wrapped in bark. They crossed to the mainland, and padded along a chain of cold, dead ponds, up into the benighted forest and then several days through the dark. Eventually they came to a vast, mad river, more like an ocean boiling over the land. From there, they scrambled upstream until they got to a cauldron of dizzying granite and spray. Today, this is Grand Falls, but to the Beothuks it was merely a pause.

This, broadly speaking, was the same route I took, as I set off in uncertain pursuit—in a car, of course, and without a rotting head.

69

I loathed Grand Falls, from my first lungful of steamy pulp to the last bungalow of its dreary, pastel suburbs.

It wasn't just that it was ninety, or that Grand Falls was shrouded in forest, or that it was eating its way through the trees at the rate of thirty-three trucks a day (and spewing out twenty-six trucks of paper in return), or that every garden had a bare-bottomed gnome, or that every duck was plastic; the town was in a state of terminal smugness. Everything was welcome-signed and pansied, and smothered in corporate values. It horrified me that I'd struggled into the wilderness only to find myself in Nicetown Limited, among lawn-sprinklers and propriety. No perfume please, said a sign in the library, "or other unpleasant smells." The politeness of it all was unnerving. I'd never seen such battery-operated children—or Stepford Mothers, come to that. "Make a path for the gentleman," they piped, as I panted around, light-headed with pulp.

Heat and hubris trickled after me wherever I went, down avenues of identical chalets, along a high street of faded shops, past temperance halls and eerie parks, right to the gates of a gargantuan mill. This was the engine of Grand Falls's pride, built by the man who'd re-shaped Edwardian morality in pulp (whilst never neglecting a little adultery of his own). In 1904, Alfred Harmsworth—later Lord North-cliffe—bought over 2,300 square miles of this forest to sustain his voracious halfpenny squib, the *Daily Mail*. Although there was always a prissy, outraged tone to Northcliffe's newspapers, Churchill saw them for what they were, "cheap imperialist productions . . . produced for thousands of people at a popular price." Grand Falls was to be a place commensurate with its product. Fishermen would be tempted away from the sea, owned and moulded into model, tabloid citizens. Even Northcliffe's mistresses cooed at the prospect. "The establishing of a town," wrote one (who was also his secretary), "is surely a romance in itself."

Millions of tons of sawdust later, it was hard to see the romance. Whatever had given Northcliffe his glint now seemed just bleakly corporate and tawdry. His hideous log palace had survived, of course, but so too had Windsor, the ghetto across the tracks. Here, Nicetown had housed its Jews and foreigners, and others not quite up to scratch. With this sort of splendour, it was hardly surprising the company had collapsed. In 1964, Grand Falls had been sold off for a dollar a house, leaving only the pulp and the suffocating values. Not even my themed motel could raise my mood; after a Friar Tuck breakfast and a Robin Hood bill, I decided I'd had enough.

There was one last thing that troubled me. I seemed to have lost the river. Perhaps Grand Falls had thought it uncouth and sent it out to the country. I scrambled across the dunes of sawdust, and out through an Edwardian dump. There, suddenly, I was alone, picking my way through tall cool weeds, no sound but the grasshoppers and a reassuring groan. Then the earth and rock rose to a lip, and crumbled away. I sidled to the edge and peered down, into a chasm of foam: the Exploits River.

In August 1768, it wasn't just the Beothuks clambering along these cliffs. Some way behind them was a curious gaggle. Although their intentions were good, their footwear was useless, and a great expedition was about to end in blisters.

70

Despite poor shoes, this expedition was the best of those in the Age of Curiosity.

For some time, the Governor had been contemplating the Beothuk tragedy. It made little sense. This strange, shadowy people seemed set on extinction, shrinking from all sociable contact with the world and hell-bent on revenge. If only his men could contact them, perhaps civilisation could save them. But how? Still, no one knew anything about them. A study of the Beothuks had become a matter of national curiosity, not to say urgency.

In finding men of courage and spirit, the Governor cannot have improved on the Cartwright brothers. This extraordinary family from Nottinghamshire seemed determined to alter the course of the eighteenth century. Charles was a distinguished soldier, Edmund invented the power loom and John would one day be known as "the Father of Reform," credited with so many of the upheavals that we now take for granted (the abolition of slavery, for example, ballot reform, the liberation of Greece and annual parliaments). In 1768, John was a lieutenant on the Newfoundland station, where he was joined by a fourth brother, George.

George is probably the least well-known of these brothers, and probably the most enjoyable. He was canny and strong and fond of top hats and dogs, but hopeless with women and money. For a moment there were signs of military greatness. After Plassey, he fought through Germany with the Marquis of Granby, but was driven home by the debts forced upon him by so many servants and horses. Drifting around on half-pay, he took to Scotland for a while with "a lady and two dogs," but the debts soon found them. After that, he decided to head for Newfoundland, on the promise of plentiful bears. It didn't take much to coax him onto an expedition "against the wild Indians."

The party set out at the height of summer: John, George, a vicar, a "furrier" and eight grumbling sailors. They split into two parties, scrambling along opposite banks. George was an enthusiastic explorer, even though his shoes were the first to give. The sailors were made of frailer stuff, and simply fled, limping off down the Exploits. More disappointingly, the brothers never met any Beothuks although—being Cartwrights—even this was only a set-back. The report they wrote, *Remarks on the Situation of the Aborigines of Newfoundland*, would be the most intelligent, contemporary study of Beothuks ever produced. No detail escaped them: amulets, talismans, "deer fences," weapons and "whigwhams." Not only that, they also produced a map of excruciating accuracy, and forced through a new law: from now on, the killing of Indians would be punished as a capital crime.

There was less intelligence after that. Although the Cartwrights continued to campaign for a reservation off and on for the next twenty years, John went home and George wandered up to Labrador. I had a feeling I'd be hearing more of him as I made my own way north. Apart from anything, I could see a "Cartwright" half-way up the Labrador map.

In the meantime, successive governors blundered around the Beothuk problem. One of them thought he'd coax them in, by leaving a charming painting by the Exploits: whites and red men in convivial discourse. Others just relied on bounty hunters ("£50 to him that shall bring a Red Indian"), but the bloodshed merely doubled. Even renewed forays by the Navy were little more than clumsy. In 1811, Captain Buchan set off up the Exploits, determined to try out the Red Men in Norwegian and other exotic tongues. He did encounter a tribe, but their meeting was predictably confused. It ended with the older huntresses sawing the heads off two marines, and impaling them on stakes. Worse, Buchan brought the Beothuks tuberculosis, and so within a year another twenty-two of them had coughed themselves to death.

Unhappily, the Age of Curiosity didn't end in wisdom. It was merely a moment of reflection before the last scenes of this awful burlesque. Ironically, the main player in the final tableau was a protégé of the Cartwrights, a man who'd sailed with them in his twenties. Everything about him suggested gentility—a business in Fogo and a leafy home in Dorset—but beneath it all was dangerous brutality. He killed his first Indian in 1781, by smashing his head open with a trap, and would have killed them all ("Big and Small") if only he could. With him were the last gasps of the Beothuks, and the beginnings of a family curse.

He was John Peyton, a gentleman of Wimborne.

71

One of the few exhibits of the Grand Falls Museum was John Peyton's spoon.

Despite the violence of its shiniest years, it was a pretty object. In its dappled surface, I could still make out my reflection, just as the Indians had made out theirs, hammered and polished by an Exeter cutler. He'd hallmarked his spoon "1813" and sold it to a man who saw the future in fish, and who'd sailed off to the Exploits. There, four years later, the spoon was stolen by the shadows, and tiptoed away into the balsam firs and spruce. It was now a magical thing, like ice that never melted, or a sliver of the sky. It was something a chief gave to his young bride, and so the giant Nonosabusut gave it to Demasduit. She kept it with her always, a mirror, a token of love, a scooper, a blade and a scraper. I could still make out Demasduit's work, a weft of tiny striations worn into the cup by hours of scouring hides.

She even had it with her when John Peyton panted up the river for the kill. The theft of white men's property had always provided a thrilling excuse for a hunt. When, in 1818, Peyton's son—also John—was ransacked by the Beothuks, and lost guns and watches and bits of boat, he called for revenge. That's not, of course, how he sold his expedition to the governor. If it will foster brotherly relations between our people, said the old dodderer, it has my endorsement. The Anglican Church added its own blessings. The Peytons, they said, would raise the savages from "a state of darkness and wildness." Of course, said the Peytons as they set off the following March—with eight murderous furriers, and guns enough for a war.

Some weeks upriver, they found Demasduit, who'd just given birth, and decided to appropriate her (for the reward in St. John's). The giant Nonosabusut then crashes into this scene, scattering the historians and the truth of what happened next. In the Peytons' version, he seizes the elderly Peyton "by the throat," and in the struggle that follows a gun goes off and the unfortunate brave is killed. In the untidied versions, he bellows for his wife's release, is torn open from behind and dies with "his eyes flashing fire" and a "yell that made the woods echo." As the last of the Beothuks flee, the Peytons see them on their way with fusillades of thunder and fire. More fall, the forest screams and Demasduit's baby loses a tussock of his soft, new flesh. That leaves only twenty-seven Beothuks alive, and their chief's wife in the hands of the Peytons, a silver spoon tucked in her tunic.

The Peytons' version makes no mention of the murder trial that followed, despite their acquittal. Perhaps a Newfoundland jury weren't yet ready to see a man hanged for acts committed among all the uncertain motives of the Red Men. It was held that Nonosabusut's death was caused by "his own obstinacy in not desisting when repeatedly menaced." The Peytons were freed.

Along the road to Beothuk extinction, it is the injustice of these side-shows that still taunts the Newfoundlanders. Liberals of the sixties toyed with the notion of Newfoundlanders having killed "over 50,000" Beothuks "for fun." Others heated up the story during the seal-hunting controversy, depicting Newfoundlanders as lawless rogues who were clubbing their wildlife to pulp, just as they had their natives. It all seemed a little simplistic. Weren't the Peytons Englishmen? And hadn't the Newfoundlanders put them on trial? Others would prefer to see the disappearance of the Beothuks in more grandiose terms: here was a race incapable of adapting to the stress of contact with other humans. Perhaps this incapacity was physiological, perhaps it was ideological (although their beliefs remain a mystery).

Either way, their time was ticking away in seclusion and revenge.

Meanwhile, the Peytons' princess was led away into servility. Demasduit was taken first to Twillingate, the capital of the northern coast, and given a new name to remind her of the atrocity: Mary March. Although she bore the curiosity well, she was never happy and "seemed to drag a lengthened chain." Then for a while she was sported among the Quality in St. John's, and Lady Hamilton (the governor's wife) painted a portrait of her nestled in fur and improbably happy. Too late, the governor realised that if there was to be any rapprochement with the Beothuks, Miss March had to be returned to her people. She already had tuberculosis.

Ironically, it was left to the hapless Captain Buchan and John Peyton Junior to carry her back up the Exploits. A vast procession tripped its way along these banks, fifty soldiers and an ageless native girl rattling bones and lungs. It was a futile slog. Demasduit died beside this furious torrent, almost exactly ten months after her capture. In early February 1820, she was abandoned in a derelict wigwam at the head of the river.

With her death, the silver spoon passed to John Junior. One would have thought that—after Mary March—the Peytons would have wearied of experiments with Indians. But John Peyton Junior would make a servant of just one more wild princess. She was, as it turned out, the last of the Beothuks, and the most cruelly-named: Nancy April.

72

The acquisition of Nancy April has a brutally familiar ring about it.

By April 1823, there were only a dozen or so Beothuks left, foraging in two groups on the shore. The first group ran into two witless, forest-maddened trappers called Curnew and Adams. Although the women adopted the attitude of submission—breasts exposed, heads bowed—the trappers still blasted holes in them and splashed them across the ice. The other group were hardly more fortunate. One of the Red Men drowned as he tried to escape, and three women were captured. Each had consumption, a mother and two daughters. The older woman and "Easter Eve" died within days but Shanawdithit survived. She was committed to the magistrate, who—as luck would have it—was John Peyton Junior.

Peyton kept her as a servant for five years. She was an intelligent and striking woman of twenty-three, and usefully complemented Peyton's wife, who was only seventeen. In the Peyton history, these were enchanting days; three children and a loyal native nanny, aprons, deportment and service, and a room in the eaves. But for "Nancy April," there was never enchantment. She was a consumptive, caught in a world she didn't understand and where she wasn't understood. There could be no going back. Even if there were any Red Men left, they'd kill her for her collaboration. Nor was there an afterlife any more; her complicity with the white man meant she would never make the Island of Contentment. The anger never left her. "The savage eye," noted one observer, "darted fire and vengeance."

She was rescued in 1828 by William Epps Cormack, a philanthropic merchant who'd searched the island for *Boeothicks,* and found none. Shanawdithit was the last one left, he declared, and—in the name of "The Boeothick Institution"—he took her to St. John's to make one last map of her culture. He only had a few months in which to work, before debts forced him back to Britain. In Shanawdithit's fastidious drawings are the only clues to this ephemeral race: the curious decapitated heads, the paddles that were worshipped, and the world that began where the arrow fell. By the time he left, Cormack had gleaned a mere 325 words from the growls and whispers of the last Beothuk's language.

Then Cormack was gone, and six months later Shanawdithit drowned in her disease. Her obituary appeared in the London *Times,* written by Cormack: "There has been a primitive nation," he lamented, "once claiming rank as a portion of the human race, who have lived, flourished and become extinct . . ." Meanwhile, the Johnsmen had no idea what to do with a savage and so they buried her in a Protestant cemetery, even though she'd resisted evangelism with every last gasp and scratch. Her grave doesn't exist any more. A century after her death, it was torn up to make a road, and the last of her kind was ground up into gravel.

As for John Peyton Junior, he was promoted to Chief Magistrate for Twillingate, or *Toulinguet* as he preferred. But it was only a moment of triumph. It wouldn't be long now before misfortune was among the Peytons.

73

I arrived in Twillingate to find it dreaming away its days as the capital of the northern coves. It was an archipelago of old sea captains and cabins as white as starch, of sailors' memories, and of parrot-cages and old zithers, cruets from Poole, treasured shrapnel and Zanzibari arrows. I half-imagined a troop of ramrod Orangemen to come fluting up Stuckless Lane, or a temperance band to burst into *Lo, Hear the Gentle Lark*. Twillingate seemed so oddly awkward in the present, and so oblivious of the north. Although it had once enjoyed cricket and trams, in reality it was deep within the ice lanes, extreme enough for polar bears. I was even shown one, up at the old drill hall, a shaggy,

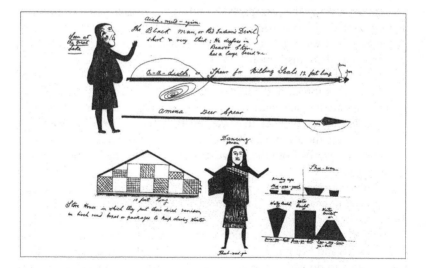

Shanawdithit (or Nancy April's) sketches

bug-eyed monster frozen in mid-swipe. It had only been upholstered two years before.

"She came up Sleepy Cove," they said, "and was makin' for the Chinese."

This was an appealing thought, as I tramped across North Island to Back Harbour. The Peytons had had the Magistrate's House here, on a gentle slope of lawns and rocks brocaded in kelp. The garden, where they'd grown potatoes and turnips, was still there, and so too was their root cellar, like a doorway into the world below. But the house had long ago rattled itself to pieces, and with it went the curse of the Peytons.

I stood at the palisade, trying to disentangle fact from Faust. Although John Junior had somehow crabbed on into the late 1870s, the destruction of his family had been breathless and thorough. His first son had choked during infancy, and his second was drowned on his way to an English education. Then three daughters were stifled, throttled by diphtheria or rotted down with smallpox. Only his daughter Anne (who'd been swaddled and cooed over by the last of the furious Beothuks) survived him. But, within three years of moving into the house, she too was dead, her arteries frozen with grief. Misadventure had already begun to seep among her children. Her only son had toddled face-first into a puncheon, and gurgled away his life. As to her seven daughters, fate left them a choice: leave Newfoundland forever, or die here, unmarried and in black.

The seventh daughter, Georgie, almost survived her Twillingate destiny.

She'd leave Newfoundland, and become—momentarily—one of the greatest mezzo-sopranos in the world, "the Nightingale of the North," the diva who brought La Scala to tears in January 1901, on the night Giuseppe Verdi died. She'd wear velvet and mink, and garlands of lilies and live canaries and doves. She'd call herself Mademoiselle Marie Toulinguet, and would tour the world, reaping devotion from Arizona to Milan. "She suggests the tropics," the critics would gasp, "and yet she's from Newfoundland." Although there was never love, there'd be no end to the adoration. *Conquista rapisce il pubblico,* proclaimed the Italians—She conquers the people and steals their hearts.

But then the icy shadows had gathered and hauled her home.

I walked back down the lane to the church where Georgie had found her voice. Inside the air was cool, and light with beeswax and polished reflections. This was the Old World, I realised, Norwich organ-pipes and a blaze of Dorset brass. Perhaps the same thought had occurred to Dr. Stirling as he listened to his daughter's voice, maturing and mellowing in the wood. Although he was a durable physician, ruthless with the chloroform ("Kill or cure," he'd say as his patients slipped away), he knew beauty when he heard it. In 1888, at the age of twenty-one, Georgie was sent to Europe, to the École Marchesi in Paris.

These were the best years. Although, in her portraits, Georgie was never an attractive woman—puggish, currant-eyed, with a hank of autumnal hair—no one doubted she was a diva. Men were spellbound, though never infatuated, and women felt admiration though never envy. "A voice such as hers," reported the *Boston Globe,* "one hears only once in a lifetime." To my surprise, a recording of the diva had survived, at the old Twillingate Rectory. Among all the crackles and spits, I could hear an exquisite note rising and falling and falling like crumbling birdsong. Everybody wanted this sound, and soon Mademoiselle Toulinguet was touring France, Italy and the world. Her glory was never greater than the day she was invited to sing the magnificent 1898 Mass at Chioggia: "Orchestra and chorus refuse to play without you," said the telegram. "Everything in confusion. Utterly ruined unless you come. Don't refuse."

Georgie was never too grand for her old home, although—like grandfather Peyton—she tended to recast it as "Toulinguet" and "Terra Nova." Almost every year, she rode the ore-carriers home, to the copper mine at Sleepy Cove. Wasn't this where the polar bear came ashore? It was an uneasy thought as I bedded down in the moss, among the echoes, and the rusty old bones of winches and cogs. The cove had always seemed more skeletal than sleepy. Georgie would remember families who wintered on molasses and potato mould, and who buried their own dead for fear of disease. She no longer knew how to live with such poverty, and would send them Christmas trees and hampers. Then she'd sail for St. John's, to cream off the applause. In the year my great-grandfather called by, she sang an aria from *Aida* to the charred city, but Curwen was already on his way, ploughing up to Labrador.

The adoration of the Johnsmen would be the most enduring, and the last. On 24 October 1904, their diva's enchanted voice had simply spluttered out, leaving an audience blinking in panic. It was as if she was smothering, or as if her throat had been seized by icy hands. From now on, the only way to calm the demons was in gin.

I went out to Mademoiselle Toulinguet's grave on the headland, behind the church where this opera began. To begin with, the people of Twill- ingate had buried their prima donna with shame, lowering her into a frozen, unmarked grave during Easter Week, 1935. But then, in the sixties—when it was good enough to have been merely enchanting (and not much more)—Georgie was heaped with granite and birdy praise. "Nightingale," I read, "fairer than all the larks of Italy."

Although this was a life that ought to have concluded with an asp or a dagger, the end was a torment. Georgie spent almost thirty years in England, fifteen of them in a home for "Inebriates and Unfortu- nates caught in Vice," and the rest in a haze of dreary, Purley drudge. Finally, in 1929, she gave in to the demons, and came back to Newfoundland—fat, unwanted, unrecognised and battered by drink. There was only one sister left at the Magistrate's House—Rosetta, a viperous spinster who'd scowled away her life in Naples, and then returned to Twillingate as black as grief.

I met an old nurse once, who remembered their fights. It was always drink.

"Eventually, they divided the house," she said. "Wouldn't even share the stairs."

The last moments of this masque are blurred and unhappy. The nurse remembered the embattled house filthy with pigs and ducks. Under the bed were two sled dogs—Whisky and Brandy—and a demented cat called Marchesi. Georgie fed them on butter and veal, and would drink coffee with a spoonful of mustard. Occasionally, she'd take out an exquisite gown of georgette and seeded pearls, and haul it on over her sweater. Then she'd ride along the harbour on a sledge pulled by her goat, Garibaldi, and the townsfolk would stiffen with shame. Some remembered how Georgie had once tried to teach acting to the Hustler's Club, but no one had believed her, and so she'd tottered home.

"According to the doctor," said the nurse, "she had *general paralysis of insanity*."

But, in the end, it wasn't the hands at her throat that killed the prima donna. Georgie was being eaten by cancer. "Leave me alone," she bellowed at the doctor. "Let me die!" It was almost as if he too was a tormentor. Perhaps she thought he'd keep her in this purgatory, depriving her of the peace she'd sought for the best part of her life.

74

The ice had cleared. It was time to leave the north coast, and follow Curwen up through the Labrador Sea. All that remained was to drop the car at Gander.

The dream of every outporter—that he is no longer at the edge of the world but can somehow feel its pulse—is almost fulfilled in Gander. Although there is little there but an airport, every day the events of the world come plunging down the runway, and the town is swamped in adventure. On the morning I was there, there were calls from the RAF, a plane full of cows, and two F15s hunting the ocean for extremists. Then a planeload of desert troops arrived, still powdered with Afghanistan. What the fuck's this place, they grunted, as they pounded around looking for fries. No sooner had they gone than there were more peacekeepers, with Macedonia on their boots—or Germany or Turkey or perhaps a spot of Kosovo.

"Is it always like this?" I asked the sergeant on the gate.

Harry, it turned out, saw life as a moose-hunt, interspersed with foreign farce. "Jasus, no," he said. "We're usually arse over kettle. This is quiet, sure. Last week, we had two airliners diverted off the Atlantic. One was an air rage—a couple of French doxies fightin' it out with the trolley girls—and the other was for a feller who'd swallowed eighteen balloons o' coke, and one of them had burst ..."

Soon the stories were singing along. Harry's wife, who was a corporal in the guard, added her voice to the chorus. "Another time we found $30,000 stuffed down the toilet ..."

"Then we had Stirling Moss' cars here once ..."

"... and a plane full of polo ponies ..."

"... which me father had to feed for a month ..."

For Harry the best of these visitors were the statesmen. Their fleeting visits to Gander put Newfoundland momentarily at the centre of the world.

"I've met Fidel Castro," he said. "Nelson Mandela and the Queen ..."

His corporal preferred the film stars.

"Woody Allen, John Travolta, Marlene Dietrich . . ."

But, as always, they were only passing through, like the people that pop up in our sleep. Although, in 1936, Gander was the biggest airport in the world, it had never been more than a diversion, a fuel pump, or a slammer for drunks. Only rarely were the planes seeking out Newfoundland itself—Hollywood jets here for the hunting, or Concorde nosing out the icebergs. Mostly, these visitors brought the news with them to the Rock, rather than making it here. The exceptions were usually poignant, like the Bulgarians who'd defected on the way to Cuba, or the U.S. 101st Airborne Regiment which had missed the runway in 1985, and had cremated itself in the forest. But these incidents were soon forgotten in the world beyond.

It wasn't until the Twin Towers disaster that the North Coast felt any hint of acknowledgement. When Washington switched off its airspace, there were thirty-seven airliners dangling—homeless—over the Atlantic. They turned, and settled on Gander like an aluminium swarm. At first, the Newfoundlanders didn't know what to do with such an extravagant migration, and the two sides peered at each other through the portholes. But then the rescue began.

"We're maritime people," said Harry. "When there's a disaster, we all pitch in."

"Every mealtime, we had to find another 7,000 dinners . . ."

". . . including kosher and halal . . ."

As Harry said, everyone pitched in. Fifty new telephones were installed to link the castaways to their world, and the truckers called off their strike. The tiny Newfoundland army arrived, and every spare toothbrush in Gander was requisitioned, along with several trucks of diapers and soap ("By now," said Harry, "they was all a bit hummy"). Then, the passengers were dispersed to the outports; Africans in salt-boxes and Finns in schools, Greeks along the Exploits and mums in Orange Lodges, Irishmen tucked up in the attic and Americans in the eighteenth century. It was hard to imagine all these people scattered through the journey I'd just done. "Where are we?" they kept saying. "What is this place?"

They'd never forget their time on the edge, and nor, I suppose, would I. A year on, gratitude was still pouring in from the States, enough to rebuild schools, and clubs for the elderly. Some even saw the beauty of the place, and caused a tiny blip in the price of a saltbox, which had hardly changed for centuries. Even the Nigerians turned up for the first reunion, a thought which still causes me to question my own gratitude. I can hardly remember having been so generously treated before, especially by a people who had so little to be grateful for themselves.

On the bus to the coast, I wondered how Labrador would compare.

"It's fucked," said the boy next to me. "Nothing there but rocks, bears and drunks."

Act IV: Down Labrador

Labrador was discovered by the English; there is nothing
in it of any value.

—Spanish map of the New World, 1529

The whole land is strewn with boulders. Language fails to
depict the awful desolation of the interior of the peninsula.

—Professor Hinde, Victorian explorer

Labrador land as a farming proposition would unquestion-
ably appear discouraging. Not only John Cabot but the early
Vikings were pessimistic about it. Seamen as a rule are not
attracted by digging.

—Sir Wilfred Grenfell, *A Labrador Doctor*

Melancholic insanity is not uncommon.

—R. D. Graham, *Rough Passage*

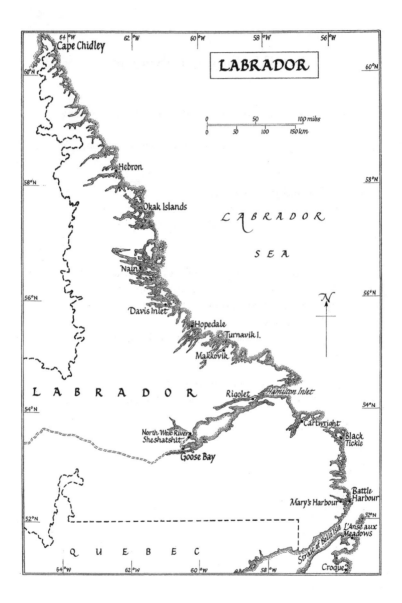

LABRADOR

0   50   100 miles
0   50   100   150 km

Cape Chidley

Hebron

Okak Islands

LABRADOR

SEA

Nain

Davis Inlet

Hopedale

Turnavik I.

Makkovik

LABRADOR

Rigolet

Hamilton Inlet

Cartwright

Black Tickle

North West River
Sheshatshit

Goose Bay

Battle Harbour

Mary's Harbour

L'Anse aux Meadows

Strait of Belle Isle

QUEBEC

Croque

N

75

I'd booked my passage to Labrador some weeks before, in St. John's.

"It should be clear by the end of July," said the clerk, "but there's over five hundred bergs headin' this way. Big ones too, like 200,000 tons."

It was an uncomfortable thought, throwing a ferry down Iceberg Alley.

"I hope," I said, feebly, "that she can find her way around them."

"Better than the last one," tutted the man behind me. "She went down in the ice."

I managed a smile. What other perils, I wondered, might I expect? There were plenty of suggestions from the queue.

"This time of year, the stouts and flies are as big as buzzards . . ."

"And I heard there's a polar bear tryin' to get home down the shore. So you want to take care if you're out in the tucks. She's proper hungry . . ."

". . . hungry enough," howled another, "to eat the arse off a flying duck!"

The clerk steered us back to the question of tickets.

"Do you want a shared cabin, or a single?"

I hesitated. "What if the other fellers want to drink their way to Cartwright?"

"What d'you mean?" said the man behind. *What if?*

76

Labrador, as Newfoundlanders so often told me, is just a waste of space.

To the older generation, it had been the hard, outer rim of their fishery, but without fish it was hard to imagine it being anything at all. No one could remember much about it except the rock and mollyfodge, and the flat-faced natives who could smell their way up the coast. To the younger generation, it was even more skeletal than their own hungry island. There was no work to the north, no future and no need to go there. Although they'd heard of the great new nickel mine at Voisey's Bay, it seemed to produce more rancour than dirt. Every day, the newspapers carried stories of ancient land claims and angry aboriginals. Even the provincial government showed little stomach for Labrador: St. John's had simply sold off its airspace to foreigners training in the art of war, and had sold off its rock to anyone brave enough to mine it.

Many people I met excused their ignorance of Labrador by assuming it was just demented. There were always the stories about bugs and drinking, of course, and the intractable natives. But there were also tales about strange mythological creatures—like the ferocious (but as yet unseen) Ungava grizzly—and about settlers so genetically interwoven that they were now little more than half-wits scratching around on the rocks. There was much satisfaction in these stories: at last, the Newfoundlanders had found a vessel for the jibes that had taunted them for years; the Labradorians were runts, scroungers, toothless, fish-faced, feather-brained dolts. They're not like us, people said, many of them were straight from the old countries, and were never Newfoundlanders.

Why go *there*? they said. *The place is empty.*

On the map, Labrador even looked like an unfinished version of Newfoundland. It covered an area bigger than the British Isles—about the size of Italy—and yet there were only thirty-one communities, all but a handful barnacled to the shore. With only 30,000 people to fill out this coast, it was, perhaps, the scrawniest land in the world. There were no railways or bridges and only two short roads. The outports either faced the ocean alone, or were linked by dots marked "Snowmobiles with emergency shelters." As to the interior, if there can be degrees of nothingness, it seemed even emptier than Newfoundland's, just blank squares and the occasional shiver of blue.

Among the cracks and shards of the southern coast, I could see old English and French names like Snug Harbour and Chateau Bay, but as the land tapered north into a gnarly spike, so the names thickened and baffled: Opingiviksuak, Kikiktaksoak or Tunungayualok. In these northerly reaches, human intervention was so sporadic that, when the Nazis set up a weather station here in 1943, it wasn't discovered for another thirty-seven years.

It wasn't hard to see why mankind had shrunk away from Labrador. Although it sat at the same latitude as Scotland, its coast was frozen solid for six months a year. Then the storms would roll in, grinding and splitting their way along the shore. Little could survive such a mauling, especially trees. In fact, along this entire 1,000-mile wind-cracked, ice-chiselled, bear-infested coastline there was barely a twig to be had. God built the world in six days, say Canadians, and on the seventh he pelted Labrador with rocks. Here is the geological front-line in the Atlantic's attempts to reduce America to pea-gravel, and no place for a twiglet.

77

An absence of trees was one of the first things the discoverers noticed as they found their way to Labrador. The accounts they left are hardly cheering.

The first to report back was Bjarni Herjulfsson, at the turn of the eleventh century. Even for a Viking, the prospect of so much rock was horrifying, and he declared the place "a worthless country." Then came the fishermen, who'd leave nothing but a name. The French would say it was they who thought of *Le Bras d'Or* or *Le Bras d'Eau*, but the Portuguese have a more convincing claim: the *lavrador* was the "landowner," João Fernandez, who'd sighted the coast on an expedition in 1508. Having named it, the Portuguese then sensibly veered away, to more sensual territories to the south.

It was left to a Frenchman to provide the first and most discouraging descriptions. Jacques Cartier sailed through here a quarter of a century later, writing furiously and eating polar bears ("flesh as good to eat as any two-year-old heifer"). He was looking for a north-west passage to the Great Khan but, instead, found himself in an appalling land of "stones and horrible rugged rocks." Like my Newfoundlanders, he saw only emptiness and moss. "I could not find one cartload of earth," he scrawled, "though I landed in many places."

But it was Labrador's first English tourists who showed that it was no place for fools. They were a crew of barristers, under the command of a velveteen fop called Richard Hore. In April 1536, these gentlemen "mustered in a warlike manner" with a view to capturing a few human curios in the New World. They can hardly have looked warlike as they limped down the Thames, leaking, under-supplied, and dressed up in silk bonnets and ruffs. They were even less impressive when, after two months, they landed half-starving in Labrador.

Without the wit to fish or the strength to chase natives, the barristers began to fall apart. For a while, they ate moss and roots and bits of fish stolen from an osprey's nest, but then they started on each other. It took Hore some time to realise that his company was self-digesting. It was only when he caught one of his men grilling a slab of juicy steak that he started some enquiries. "If though wouldest needes know," confessed the accused, "the broyled meat that I had was a piece of such a man's buttocke." Such candour only encouraged more roasting, and the men drew lots as to who'd eat who. It's quite possible that this barristers' lunch would have consumed every last bit of itself had rescue not arrived.

Certainly, after that, the English had no appetite for Labrador. As it happens, it was a French ship that rescued Hore's cannibals, and it was to the French that *Le Petit Nord* now passed. There it remained until 1763, when it was tossed back to the English as part of the spoils of war. Even then, they were unable to muster gratitude. Labrador, ran one Admiralty report, is "a country formed of frightful mountains, and unfruitful valleys, a prodigious heap of barren rock." Perhaps most discouraging of all was the verdict of a man who'd give the best years of his life to Labrador. It was our old friend, the superbly top-hatted George Cartwright:

> The astonished mariner is insensibly drawn to a conclusion that this country was the last that God made, and that he had no other view than to throw together there the refuse of his materials, as of no use to mankind.

This was not the sort of encouragement that Curwen and I needed, as we clambered onto our boats. My great-grandfather was already bouncing through lumpy seas, heading north aboard the *Albert*. Now, a hundred and nine years and three weeks later, I was setting off after him, on the MV *Sir Robert Bond*, out of Lewisporte.

78

Unsurprisingly, there were few Newfoundlanders on the ferry.

The saloon deck was a Noah's Ark of Labradorians, every variety assembled. There were Celts two by two, pairs of blondes, pairs of Indians, a brace of hunters and thick, hot knots of Inuit and icemen. Often there were combinations of reds and Celts and, often, these were the most beautiful people of all, the *metis*. It was almost as if a long-lost race of antiques had been rescued from The Deluge— people coloured mahogany, lamp-black and gilt. They even looked like survivors, dug-in behind stockades of boxes and barrels, bullets, bits of engine and Wiener sausages, or "wienies." Occasionally, little Labradorians wriggled free and were hauled back with long-lost reproof.

"Pearl, knock off *tarmintin'*!"

". . . and, stop that tissin' or I'll *trim* yer!"

The sensation that I was among intriguing species continued as I made my way down through the ship. Because the *Bond* had been hastily converted from a railway carrier, both elegance and daylight had been lost along the way. One layer down, it was vaguely rabbity, but, by the lower deck, I was among the deeply subterranean. To begin with, all I could make out were growls and bristly outlines, but, as I burrowed on, I found my cabin. It was already being picked over by two ferrety *Québécois*. The older one said they were scrap-dealers, and had bloody eyes and a nose for a carcass.

"Nice, isn't it?" I said awkwardly. "Good clean sheets."

The scrapmen looked uncertain, their noses wrinkling at such cleanliness. Then they scurried off back to the truck-deck, to sleep with their rust. To my relief, I never saw them again. I think if I'd had to cosy along with those two carnivores, I'd have been the one drinking away the next twenty-four hours to Cartwright. As it was, the night would be only mildly disturbed. The fourth occupant of the cabin was an old Canadian soldier called Joe, who snored like a kitten.

I sat on my bunk, leafing through Curwen's journal. He'd only used the Labrador Coastal Service once. Although it was then still a new service, the only boat was a filthy tub called the *Windsor Lake.* Curwen had heard that the bunks had a "bad reputation," and so he took his chances with the Labradorians upstairs. It was never going to be a comfortable ride. The crew were exclusively Catholics, he noted, "and all hate us." They were always stealing Mission property—newspapers, Curwen's *British Medical Journal,* anything not bolted down. Even the Captain was tirelessly opposed to Grenfell, accusing him of "pauperising the coast." As for the ship's surgeon, he had a well-earned reputation for being ten thumbs in a crisis, and his sickbay was grotesque. Curwen spent much of the night reassembling one of the patients, who'd fallen from the mizzen-mast and flattened himself to the deck.

It was heartening to think how much had changed since Curwen's time. Disaster was no longer the casual punctuation of the day. Scurvy, lice and sectarian fist-fights were now just part of a rich past. These days, there were showers and videos somewhere down in the bowels of this unlikely ark. Only the food had remained obstinately nineteenth-century—boiled cod, salt beef soup, tea and preserved fruit.

The Noah of this strange voyage lived near the bow, in a deep, white labyrinth of pipes and girders. After the *Bond* had extracted itself from the Bay of Exploits, I was allowed down there to see him. This was the bears' quarters, where the crew lived. Captain Stuckless said that his men only worked half the year, during the thaw. Perhaps they hibernated for the rest, I thought (although it seemed unwise to say so. Even the Captain was more bear than Noah, with his huge, hairy paws and grizzly watch).

"They'll have to find new work next year. The Coastal Service is finished."

His Chief Engineer had been coming to Labrador for fifty-three years, first as a stationer. "Every spring," said Mr. Pye, "we sailed out on the *Kyle*, with all our gear: tilts, window-frames, guns, lamp oil, fish-barrels. Everything ye needed for the next three months."

These were uncomplicated summers: of roasted sea-birds, seal-shoots, and Northern Lights. "There's nothing like puffins," he smacked, "with pork-fat and tatie-cakes!"

At the porthole, the Captain growled.

"Well, here we are," he said. "Still plenty of ice . . ."

Outside, pale slashes of light were floating through the dusk.

"Don't they worry you?" I asked.

"We've always got someone on look-out."

I felt a little nip of panic. "But you've got the fog-horn on?"

"Sure, boy, the visibility is not as good as we'd like it."

This, twelve hours later, is how we found ourselves off Labrador: an ark of exotic misfits, bawling its way through the ice.

79

Now, we were out in "Iceberg Alley," riding among the great towers of ice that had ripped themselves off the flanks of Greenland. Each was its own world, twenty times the weight of our ship, and each had its own frozen aura, the air stiff and raw as the *Bond* crept by. The planters had called them "islands of yce," and Captain Stuckless told me that they still brought polar bears and colonies of birds. But, he said, if they ever found the sea-bed, they'd rip it up, leaving a trench as deep as a house. Icebergs, I decided, were almost too much to comprehend. I spent the morning peering up into the peaks, clipped with cold and disbelief.

Every year some 3,000 of these exorbitant powder-blue stacks come cracking and groaning down the Labrador Sea. There were seldom less than five in view (Curwen told his sisters he'd counted 147, on the day he climbed the mast). Perhaps one in ten of them would make St. John's, and then drift on, into the Atlantic. In their two years of wandering there would be moments of serenity and then, with a boom like naval guns, 10,000 tons of ice might shear away. The giant, unbalanced by the loss of a cheek, would totter for a moment and then throw itself face-down into the sea. Curwen often tried to provoke these spectacles with his explosive bullets, but nature would not provide its tantrums on demand.

Let no one think that an iceberg is just a lump of cold water. Here were exquisite crowns, hands, cathedrals and pyramids. Curwen even saw Fountains Abbey floating out of the mist. Sometimes, they were shot with streaks of ultramarine, or they lit up the sea like jade. By day, they tormented the horizon with fancy mirages—mushrooms and hammers and Dali's ears. By night, they glowed like planets. The Labradorians never came out to watch them. They had their own language for the ice, which often reflected their anxieties: *slob, blocky, quarr, growlers* and *blue drop.*

Perhaps they were right to be anxious. The ice was forever disembowelling the government's ferries. Three years after Curwen sailed on the *Windsor Lake,* she was crushed like a tin of clams and sank. The *Patrick Morris* was lost in 1970, and the latest to go was the MV *William Carson,* sliced open in 1977. The *Bond,* I learnt, was its successor. I asked Captain Stuckless about our prospects.

"Unsinkable," he said.

Hadn't *The Titanic* been "unsinkable"?

So she was—until she lost her belly to Labrador ice.

80

Whilst we were hooting our way through the soggy, purple islets of the south, Curwen and the *Albert* were making uncertain progress ahead.

Captain Trezise was now shrivelled with fear. He was back among the most dangerous waters in the world—seas that had almost swallowed him once already. Here, summer became winter within a matter of weeks, and the ocean could swell from calm to fury in just a few hours. Although it was quieter in among the islands, the water here was barbed with vicious reefs, known—economically—as "sunkers." Captain Trezise had no real idea what lay ahead—or below (some of his charts dated from Cook's visit in 1765). Wherever they went, his sail-maker was always up the mast, keeping an eye out for disaster.

The *Albert* wasn't just blind, she was also clumsy. She had no steam-power, and she'd have to weave her way through the Labrador maze on sails alone. As if it wasn't bad enough wearing a straitjacket of oak, she was also stuffed with charity. The Mission had filled her holds with a bizarre cargo of cast-offs for the poor—old military tunics, cavalry mess jackets, Eton coats and hunting pinks. These clothes alone caused the *Albert* to settle another eight inches in the water, and were supplemented with bales of tobacco and religious tracts. Blinkered and cumbersome, the *Albert* groped on through the tickles, in a squall of horn-blasts and rockets.

Although the nurses and stewards were energetically seasick, Curwen seems somehow detached from the trials of this voyage. He developed his photographs, shot icebergs, and fed the chickens he'd bought in St. John's. In his immaculate letters home (lucent paper, engraved headings and waxed seals), there is no hint of his own frailties, of suffering or pleasure. He describes a night trapped among the icebergs as "not an over-pleasant situation," when what he surely meant was "terrifying." It's almost as if he is writing in the third person, about an observer of unembellished fact. With so much left undefined, I found myself wandering freely between his travels and my own. Even his first descriptions of the Labrador coast were tantalisingly equivocal: "When the sun has shone, the islands have looked beautiful although absolutely devoid of trees—nothing but bare rocks covered with mosses, lichens & low-growing, berry-bearing plants."

Not all his contemporaries were so restrained. One visitor, a naturalist, was moved to describe Labrador in terms of a good thrashing: "Angry waves, paled with rage, exhaust themselves to encroach up her stern shores, and baffled, sink back howling into the depths. Winds shriek as they course from crag to crag in a mad career, and the humble mosses that clothe the rocks crouch lower still in fear." Grenfell, on the other hand, liked his readers to think he'd found a more alluring mistress: Labrador, he said, "like some diffident virgin, is still wrapped in garments of isolation, having turned away her wooers..." In his more prosaic moments, she was simply the land of "Fog, dog and cod."

The absence of Grenfell was about the only feature of this voyage that Captain Trezise enjoyed. The Superintendent was making his own way up to Labrador, crashing launches and ruffling feathers. If he'd learnt anything at Mostyn House School, it was *not* how to sail a boat.

81

Another twelve hours on, we arrived at the headland George Cartwright had called home, and which still bore his name. The settlement he'd started had somehow survived, shrinking beneath a great whale of granite known as Signal Hill. I said good-bye to the captain and Mr. Pye, and disembarked.

"We admire your spirit," they said, which made my heart sink.

But Cartwright was more robust than they'd imagined.

"Most of us came from the islands," said the harbourmaster, Tom.

Most were descendants of stationers who'd stayed on, to become *livyers* (literally, we live 'ere). For them, living with scarcity was like learning to walk, and they could divide their lives into the Time of the Fish, and the time After. At the beginning of the After, they'd floated their homes in from Horsechops and Spotted Island, or built new plastic ones on the shore. Cartwright was not a pretty place—"a loop of battered boxes around the bay"—but it had a cheerful obstinacy about it, which was hard to ignore.

"And soon," said Tom, "we're getting a road to replace the coastal service."

This road, I soon realised, was a source of almost supernatural hope. People imagined that it would burst out of the muskeg any day now, and transform their lives forever. There'd be cream and peaches in the store, instead of just boots and drums of orange. Everything would be freshly painted, and the rust swept away. It would be the end of boil orders, the old town track, dust and unemployment. How much longer? they'd pester the contractors. When does the future begin?

The contractors were staying in my hotel, which was a large hut at the end of the track. Every evening, we sat down to a road-gang's tea of turkey sandwiches and gravy (or "Labradorian cuisine," as it was called). Then the labourers would kick back their chairs, and stamp a new muddy track through to the bar. Not that the Lethbridges minded; it was business. Theirs was the only hotel I'd ever known to sell gearbox oil on reception. Never again would they let an opportunity pass them by.

"Not like my great-uncle," said Woody, "who was a trader at Muddy Bay . . ."

Woody Lethbridge had a hungry walrus face and his uncle's muddy luck. "Uncle Garland knew everything there was to know about freezin' food."

He even taught it to his trappers, said Woody. "And that's where he went wrong—'cos one of them was Clarence Birdseye."

By 1925, Birdseye was back in the States, getting rich on super-cooled fish. Woody scowled at the thought of so many frozen dollars slithering from his grasp.

Others in the town were more forgiving of misfortune. There was a plague of bears but few complained. "We try to tranq 'em and take 'em away," people said, "but they always returns." The contractors said it was bears stealing their gloves, and Mrs. Knee, at the Post Office, said that eight of them came every night, and that they'd eaten her shed. Others had torments of their own. For the rubbish-man, Clarence, it wasn't bears pulling his life apart, but a strain of hereditary "lupus." There's nothing to do, he'd say, it's just the way we are.

Perhaps most forgiving of all was Mr. Fequet, whose family had once owned a chain of stores from Horsechops to kingdom come. Nowadays, he was the gas-pump attendant and Justice of the Peace, a relic of the schooner years, with waxed moustache and overalls spattered in boat. I met him in the wreckage of his last store, knee-deep in old till-rolls and writs.

"One day," he said, "this'll be a museum . . ."

There was no end to things Mr. Fequet thought sacred: old spades, nets, Orange regalia, broken bottles, clay pipes and bayonets. If they weren't *wonderful gosh*, they were probably *awful shocking*. He even had a few unlikely stories which he was ripening with age. In one of them, his uncle is stabbed in the back by a porcupine, and—after many adventures—the quill works through him, before finally bursting out of his toe.

George Cartwright

Naturally, I was thrilled by Mr. Fequet, and we spent the afternoon together rummaging through Cartwright. We found a bear-trap, the old Grenfell orphanage and the tombs of two uncles who'd perished on a picnic some ninety years before. On the other side of the bay was an old sea-plane base, where one General Balbo had landed in 1933, along with half the Italian airforce.

"They were on their way to the World Fair," said Mr. Fequet. "In Chicago."

The Italians had had a curious reception. All the men were away, fishing, and so their planes were refuelled by women. Then there was a banquet on the wharf, with Chianti and portraits of Mussolini. In his old age, Grenfell claimed that the airmen were welcomed by his orphans in black shirts, "bearing the fasces of lictors." Even by Mr. Fequet's standards, this was extravagantly surreal. General Balbo, he said, must have been a very great man (and so he was—until brought down by his own guns, over Tobruk in 1940). Sadly for Mr. Fequet, this strange, Labradorian *avventura* seems to have moved on, without scraps or bits for his museum.

Our walk ended with three large boulders, at the tip of the headland.

"Caribou Castle," announced Mr. Fequet. "Captain Cartwright's home."

82

George Cartwright was still eager for adventure after losing his shoes on the Beothuk expedition. Within two years, he'd thrown in his commission with the regiment, and his eye had settled on Labrador.

It wasn't a tempting prospect, even for a man hardened by the bloody 1760s. The French had just been winkled out, perhaps gratefully. They'd been continually at war with the Inuit, or *Esquimaux* as they were known. By 1770, the entire Labrador coast was thick with "savages" (it was not until later that the Esquimaux pulled back, north of Hamilton Inlet). They were adept killers, half-animal in the ice, half-mad on the land. They could survive for weeks on a bag of rotten flippers and bits of gut, and still deliver a fearful volley of harpoons. They were, wrote Cartwright gleefully, "the most savage race of people upon the whole continent of America." No one had yet survived a meaningful encounter.

DOWN LABRADOR

The Esquimaux weren't the only threat to settlement. There was another dark presence on the Labrador landscape: it was the New Englanders, or "Americans" as they'd become. They were lawless, pickled louts, slavers and freebooters, forever tormenting the aborigines, and stirring up revenge. Governor Palliser called them "the very scum of the colonies" and, in his reports, they "swarm upon the coast like locusts." For Cartwright and his fellow-venturer, Captain Lucas, it would not be an easy sojourn.

They arrived in Labrador in July 1770, a curious entourage. George himself made a formidable sight. In his portraits, he is splendiferous and gallant, built like a ship and flying full colours. He's wearing a white top hat, northwester, wrappers, cuffs, breeches, buskins and bandoleer, and carries a knapsack and German rifle. People would be overwhelmed by this apparition and would stutter and obey. Bobbing along behind him were the rest of his camp; there was his "housekeeper" (or mistress) Mrs. Selby, soldier Atkinson of the 39th, a gamekeeper, three foxhounds, two bloodhounds, a greyhound, a pointer, a spaniel and "a couple of tame rabbits."

Captain Lucas was altogether less impressive than his partner. He seemed distracted, and had with him an inebriated goat that was drinking rum by the gallon. Lucas hardly noticed. He was in love, tormented by the memories of an Esquimau girl called Mikak. He seemed unable to forget her, and friends worried whether he'd get through the winter without her. In his mind he was bathing in her scent, in warm brown body and sealskin.

Mikak had entered his life as a captive, the booty of a Royal Navy mission two years earlier. Although some (like George's brother, John Cartwright) thought her "hideously ugly," Lucas was bewitched. He learnt Inuktitut, and taught her English. Then he took her to London, the first such savage in England. There, she was introduced to Augusta, Dowager Princess of Wales, who fitted her out in velvet breeches and a *silapaaq* of lace and gold. John Russell painted her portrait (which still hangs in the Royal Academy, her eyes as black as the sea). Lucas was by now haunted by her vicious love, aloof and predatory. But, on their return to Labrador, she vanished.

Lucas spent the rest of his life in the search for Mikak. It was a futile endeavour constantly stalked by misfortune. First, he abandoned his promising career in the Navy, and then he threw in his lot with a hapless Newfoundlander called Nicholas Darby. Darby had been picked

Labrador "Esquimaux"

clean by Esquimau warriors, and was already ruined. Even his daughter was appalled by his folly and abandoned this drama, to join a real theatre (as Mary Robinson or "Perdita," she even enjoyed a flash of glory. She became David Garrick's charge, and mistress to the Prince Regent and had her portrait painted by Reynolds, Romney and Cosway. Naturally, it couldn't last; at the age of twenty-four she was levelled by rheumatic fever, and died in penury twenty years later).

George was pleased to take Lucas on, with his grasp of the language. But there was no place in this tableau for a dreamer, and so—the following winter—Lucas was caught in a storm and washed away.

George settled first at Cape St. Charles, in what he referred to as the Last Country made by God. His brother, John, helped him build a cabin, and then sailed off to his life of politics. For George, this was merely the beginning of an excellent adventure, which he recorded in his journal, *Transactions and Events During a Residence of nearly Sixteen Years on the Coast of Labrador*.

George soon realised he was not alone on this coast although he saw himself as its squire. Around him were some eighty settlers "of the lowest types," Dutch drunks and Irishmen who fought all through Christmas. In his relations with these, his subjects, our gentle giant was often less than gentle. George carried a stout stick, with which to give his men a good "dressing" or a "trimming." The worst offenders he chained to his bed, thrashing them until they could be brought to trial in St. John's. One man was foolish enough to raise a hatchet at his master, provoking an awesome response. "I gave McCarthy twenty-seven lashes with a small dog-whip on his bare back today," noted George, "and intended to have given him thirty-nine; but as he then fainted, I stopped and released him, when he thanked me on his knees for my leniency . . ."

But George was more than a scourge to this coast. He conducted marriages, and was the trader, the government, the sexton and the priest. When the naval surgeon from Fort York froze to death on a visit, George buried him on the beach, and became the physic too. He administered jalap for boils, warm vinegar for a crushed head and bleeding ears, laudanum for snow-blindness, ipecacuanha for *cholera morbus*, guaiacum and camphire for sciatica, and James' Powder for everything else. The master even set bones and delivered babies. His maid told George that, of the six babies she'd had, he was the best midwife she had. "But," he noted, "I was obliged next to act as nurse, and take the child to bed with me . . . an office I never wish to resume."

Not all were so lucky. His servant, Charles, caught frostbite in bed, and rotted to death despite the ministrations of his master. Yet somehow life went on. George learnt to eat polar bears and porcupines, and fought a war with the flies. He wrote rhyming letters to his famous brothers, and—every other year—visited England, to fight his rivals in the courts.

In time, he moved his settlement north to Caribou Castle, always in pursuit of fur. He was now well within Esquimau territory and took to wearing their clothes, together with a top hat and a sash. Every day he lolloped up over Signal Hill, trailing a pack of greyhounds. On one occasion, a bear killed his Newfoundlands, and so George seized it by the neck and ripped it open with his knife. "This method I learnt from His Majesty's Jagurs [*Jägers*, or hunters], in the forest of Linsberg, in Hanover, at the conclusion of the German War . . ."

It was impressive stuff—and it terrified the Esquimaux, a people not used to being afraid. To begin with, George found them merely revolting. They reeked of seal, he noted, and their babies sucked raw sculpins. George found himself wrestling with nausea, but the Esquimaux chose not to kill him. A friendship developed based on games of leapfrog, archery contests and pints of callibogus. They began to trade, silver fox pelts for tuppenny combs. Only once was an Esquimau tempted to steal, and George was quick to respond.

"I gave him a cross-buttock—a method of throwing unknown to them—and pitched him headlong out of my tent . . . I seem to have established an authority . . ."

But the savages' admiration was not always welcome, particularly when George was ill. At night the *Angekoks,* or witch-doctors, gathered around him. "They were accompanied by such horrid yells and hideous outcries as I never heard before from the mouths of the human species. These dismal notes continued till daylight; added to this their dogs were continually fighting and tumbling into my tent . . ."

This wasn't his only concern. The Esquimaux told their new friend that they could overwhelm the English any time they chose ("An opinion which could not fail to produce in me some very unpleasant reflections"). To demonstrate that his countrymen were more than simply stragglers, George decided to lead a party to England—Attuiock and Tooklavina, and their wives Ickcongoque and Caubvick, and an infant, Ickeuna. In November 1772, they set sail for Waterford, where George found himself "teazed to death by the curiosity of the whole town . . ."

London was no less agog. The savages were a sensation. Even Dr. Johnson refused to believe the reports coming back from Mr. Boswell ("No man," wrote Boswell, "was more incredulous as to particular facts which were at all extraordinary . . ."). The Esquimaux were indeed an outlandish spectacle. They were dressed in sealskins and accompanied by "a beautiful eagle" and an Esquimau dog "which has the resemblance of a wolf." The crowds gasped, and the streets were choked with astonishment. Leicester Square seized up with curiosity, carriages full of spectators blocking the side-streets. At the Covent Garden Opera, the audience rose in standing ovation, and, on The Mall, the King ordered his troops to salute the savages. They were feted at the Royal Society, and examined by the great surgeon, John Hunter. It was only when they saw all his skeletons that a good dinner turned to terror.

"Are those the bones of Esquimaux whom Mr. Hunter has killed and eaten?" wailed Attuiock. "Are we to be killed?"

George tried to reassure them. "Those are the bones of our own people," he said, "executed for certain crimes. They are preserved that Mr. Hunter might better know how to set those of the living . . ."

Unsurprisingly, the Esquimaux remained wary. They thought St. Paul's was an enormous cave, and that pet monkeys were their own people shrunken with contempt. Even cultivated land appalled them: how can men eat all that food in a year? Worse, their sealskins now stank, and they'd seen enough.

"I am tired," said Attuiock. "Here are too many houses, too much smoke, too many people. Labrador is very good; seals are plentiful. I wish I was back there."

Not long, promised George, and took them to his family estates to recover. The Esquimaux discovered horses, and rode to foxhounds. In their greatest moment, they crashed across twelve miles of Nottinghamshire forest to be in at the kill. This might have been the crowning moment in this charming tale—except that it was bound to end in tragedy.

On 8 May 1773, the group prepared to sail for Labrador. In the English Channel, they paused to shoot murres on Portland Bill, and then Caubvick erupted in smallpox. Soon they were all reduced to skeletons and boils. George pulled into Plymouth, and rented a place in Stonehouse where his friends began to shrivel and die. Only Caubvick survived. Although George managed to shave her head, she would not be parted from the filthy, matted hair. "Each time," wrote George, "she flew into a passion of anger and grief . . ."

More grief awaited them in Labrador. When the Esquimaux saw only Caubvick on deck, they beat their faces with stones. One girl almost smashed her eye out with a rock. Then they saw George's tears, and they gathered round to comfort him. "The whole of the night was spent in horrid yellings, which almost petrified the blood of the brig's crew."

No one would speak to Caubvick. She returned to her own people with her poisoned hair, and within a year they were all dead. Only her cemetery-home remains, still Caubvick's Island even now.

As for George, his great venture began to collapse.

First, his love-life began to warp. Grenfell once wrote that, with regard to women, Cartwright was "frankly immoral." True, he never formally married but his affairs were surprisingly orderly. Besides, this time it was actually his mistress, Mrs. Selby, whose eye had settled on a new lover, a trapper. She refused to admit to her "criminal connection" and so George had her publicly "tried." He found her guilty (and ebulliently pregnant), and announced Labrador's first "divorce." The baby, born that winter, died of the cold, and at the first thaw George deposited Mrs. Selby back in England, on retirement pay. Then, with long nights ahead and a cold bed, he began to dream of Esquimaux. "The ladies had very soft and musical voices," he noted, "but, as to their dancing, one would have supposed that they had learned that art from the bears."

He had a stab at immorality but his efforts were hardly Grenfellian. "Eketcheak last winter married a second wife of about fifteen," explains George. "I took a fancy to her and desired that he would spare her for me." Eketcheak told him he was welcome but that the girl was idle-tempered and useless, and offered George his older wife instead.

George laughed this off. "I am contented with the bad one!"

Sadly, "the bad one" was less than contented with this proposal. "You are an old fellow," she told George, "and I will have nothing to say to you!"

"And so there," noted George, "ended my courtship."

. . .

Far worse was to come, in the shape of the New Englanders. In August 1778, they appeared in the bay. With the American colonies in revolt, their piracy had become a matter of duty. Four Esquimaux were captured, and sent for slavery. George was stripped of everything—his ships, stores, trade and furs. Half his servants were tricked into desertion ("May the Devil go with them!") and would spend the next few years in a Boston lock-up. George was left with just enough to live, but, for one of the pirates, even this was too much.

"God damn you, Sir," said one Carlton. "If I commanded this ship, I would not leave you a rag to your arse, by God."

Although he faced ruin, George managed to draw a line under this catastrophe with a simple entry in his diary: "I shot a brace of curlews today . . ." But phlegm alone would not sustain him. George spent the next seven years fighting off creditors, and parts of Marnham Hall were sold to pay off his debts. Then, finally, in 1785, he set off again, to rekindle Cartwright Harbour. This time, he had with him four convicts on loan from Newgate Gaol ("Good only for the gallows").

It was an ignominious end. Back at Caribou Castle, the convicts proved merely foul-mouthed and idle. Soon winter was among them, and "the castle" was chopped up for firewood. Convict Thompson, who'd been a Thames water-pirate, was caught in the ice and got the death he deserved. George decided he'd had enough, and that it was time to pull out. As they passed back through Newfoundland, another convict escaped, taking his chances among the outlaws. Then, outside St. John's, the ship was swamped, and the last of the old settler's chickens and sheep were swept away and drowned.

George never returned, although he never forgot Labrador either. For the rest of his life he campaigned for the Beothuks and the Esquimaux, and in 1792 he published *Transactions*. It was subscribed by many old friends (not least the King, Sir Joseph Banks, Thomas Coke, Dr. Hunter and William Wilberforce), and among its admirers were Southey and Coleridge, praising a work of rare originality— and Pepysian candour. Meanwhile, "Old Labrador" himself was indomitable. He invented a lifeboat, and became the Barrack-Master of Nottingham until the age of seventy-nine. Even on his deathbed two years later, the stories wrestled and snapped in his mind, as his brother discovered.

"His voice is strong," noted John, "and although not much inclined for conversation, he can occasionally talk with much animation of Hudson's Bay and a North-west passage ..."

But, in March 1819, even this voice was silenced, bringing to an end the Cartwrights of Labrador. Or did it? A few years later, Frances Cartwright, the brothers' niece, arrived with a block of marble as white as an iceberg. It's still there—behind Mr. Fequet's store—carved with Cartwright pride:

> To these Distinguished Brothers, who in Zealously Protecting and Befriending, paved the way for the Introduction of Christianity to the Natives in this Benighted Region.

83

From Cartwright, I flew south aboard a Twin Otter. Although Curwen may have been undecided about Labrador, the experience of aviation would have left him speechless; a vast pewter landscape gouged by ferocious rivers of tea; bays of peacock-green trimmed with beaches of bleached shell; the ocean scattered with colossal crumbs of ice. Such grandiose isolation was a sure sign of the eccentricity to come.

84

At Mary's Harbour, I attended the coronation of the Crab Queen and the Blessing of the Fleet. A Mountie turned up in full ceremonial dress, and the mayoress barked out a speech in old Wessex. Her shorts were so tight that she couldn't sit down, worried perhaps she'd shoot someone with a rivet. Hardly anyone noticed. Soon, they were puddled with laughter at the crab-workers' skits, an impenetrable torrent of yaps and quips, about the dole and Sharon's shaved legs.

"And Ronnie's so cross-eyed he's got tears running down his back ..."

"And his dog's as saucy as a crackie ..."

Then, as the sun shrivelled to a evening wick, everyone filed out into the mosquitoes. There, at the flag-staff, we ground our way through the national anthem, *The Ode to Labrador*. Written by another of Grenfell's doctors, it was a shapeless dirge, sung to the tune of *The Red Flag* ("Thy stately forests soon shall ring, / Labrador, Our Labrador, /

Responsive to the woodsman's swing . . ."). Duty done, everyone rushed home before the bears appeared.

I clambered back over the rocks to my lodgings. Although the "Bed & Breakfast" was the only "place of interest" listed by the town (apart from the crab plant), it was determinedly Labradorian. Like every other house, its owners tended to think of it much as they'd thought of their boats, clinker-built with a "funnel" and a "bridge." Outside, there was a fossilised garden of bones and harpoons, and inside a stuffed pine-marten and a Bible the size of a mounting-block. My hosts, who were crab-packers, also kept a large scarred beast chained to the rocks. Smut hated me with his sulphurous eyes, and all his yellow teeth.

"He keeps the wolves *oot*," said the crabbers, "but he wouldn't harm a flea."

This intriguing paradox was as brisk as our chats ever got. My hosts weren't alone in their reticence; Mary's Harbour was in a state of chronic withdrawal. The skits had been an illusion, not extroversion but the banter of islanders. There were few words to spare for outsiders. Even my great-grandfather (who was hardly effusive) was troubled by the ghostliness of the livyers. "Should I hail any of them in a boat," he wrote, "with 'Good morning' or 'What cheer, Old Skipper?' I have learned to expect stares and not words or signs in reply." Little had changed, it seemed. I could feel people curling up with shyness, paring their words down to the essential or the marginally polite. Perhaps I shouldn't have been surprised; most had grown up never having met more people than one might expect to find on a single London street. Newcomers could not be "read," and could only be known with wariness and time.

Fortunately, there were exceptions. Everyone agreed that the Spearing brothers talked. They've known this coast nearly eighty years, people said. They'd lived at Battle Harbour when it was the capital of Labrador, and were among the last to leave.

"You'll find their place at the end of the harbour."

I found it immediately: a hut, an old trap-skiff and a privy hanging over the water.

"You're kindly welcome," said Alfred, hauling me in off the stage.

There was a scuttle of excitement as the brothers settled me in—a chair, another log on the stove and plate of bony smelts. For the Spearings, austerity would suffice for silence. Their parlour had pale, colourless walls, a few stools, a bed, an oil-lamp and a skirt of lace across the window to filter the glitter off the cove. But it was warm, and smelt of potatoes and afternoon sleep, and from here I could see through to the other two rooms (the brothers had never seen the need for doors). In each, there was an iron bed and a goose-feather mattress troughed with age. The only pictures were hung high on the wall, near the ceiling; Battle, at about the time of Curwen's visit; the SS *Kyle*, plunging through a storm; grandparents in oilcloth and scollies.

The brothers were back at their positions. Each wore slippers cut from boots, and plaid shirts tightly buttoned at the neck and wrists. Albert had a head of wild silvery pins, and Levi was missing an eye. Only the youngest, Alfred, now got up and hopped around, the strongest at last. None of us has ever been married, he said; we've always lived together in three small rooms. Because each knew the others' thoughts, they had to shout to overwhelm them. Soon the stories were emerging three at once.

"Our people was English once, from Dorsetshire ..."

"Poor father! He was always given us a good lacin'..."

"We didn't get a cod-trap until 1955. Till then we was just jiggin' ..."

"And in winter we'd come up the bay to cut junks and billets."

"We still cut our own! And catch a few smelts through the ice!"

But the stories always came back to Battle. When we discovered that my great-grandfather knew their grandmother, there were howls of pleasure. "Mrs. Ash," wrote Curwen, "is the proud possessor of the only fuchsia on this part of the coast; she grows balsam, asters, & even sunflowers ..." Real gardens, I said, not propellers and bones, and they howled again.

I told them I was off to Battle the next day.

"You'll be goin' on the *Iceberg Hunter* with our nephew, Jim Jones."

Alfred was suddenly serious. "His poor father was killed there in 1983."

Sometimes their genius for detail tormented the Spearings.

"Ripped his arm off in a winch," said Levi, "and bled to death on the wharf."

85

Jim Jones steered a thoughtful path through the last of the season's ice.

"This is all frozen over in the winter," he said, distractedly. "When

I was a child they used to drop the mail over Mary's Harbour, and then a dog-slide would bring it out to Battle."

It was a twelve-mile journey. After the open water, we shrank into the flanks of Great Caribou Island, the *Iceberg Hunter* creaking and groaning with the surge. Jim said she was launched in the sixties, but with her funnels and copper pipes she seemed so much more Vintage Steam than Space Age. I thought of Curwen belting up here on the *Albert,* a record four days out of St. John's. Two days behind him was Grenfell, lurching along in his steam-launch, not unlike our own.

Great Caribou rolled and sprawled, and cracked and frothed, and then ended in a full stop. This was Battle Harbour, a third of a mile long and an eighth wide. Between the islands was a channel, big enough for a hundred schooners, too shallow for the icebergs to get among them.

Batal, the Portuguese called it, the Boat. Then came the horse-faced Basques and the scraggy livyers, landless Scots and bony Norwegians, merging their fortunes with the Esquimaux girls. By 1862, Battle was the capital of fish, and "the most lawless and disorderly place on the whole coast." By the time Curwen appeared, there were three hundred permanent residents—"the Wintermen"—and ten times that in summer. There was no law, no police, no representation, and the place was terrorised by dogs. But the killing and "making" of cod was industrial; over two-and-a-quarter million pounds of "Labrador Cure" were being shipped out every year, along with 5,000 barrels of herring for New York. The stink of fish pip and gurry carried way out to sea, and the rocks were rotten with slime.

But—despite itself—Battle had never ceased to please. Grenfell was so delighted that he chose it as the centre for his Labrador, even though it was solid half the year. Curwen was more circumspect in his praise: "An odd-looking place," he wrote, "but picturesquely situated on the rock."

But what was merely surprising for Curwen left me gaping with disbelief. Of course, I'd lived with his photographs all my life, and now here it was, almost exactly as he'd left it. I had a feeling not unlike homecoming, even though the place I'd known was fogged with sepia and age. Now here was Battle transfused with colour; seal-oil scarlet, cavernous white fish-sheds, wharves, salt warehouses, a tiny church, and the hillside writhing with sundew and vetch. It was like memory in reverse, faint recollections bursting into life.

Jim dropped me at the empty stage.

"They nearly burnt it all down," he told me, "in 1992."

With the cod gone, pretty Battle was almost lost. Even the Spearings had stopped visiting their old home, and the Victorian woodwork had begun to flap apart. But then, unable to watch it perish, the Labradorians had restored it. A handful of them had even stayed on—cooks, boatmen, joiners and clerks—to feed the curious and sustain the myth. It was an uncanny resurrection; Battle much as Curwen had described it but without the fish, of course, and the tuberculosis. Someone had hung copies of his photographs in the net shed, a reminder that life hadn't always been so quaint.

I climbed upwards, through a mercantile complex known as "The Room."

"It was all made in England," said the carpenter, "two hundred years ago." Every knee and joint was shipped over, he said, and slotted together without a nail.

Most of the stores still smelt of industry, of seals and pine, salmon, flour and herrings. "No spitting," said the signs, although the salt had gone; drifts of seven hundred tons once loomed out of the darkness like alps. Curwen had often held services in here, among the stench and grind. It was a bleak ordeal, he noted, the men "sleepy and unresponsive." The floorboards still bore the mark of their exhaustion, furrows sculpted by seaboots and heavy feet.

"Most think of nothing," wrote Curwen, "but fish, fish, fish."

Only a fraction of the fish flake had survived, a platform of latticed spruce. In 1893, it had sprawled up the hill like a basketwork rash. To the armies and workers of Europe, it truly was a bread basket, crusts of fish warming in the sun. Three-quarters of each fillet would evaporate, leaving a husk of concentrated protein (it took 75 lbs. of salt and 225 lbs. of fish to produce 112 lbs. of Labrador Cure). The Spearings explained the metamorphosis. First, they said, the fish was pitchforked from the boats, split and lightly salted for twenty-one days. Then, the "beach women" spread it on the flake, flipping it skin-up if it rained. There it dried for up to four days, until an aromatic amber.

"Too much salt, she burns," said Levi. "Too little she had redshanks."

Finally, the fish was sorted for export: Choice and Prime for Europe, and the broken cullage for the Caribbean. Battle carried on like this until the age of fridges. "We stopped makin' fish in about the fifties," said Alfred. "After that, people wanted it frozen, see."

· · ·

Elsewhere, there'd been a few refinements since Curwen's day.

The Doctors' House, I noticed, was new. As the Mission had grown, Grenfell had had it shipped out from England, complete with gingerbread gables and leather-buttoned chairs. The "Big House" too was enjoying a little splendour; there was William Morris wallpaper, and linen for the guests, and polish and caribou cutlets. Even the Battle Store was in the throes of renaissance. There was still the old counter, of course, and the brass scales and bags of split peas and hardtack, but there were apples too, and tins of meat. Curwen would remember just the caplin and "porpoise chops," all emphatically fishy.

"Anything by way of fresh meat," reported Grenfell, "is a treat in this country."

Only Curwen's tiny hospital was missing. In his photographs, it's all new; walls of rough-hewn planks caulked, or *chinsed* with straw and felt, eight iron beds, biblical tracts and a shelf of unguents. It will be the first hospital outside St. John's, but already things aren't right; they realise—too late—that it'll have to close for winter, and the *Albert* has brought the bacon instead of the drugs. It's an inauspicious start, but the hospital will do brave work—until it's carbonised by a careless cigarette in 1930. The Spearings had watched it burn.

"It was a bit o' fun," said Albert, "'til we heard about the gunpowder..."

"Then we was running," said Levi, "like pigs before thunder..."

But the Rooms didn't blow. The fire moved off harmlessly, into Battle's miniature barrens. The only other casualty was the Marconi station. "Battle Harbour Burning..." it squeaked as it melted into the rock. Now, there was nothing left but four blobs of metal in the moss.

I often took the same path as the fire, out into the muskeg. Battle's barrens made up for their size with their ferocity. There were always signs of struggle; kittiwakes bombing the sea, fierce golden rod and snarly dogwood, pieces of an aircrash, and the icebergs booming like artillery. It was easy to see how Grenfell had been ignited by such beauty. Curwen was different; his curiosity endlessly stimulated, but deep affection never aroused. I decided that nowadays it was possible to feel all these things; Battle had ironed out its cruelty, but was still as savage as ever.

That night, I slept out on the headland, above the battle of the hulks. They fought through until dawn, roaring and imploding, and collapsing in clouds of diamond dust. Then there was a lull, and a new cathedral floated into the bay.

86

Without trying, I found I was re-living Curwen's Battle.

His patients had lived at the end of the harbour, away from the explosive Room. Their homes had been built for storms rather than admiration, with schooner walls and tarpaper roofs. Now, these shacks were barely visible above the weeds, and were crusted in lichen and thick scabs of paint. Alongside some, I could just make out the shadows of a turnip patch. Horticulture had always been a struggle with ice and rats, and the hay was too sick for cattle. Sheep might have flourished but the dogs usually killed them. In 1893, Esquimau dogs ate twenty-seven of the Mission's forty sheep. In fact, nothing was safe; the turnips had to be fortified against the huskies, and Curwen's chickens clucked themselves to death.

I found the Spearings' cabin, much as they'd described it. Their gear was still heaped up under the deck, as if they'd return, and row off again after the cod.

"We'd kill fish all summer," said Alfred.

". . . and then we laid nets for the seals," said Levi.

Which was where the dogs came in, I'd heard, to haul the seals ashore.

"How many hours did you fish?"

The boys whistled. "We was up at three, and stayed out til the next night."

Curwen was horrified by the casual brutality of this work. Men might row fifteen miles out into the current, and stay until they had a boatful. If there was "a poor sign of fish," they'd simply wait. Sometimes, they'd be out for three days, wrapping themselves in a sail if they had to sleep. It was then twenty hours home. That year, 1893, was one of the worst seasons ever, and fatigue was epidemic. Unsurprisingly, there were accidents, plenty of work for a doctor: breaks, strains, burns, festering "water pups" and gangrene. Often people had waited all winter for treatment, like the girl with the frozen feet. Eventually, her father could wait no longer, and lopped them off with an axe.

Curwen saw over a thousand patients that summer. Not all were so florid. Some were shamming, desperate to be packed off home (deserting a fishing boat was still a criminal offence). Others were merely the victims of penury—gummed up on flour and molasses, infected by midwives, infested by their tilts, or just rotting in their boots. Every day, Curwen would find exotic new diseases—scurvy, beri-beri and pellagra—and, every night he was pulling teeth.

Although death was frequent, Battle had never stinted on funerals. In the absence of a minister, Curwen had often had to lead these spectacles. For most, there was a procession of boats, led out to sea by a mournful bell. But, for those able to afford a stone and a bit of soil, there was the cemetery, which was exactly as Curwen had described it ("a peaceful spot" squeezed into a rocky cleft). The inscriptions were as stark as winter: "Mourned by his sorrowing owner," read one. "His merits were many." Here too I found old friends of Curwen's, like Mrs. Ash, and Mrs. Smith who'd given the hospital some kittens. Her great-grandson, Terry, was now the mechanic on the wharf, and was in charge of throwing sticks for the last of Battle's dogs.

"Looks like we got some weather," he'd say. "Something dirty about."

87

The storm that Terry had predicted came that night.

I moved to the fishermen's bunkhouse, and settled in a box on the wall. There was a draughts board on the table, and curtains around each bunk. Once, a tract had hung over the stove: "Please do not use Profane Language when Eating. Respect your Food. Mug up period 10 minutes." It all seemed unfeasibly cute, like a house for the Three Bears. Then—just as I was beginning to feel a rosy, Victorian glow—the storm tossed two Metís off the ocean, and they came crashing through the door.

"Get de fuckin' grog goin'," they said, "and we'll stay till de coast's clear."

My fairy-tale evening had just turned into a Western.

Slab and Chuck said they'd been out in a rubber boat.

"On our way to Newfoundland . . ."

"*Why?*" I squeaked.

They weren't sure. Slab and Chuck weren't sure of very much. They weren't even sure they were Metís, except when it came to the hunting laws ("Metís get all the caribou, the rest can fuck off"). They certainly didn't look like Curwen's Esquimaux, but then even a century ago there were few pure-bred Inuit this far south. No, Slab and Chuck didn't look like anything much—babies with red whiskers, perhaps, or experiments thrown up by the sea.

Slab was looking at me suspiciously.

"We isn't de sharpest knives in de drawer."

"STDs!" snarled Chuck, and laughed. "Small Town fuckin' Drunks, dat's us."

Soon there was a feast spewing across the table: Screech, cod's tongues and dandelions, smelts and tins of fatty Klik. As the Metís scooped it up in their paws, an uneven tale emerged.

"We clears snow in de winter," said Chuck.

"Clubs a few harps in de spring . . ."

" . . . and collects UI all summer."

Both were married to Inuit. They made better wives than the Innut.

"Innu girls is dirty. Beaters . . ."

"Thieves."

"More Screech!"

"Pass de Klik, John. You not eating de tongues?"

"My girl can't cook, de lazy bitch," said Chuck. "De only thing her cookin's good for is keepin' de bruins off de garbage!" He took a long thoughtful swig of rum. "So I just cooks for meself and me dog, Snatch. He's all I got."

Slab lit a fag, which he puffed through a mouthful of smelts.

"You hear about de German submarine, came in here in de war . . . ?"

"Dey drank all de fuckin' wine! *And* danced with de girls . . ."

"Holy Moses! Some story dat."

The Klikking and Screeching went on most of the night. Then Chuck said it was time to sleep, and slumped across the draughts board. Cocksucker, he muttered, as he drifted away.

By dawn, the bunkhouse was airless and blue. Slab unlatched the door.

"Get out dere!" he said. "And let de wind blow de stink off yer!"

Soon Battle was smelling as it always had: of smoke, of Slab and Chuck, and fish.

88

In July 1893, Battle was visited by a man no one knows whether to love or loathe.

"The great event of the day," wrote Curwen, "was the arrival of the *Falcon,* a sealing steamer which is carrying Lieutenant Peary . . . and the eleven members of his expedition to North Greenland."

Robert E. Peary was already a super-hero of his age. Not only was he physically stupendous ("a big, powerful man of about 35," says Curwen), he'd also developed a reputation for never doing things by halves. His baggage train for the Arctic comprised over a hundred dogs, eight Mexican *burros* and a collapsible house. On his way from Philadelphia, he'd charged sightseers 25¢ each to come and gawp at it, and had raised a whopping $5,000. We'll be away two and a half years, he told Curwen, and prove that Greenland is an island. It didn't seem to surprise anyone that—in addition to his boffins—Peary had also brought his wife, Josephine, and a maid.

So far, the expedition had been more heroic than inspired. The donkeys had contracted pneumonia, and Peary's favourite Esquimau dog had taken one look at Labrador and jumped overboard. The others looked like following. There was no alternative other than to stop at Battle, and shop for more.

Curwen and Peary disagree as to whether dogs changed hands. Curwen describes a tour around the *Falcon* on the day they started shooting donkeys. Peary's dogs, he says, "gave us many opportunities of examining their teeth, as they snarled at the newcomers just bought on shore." But for Peary there were no purchases, and he sailed the next day. Curwen was up, to see him off. As he left, Peary fouled the *Albert's* anchors, adding another three hours to his great expedition. After that, he'd have little to say about "desolate" Labrador, and would be vicious about missionaries in particular.

But it wasn't Peary's last visit to Battle, although Josephine would never return. From now on, the expeditions would be rather less domestic. In one sense, they were hardly family outings; the 1898 expedition was four years on the ice, and Peary was always in debt and lost all his toes. "Josephine"—on these expeditions—was merely the sledge that her husband rode.

In every other sense, Peary was overwhelmed with family urges, and had started another one among the Inuit. Their sex lives had always fascinated him; the experimentation, the shameless hospitality, and the proximity between puberty and experience. The women had become strangely irresistible ("buxom and oleaginous"), and Peary's first book is full of their plates—naked, except for some titillating wisps of fur. Even now, the captions would raise an eyebrow ("Ahtooksungwah—Her Curves were a Trifle Heavy"). In 1898, they raised a storm, and yet Americans still didn't know the half of it. Peary's first mistress, Alakasingwah, was only fourteen when he met her. There was a moment of willpower ("My years will, I trust, protect me"), and then several babies. Peary ignored them all magnificently, never even troubling with their language.

Josephine was finding all this harder to ignore. There was less rigor mortis about her than her portrait suggests. At one stage, she even made her own way up to Etah to find out exactly what (or who) her husband was up to. As soon as she saw Alakasingwah, she made the wise decision that polygamy was better than infamy. She then spent the rest of the winter with "Ally," before sailing home in the spring.

Peary's last visit to Battle was in September 1909, after his most questionable triumph. Did he reach the North Pole before his rival, Dr. Cook? Did he reach it at all? The National Geographical Society says he did, the Soviets said he didn't. Either way, he wasn't going to lose the publicity war. He tore back to Battle, to commandeer the Marconi and bellow his case to the world. "Do not trouble about Cook's story!" he roared. "He's simply handed the people a gold brick!" This time, it was Grenfell on hand to watch the fluster. He even intercepted one of Peary's cable's to his sponsor: Should he leave his spare supplies with the Mission?

Grenfell sent the "reply": "Give it to them, of course, Washington" (which is how he ended up with a pallet of tinned bread and Peary's sledge).

Hapless Peary—even missionaries mocked him now. He seldom raised his head again, and eleven years later he died, "lying on a musk-ox skin," says one biographer, "staring out over Chesapeake Bay."

89

Slab and Chuck had no intention of leaving, and so I decided that—between the Kliks and Screeches—I needed some air.

The boatman, Tony Rumbolt, took me across the channel to Great Caribou Island.

"Ye gonna twack over to Indian Cove? On *foot*?"

Tony was a big crusted man, born to boats (like his father, who'd drowned in one). I told him about Curwen. "He had a patient there, called Robert Rumbolt."

"Happen he was my great-great-grandfather."

I told him about the diphtheria, but not the rest. Curwen had been unusually blunt: "Robert R is a lazy, thriftless man and his wife does not help him . . . A dirty house and dirty people." Tony was a generous lad; it seemed unfair to visit him with ancestral vices.

"I'll drop ye at Trap Cove," he said. "From there, ye walk straight. Can't miss it."

I told him of my family tendency for getting lost on Great Caribou, and Tony gave me his radio. "No one lives here any more," he warned.

Trap Cove had already been picked to the bone. The schoolhouse was now just a spine, its desks scattered through the sorrel. I found a fragment of a child's writing: "Trap Cove is a beautiful place. In winter we see bears." Curwen's seamen had refused to accompany him any further. "Dr. Curwen," wrote Captain Trezise, "is on an eight-mile tramp to a sick family, and will not return until midnight. There is no road, and the ground is rocky and boggy."

It was a remarkable walk, not midnight but a freshly minted day. I waded up through a flash of green, a weedy droke leading to a ridge. At the top, I stopped to take in the view; hot wind seething through lichen, yarrow and dock; an osprey snatching at the surf; fifteen dazzling storeys of ice. It was all so impossibly pure, like the draft for a new planet. But, from here, the land tumbled away to the west, in shape-less folds of sphagnum, crackerberries, ponds and sedge. George Cartwright had often hunted on Great Caribou. He'd had a warning for the walker: "He will find the ground gives way under his feet as if he were walking upon a bed of sponge; and he will be necessarily tormented by millions of flies."

Black-flies. At their very mention, I was infested. These weren't ordinary bugs, but a vast peppery cloud, each insect shearing off a tiny snip of flesh. They got up my sleeves and in my eyes, and even found my nostrils. Men have been known to go mad like this, dogs die, moose have breakdowns, and lynx leap into rivers. Now I knew how it felt; you just wanted to tear your skin off and run away. Had it not been for Cartwright, I might have been unprepared for this assault. Instead, I buttoned everything up, covered myself with a net and dope, and floundered on.

It was slow going. I stopped, and ate a fistful of cold blueberries and a hunk of Battle cheese. The land looked as shapeless as ever, except for the distant specks of Indian Cove.

Then a storm erupted, drenching everything black.

Soon I was a torrent of dope, and dead flies and cheese. I surprised myself by how quickly enthusiasm could turn to damp. I also felt a spasm of irritation, wildly directed at my ancestor. What were we doing out here? Why couldn't Curwen ever admit that he was cold or fed-up? Or that he hated porpoise chops, or cheese? Why did he have to be so doggedly *Victorian*? After a while I realised that I wasn't making any sense, and turned and sloshed back towards Trap Cove. This time, I'd have been wise to heed my forebear's words: "Walking back," said Curwen, "was a very different thing to walking there."

By now the sky was cracked and furious, and it was raining pianos and ships. The air was so electric that I could feel the hair springing out of my scalp, and my radio simply whimpered and died. I now started making exactly the same mistakes in daylight as Curwen had made in the middle of the night. I took the same wrong turning and slid into the same wrong valley. Then I tumbled down some scree, fell in a bog, got out and climbed up onto a hog of granite, where I tottered for a second before slithering down into the Trap Cove cemetery, head-first and on my back.

Tony Rumbolt was already there, waiting. "Looks like you had a nice walk, boy."

The next day, we took the boat.

90

I was unsure what to expect of the Rumbolts' island home.

Curwen's experience of the livyers' tilts was invariably grim. The worst ones were no more than scrapes, with an open fire, turf walls and dogs falling through the roof. The better ones were made of old boats and flour barrels, and had a rack for the musket, and a shelf for the clock. In most, the families slept on shelves around the stove, and the damp was perfect for consumption. Curwen realised that the livyers were living in conditions far worse than the pure-bred Inuit, perhaps because they'd failed to adapt. The Rumbolts' place in Indian Cove was no exception:

> The house consisted of two rooms, the bedroom measuring 10 x
> 5.6, in one end of which was a bed; this bed is 5ft 6 in long and
> 3 ft 4 in wide, and on [it] sleep husband, wife and two boys, all

under one wool coverlid they had from the Mission last year. The man told me he had not eaten any meat (save seal in the spring) since his nets wore out 3 yrs ago, and that he had in the house only enough biscuit & tea for two meals.

"There it is," said Tony, as we entered Indian Cove.

The Rumbolts' house was one of several derelict cabins, weeds up the windows. The last people to live in it, said Tony, were Sam and Eliza Rumbolt, and they left in the eighties. It's hard to say if this was the house of the "lazy, thriftless Robert." If it was, a linny had been added to the back, with two more stunted rooms.

I followed Tony through the open door, and was surprised by the sight before me.

Time had stopped on a day some twenty years before. An ordinary afternoon had simply been deserted, darts rusting in the dartboard, a book left open to the weather. There were still clothes in the wardrobe—rotten with snow—forks in the drawer, and a streak of zips and fur still loyal to its peg. I could just make out ticking and blankets around the stove, and wallpaper pouring down the walls. The windows had long since burst their cords, and the lino had risen and cracked like mud. By the stove was a pair of boots, as if some feet had just stepped out.

"What *happened?*" I gasped.

Tony shrugged. "Their little Anthony drowned in the cove. They wanted nothing more to do with the place after that, see. Just doused the lights and shut the door . . ."

So it was that the Rumbolts had abandoned their lives, Sam's glasses on the table, the chamber pot under the bed.

The end for little Anthony was also the end for the islands.

Battle had been steadily failing since the twenties, and then the men abandoned it to build runways in the war. It never recovered; no one wanted stockfish any more.

"By the time ye paid for yer salt," said the Spearings, "there was nothing left."

In 1968, they stopped living there all year, and built their hut on the mainland.

"We was the last three families to leave."

Twenty-four years later, the Minister of Fish shut down the sea.

"That was it," said Alfred. "We never went back."

But the demise of the islands had left me with one loose end. At the end of 1893, the *Albert* had sailed home with a new protégé: one Lorenzo Rumbolt, aged 9, of Indian Cove. Did this story have an ending, I wondered, or—like all things Rumbolt—would the trail run suddenly cold?

91

Back at Mary's Harbour, the Spearings laughed.

"You'll never find your Rumbolt!"

At first, I didn't believe them, and set out to explore the Rumbolts alone. There was a whole page of them in the phone directory. For a town that could barely fill its church, there were fifty-seven Rumbolt families. The director of the coronation was a Rumbolt, and so was the mayoress, the waitress at the diner, and the people next door, Adolphus and Daisy. Both the town's "variety stores" were called Rumbolt's, as were the garage, the nurse and—of course—the boatman. Rumbolts were everywhere. They were about the only people who'd featured when *National Geographic* called: Rumbolts looking grimy, benighted and hard. Perhaps they'd been all these things. They were certainly numerous.

"Every other person's a Rumbolt here," said Alfred. "You'll get lost."

Only the Spearings could chart their way through the Rumbolts.

"People come to us to find out who they are . . ."

It wasn't just numbers, they explained, but the way life is. Rumbolts married Rumbolts. Then they drowned and their widows married more Rumbolts. Or perhaps a Rumbolt might marry his way through a pair of Rumbolt sisters, losing each in childbirth. As if this wasn't difficult enough, illegitimate children often took the names of their mother's former husband, without a drop of Rumbolt of their own. People could lose themselves in a torrent of Rumbolts and then re-surface dangerously close to their cousins. The only way to understand the Rumbolts, said the Spearings, was to think of them in terms of their original coves: Indian, Trap and Matthew's.

Soon genealogy was gushing free, with genius.

"Tony's father—who drowned in the harbour—was John Hope Simpson Rumbolt, son of William Rumbolt of Matthew's Cove, whose grandfather's sister married Henry Rumbolt of Indian Cove, and they had a son, Lorenzo, but he's not the one you're after because he only died four years ago at the age of 92 . . ."

For a while, I tried to keep pace with a chart. It makes little sense even now, more like a tube map than a family tree. There are branch lines and sidings, cousins left at the depot, and others going round and round in circles. Rumbolts seem to set off in one direction and then meet themselves coming the other way. I tried to identify them by their footnotes; there was one who hanged, several more drownings, and George "who was not the man his mother was." Then there were various Toms, who I began to suspect were one and the same, marrying all his cousins at once.

Somewhere along the line we came across the right Lorenzo.

"What relation is he," I ventured, "to, say, Little Anthony who drowned?"

"Anthony's uncle Bruce Rumbolt was the grandson of Lorenzo's brother, Henry."

I had a weary feeling that this was as close as I'd get.

"Does anyone know what happened to him? Did he come back from England?"

Levi nodded. "He was back for a while . . ."

"But he did what they all do eventually," said Albert. "Headed south."

Lorenzo had moved beyond the Spearings' reach, a life reduced to myth.

"Heard it said he was got by a moose."

"Heard he was killed in France."

Alfred shook his head. "Moved to the Boston states more like."

92

After a day of futile Rumbolting, I caught the next ferry north.

The *Northern Ranger* was smaller than the *Bond,* better suited to wriggling through the islands and tickles. For the outporters this made it a local bus, and for outsiders a cruise. But being glamorous was never going to be easy for the ferry; she had a crane on the front, and below decks she was so uniformly plastic that she'd have looked exactly the same even upside-down. There'd been few concessions to luxury; some snarly televisions, a painting by an Inuk, and poached salmon for tea. In every other respect, the Labradorians would have recognised the ship as their own, with its staunch temperance, and plates of Klik and chips.

Just like the old Coastal Service, there was still scope for camping. Most of the bodies in the lounge were Metís picked up along the way but there were a few travellers from further west. They were a curious lot. Mostly in their forties, mostly from Ontario, they all seemed to be running away from something relatively innocuous: in-laws, Toronto, anti-perspirants or a teaching post. Lloyd was seeking the wilderness, even though emptiness just made him talk faster and faster. Matty was already wild, having reverted to baked beans and bare feet. He had a conspiracy theory, and Warren was a biker (although he owned a block of flats). Everyone was deeply intense, even over the details—like their feet. It all seemed to confirm my worst fears for Canadians: that they're constantly taunted by the idea that they're neither one thing nor another.

I felt more at home with the Americans, in the cabins. It horrifies me, the ease with which I like the elderly and Americans. Being both, my new friends knew exactly when to be serious, and had no truck with bare feet. They were insatiably curious, and had names as uncomplicated as a day in the garden: Bud, Spike, Rose, Iris, Frosty, Pete and Doug. We often shared a furtive bottle of wine together. Here were lives which ought to have been intense but which were oddly self-assured; Bud had been at Dachau on the day of its liberation, Spike had a ranch the size of Wales, and Iris had leukaemia. The trouble with being American (it's always seemed to me), is that it's so time-consuming that you're not allowed out till you creak.

The crew were also fond of the *Northern Ranger,* although they knew she couldn't last. There'll be no need for a boat on Labrador's south coast, they said, once the new road's through to Cartwright. They didn't know what they'd do afterwards. They called unemployment "walking about." But that's next year, they said, and now we got a job. With only forty passengers, they tended to regard us as family, addressing everyone as either "Boy" or "Girl." Every afternoon, Kitchen Mary came round with a sack of boiled sweets, as if we had children or popping ears.

The Americans loved it. Some were on a second or third voyage. Only one of them missed the point: it was Conchita, Spike's fourth wife.

"There eez nothing here," she sobbed, "but rocks."

. . .

Curwen, too, was worried about the rocks.

After Battle, he was ordered back aboard the *Albert*. As Curwen's own hospital (on an island to the north) was still not ready, Grenfell wanted him to cruise the coast as a floating hospital. Floating hulk, thought Curwen, but held his tongue. He knew the *Albert* was far too lumpish for these shoals, but Grenfell's orders were not a matter for discussion.

There was also some anxiety about what he'd find on the rocks. How would he be received? The Coastal Service—the SS *Windsor Lake*—was already steaming ahead, churning up venom. The Mission had made enemies everywhere. The government resented the accusations of corruption, the fishocracy resented accusations of any kind (particularly those being published by the Mission, of slavery and fraud), but the most vicious attacks came from the churches. Grenfell had made a wild swipe at them, saying that the livyers "lived and died without the knowledge of God."

The Catholics responded by saying that the Mission was "not only useless but worse than useless." Officially, it was to be regarded with "tolerant amusement," but Archbishop Howley was already tickling up some nationalism: "There is nothing in the circumstances of Labrador, that calls for extraneous help." Grenfell blundered into the counter-attack, blasting Howley with the charge that he was a "mean, sordid, bigoted prelate, aided by rum sellers and barrators."

Things were no more congenial with the Anglicans. Relations that had started a little untidily in St. John's were about to turn volcanic, with the visit of the Anglican missionary. The Rev. Arthur Waghorne was only an occasional missionary, who used his visits for collecting plants. Full credit to him, he was one of the few people ever to make my great-grandfather over-boil. ("A more pitiable object I have not seen for a very long time," wrote Curwen. "He is interesting as a pathological specimen but a deplorable specimen of man.") Waghorne accused him of being superfluous, and Curwen responded with a charge of neglect.

"There's been no clergyman on the coast for *eighteen* months! The last man in Battle was not all he should have been—and another late clergyman on the coast is now in gaol! What's more, a harbour ten miles from here has not been visited by a minister of any kind for *seven years!*"

"Not at all!" shrieked Waghorne. "These are only isolated instances! You have no right to say the people are neglected! It makes us mad to hear it..."

The row swept through the *Albert* for an hour, before Waghorne repaired to the ferry. "It is sad to think of this man," concludes Curwen, "wandering about in Labrador botanizing & spreading misrepresentations... Where he is known he is harmless, where not known poisonous."

It was more than sad, it was worrying. Had the livyers already been poisoned? What would they make of Curwen, with his gifts of tobacco and hunting pinks?

There was only one thing he could be sure of in the voyages ahead, and that was rocks.

93

For us, the passage north was eerily calm.

Sometimes, the surface was creased only by dolphins and potheads, and at other times it was washed away in mist. One moment we might be hooting along through a fortress of beryl and ice, and then it would all be rolled up in a deep white sleep, and we'd wake to find ourselves in a cluster of rocks and stilted sheds. But it was invariably serene, "hardly a flobber" as the crew would say. This wasn't what I'd expected. What had happened to the Swells? Sir Joseph Banks, the naturalist, would remember his 1766 Labrador cruise as "one continual puke."

Only once did the seas rise up like mountains of coal, and smash over the decks. It happened to be at the moment of the crew's cabaret, and the singer turned to chalk. Through waves of nausea she belted out her songs, ballads of whalers and "salt-water cowboys," and cod cooked in maggoty butter. In the final rousing choruses, of course, the hero always drowned.

94

But Labrador life wasn't all singing and drowning.

Our cargo spoke of cosy cottagey lives, well-defended against winter; we carried onions and double-glazing, huskies, pallets of cake-mix, skidoos and wallpaper. For the outports, our visits were their only contact with the outside world, perhaps an hour a week. Sometimes, it wasn't even that: if it was too dangerous to dock, the freight was simply carried away in lighters.

Whenever we docked, I climbed up, through the outports. Some were so deeply embedded in the flanks of Labrador that they'd ended up in forests. But most were out on the ocean, nailed down to a knob of rock. I always enjoyed these places and felt that, somehow, people here had known Curwen, and had survived the century unscathed. They said things like "Hearken!," and still sold cough syrup at the inn. I often came across men with whiskers like Prince Albert, and even their names were redolent of the age of sail; Alphaeus, Julius and Job. Life, they told me, was as bloody and rhythmical as ever; seals in the spring, fish all summer, turrs in the autumn, and caribou in winter.

Dependence on a surly ocean had left the outporters fatalistic but they seldom grumbled. Whenever they did, I wrote it down: "You can't go out at night for the freckin' bears"; or "The wolves just ate my dog."

Life had never been frilly.

Out on the islands, Curwen found destitution worse than he'd imagined. The Truck System had left no one with cash. "God knows when I last had any money," said one old man. "Afore I was married I had a scattered shilling."

Curwen's photographs find the livyers barefoot, children dressed in flour sacks and a girl in just a coat. Clothes were so scarce that they were stripped off the dead—even the drowned—and passed on. Often, people wore everything they owned at once, and on washdays they wrapped themselves in a quilt until their "duds" were dry. Few had any experience of towels, and there was utter disbelief when Curwen changed into a night-shirt for bed. He needn't have worried about his gifts; for years to come, the livyers would be wandering around, gratefully kitted-out in scarlet and gold braid.

What was killing them was the dearth of food. Unlike the stationers with their fancy new nets from Newfoundland, the livyers often didn't have the gear to fish. If they were lucky, they'd have a bit of powder, to take a seabird or "a spruce pig," a porcupine. Otherwise, they'd have to get by on their autumnal ration. Here is the caption to the Blomfields' family portrait, with eight mouths to feed:

> By October they had already started their winter diet (4 barrels of flour, 1½ lbs of tea and 8 gallons of molasses), which has to last until July.

By comparison, their spiritual neglect might have seemed trivial, but here the livyers were richly adaptive. As "half-breeds," they'd simply married up their Inuit beliefs with the superstitions of Old Wessex. It was a life infested with fairies, and the only creatures that truly knew the way ahead were old black cats. Every aspect of the day was rich in magic. Even determining the direction of the wind was a matter of sorcery, dangling a fox's head on a piece of string. It was often a grotesque world (a pregnant woman would have a hare-lipped child if she saw a hare) but the cure was usually simple (she should cut a piece from her skirt, and keep it till the birth).

With so many pixies of their own, the livyers were spiritually replete. Curwen found them a poor audience. Occasionally, he met outright abuse (although it was usually fuelled with grog). Even today, there were plenty of Labradorians suspicious of the Mission. I once asked a man in Black Tickle what he thought of Grenfell.

"Had all those nurses, didn't he?" said the islander. "Bet he had other women too."

I told him my great-grandfather had been with the Mission.

He shrugged. "He's probably got a few kids along this coast as well."

95

As we picked our way through the islands, we were joined by other characters from coastal society: a sculptor, two drunks (calling everyone "skipper"), a cribbage team, a story-teller, an engineer and a basket-maker.

Each basket took three months to make, she told me, and was the size of a tea-cup. "They's woven from grass, so fine they'll hold water, sure."

The engineer was from Newfoundland, and despised the Metís. "They got more rights than we has, and the government spends *swarms* on 'em."

Other than that, the charges were unspecific.

"They's all bow-legged," he said, "and the people from Black Tickle are *dwarfs*."

One of the bow-legged Black Tickle "dwarfs" was the sculptor, who came aboard beneath a sack of whalebone. There was a smack of the Irish about Johnny Neville, even though he saw the world in

Inuit, and wore an old squadron-leader's tunic. The crew adored him, and were always fixing Johnny bits of food. He plays nine instruments, they told me, lived all forty years at Black Tickle and can't read a word.

Not forgetting the year at Mount Cashel, said Johnny, which is why I drank.

Although the demons were always there, Johnny had found expression in sculpture, in the bones washed up on the beach. He was always looking for meaning, and never certain if he'd found it.

"I'm not religious," he'd say, "but I goes to church and I love God."

We often talked about Black Tickle. It was an uncluttered childhood; soil in which nothing grew; fourteen children fighting over roasted auks. Johnny also remembered Aunt Lucy, who'd sewn his brother's arm up when he blew it off with a gun. Aunt Lucy had cures for everything; cobwebs for cuts, Sunlight soap for constipation, porcupine grease for impetigo and redberries for colitis. She would make poultices of flour, cod oil, "Sloan's Liniment" and turpentine, and could clean the blood with juniper.

"She fixed up this hand," said Johnny, "by sewing tobacco in the wound."

We worked out that Curwen had known Aunt Lucy's mother, a "wise woman" called Mrs. Keefe. I read Johnny the account of his visit:

> She was outside her house—short, broad, flatfaced & darkskinned as all Esquimau are—surrounded by her pack of Esquimaux dogs when we arrived, but she asked us in and it was not long before I got her to tell me about her cases & principles of treatment. She tells me she has never had a patient she has not cured . . .

It was a remarkable claim. So often the older generation of Inuit had seemed more reliant on experiment than principle. Babies had sugar blown in their eyes, flu was treated with lice, and "the itch" was soothed with soot and lard. Grenfell even had stories of wounded hands sewn up with chicken meat, and abscesses slapped in paint and herbs. Aunt Lucy's cures had been almost humdrum by comparison.

"I loved her," said Johnny, fondly. "But swear to God she looked like a witch."

He was thrilled that—somewhere in the past—our lives were linked, and was always trying to marry up the ends. When we stopped at Cartwright, we got out and ran through the outport, looking for the heirs of Sam Holwell. Johnny said the Holwells were friends, although Curwen had known Sam better as "the King of the Esquimaux":

His father was an Englishman and, his parents refusing to allow him to marry a lady he liked, he left home, saying he would marry the ugliest woman he could meet. Those who saw his Esquimaux wife say he could not have found one of less prepossessing appearance . . .

When they died, [they] left their son, Sam Hallowell [sic] with a store & a schooner. He gave us some tea & cake, and his third wife waited on us. His second wife died last year, and he wanted to marry her sister. But, the minister who came down from Rigoulette refusing to marry them, he chose one of the girls "out of the crowd" and married her on the spot . . .

We found their cabin but too late. The Holwells had already left for the summer, returning to their old kingdom on Spotted Island.

96

A mile north of Black Tickle, Curwen found himself among a fearless clan.

The Bartletts were ugly people, ox-bodied and plough-faced. Some think they were descended from the Basques, which is why it never worried them sailing off the map. The Bartletts, however, simply saw themselves as Newfoundlanders, always defying the sea. In the 1790s, William "Follow On" Bartlett was advancing his fishing "stations" further and further north, into Labrador. After that, the family set out every summer in twenty schooners, to push their luck even further.

Curwen had often found himself sailing amongst William's great-grandsons. The youngest, Henry, had been the captain of Peary's exploration ship, *Falcon,* and was proof—if proof were needed—that good luck makes a poor mistress; having safely returned Peary to Philadelphia the following year, the *Falcon* had tried to slip home through a squall, and was lost with all hands. William and Isaac were just as gristly as Henry. The former was the *Albert*'s pilot for a day, and took her for the roughest ride she'd ever had. Isaac, on the other hand, lived in a fish-shed out near Black Tickle. Curwen and the nurse had once had to spend the night there:

> Sister was to sleep in a little room with the two maids, & I was told to share a room with Mr. B . . . In one bed I found Walter & another man and into the other I crept after partly undressing & was followed by my large host; we lay shoulder to shoulder under a blanket and three thick bedcovers. There was only one lamp in the house so, when I had turned in, Mr. B took up a plank & let it down to the ladies in the room below. I had a fairly good night but often woke to hear my neighbour's snore, or the rain falling heavily on the birch-bark roof which slanted up within six inches of my head. At 3 all the men went off to haul their cod traps.

By contrast, Tom—at Batteau—was a more domestic character, and had invited Curwen to tea. It says much for the Bartletts that a good tea was only slightly marred by the fact that the night before a hurricane had ripped through the house, and torn down all the wallpaper. Curwen was unsure how to repay such hospitality, and so he gave Mrs. Bartlett the last of his suicidal chickens.

But perhaps the greatest of Curwen's Bartletts was William's son, Robert. In time, he'd become one of the most unforgettable, forgotten heroes of the Arctic; the master of over twenty-two voyages of exploration, the first man to get to 87°48', holder of the Hubbard Medal (and a handful of others), honorary Lieutenant-Commander USN, the survivor of three shipwrecks, and the brawn behind the three greatest Peary expeditions. He even featured in one of the first sound-synchronised movies, *The Viking,* in 1930 (faring rather better than its director, who was killed when his sealing ship exploded). To many Newfoundlanders, "Cap'n Bob" was what they were in their dreams.

But in 1893, he was little more than a truant. Although Robert could read his way from Austen to Wordsworth via *The Rubaiyat,* he had no use for school. At the age of sixteen, he threw everything in a nonny-bag, and ran away to The Ice. Two years later, he was skipper of the schooner *Osprey,* which is how Curwen met him. On 23 September, Robert and his father took Curwen to see "some old Esquimaux graves" out on the islands. They found two skeletons—a man and a woman—as well as huts, buttons and pieces of kayak. For Curwen, the day coincided with the awakening of his lifelong passion for archaeology.

For Robert, it was merely a taste of the adventures to come. Five years later, his effrontery was spotted by Peary, and "Cap'n Bob" was made.

His greatest—and his worst—moment came with the *Karluk* expedition of 1913. It all began well enough, with some Canadian nationalism, a gramophone, and the anthropologist Stefánsson Vilhjalmur. But the *Karluk* was only a wooden barquentine, and 500 miles northwest of the Bering Straits, she was caught in a sunless, midnight icefield. Vilhjalmur took off on a sledge ride that lasted for five years, leaving Bartlett with twenty-one men only two of whom had ice experience. It was -40°, and as the ship began to crack and scream, Bartlett fed his old 78s into the stove. He kept until last Chopin's *Funeral March,* which was playing as the *Karluk* sank.

Perhaps he should never have been there in the first place, but Bartlett's escape was Homeric. He walked 1,300 kilometres to the coast of Siberia, met a Russian aristocrat and then sailed back, seven months later, to rescue his crew. Ironically, the only members of his team to perish were the two old hands, veterans of a Shackleton adventure; they'd refused to follow Bartlett, and wandered off to a death of their own.

No one wanted to know about this failure, and Canada never honoured Bartlett. Even Curwen let the story go. He'd often kept clippings on Labrador (like Birdseye's *Camping in a Labrador Snow-hole*) but I could find nothing about his old friend, Robert. After the *Karluk,* Bartlett—like Peary—had suffered the only fate he truly feared, which was to be forgotten.

In 1914, he set off for New York to begin the end of his life, as an American and a drunk.

97

The voyage up Hamilton Inlet was played by a cast of improbable trappers.

On the map, the inlet looked like a wound penetrating deep into Labrador's side. Although the fighting was long over, it was still the *Baie des Esquimaux* in spirit; the southern limit of the Inuit. Johnny Neville told me that the Inuit often sang of the battles they fought, and of how they stole nails and tormented the French.

"And that's Eskimo Island, where they all died of the pox."

Others call it Caubvick's Island, because the smallpox was hers, from London.

"Nothin' there now," said Johnny. "Nothin' nowhere."

This was true. The emptiness of the inlet was compelling: a corridor seventy-five miles long, the colour of amethysts and Labrador tea. It's hardly surprising that sailors once thought it led to China. But now the terror had receded and the water was inky-calm and flecked with puffins and seals, and the rock had cuddly names like Rabbit Point and Beaver River. And, said Johnny, you'd never guess the creatures we got in The Bush: we got flying-squirrels, a tiny kangaroo-thing called a redskin, and a mole with a star on the end of his nose.

The heat and tranquillity soon brought the old trappers up from below.

Most had mixed blood, their families part of this wilderness for centuries. Horace the Furrier had survived the thirties on a diet of squirrels, Joshua built cabins and shot wolves, and Big Austin ate raw caribou to show he was an Inuk at heart. But really, we're Scottish, they'd say, brought over by the Hudson Bay Company to bring in the furs.

"There's only about ten names along the inlet . . . ," said Bert.

"Baikie, MacLean, Goudie, Montagu . . ."

"And Blake!" said Horace. "We got a hundred and fifty miles of trap-lines . . ."

Horace Blake was a giant of a man shrunken into an old trapper's frame, hands too big, eyes nostalgic and pale. Once, he said, there was a time he'd spend five months out in the bush, from the September freeze to the spring thaw. Even his own lines took weeks to cross, dragging the canoe out of the water thirty-six times, and hauling it to the next icy gush. But such days had a natural rhythm; waking in a sealskin bag, a new day at the traps, smashed rabbits and foxes caught in iron teeth, a boil-up of doughboys and porcupine, the long haul to the next tilt, a blast of Winchester and the evening kill. It was a wilderness sure, but not without rules.

"If ye find live game in another's trap," said Horace, "ye'd kill it, and hang it . . ."

"Ye never took it," said Bert.

"And if you did?"

"Ye was like filth, a *carajou*," he said. "A wolverine."

"But," continued Horace, "if the trap was on *your* lines, ye could spring it."

"And if it happened again," said Bert, "ye could beat it up."

"And what if they built a tilt on your lines?"

The trappers looked at each other and laughed. "Ye burnt the fucker down!"

We spent the rest of the day in the sun, calling out names in Labradorian—"Jumpers!" (dolphins), "Tinkers!" (razorbill auks) or "Grampus!" (pilot whale).

More trappers got on at Rigolet, the world's most southerly Inuit town.

It was still the *rigoulette,* or channel, that the French had intended, a confluence of water and races. As the ship slid alongside, everyone brought their business to the wharf; Metís traders, almond-eyed stevedores, hunters with rifles and canoes, and the curious, as plump and sleek as puffins. For many, it was grocery day, and a long voyage down the inlet to Goose Bay.

"It's easier in winter," said Big Austin. "We goes by skidoo."

One of the Inuit had shot a seal, and was ferrying it away to be skinned. It sat upright in the back of his punt like a thoughtless passenger, its brains pouring down its front. This was an unremarkable sight to the people of Rigolet, which owed its prosperity to skin. *Pro Pelle Cutem,* as the old Company motto went, Pelts Into Leather.

Curwen had been delighted with Rigolet, and stayed with the company agent. Perhaps it was the vigorous life that appealed (every morning in winter, the agent's children went for an eight-mile run in snowshoes). More likely, it was the prospect of meat. Curwen was by now craving a juicy roast—"even seal chop"—and was always loosing off at tickleasses and harps. Exploding bullets, he discovered, made a poor impression on the seals ("They didn't like the whiz," he observed as they ducked). Undeterred, he bought his sealskin outfit off the peg; *"netsek, karlik, kamiks* and *pualo."* In his self-portrait, he looks happy but unable to move, as if he's wearing a suit of shagpile armour.

Naturally, he was deeply impressed by the trappers. He spent a whole day hunting with the barefooted Parrs, and caught a muskrat with Charlie MacNeal. But best of all was Hannah Michelin, aged 82:

She is a half-breed Esquimaux & is a fine specimen, doing the work of two or three others. Last winter, she shot a great number of partridges, walking twenty miles in a day, and would dig herself a hole through 3 or 4 feet of ice to fish for trout . . . She used to hunt & trap animals & drive the *comatic*, or sledge, but has had to give that up the last few winters.

What Curwen didn't know was that Hannah's hunting was but the epilogue to a curious saga. Her mother was an Esquimau born in around 1792. When she was fourteen, it was thought that she was the curse of Eskimo Island, and so her people decided to rip off her finger and bleed away the evil. At the sight of the sharpened *ulu*, the girl fled, and ran and ran until she fell into the knobbly arms of a stowaway, an Englishman called Ambrose Brooks. Ambrose was twenty-six and had thought he'd never see a woman again, but when this fiery, blackened creature swooned into his grip, he knew his luck had changed. He called her Susan, and, as soon as she'd learnt enough English to recite the Lord's Prayer, he married her in a ceremony of sea-wrack and shells. Hannah was born five years later, in 1811, and would be as expedient as her mother in the matter of marriage. Her first husband was a livyer doomed from the start, and her second a rickety Indian from Québec. In Curwen's photograph, he looks like the wreck of an old chair alongside Hannah, his craggy huntress-wife.

By a strange coincidence, Hannah's great-great-grandson was one of those getting on at Rigolet. His name was Max.

98

Max Blake was angry although, at first, this wasn't obvious. Johnny introduced us, parked me in front of him, and vanished. To begin with, Max seemed oddly senatorial: soft white hair, a plutocratic tan, and the aquiline cunning. It was only when we stumbled into politics—two minutes later—that he began to simmer.

"I don't care a shit," he said, "what happens outside Eskimo Bay."

But what he meant was he cared too much. Max loathed St. John's, and hated Newfoundland. He also hated the province that lumped it together with Labrador, and despised its flag of "spears and spikes," bits of the Union Jack and "nothing to do with us." He hated all Newfoundlanders too, especially the "parasitic bunch of thieves" in charge. Hadn't they sold off the mines at Voisey's Bay for a scroddy eleven million? And what did Labrador get?

"Nothing," growled Max. "We always pays X and gets the Moses' share."

Max cared alright. He cared so much that he'd like to have seen Newfoundland wiped away, and Labrador casting off alone. But this thought too made him angry. The separatist parties were as thievish as the southerners, took the money and ran for Florida. Max hated them as well. But what made him even more angry were the alarming divisions between his people—the Metís—and the aborigines.

"The Innut and Inuit can hunt on our land, on days we can't even hunt at all!"

"But how can you tell who's a Metí, and who's pure-blood native?"

"Y're fuckin' smart, you tell me."

Occasionally, Max's stories made him angry. "Why am I telling YOU this?" he'd suddenly snap. "This is MY research! And. It. Will. Be. MY. Book."

After that, I shut my notebook, and listened as the anger rushed back to St. John's.

"Ye know what they're doin' now?" he snarled. "Shutting down the only chicken farm we has in Labrador. People is uncontented. We don't want no freckin' Newfie eggs. Truth to tell, there's goin' to be trouble, and I ain't feared to say it."

Perhaps it would be the war that Swift had imagined; little people fighting over eggs. The conspiracy theorists on the camping deck were already cooking up their fears.

"I feel a friction," said Matty the Bean, "from here on, north."

99

In Goose Bay, I stayed at a refuge for the war-torn chickens.

Goose, as they call it, was deep in a conflict of its own: a war without enemies.

Every few moments, the air burst, and the sky was ripped apart with sound. It was like artillery or thunder and cavalry, lorries and earthquakes, all at once. One minute, there was the scent of pine, the next the world seemed to shudder, and turn black with noise; a swollen, oily booming in ears, eyes and throat, and shuddering through the bones. There was then a moment of excruciating sensation—every faculty stretched to red—and then silence. In the blank, machined moments that followed, I couldn't feel anything much except a vague whining and a crackle of sparks, as if the day had fused.

To people who understand fighter-bombers, this is known as the Startle Effect. On the ship, I'd met some French *missionnaires* who said this sometimes happened sixty times a day. "Or at least 8,000 times a year," they said. "Planes from everywhere: *les Anglais, Allemands, Italiens, Hollandais—tout le monde.*"

"Why *here?*"

"They thought we looked like the Soviet Union . . . ," said Claude.

"And the airport," said his wife, Muriel, "is the sunniest in Canada."

Sun and Soviet good-looks had made Labrador the biggest simulated battle ground in the world. From here, the war-zone sprawled into the muskeg; an area the size of England sliced into bombing-runs, and seething with divisions of heavily armoured cardboard. Even Goose had a muscley name—the NATO Tactical Fighter Weapons Training Centre, or "5 Wing" as it was known in the air.

"They were going to double it once," said Claude, "enough for 60,000 pilots . . ."

"Ninety fighters in the air at once," said Muriel. *"Comme à la guerre . . ."*

BOOM! Numbness again.

Claude winced. "You want to look around?"

As the ferry was docked for the night, I was pleased to be out with the Quevals. They told me they were Mennonites, and they'd left Strasbourg thirty years before, with nothing more in mind than to relieve suffering. Although Claude was a huge man, who'd worked on ships, it was an endlessly daunting task. Muriel was lighter on her feet, and lighter in spirit, but I became equally attached to them both. Muriel once told me that Claude's father had been a prisoner of war for five years, and that he'd spent the rest of his life drinking away the walls and locks. Perhaps that's why Claude needed to travel, so that, in his own way, he'd never feel enveloped.

Perhaps also that's why he liked Goose, which had a transitory feeling like a camp in the middle of a long campaign. It was a momentary settlement—like an outport, except open to the sky, of course, and not the sea. Everything was poised for sudden departure, gigantic metal tents, huge green bladders of aerofuel, and the silvery swarms bristling across the airfield: Alpha jets, F-16s, F-4s, F-everything.

BOOM!

Unsurprisingly, the airmen had done what they could to make themselves at home among the sand and the shallows of an undecided river. The Luftwaffe had built itself a little concrete Dortmund, and the RAF had run up some suburbs with lawns and a "Spitfire Place." There was even a "Hilton" for the USAF, built with pride and abandoned to vibrations. I didn't see the Italian quarters. Perhaps they didn't have any. It was said that they spent half the year in sports cars, and the other half on snowmobiles. It surprised me that anyone could have enjoyed such a portable town, but some of the airmen had even stayed on. We found several German car dealers, and a strange alpine chalet that seemed to have mislaid Obergurgl.

"Only the Belgians were unhappy," grinned Claude. "Didn't like our *frites* . . ."

The Labradorians lived in a sprawl, which unfurled from slum to scattering as it spread out from the runway. I imagined this is how it must have been for the minions who'd followed the great medieval armies around. If the signs were to be believed, everybody here either repaired tents or cooked "Jigg's dinners" and pea soup. One in ten of them, said Claude, worked on the base.

Military babble had leached into everything, even the sale of ice-cream.

"Try our frozen explosion! Razzle and flavor-burst cones!"

Our tour ended at the Quevals' house, at Skunk Hollow.

Nowadays, the airmen called this area "Happy Valley," although it didn't seem to be either. It was just a drift of sand and lank, dusty weeds. The Quevals had hacked the undergrowth back—so the Mission House could breathe—and then they'd planted it with grass, and peas, beans and marrows. To the aviators, it must have looked like a bright green stamp on their great flat lump of manila.

There were gobbly voices from the woodshed.

"Nous avons quelques réfugiés," said Claude.

It was the chickens from the outlawed egg farm.

"We rescued them," said Muriel proudly.

"It's not much," said Claude, "but at least they now learn to be birds."

When I returned to Goose several weeks later, I stayed out at Skunk Hollow.

Claude said there'd been a protest in my absence.

"When the Premier was here," he said, "we ambushed him with the dead chickens from the egg farm. *C'était un moment de surréalisme divin!*"

Chickens. Bombers. Skunk Hollow.

I soon began to discern a recurring theme. Eggs today, but once this was the hub of bomber fury. A decade ago, the Mission House was full of Indians, who'd marched on Goose to close down the airbase. Claude's predecessors had fed them, and packed them round the furnace, and in the bedroom where I now slept. Then, at night, the Innu had padded off across the weeds, to cut their way through razor wire, and throw themselves in front of the planes.

"They said the planes were ruining their way of life," said Claude.

The trout are poisoned, said the Indians, the spruce pigs go deaf, the muskrats kill themselves, and the fox eats her cubs.

"Et les caribous ont disparu dans cette région . . ."

Both sides were guilty of embroidery in the skirmishes of the Deaf Pig War. The protesters said that jets were swooping down on caribou, and tearing their heads off with their wheels. No doubt the aviators wished their 20-tonne machines could have gone through such 900 km/h acrobatics—but they hadn't. Nor had the caribou disappeared; they were simply varying their migration routes, as they always had.

The government's sophistry was no better, just slicker. They said even their researchers were more intrusive than the bombers (a startling thought as the ears liquefy under another 120 db of sound). Their brochure described Labrador as a "fitting location" for practising warfare, but fitting for who? None of its native inhabitants had ever been asked what they thought. All enquiries, I noticed, were to be directed to Colonel Rooke, Mr. Bird and Lt. Col. Pigeon. Was someone having a joke?

The Innu way of life, said another brass hat, is already doomed.

"Is that right?" I asked the Quevals. "Have the Innu had it?"

Claude heaved a giant sigh, but he was being more than merely Gallic.

"We better take you out there. You can see for yourself."

100

For thousands of years, the Innu lived in a world that was back to front.

They believed that existence began with death, and ended in birth. Between these states, nothing ever quite resembled life as others saw it. The Innu hunted but were not the masters of their quarry, but its servants. Killing was an act of reverence, and hunting a ceremony of exacting ritual. Even their cosmos was different, not a creation but a remnant of destruction. It had been seized from a flood by a muskrat, who then choked on her mouthful. Seeing this, the wolverine blew up her backside, and the muskrat coughed up our universe.

In such a world, the natural order of things was bound to seem distorted. Leadership was a vice, and the idea of command was repulsive. An Innu could accumulate wealth but it impoverished him in the expectations of his peers. He might acquire seniority but his authority was dissipated throughout the band. Every man was a terrified subject of Katipinimitaoch—the caribou god—and of no one else. Even children could not be insulted with authority. Society, if it can be called that, was not a structure at all, but a series of impulses pulling away from a non-existent centre. There were no rules, no law, no sense of obligation and no process of decision. In deciding the tribe's future conduct, that therefore left only luck; the Innu were ruled by scapulimancy, the reading of old bones.

For centuries, the only threat to Innu life came from the *Ashkimow*, or Inuit. Even now, people tell stories of the savage clashes between these races, but by A.D. 1400 territories had begun to emerge from the bloodshed; the Inuit took the coast, and the seal hunt; the Indians were forced inland, condemned to traipse across the tundra after the caribou. In time, the Innu would adapt to this, one of the most ruthless corners of our planet. They lived a nomadic life, tent-dwellers owning no more than could be packed into one canoe. As an adaptation, it was perfect—although later scholars, like V. Tanner, were inclined to see it as simply primitive. "Never before," he wrote in 1937, "have I had such an overwhelming impression of standing face to face with Stone Age people, with veritable cavemen."

Such a strange topsy-turvy world might have gone on forever if it hadn't been for the next arrivals: the *Akaneshau,* or Europeans. When Jacques Cartier turned up in Labrador in 1534, he found the Innu in rude health:

There are people in this country with a splendid physique, but they are wild and savage. They have their hair tied upon their heads in

the fashion of a fistful of hay trussed up and a nail or something
passed through it . . .

But unlike the Inuit, the Akaneshau would be a more insidious foe.
There was no war, no scalping, not even massacres or clearances. The
Innu are probably the only Indians in North America never to have
signed a treaty. No one saw the need; they were simply overwhelmed
with trade. Here is a Hudson Bay Company report from the mid-
eighteenth century:

> They begin to like our commodities better, the women like our nick-
> nacks and guegaws, and the men begin to love brandy, bread and
> tobacco, so that a little address and management will bring these
> happy drones out of their profound lethargy.

Soon, such abundance began to kill the *Montagnais* or Mountaineers
(as they'd become). Stored food blunted the appetite for hunting.
Guns replaced teamwork in the wilderness, and complex relationships
began to fall apart. For the wily, there was money and biscuit, and the
shaky concepts of capital and power. For the rest, there were easy
scraps at the trading posts, and grog. Labrador had slums long before
it had settlements. Even within thirty years of the HBC report, the
future for the Indians looked verminous, as George Cartwright records:

> Not theirs the friendly visit; nor the feast
> Of social intercourse; but like brute beast,
> They greedily devour the reeking meal;
> And then get drunk and quarrel, lie and steal.

Although the Indians despised the Europeans for their stupid faces
and revolting bodily hair, they were addicted to the trimmings. From
now on, values that had seemed intuitive—such as sharing and
equality—were in permanent conflict with the desire for possessions,
a struggle that remains unresolved three centuries on. It's a lethal
struggle too; failure in this competition might easily mean death, usually
in cheap grog stiffened with lacquer or anti-freeze.

Of course, grog and biscuit weren't the only imports thinning out
the Indians. The Mountaineers had sweated themselves to death on
a range of exotic Georgian diseases—smallpox, measles and diph-

theria. By the twentieth century, it was mainly tuberculosis. This disease didn't often get the opportunities it found in Labrador in 1950; hot damp shacks, foul drainage, and a malnourished proletariat already rotten with drink and sugar. That year, the successor to Grenfell's medical empire, Dr. Paddon, decided to gather the diseased tribe in one place for treatment. It was at the mouth of an inlet called Grand Lake, forty kilometres from Goose. They called it Sheshatsit, a town that was already sick before it was even built.

It was to here that Claude was taking me, none of us saying much on the way.

I am surprised by how often poverty can seem immaculate.

Not Sheshatsit. The Innu had been auditioning for this tragedy for centuries, and had left nothing to make-believe. Their village had imploded, almost as if it had suffered a complete failure of entity. Nothing had any structure any more, it was just a coincidence of things. The cabins had long shivered off their paint and cardboard, and stood in bones and disbelief. Everything was broken, not merely decayed but smashed with hazy determination; windows burst, fences ripped up, doors punched, skidoos peeled of rubber and burnt. Somewhere, I found a pile of dolls' heads, and the back legs of a dog. If Sheshatsit had ever been a community, it didn't feel like one now—just a streak of dust marked with inhabited wreckage.

"They hate it here, don't they, Claude?" I asked.

"Everything. They hate doors, windows, walls. Everything."

To begin with, we saw no one, just a bun-face peering through the shards. Then Claude met some people he knew, not Cartier's Splendid Savages nor the Veritable Cavemen, but awkward, bloated men. For a moment they hesitated, cumbersome and expressionless. One of them spoke a form of English, the parrot-talk of welfare workers.

"We're in a time of transition . . ." he said, and then they heaved themselves away.

Muriel frowned. "The Innu hate Sheshatsit, and yet it's all they've got left."

They saw it as a concentration camp, she said, a human dump. Here, they were overcrowded, forced to live in groups they didn't understand, banned from cutting wood and—for a while—banned from hunting. Until someone challenged them, Labrador's hunting laws were the most restrictive in Canada. It was the only place where porcupines couldn't be killed, even though that's what people ate.

"But it's too late to return to the bush," said Claude. "They couldn't survive."

Muriel agreed. *"Ils ont oublié comment vivre."*

"And yet they can't live in a white man's world either," said Claude. "Everything's the wrong way for them. No one's in charge. They don't know what to do with money, and no one can control the children. So what happens? They can't see their way out, and they kill themselves. Literally, they *kill* themselves. When I first came here, the suicide rate was the highest in Canada. Seventeen times the average! All kids. *Que les enfants!"*

I asked Claude if some races were doomed to fail, whatever happened.

"I often wonder the same, but I have to resist this thought."

Just outside Sheshatsit, we stopped at a treatment centre for addicted children.

"They say the worst time was the seventies," said Claude. "It was madness here. People drink and fight, and die in the fire. Maybe they drank because we said they couldn't, or maybe they didn't know how to stop. They drank everything—even the stuff in the skidoos—and the kids were on solvents. It's no better now; there are just fewer kids. *L'alcöolisme est systémique."*

The clinic was closed for the day. Although I could still see the alarms and wired glass, it had been built in the manner of an Innu camp, with bearskin rugs and healing circles. This time, said the Quevals, we're doing it their way. Everything else has failed.

"Only one in ten of the children go to school, and not even the same ones."

It wasn't much of a future for a people who'd collapsed under the pressures of the eighteenth century, and who'd never recovered. Perhaps they never would? Perhaps they'd never negotiate the modern maze, and would simply shake themselves to bits like Sheshatsit? The Quevals liked to think there'd been a moment of hope in the runway protests.

"Fighting authority made them feel better . . ."

"More than seventy were arrested . . ."

"They founded the Innu Nation, and fought the government in the courts . . ."

There was victory too, of a sort. The prosecutors couldn't find anyone willing to translate their trials into Innu-Aiman, and so the last cases had collapsed. The Indians had also sensed triumph in the reduction of bombing-runs, but what they didn't know was that, on the other side of the world, the reason for it all—the other Cold War—had ended. From now on, the imaginary battles of Goose would be smaller, but it was war as usual.

That night, I helped Claude gather up the eggs.

"Ce n'est pas facile d'accepter une vie qu'on ne peut contrôler."

"True," I said. "Unless you're a chicken."

They'd already adjusted, bedding down to a life in the Luftwaffe's sawdust.

IOI

My last day, we had a picnic at the end of a story as daft as any.

Most of this tale can be seen from the top of Sunday Hill, and so, that morning, we climbed up there with a basket of camembert and home-made brioches. The flies were soon upon us, snipping away at the flesh, and notching the ears. Doctors always like to tell you about the Labrador flies. Once, a dermatologist worked out that, if you were naked, the Labrador mosquitoes could bleed you dry in a matter of hours, and Grenfell often embellished his adventures with bott flies that could shin up your nostrils and burrow through the brain. Facts like this just make me panic, and so I'd hardly noticed the whisky jacks; they were also onto us, pecking great gouts out of the cheese, and ransacking the salad. Suddenly, the wilderness didn't seem so empty.

If I'd been here enjoying such pandemonium on 15 July 1903, I might have missed two Americans paddling along the shore. They were eating flap-jacks and reciting Kipling. Had anyone popped their head out of the forest and asked what they were doing, they'd have said they were writing a Bully Yarn, and were going to do The Big Thing. By this, they meant they were going to try and walk across Labrador in moccasins, with just a few tubs of pea-meal and lard. They hadn't even bothered taking coats and it never occurred to them that they'd get lost (even though their guide was an Indian from the wrong country, two thousand miles to the west). Their only map was made by a man who'd never seen the river system, but who'd relied on geographical gossip.

To begin with, all went well, and they bobbed along and found the bottleneck that led into Grand Lake. This was another long dark-green alley, and—from our mutilated picnic—we could see all the way up it, towards a faint gritty blur, which I imagined was The Interior. I also remembered that this was where Horace Blake, one of the old trappers from the ship, had had his lines.

"And me father, Gilbert, knew o' those fellers. Never forget 'em."

Particularly the day their guide fell though his door, and almost died on the rug.

Leonidas Hubbard was twenty-nine when he decided to throw himself against the tundra. He was a straggly boy, both in body and in spirit, always bounding off after his first idea. Up until then, he'd had little experience of hot and cold; he'd been a Sunday school teacher and the sub-editor of *Outing,* a magazine for those who dreamed of being elsewhere. Even at this stage, his wife, Mina, seemed so much more impressive than Hubbard. She was a nurse who'd rescued him from the New York typhus, and who would spend her married life enduring her husband's folly, and her widowhood denying it.

Our other hero ought to have been a sturdier figure. Dillon Wallace had been clambering upwards all his life, starting as a miller, then a telegrapher, and finally a lawyer. Although he was ten years older than Hubbard, in their photographs the two are almost indistinguishable; both wear thick moustaches and an expression which says We Don't Know Why We're In This Story Either. Apart from looking uneasy, they also bear an absurd resemblance to Tintin's friends, the Thompson twins, except of course that they're in knitwear and pork-pie hats.

It wasn't long before this adventure lost its wheels. The first day, paddling up Grand Lake, was the only one that went to plan. This ought to have been the moment to stop at Gilbert's tilt and ask the way, but Hubbard didn't (he thought "the breeds" were just a bunch of hicks). Instead, Hubbard took the wrong turning, up the wrong river, in the wrong direction. The fact that the Susan was steep, shallow and rocky ought to have been a clue that this was not the trappers' river, the Naskaupi, but it was a hint that wasn't taken. Instead, our boys carried their canoe for two weeks, covering only twenty-four miles. By the time all the flap-jacks were finished, they were still barely out of sight of Sunday Hill, and already beginning to starve.

Then things got difficult. First, their moccasins rotted away, and Hubbard's toenails fell out and a crack opened across his heel. They were also breathing flies and the temperature was ninety. Then Hubbard developed extravagant diarrhoea, followed by depression. At night he called out for Mina, and everyone began to have unnatural thoughts of food. Now they were eating moss-berries and whisky jacks, and smoking bits of trees. There was nothing heroic about this failure—except that they persisted. Finally, after two months of wandering into nothing, they decided to turn back.

It was now winter, and the game had vanished. All there was to eat was the rubbish from the journey up; a pair of rotten hooves, a fly-blown skin and some mouldy flour. There was a feast the day they found some putrid offal. Wrote Wallace: "As Hubbard said, the maggots seemed to make the broth the richer." If nothing else, at least such fare had cured them of adventure. "What does glory amount to after all?" scrawled Hubbard in his failing hand. A few days later, his legs failed altogether, and the other two left him behind in a tent.

Hubbard's last plan was to eat the rest of his shoes. Even in that he failed, because he was overwhelmed with fantasy. "I am not suffering," he wrote. "I am sleepy. I think death from starvation is not so bad."

For the others, an over-ambitious picnic had become a death march. Two days later, Wallace developed snow-blindness and wandered off, groping through the trees. That left the guide free to make a run for the Blakes. It took him a week, surviving on a partridge, which he ate still warm.

Horace the Trapper told me his father was in the rescue party, aged nineteen.

"They left next morning, and did forty miles in two days."

Gilbert and the other Blakes soon found Wallace, blind as a puppy, half-naked and mad. Hubbard was harder to find, under eight feet of snow. They decided not to touch him (he was already inhabited by spirits), and so it was only Wallace that they hauled back home. "God knows how they starved," said Horace. "There's always s'thin' to eat out there."

Five months later, Wallace had recovered enough of his wits to arrange a funeral. By then, the Grand Lake was as hard as a hammer, and he slid through the bottleneck on a dog-sledge with his old friend packed in salt. This curious cortege then swished past us, and on, 325 miles to Battle. From there, they took the steamer on to Newfoundland and New York, and the grieving Mina.

An unhappy conclusion wasn't the end of the dramas in the bottleneck.

Two years later, Wallace paddled back up here, to make the same mistakes.

Close behind him was Mina. She was angry that Wallace had made a best-seller of the earlier fiasco, with *The Lure of the Labrador Wild*. Now, Mina was determined to recast her husband as something other than a fool. In fact, she managed exactly the opposite because over the next two months she crossed 550 miles of tundra, and arrived in Ungava Bay looking hardly ruffled. Wallace arrived six weeks later, having almost drowned, frozen and starved. Mina's contribution to the exploration of Labrador was far greater than anything he or her husband had ever achieved, and yet she was only an extra. She'd brought back some of the first accounts of the Innu hunt and the caribou migrations, and had made a map of the interior. Her secret was simple; she'd got Gilbert Blake to show her the way.

Horace giggled. "She'd an eye for my father, sure. Always put her tent up he did."

But the extra never played the love-scene. Mina went home to the fame she deserved. Wallace went back to his practice, and Gilbert Blake carried on trapping until his death at the age of ninety-four.

Oddly enough, he'd been there for the postscript in 1913.

It was Wallace again, puffing through the bottleneck. This time, he had with him a judge and a vast memorial tablet. Gilbert offered to take them back to the place where Hubbard had died but, on the way, their canoe tipped up and the tablet was lost. Instead, the party said their good-byes in canoe-paint with a brush made of Gilbert's hair. Then, as they left, they picked up the remains of Hubbard's effects, including the last of his shoes.

Somehow these had ended up at the local store, which is where we found them.

Looking parboiled, of course, and thoughtfully chewed.

102

I continued northwards on the ferry, back out to the coast.

It took a day to get out of the inlet. Although it was calm (like a day next summer, said the purser), the crew practised their lifeboat drills, and the portholes were sealed. We were told there'd be no drinking from now, although this didn't stop some of the younger Metís getting chatty on cans of altered Coke. For everyone else, there wasn't even a glass of rough with their fritters.

"We's goin' to be in native territory soon," said the cook.

Although this sounded alarmingly Victorian, it was true. From here, a vast unofficial, unmarked homeland spread out north-east, taking in Greenland, and curling up though northern Canada and Alaska, and into Siberia. This estate ranges from 54°30'N to 79°N, and covers tens of thousands of miles of coastline and ice. Apart from their solitude, its inhabitants, the Inuit, are linked by a common language, a flair for engineering and the same outlandish nightmares. Despite their obvious talents, it's often said that they can't survive anywhere else but in their frozen lands, and throughout their entire range they've never exceeded 100,000 souls. But at least they're sure it's *their* territory, and so—two centuries on—whites and half-breeds here are still known as "settlers."

"De Inuit's not too fussy about de white man," one of the settlers told me.

Burt wore a sea-captain's hat, and said he'd been hunting polar bears for seventy years. Nowadays, his nose was tattooed with rock and soot, and his tiny winter-burnt eyes were always flooded and trickling down his chest. Got no eyes, he said, and no teeth but I still shoot.

"And last winter I skidoo'd up Cape Chidley to get me some bunnies, and a bear."

Burt was travelling with some new walls for his house.

"I can get $80 for a bear," he said.

As we went out past Eskimo Island again, I mentioned the smallpox which had come from London with Caubvick.

"Dere was no smallpox, boy. Our elders say dat was de Indians, came up 'ere one night with der French friends. Shot everyone in de head before dey was even out der beds. Me grandfather saw de graves— he'd tell ye."

It had been a savage past. As we turned into the ocean, furious sparks of phosphorescence folded themselves into our bow-wave, and the rocks turned black, and were streaked with slashes of crimson ice. Burt told me their old names, as if that explained it all; Smokey Run, Dark Tickle and Cut Throat Island.

Nothing in Labrador's early history gave me much hope for what lay ahead.

To begin with, Europeans saw the Inuit simply as repulsive curios to be collected. Hore's man-eating barristers had been on a hunt for savages, before their larder let them down. An expedition in 1567 was more successful, and returned to Antwerp with a female dressed in seal-skins "almoste more wickedly than the beastes." Her exhibitors were able to turn a good profit on this venture, particularly when they told people she was a cannibal and that her husband was twelve feet tall. After that, the race was on for the most amusing savage.

But the Inuit too had been learning, and had developed their ruthless guile. When Frobisher landed in Labrador in 1576 he was initially well-satisfied with what he found: "Tartars with long black hair, broad faces and flat noses, and taunie in colour, wearing seales skinnes." They mooed like bulls, cut their coat-tails off as presents and appeared to be riding around on fish (although these turned out to be kayaks). Such delight only turned to horror when the "salvages" chopped up five of his men, forcing Frobisher to retreat with just one captive—who bit his own tongue off on the voyage home, and then died of a cold. Frobisher was barely more successful the next year, capturing a mother and baby—although it cost him an arrow in his buttock. To his astonishment, the woman healed her child's bullet-wound by licking it until it healed "not much unlike our dogges."

Duplicity continued to be the best defence for the Labrador savages. Although John Davis had found the Greenland savages amenable to a little Morris dancing and football, it was a different story when—in 1586—he tried the same in Labrador. His men were ambushed and cut down with arrows, without even "parley or speech." Jollity then slaughter, it was the same for all who followed; Hall, Hudson, Button, Gibbons and poor Captain Knight, who was ripped apart in April 1601.

Apart from dampening the enthusiasm, these attacks left the English with only a patchy understanding of the Inuit. Frobisher thought they ate grass and ice, and drank salt water. Davis said, "They are never out of the water, but live in the nature of fishes." Others assumed they were half-man, half-beast, probably seal. At least they had a new name. The word *Esquimawes* ("raw-meat eaters") first appeared in Hakluyt's *Discourse of Western Planting* in 1584, via the Basques. The Inuit have always hated it because it's Indian, not because it's untrue (in one of Curwen's photographs, a family is sitting on a beach in their Sunday best, eating an uncooked walrus head).

The Inuit's understanding of the Europeans was hardly any better.

They were surprised to find anyone in the world apart from themselves and the weaselly Innu. Then they remembered the legend of the woman who mated with a dog. She sets her litter of half-puppies adrift in the sole of a boot, which becomes a ship, and they become *Kablunaets*. Although the Asiatic origins of the Inuit are still debated, it's a curious fact that the Japanese have a similar explanation for the Ainu of the Kurile Islands.

Naturally, the half-dogs had to be tricked, lulled and killed. But the *Kablunaets* were almost nothing in a world beset with monsters. There were mermen, dwarves, high-speed worms, a witch who could seize the entrails of a laughing man, giant kayakmen and wolves, more half-dogs and—worst of all—the *Anghiaks,* abortions returning for revenge. It was like a bad dream designed by Tolkien, except that one lot of demons—the Europeans—were about to become persistent. The Inuit had not prepared themselves for such systematic killing, and didn't even have a word for "war."

The French bore the brunt of the Inuit's disgust. They believed they might have made a Peru out of Labrador had it not been for the savages. *"L'Esquimau est méchant,"* they complained, *"quand on l'attaque, il se defend."* Worse, these people stank, ate like rats and stole everything, even the buttons off the Commandant's coat. For a while, the French tried to learn the language but their intelligence was horribly distorted. The Esquimaux told them that there were three tribes: one were dwarfs, only two foot high but uncommonly vicious; another had white hair from birth; the third were unipeds, with only one eye and one arm. With mockery like this, who can blame the French for Eskimo Island, or their other reprisals? When Britain took over the Inuit in 1763, the French were the last to complain.

It didn't take Governor Palliser long to get the measure of his subjects.

They were, he declared, "the most savage people in the world."

103

It took a whole day to reach Makkovik, squeezing through the rock and ice.

My memory of this port is shot with mist, and moments of brilliant empty light. I can't hear anything in this whiteness but I'm aware of the smell of dogs, and the dirt road beneath my feet. Then the picture clears a little, and I can see two tiny girls with blue-black hair spitting and fighting with extraordinary ferocity. I want to stop them but I don't know the words, and then they're rubbed out. Now I'm in a shop, full of creatures on coat-hangers: wolves, rabbits, muskrats and ermines. I buy some seal-skin boots for a child I don't have, and then nothing again. But who's this? It's a face, an old face with an Abraham Lincoln beard. I'm Albert Andersen, he says, and I seem to be saying "I know, my great-grandfather knew yours": Tosten Andersen of Norway, "a splendid man." Want a sledge-dog, he says, and holds up a bundle like a fat, blunt wolf. What would I feed it, I ask. Flippers and moss, he says, or walrus if you can get it. We laugh. I'm enjoying this whiteness, wondering what will happen next.

Then the Bartletts appear with a message for Curwen.

Get out to Turnavik quickly, they say, there's two women murdered.

104

We passed Turnavik as we steamed north. Now there's little there but lichen.

By the time Curwen arrived at Ben's Cove, the death toll had risen to four.

The dead were all women—Tom Brown's wife and that of another Esquimau called Benjamin, an old widow in their care, and Brown's twelve-year-old daughter. They'd all suffered the same symptoms in the hours before death: our feet have died, they gasped, and our hands are as cold as the sea. They'd been poisoned. Curwen decided it was probably hemlock, which also grew on the outcrop.

He realised that, to the Esquimaux, murder was a subject of some complexity. Killing was wrong and was punishable with death, but there were subtle exceptions. It was, for example, legitimate to kill someone who was insane. It was also acceptable to kill out of revenge—a latitude which extended not just to murderers but to all their kinsmen too. Even more difficult was the rule that permitted the killing of starving children. Curwen had already seen too much of this. Joel, the man who taught him to kayak, had killed all his children, and so too had Mr. Olliver, who'd hacked up his three with an axe.

The Turnavik murders, however, were different, by any set of rules.

It wasn't hard to find a suspect. Curwen was fascinated by the forensic chase, or "ferreting" as he called it, and had soon assembled a history:

> A very great suspicion rests on Brown for there is little doubt he killed his first wife & baby: and so badly did he treat his 2nd wife that she died too; this his third wife came off the best of the three while she lived but . . . she must have led an awful life . . . He is greatly feared by the few winter settlers here, and I should not be surprised to hear next year that he has been shot; his life seems to be a long story of crime upon crime.

Tom Brown treated the Dogheads' investigation with disdain. He smoked his pipe as he dug the grave, and was already talking of another wife. Curwen took a picture of him and Benjamin standing in front of their sod-roofed tilt. They're wearing woollen jackets and sealskin boots, and Tom is grinning with contempt. Not so the other man; "Benjamin really cut up," notes Curwen, and his face is a blur of fear. There is also a boy in the picture, Benjamin's boy. Soon all three of them will go off fishing to Double Island, and the boy will be poisoned like his mother.

In the meantime, Captain Trezise held an inquest on the rock. Twelve jurymen were brought from West Turnavik, and Curwen was the expert witness (Grenfell of course was absent, still racing around in his launch). This strange fishy court opened on 28 August 1893, and proceeded with astonishing exactitude:

> It was a long weary & difficult business but carried through as carefully as possible, I think; a verdict of death from poisoning was brought in but we could not determine by whom it was administered.

The forensic evidence was sent to St. John's for analysis but nothing more emerged. Despite the lack of evidence, a magistrate and two constables were sent up to the north to round up Tom Brown. They ignored the murders and had him convicted for an offence he was supposed to have committed twelve years before. He got four months inside.

Reactions to this were mixed. Turnavik was relieved to have lost a rascal, and possibly worse. Curwen, on the other hand, was disappointed; he thought his rock justice had quite properly given Tom the benefit of the doubt. But the governor was delighted; the world had been spared an intolerable spectacle.

An Esquimau dangling from a British rope.

105

London had never had the stomach for killing Esquimaux.

This is more quaint than it sounds because, as much as the British admired the savages, the savages hated them. In their brief encounter with the Europeans, the Esquimaux had perfected their knack for deception, and were bloodily cunning. They might be all smiles one moment, as they massed for the attack, and then they'd fall back with more smiles, and they'd be charming until darkness when they'd be on to the Dogheads again, cracking bones and ripping out faces. Until Cartwright appeared, the only dialogue between the two was that of war-cries and grapeshot.

Admiral Palliser's first law of April 1765 was therefore one of desperation—*An Order for Establishing Communication with the Esquimaux Savages.* It was an outrageous proclamation for its time, forbidding the sale of grog to the aborigines, and giving them more rights to Labrador than any enjoyed by the planters. It earned Palliser the eternal scorn of the Newfoundlanders. ("No ruler since the days of Charles II," wrote Judge Prowse, "hated the country he was set over more bitterly.") But on the question of civilising the Esquimaux, the Admiral had yet more outrage up his sleeve. That same year, he delegated the entire, ghastly task to a group who'd been on the run for over three hundred years, a theocracy of Bohemians.

The choice of the *Unitas Fratrum*—or United Brethren—wasn't as odd as it appeared. In their flight to the ends of the earth, the Brothers had discovered an affinity for the aboriginal and the dispossessed. They'd established their own rigorous strain of Protestantism as far away as Tibet, and throughout the Georgian world of slaves. They were an unstoppable blaze. If you aren't a missionary, said their leader Count Zinzendorf, you need one. By 1735, he and his black-frocked confederates were refugees in London. The only thing the English knew about them was that they'd been burnt to death in Moravia, and so, from then on, they were known as the Moravians.

When it was discovered they'd learnt Inuktitut in Greenland, Labrador was theirs.

The Esquimaux had other ideas. The Moravians' first expedition ended with their seven best men dying, lopped and slashed in their beds. On their next trip, the Germans caused panic by reading out Palliser's orders, demanding of all men "the utmost probity." When they heard these words, the Esquimaux thought the book had come alive, and fled.

The third expedition was more promising. In 1765, the Moravians set out again, under the armour of HMS *Niger*. This time, the Esquimaux paddled out to greet them, in horribly cannibalised French. *"Tous cammarades,"* they squealed. *"Tous cammarades! Oui! Hee!"* The Moravians were encouraged, but the sailors weren't. The tension never eased, and when, a month later, the night-watch heard a whooping, *Niger* was cleared for action, all hands to the great guns, arms in the tops and everything in order. But there was nothing there, no kayaks and no war party. On this occasion, the Royal Navy had merely engaged a flock of whobbies.

Five sinister years passed before the Moravians got their break. It came with the reappearance of a familiar face (one that had hung in the Royal Academy to be precise). It was Mikak—Lieutenant Lucas's girl—who'd remembered her teas with the Princess of Wales, and who now came down to the shore in her velvet outfit, her Coronation medal and the Duke of Gloucester's bracelet. The Moravians had no idea that the other Esquimaux despised her for her flummery (or that she was about to renounce the Dogheads and revert to savagery). Mikak was a good enough excuse and so they established Nain.

Other outports followed, conjured from the scriptures: Ramah, Hebron and Zoar.

London encouraged these settlements with a grant of 100,000 acres and fifty muskets. The Brethren, noted one commentator, always worked with a tool in one hand and a weapon in the other.

But, gradually, the slaughter eased and—in their prayers at least— the Inuit became oddly German. However, in 1777, the Moravians noticed that their influence was leaking away to the south, and so they prepared for the building of a new spiritual fortress, between 55° and 56° North.

This was to be Hopedale, which is where my ship went next.

Hopedale was still menaced by its Esquimau dogs.

Or perhaps I should say they defined it. There were dog-teams all the way along the beach from the port, dogs on the promontories, dogs in the scrub and dogs on the outskirts. There were then a few dogless dirt roads of cabins and sheds, before I found myself back out on the rocks and among the dogs again. Although it was possible to enjoy a moment without teeth and hackles, there was no avoiding the noise. Every snarl and growl, every scratch and every chink of chain was caught in the cliffs as it tried to seep harmlessly into the wilderness, and was amplified and boomed back across the town. Along with all its grunts and whispers, Hopedale was a cage of captured barks.

But dogs defined not merely the limits to Hopedale but also the way it looked. Here man had fortified himself against his best friend, with stockades and fences and nets over anything edible, like turnips or canoes. If it wasn't fortified, it was out of reach; snowshoes, racks of caplin, boots, skins, and brilliant orange garlands of arctic char looped between the cabins. There were no cars. In summer, people churned up the dust on quads, and in winter they were out with their snowmobiles and, of course, their dogs. When I asked why *anyone* still used dogs, the answer was always the same: you can't eat a snow-mobile.

For many, the anxiety was the other way round: they feared being eaten by dogs. Once, I watched as a hunter cut up a seal for his team. Feeding dogs in summer was an innovation, and until recently they'd haunted the town with their hunger. Curwen says the "Hopedale Band" had had to get by on cods' heads and berries (although the mission often gave them blubber and caplin to keep them off the carrots). Grenfell describes how the "huskies" had eaten the Mission cat, and how they'd polish off a whole sheep overnight, wool and all. Watching them now, unstoppable and furious, this was an unnerving thought. In the days before snowmobiles—and ten times as many dogs—it was terrifying. This daily riot carried on until the Mounties arrived, and started shooting anything unchained.

"After tha, they puts 'em on the islands," said Davey, "which is crazy, eh?"

Davey was an Inuit who often appeared at moments like this. The stealth and dexterity of his appearances surprised me because Davey was missing an arm and both his feet. He was, I imagined, always on the lookout for conversation because, whenever he saw me, he slotted his stumps into shoes, vanished and reappeared at my shoulder. Although I enjoyed our conversations, there was much about Davey that I just couldn't fathom. He had a Ho Chi Minh beard but I couldn't tell if he was young or merely unweathered. Everything about him was half-said, like the tattoo on his arm, which had been sawn through the middle. He spoke every word as if it was fenced in with punctuation, which lent it either emphasis or ambiguity. I have never been less sure of anyone in my life, whether he was unusually intelligent or merely angry.

I pointed at the islands scattered off the coast.

"Why was it crazy to put the dogs out there, Davey?"

"One of our people had go out there berrypickin'. This wha's happening to us, eh? Made a good meal of her they does. It was their bloody rock. Ripped her kids apart too. Two maids, not up in age. How crazy's tha, eh?"

There was silence as the hunter teased the seal out of its fatty pink jacket. It seemed strange to be talking about mutilation with a man so badly mutilated. Naturally, I was tempted to make a connection between Davey's vicious story and his savage injuries. But this—as it turned out—wasn't how things had happened at all.

Davey's secret was Hopedale's secret.

The Moravians' *Missionhaus* was well-defended against the dogs.

It was like a tiny German hamlet-within-a-hamlet: apron-white, copper bell-tower and a hefty stockade. The main buildings were made of timber and linked by corridors, and—once—they'd sprawled off into an even larger complex of workshops, blubber-yards and tanneries. The Esquimaux of 1782 had never seen such industry, which was just what the Moravians wanted. They would tempt the Esquimaux to "Hoffenthal" by the sheer splendour of work. Once there, they'd be safe from the fish-killers' vice, from drink and flour, and from their own terrors, and they'd be re-cast as little *Deutsche*.

For the most part, they succeeded. A century on, Curwen's photographs catch the blubber-boilers in a moment of solemnity and starched bonnets. Another picture shows Herr Kastner, buttoned up in black; he is the head of a *Kolonie* of neophytes, Britain's most senior representative in northern Labrador, and *Konsul* to Imperial Germany. He wears the colours of the German flag on his sleeve, and sealskin boots made by his workers. But this uncertain paradise can't last. It will continue until the Great War, when the Moravians will find themselves "enemy aliens," and their industry will collapse.

I tried to find the remains of their garden but all that was left was the fence. Over 2,000 barrows of earth had been scraped together for this enterprise, and even the Head of Mission had taken time out to fight off the dogs. Every *missionär* grew vegetables, and some had gathered up wild seeds to investigate, or to send back to Berlin and Kew. This garden was the embodiment of their beliefs, the triumph of technology over nature, and Christianity over terror. Curwen was amazed ("gardens so rich . . . they made me think I was back in England again") and the floaters were often calling in on vegetable raids. Peary was less impressed; although he was in Hopedale only a month before Curwen, he thought the gardens were "pitiful" and identified the "dreariest of an apology for a summer pavilion." His contempt perfectly complemented his general loathing for missionaries (or, for that matter, anyone in the business of questioning his ethics).

At the heart of this dog-besieged Mission was the church. The builder, Krute, was a depressive and—in his own struggle with darkness—he'd given the place huge windows and painted everything white. It was, I suppose, the clearest expression of order and light that could possibly have been achieved using only planks and paint. It was easy to see why the Esquimaux had been entranced, and why they'd taken a course so foreign and prim. There were separate entrances for men and women, choir-stalls and special seats for nursing mothers. The Moravians had made life so uncomplicated. In this world, there were "Love Feasts" and German chorales, and the afterlife was even better. Every morning, as the brethren took their places, the Esquimaux had trilled *"Guten Morgen!"* in perfect unison, and so the day began.

On the day I went to church, there were no Bohemians and the sound of German had survived only in the name of a hymn: *Jesu geh' voran*. I understood nothing except the word "Amen," and was given a glass thimble full of wine. Then, I picked my way through "Father up in Heaven," which had been scrambled into Inuktitut:

> Atatab kilangmitub tessiutsainarmanga
> Nunab pingit tamaita ungagingilakka

Curwen heard little of this; the dogs opened up at the bells and never stopped. Then, at a given moment, they all rushed in and ate the hymnbooks.

107

I soon realised that Inuktitut was less of a scrambling and more labyrinthine than I'd imagined. Curwen describes it as a "curious tongue" but—left at that—this might apply to any set of primitive babbles and grunts. Inuktitut is more than that, a language of architectural complexity and almost mathematical logic. Words are assembled long before they're inserted in the sentence, cut and fashioned out of hundreds of components, or affixes, and built up into a concept. Linguists describe this type of construction as "agglutinative" but this is far too gluey a word for Inuktitut. It's more like masonry (which is in itself an extraordinary concept to people who've never built more than a tilt). To be a master of this language is to be a master builder, a state that—even among Inuit—is rarely achieved. To the early Moravians, it was a "cage of grammar."

I decided to test this with the only word I knew: *iglo*, a house.

I asked Davey how he'd say "houses."

"Depends wha you means," he said. "*Igluk* is two houses, and *iglut* is more than tha. But if you's talking *our* houses, it's *igluvut*."

But these were still only the foundations. The concept had yet to be assembled into "a large house," *iglorssuak*, "the owner of a large house," *iglorssualik,* or a "house-builder," *igloliorte*. There might be up to ten affixes in a word, although only the master craftsman would put together sentences of such elaborate constructions. The nineteenth-century Danish "Eskimologist," Hinrich Rink, gives us an example of a word comprising a primitive stem, seven affixes, and the flexion for the third person conjunctive with the suffix for "him": *iglorssuatsialiorfigssaliarkugamiuk* ("As he commanded him to go to the place where the tolerably large house shall be built").

Oddly, amongst all this impenetrable algebra, there was virtually no counting. The Inuit saw no need; they were hunters who lived off fresh meat; there was no place in their lives for capital or accumulation. They only had words for the fingers of one hand, like *pingasut* for "three." To express more than that, one had to use the other hand. Thus "eight" was *arfinek pingasut* ("three on the other hand").

Using all the toes, one could, by this means, reach twenty which was—literally—"the whole man."

Apart from bringing them German numbers, the Moravians made few changes to the Inuit language. They taught in Inuktitut because they believed that the only sure way of getting the gospels to the aborigines was in their own tongue. Only where Labradorian Inuktitut was lacking was it supplemented with *hochdeutsch*. It now has *Gott* (God), for example, and *heilig* (holy), and—if Grenfell is to be believed—there was a "Holy Seal" for a while because the Inuit had never seen a lamb.

Despite its sophistication, the Moravians soon had a grip on the language. By 1790, the Esquimaux were beginning to see their words in Roman letters, and thirty years later they had their own New Testament. Inuktitut was finally wrestled under control in 1864, with the publication of the first dictionary, *Eskimoisches Wörterbuch*.

This was the easy part. Taking charge of the Eskimo soul would prove harder.

It's possible that, emotionally, the Inuk is even more complex than his language.

Often, when I travel, I reach a point when I realise that my understanding of what I'm seeing is unlikely ever to get much beyond the superficial. If there's any stupidity about this realisation, it's usually that I didn't reach it earlier. At its most traumatic, this moment is simply the sensible part of "culture shock." But usually it's not an unpleasant sensation; like my great-grandfather, I feel no particular need to reduce things to answers. Whilst there's incomprehension, there's fascination, however uncomfortable the facts.

Curwen had reached such a point soon after his encounter with the serial-killer, Tom Brown. It wasn't so much that he'd discovered anything from this episode, but rather that he now knew he didn't understand the Esquimaux at all. Not that he stopped trying: amongst his papers I found wads of notes he'd taken from the English version of Rink's *Eskimoiske Eventyr og Sagn*. But the more he probed, the more he found himself bogged down in contradictions. On the one hand, their society seemed to lack any cohesion and, on the other, it was "socialism in its essence." At times, it all seemed so sophisticated, with choral music and violin-making, but then Curwen would show the Esquimaux a photograph of a woman who'd died, and their world would collapse in ghosts. Some showed extraordinary detachment over the death of a spouse, whilst others ordered two coffins and let bereavement kill them.

Even amongst individuals, Curwen found himself wrestling with the same contradictions that I'd recognised in Davey. "The Esquimaux," he told his sister, "are a curious people and a curious mixture of the callous and the emotional." One moment they were "gay, careless and thriftless," and the next they were deadly earnest (or so they seemed):

> The missionaries told us that, unwarlike as they are, they had repeatedly asked if they could help when England was going to war in Egypt, and had actually endeavoured to drill—an effort not encouraged.

Perhaps the nearest Curwen ever got to an answer was a quote he took from Rink: "The end and object of life is not to starve."

Even a century after their conversion, no one regarded the Esquimaux as convincingly Christian. In private, Curwen described their faith as "nominal." But the Moravians weren't under any illusions either, and trod a delicate path. Christianity was eased into the Inuk consciousness almost imperceptibly at first; pagan festivals re-emerged as Christian feasts, tribal elders became "chapel servants," and—at communion—traditional dress was encouraged long after the Esquimaux had taken up cast-offs and wool. Polygamy was tolerated, even as late as 1907, and the Moravian schools were re-shaped for a new pupil; corporal punishment was repellent to the Esquimaux, and even the chastisement of children was an affront to the human spirit.

The Moravians had two factors in their favour: the Esquimau's need to eat, and his fear of ridicule. Properly harnessed, he might make a convincing Christian but the terrors were never far away. He was still haunted by the last ten thousand years and, in times of crisis, he reverted to magic and not prayer. It speaks volumes for the Moravians' task that—in over two hundred and fifty years on Labrador—they've yet to produce an Inuit pastor. Nowadays failure is more readily recognised but, in 1893, abandonment was not an option. No one was going to leave the Esquimaux to the fishermen and grog, or to their wonderland-in-waiting.

The world, that is, of half-dogs and mermen, and the carnivorous abortions.

108

Like Curwen, I spent much of my time in Hopedale amongst the Moravians.

Unlike his friends, mine saw themselves as the last of the whites.

"Unless I can find aboriginal leaders," said Sam Propsom, "the church is finished."

It was a mountainous endeavour but "the Reverend Sam" was a man of alpine intent. His cabin was full of guns and pelts, and he himself was physically stupendous, all whiskers and meat. He told me he'd once been a shipworker in Pennsylvania until something in his Bohemian ancestry had ignited, and he'd joined the Moravians. When the offer came of Labrador, he'd abandoned his doctorate, and come bounding up the coast with his wife and their own little tracker, aged six. We have to be like the Inuit, he said—although Reverend Sam was hardly unobtrusive. Being with him was like being in *The Deer Hunter* with Falstaff. Nothing was too loud, too cold or too rash. One evening, I told him I'd found an Indian tent up in the hills, and the next minute we were bouncing across the tundra on his quad, off in not-so-hot pursuit. The tent was rotten, as it happens, and, in a pair of huge Moravian hands, it simply curdled and fell apart.

On the way back, Sam explained the hunting.

"We freeze a lot of meat. There's always someone without, and they come to us."

Not much change there, I thought.

But in every other respect the old lives had gone. At the time of Curwen's visit, there'd been seven missionaries: the Kastners, the Simons, the Hansens and an Englishman called Fry. The visit had begun well enough with an extravagant welcome from fifty Esquimau choristers singing *Twinkle, Twinkle, Little Star* (the previous year they'd welcomed Grenfell with a cannon and killed one of their own amateur bombardiers). Curwen repaid the gesture with a dinner for seventy-four aboard the *Albert*, followed by fireworks and a brass band. There was then a slightly less enjoyable period of dentistry as Herr Simon made some instruments, and Curwen set about a century of untended teeth, assisted by Herr Kastner.

Dentistry is probably as happy as this visit ever got. What emerged was a picture of debilitating isolation. The Moravians were dependent on supplies from England, and got a ship once a year. Each man could expect a long, empty sojourn on the coast (nearly fifty years in one case) with no visits home. If he was unmarried, he'd be sent a wife when he was considered ready, and if there were children they'd be removed to Germany at the age of six and never seen again. Curwen was horrified by such self-inflicted cruelty, and thought their sacrifice in vain. The missionaries had missed out on a whole generation of social science and their methods were "a hundred years out of date." Stale and intellectually inert, the Moravians were also critically lonely, and it wasn't long before Curwen felt the crush of claustrophobia.

"I seem to have known you for years already," said Herr Kastner, after a week.

But it was hard to resist such loneliness, and so Curwen allowed himself to become a source of constant novelty. He held lectures and magic lantern shows, and handed out gifts of jam, cigars and plums. The Moravians repaid with him with gratitude, their rendition of *Ein feste Burg* and garden teas "in the true German fashion." Curwen was up at the Provision House almost every night for a month, talking and singing and pulling out teeth.

I asked Sam if I could see inside one day.

"Sure. The Premier's on his way. I'll take you round with him."

I spent that morning clambering through the old Mission with Premier Grimes.

He and his ministers wore matching anoraks, and expressions of matching disquiet. Davey said the Inuit hated politicians, and St. John's hated them. Like everything else about Davey, his sentiments were perhaps a little mutilated but there was always some truth there. Many people thought the government just wanted to see Labrador closed down, or rented out. It was a suspicion confirmed by almost everything the government did. They'd even tried to shut down Hopedale in 1974, until they'd discovered that it was cheaper to keep it running. But what was the point in survival? To keep the last six hundred inhabitants in a state of almost perpetual unemployment? The fish plant employed three people, and was the only industry.

Grimes was keeping everyone going with hoarse, empty jokes.

They'd already been pelted with chickens.

I asked the Minister of Justice how he found Labrador.

"Challenging," he smiled, but his eyes said, "Desperate."

The Provision House came as a welcome relief. Parts of it had survived since 1782 (which was decades better than almost anything in St. John's). But it was empty now, just the clump of heels on wood, white schoolrooms, white corridors and bare rooms in the attic. We found a pram made out of fur, a map of the world in Inuktitut and a three-piece sealskin suit. It was like walking around in the mind of Man Ray, all that light and the oddities abandoned. The politicians had never believed Labrador capable of such surrealism, nor such gentility. I even found Herr Simon's dental instruments, and the little surgery where Curwen had pulled all those teeth. The Moravians had simply closed the door on this chapter of their story.

After the ministers had wandered off (to sign away more rock), I went down to the cemetery. Naturally, it was well-defended against the dogs, because the turf here was shallow, barely a refuge for the dead. Only a handful of tombs had survived, Germans in their beds of stone. Most were the children of Curwen's friends, the Kastners and the Hansens. They'd not even reached the age of six before they were lost.

This didn't trouble the Reverend Sam as much as it troubled me. "The body's just a hut," he said, "to be left behind."

And what, I wondered, had the old Esquimaux made of death?

Get out to Black Head, says Curwen, and you'll find them all still there.

109

I walked down to the area where the hunters lived, to find a boat.

In one sense, Hopedale was a town of hunters, the dust jewelled with bullets.

But it was only down on the shore that bear-killing was still a man's living. There, the shingle was greasy with meat and pelts and rotting claws. Every now and then a skull rolled out of the landwash, and a set of monstrous fangs would take one last snarl at the world before being dragged under again by the sculpins and the crabs. Once, all of Hopedale had smelt like this: *Tuktu,* or caribou, in summer, and bears and seals all year. Rink says hunting made the Esquimaux interdependent, "semi-communistic" and technically brilliant. In the absence of wood, their weaponry had been coaxed out of anything to hand: ivory, soapstone, sinews, baleen and teeth.

But now, hunting had an uncertain role. Hopedale had three stores full of Fruit Fingers and Alien Heads, and a government that handed out dole. The children had no idea how to cut blubber, or how to gnaw the meat off a skull. Much of the Inuit's brilliance—kayaks, anoraks and swivel-headed harpoons—had survived elsewhere but not here. Even the old hunting skills had been forgotten, like the way to kill a *Nanuq*. If the polar bear attacked, a knife was slotted into the end of a thirty-foot dog-whip, and the beast was colourfully slashed to the ground. These days, people didn't even eat the bears.

"Got too many parasites," said one, Mr. Lacey, "eatin' our garbage."

I asked if anyone still carved.

"Most everyone," said Mr. Lacey, and gave me a pair of earrings.

Keep them, he said. Each was cut in the shape of a half-moon knife, an *ulu*. "They's jumper bones. We shoots 'em in the bay and gives the meat to the poor."

I thanked him, and had one last request: the boat.

"Ask Albert. He's gotta skiff, an' could use a few dollars for fuel."

Albert Tuglavina often fished off Black Head, and knew all about the bodies.

He was one of the few that did. Reverend Sam had never heard of them, and there were others who'd preferred to forget. The tombs belonged to a darker age, the time of the *tunnit,* or the Dorsets and the Thule Eskimos (as we now say). It wasn't so much that they were heathen that made them forbidding, but that they were dead. The Eskimologist Rink says that—to the Esquimaux—the dead are more dreaded than killing, and that a man can become tainted by his very association with a corpse. Curwen, of course, was unperturbed by such fears, and saw it all as irresistible archaeology. He'd excavated the *koppenmödings* (or midden heaps) behind the Mission, and had read everything he could about his subject; the works of Rink, Captain Hall and Fridtjof Nansen. Then he hired two chapel servants, Joshua and Ambrosius, to row him out to the dead.

Albert said nothing as we stuttered across the bay.

It was an unforgettable morning, the skyline bubbling like silver in the heat, and the shallows an improbable golden-blue. Black Head was exactly as Curwen had described it (except hotter, and shot with breeze and colour): a high trap-rock end to a thick wedge of schist. We landed at a beach opposite, known to the Esquimaux as *Arvertôk* because it was good for clubbing whales. Immediately, we were enveloped in a swarm of stouts, but Albert ignored them and led me to a perfect diameter, sketched out of rocks.

"House," he said, "and over there is your dead people."

I walked on, alone, along the shore until I came to a small lump in the moss. I knelt down and peered inside. It was exactly as I'd expected—a skeleton piled with rocks.

Rink describes the journey from this world to the next.

A man who's led a good life will be laid out on a skin, and heaped with stones. These will keep the ravens and foxes off, as he finds his way to the Underworld, a warm place for the Happy Dead. If he's been bad, he'll be dismembered and his limbs scattered, and he'll wander the freezing Upper World forever. In this version of eternity, the sinners—or *arssartut*—will play football until the end of time, with a severed walrus head.

Peary had often witnessed these departures in Greenland in the late 1890s.

If the deceased had a dog, he says, it was strangled and crushed with its owner. But this wasn't all: "If a woman has a baby in her hood," writes Peary, "it too must die with her." The grave was then furnished with the person's possessions.

Curwen discovered that, although "the people very much dread the bones being touched," there was no offence in removing grave goods. One simply had to replace them with other items useful in the underworld, a rifle perhaps, razor blades or a cup. Under such indulgent strictures, Curwen put together one of the most important collections of Inuit antiquities ever made. Here is part of his Black Head inventory:

In one grave, evidently that of a woman, I found a number of teeth of a polar bear ... for a necklace, and several pieces of thin copper, which were used probably as ornaments, being sewn to the *sillapak;* with these were two small, triangular plates of stone used probably in the necklace; a small disc of ?lead, a ?lead needle of a large size, a bone handle for a knife with the remains of an iron rivet, the bone button for a walrus-hide sling, which connects the dogs traces with the *komatik,* and the broken remains of a soap- stone lamp ...

Dating such a grave provides us with a riddle. The presence of metals suggested to Curwen a post-European timing. But the soapstone is more difficult. A friend in St. John's—a sub-Arctic archaeologist— told me only the Dorsets had worked in soapstone, and they'd vanished by A.D. 1400. Perhaps these rules were too rigid? Or perhaps the graves had been in use for several hundred years? Or maybe it was just the grave goods, in a constant state of trade?

Whatever the answer, it wasn't as puzzling as the bones. Albert and I found six of the cairns examined by Curwen. In such a mineral-starved environment, the fact that *any* of them still contained human remains seemed beyond sober explanation. Even in death, the persistence of the Inuit was astonishing.

But for how much longer?

Curwen had spotted trouble ahead.

110

In 1893, it was only the white man's curiosity killing Inuit.

The fantasy of the Esquimaux as quaint and collectable had survived. For over three hundred years they'd been exhibited at fairs and royal parties, and now they were needed for the circus. As performers, they were thrilling although these acts always killed them. In 1881, the great Hagenbeck had recruited a troupe for his display at the Berlin Zoo, but none of them had survived the German coughs and colds.

The year of Curwen's visit, there was a more ambitious scheme; the whizzy, wacky, unthinking Charlie Martin planned to bring fifty-seven Inuit back to Chicago for the Great Exposition. His "Eskimo Village" became a star attraction; savages flicking coins with whips, and *komatik* rides around a little railway, pulled by dogs. Such hilarity might have made Charlie rich if they hadn't all caught typhus. He dumped the Esquimaux back in Newfoundland (which was near enough), leaving them to make their own way north, along with their disease. That Christmas in Nain, ninety out of three hundred and fifty local Inuit died. The only good to come of this was that one of the performers was a child, rescued and nursed by Grenfell until he died. His story, *Pomiuk, the Prince of Labrador*, was a sensation and awoke the West to its folly (and, as it happens, edged Grenfell nearer sainthood).

But despite the protests, the shows went on. Charlie Martin was back in 1898, and talked another thirty-three Esquimaux into a European tour. The first three died at the London Olympia, and the rest weren't heard of again until they turned up in Algeria in 1901. Two years later, the last six returned to Labrador in a blaze of syphilis. The infection raged along the coast. By 1907, it was so out of control that a gunboat full of doctors had to be despatched to restore some semblance of health.

Theatre and mummery were now wiping out a race, or so it seemed. Of course there were other factors too—the change from meat to flour and sugar; the move from annual homes to stinking huts. But whatever it was, the Inuit population was in freefall. In the beginning, the French had made a wild estimate at 30,000 Esquimaux. In my great-grandfather's time, there were around 3,000. Now, there are less than half that, at around 1,200.

Curwen knew, when he left Hopedale, that life for the extraordinary Esquimaux would be harder from here. As always, he left it to his contemporaries to come up with wild solutions. W. G. Gosling, Labrador's first historian, campaigned to make it a criminal offence to remove an Esquimau from the coast. Grenfell, of course, went further, suggesting that Labrador be shut off from the world, a "closed zone" for its Esquimaux. Curwen made no suggestions, but was busy filing observations until it was time to head for home. The day of his departure was as baffling as any before. After the *Albert*, there'd be no more ships for eight months. There were rockets and flowers, of course, but then the women queued—in tears—to kiss the buttons of his waistcoat.

Aksunai! shouted Curwen, as the boat moved off—Be strong!

Akshuta, came the reply—Let us be strong!

There were still hard years ahead. For the Inuit, their emergence from the Stone Age had been fraught with peril. The Moravian period had been one of hiatus, a time of German teas and nursery rhymes.

Now, Hopedale was to face the next stage alone, which was adolescence.

III

As the hotel was full, I stayed with the wreckage of a family on the hill.

The apartment was small and shabby and smelt of unspecific effort.

I shall call the tenant Madge. She was a short, oily woman, half-Inuit and unsure of the rest. She said she had two teenagers somewhere, and waved me into a bedroom that was acridly male. She had the only other bedroom, across the kitchen. There was little furniture, just a couch, a poem to a dead baby, and some ashtrays full of stubs and bullets. We don't have a phone, she said; they took it away.

Family life—if there'd ever been one—had long since lost its shape. No one ever spoke and there was no sense of time. The lethargy was compelling, like a clock whose hands keep sliding backwards. Madge ate a saucepan of pork and margarine in the morning and then nothing until her sweet tea at night. She always gulped it down, as if someone might take it from her. There was no curiosity for either me or them, and no one seemed to sleep. The boy returned every day at dawn, and watched a horror film. His name was Garn, and so were all his teeth. He seemed to despise his mother.

There was also a daughter, a fat unhappy girl called Daze. She called in only when she was sure the others were out. Although she was cunning, she told me she was always committing suicide and was often raped. She made out a powerful case for municipal neurosis. Everyone's weird here, she said.

I tried my best to avoid Daze after this, which meant avoiding the cabin. It was now a powerful force repelling four people in opposite directions, all for different reasons. Out in the town I was less safe. Daze often found me, and would stare right into my eyes and beyond, as if she expected to find me there, with her grimy mother.

"Ye *like* her?" she'd snarl.

"Well, I . . ."

"Ye doan *know* 'er."

I saw even less of Garn. He slept all day—somewhere—and was out all night, roaming the town with the bears.

Each morning, I escaped early.

For Hopedale, every new day was a morning after. I often passed the children as they scurried home, before the light. Every day, their town was slightly different. More broken windows at the school perhaps, or the burning question in fresh, dripping letters: *WASS SAPPENING?* Occasionally, the night-spirits stopped me, demanding a dollar for pop. I never gave in; it was said that diabetes was running at thirty per cent, and was already eating through the children.

I walked on, Hopedale waking to the sound of scratching dogs. At the edge of town, I climbed up the rocks and into the hills. Sam wasn't in favour of these walks and said they'd shot thirty wolves that year. For a while, I carried a piece of rusty cable until this seemed even more foolish than the walk itself. I was frightened but also relieved, glad to be feeling something other than torpor. The official advice in "bear country" is to be conspicuous, and to sing. I didn't feel like singing, and so I coughed. It was a terrible noise for such a magnificent wilderness and so, after a while, even my cough was abandoned. Now I had the tundra in silence, the sea below crackle-glazed with islands, and the land raw and newly cast.

At the top of a ridge was a set of giant concrete cups and saucers. Although they didn't look like them, these were America's ears, built to listen for Soviets creeping over the Arctic. For almost twenty years, from 1951 onwards, a tiny American town had perched up here in the teeth of the wind. It was part of "The Pine Line," a string of very cold men and bowling alleys waiting for something that would never happen. Now I found myself amongst its ruins. This tea-party was of course a work of madness, and—as if to prove the point—a bearded head popped up and screamed at me in Inuktitut. I was so startled, I couldn't think what to reply, except something I'd seen on a t-shirt. *Kuvia sulautta*, I shouted and, absurdly, the head disappeared: "Let's be happy."

As I made my way—very quickly—down, I almost stumbled into a lake of broken glass. Thousands and thousands of beer bottles. Some say this is where Hopedale all went wrong. The base, a "Distant Early Warning" post, was none of these things, but a sudden and catastrophic intrusion in their lives. They say it was the beginning of the drinking, the feuds, and the indiscriminate, unwanted sex. Others say these things were inevitable, and that—eventually—modern times would have found Hopedale even if they'd not arrived in khaki.

Back in the town, Davey appeared at my side.

We sat down on an old sledge daubed with the words *FUCKIN EAT ME*.

"We once lived off de land," he said, "and now we lives off pizza."

Davey was despondent; people don't go to the bush any more, not even for wood.

"We should never left de bays," he said. "Now we's just twiddlin' our thumbs."

It was a macabre thought, a nation of Daveys just twiddling thumbs. Because for him, of course, even this was impossible.

112

My last night, I discovered how Davey lost his hand and his feet.

The whole town was in the grip of bingo, numbers spitting off the radio.

I went to the hotel bar, and ordered a beer. No one spoke, which made the place more lonely than being alone. I was even relieved when Madge walked in with her cousin, SWAT. I'd often seen him around. SWAT wore combat boots and battle fatigues, and his long blue hair was tied back in parachute-cord. I envied him because SWAT wasn't here at all, but was on a mission of his own imagination. He even wore his blood-group on a dog-tag around his neck. He said nothing, just kept guard.

Madge too was wary of conversation. I disliked her more than I can rationally explain. Perhaps she had an aura of loathing, and I'd been somehow tainted? She hated everyone in this episode: Garn, Daze, the Reverend Sam and especially Davey.

"If he hadn't got so corned, he'd still have his fuckin' feet!"

I asked her what she meant.

"Dem guys is trouble, Davey an' his buddies. Once dey gets drinkin' it's all over. It's like dey got nothin' in their fuckin' heads say *Stop!* Dey drinks all deir dole, and dey drinks till dey can't even piss. Den, one night, Davey gets himself out in de blizzard, falls in de shit and it's minus forty. Doesn't know if it's Christmas or fuckin' what, and he's lying dere eight hours. When dey gets to him, even his guts is frozen fuckin' solid . . ."

Then SWAT spoke for the first time. Our plots must have merged.

"Needed a chopper get him out."

"Dey cut out all de bits as was rotted," said Madge, "and Davey's all dat's left."

I made a remark about what a shock it must have been, for everyone.

"Whaddya mean? It happens all de fuckin' time."

The morning of the ferry, I asked Sam if alcohol was the new plague.

"I guess so," he said. "Seventy per cent of Inuit lives are ruined by drink."

"Madge told me if you don't drink in Hopedale, you're on the outside."

"Did she?" said Sam, wearily. "Then she's probably right."

I wondered if he'd ever find a pastor to continue the church.

"Sometimes, I think I'm getting close," he said.

We shook hands. A big, de Niro grip, but Sam's expression was less sure.

"We get near, and then the drinking starts again, and we're back at the beginning."

113

Further up the delinquent coast, we came to a town lost before it had begun.

Like Sheshatsit, it was a place of broken pieces. It too was Innu— not Inuit—but, unlike Sheshatsit, it'd been cast adrift from the tundra. Muddy paths had oozed out of the forest, trickled down to the shore and pooled above the landwash. A froth of wreckage and huts had formed—but Davis Inlet had never been intended as a home. It was only ever what it said it was: a deep, blue fissure in the rock. The Indians had first arrived in 1916, running before a famine. After that, the inexplicable kindness of the Catholic Mission had brought them back every year. Then they'd abandoned hunting, and settled down to live the life of those mislaid.

This state of perdition had continued ever since. Only the rock belonged, the beautiful coils of smooth, metallic rope. Everything else seemed to waft around, detached and torn: wrappers, scraps of cabin, rags, tufts of smoke and bits of anger. *FUCK YOU ALL,* it said along the wharf. Here was another town for the Indians to hate, and they didn't even think it was theirs. They called it *Utshimatshi,* the Place of the Boss. Even worse, they'd never liked the sea, and now they were on an island. But there was nowhere else to go. The nearest towns were sixty miles away—Hopedale to the south and Nain to the north—and both were Inuit, which was even worse than nothing. For the Indians, the only way to live with dispossession was to reduce their hated town to nothing.

The crew were terrified of Davis Inlet.

"We're not stopping," said the deckhands. "We just chuck the freight off, and go."

The stage was empty. The ferry always got in early.

"Otherwise the kids is out, chuckin' rocks and smashin' all our windows."

"And if we puts the gangway down, they're all over us, lootin' what they can."

Other passengers appeared, to gaze into the smouldering debris. Mr. Parsons, the storekeeper from Hopedale, told me he'd once worked here as a development officer. He described the way the Indians had drifted into nothing—no hunting, no ritual and no migrations. We made them live in whiteman's homes, he said, but never told them how.

"First thing they did was pulled the walls out, and put up their tents..."

Then came the drinking, three out of four adults an alcoholic.

"But I was the first to notice the kids sniffing gas. They was carrying it in bags, down the front their sweatshirts. Got any idea how messed up you've gotta be to start sniffing gasoline? It burns your head out. I don't know if it hurts but soon you're not makin' any sense, eyes all bloody and blisters round your mouth. And the brain damage is pretty much permanent..."

Across the town I could see a dark hump of rock, now known as Sniffer Hill.

"One night," said Mr. Parsons, "they counted 109 kids up there, all on gas."

I asked him what he thought should happen.

He shook his head. "Let em go? Hand it all back? That's what some say."

The Newfoundlanders from below decks were less sympathetic.

"Thirty years ago," said one deckhand, "these Innu had jackshit. So if they wanna go back to playin' cowboys and Indians in the bush, that's fine, but they can start by givin' their skidoos back."

His ginger-haired friend nodded. "We gotta stop spendin' money up here."

"The native people is gettin' *everything*..."

"And they're out of control. You know what? The cops can only do a couple of weeks each at Davis. It's *that* crazy! And last week they actually burnt the police post down."

What's the answer then, I asked. The deckhands shrugged.

One politician had suggested parachuting whisky and rifles into Davis Inlet.

"And then," said the ginger sailor, "you'd let evolution do the rest."

. . .

That night, the ferry moored off Sango Bay.

The liberals had defeated the whisky school, but their solution was bizarre.

"They's building a new town here, six kilometres inland. Costs two hundred million dollars!"

Mr. Parsons said it was supposed to be a fresh start. Davis Inlet would disappear.

"It's madness," said the Newfoundlanders.

Ginger spoke for all: "Ottawa is givin' each Indian a new house—with everythin' in it: telly, carpets and every last freckin' teaspoon. We never had that in our lives . . . You'd never believe what's bein' spent. Last month, the construction workers were out of fries so we brings a couple of pallets up from Newfoundland. The fuel for that trip alone cost forty thousand dollars . . ."

We'd give Sango two years, they said, before it's like Davis.

"Everything busted. Nothing there but bits o' draff and smatch."

<h1 style="text-align:center">114</h1>

Nain took all this to extremes.

It was the most northerly of the Labrador outports, the wildest, and the most picturesque. In winter, many thought it was where the Atlantic tried to smash its way inland. The Esquimaux had always called the inlet "the Long Valley," not because it was shelter but because it was relentless. Every year, a flurry of boats was cartwheeled across the water and smashed against the cobbles. But on a hot summer day, like the day I arrived, it all felt different. Nain looked like a streak of sugar, at the bottom of a deep silver fjord.

It was also the oldest of the Moravian missions, at various times the most quaint and the most flawed. Settlement began with treaties and gifts, and then bewildering treachery. In 1770, Mikak had greeted the missionaries with white fox for her old friend, the Dowager Princess of Wales, and red fox for the governor. But in no time at all she was back among the sorcerers, cursing the Mission and damning its plans. She died in 1795 but her malevolence was almost as persistent as her outfits. Thirty years later, at the lowest point in Moravian fortunes, her family were still wearing the velvet and gold lace that she'd picked up in London, three generations before.

Even now, people spoke of Nain's "aura of negativity." I'd often be told the same story: of how the missionaries voted three times on whether to stay, and of how they voted "No" twice, before a grudging assent. Sometimes, it seemed as if only the negative had survived this election. Even its title—Nain—sounded like denial: nothing, nowhere, never.

The first two centuries would be an endless struggle against nothingness, a constant fight for structure against nullity. Occasionally, the emptiness was simply hunger, as it was in 1816 when the supply-ship *Harmony* failed to call, leaving nothing but berries and rotting whales. At other times, the subtraction was more malicious: floaters with their grog, or Americans after spoils. Looting the *Harmony* was considered fair game in Boston until 1779, when it was granted an American "passport" (by the ambassador to Paris, as it happens, one Benjamin Franklin). After that, the annihilation was more biblical; in the first hundred years, there were eight epidemics—each bringing Nain to the brink of non-existence—a plague of mice, and two outbreaks of canine distemper, both of which killed all the dogs.

These days, all that remained was a lonely Silesian church, and the charred stumps of the Mission. Arctic poppies and cotton grass now swirled along the foreshore, which had once been marshalled into stern displays of rhubarb. Nain, it seems, was still determined to be no one and nothing. There were no gardens any more, just plots of dust. Even odder, the beach was littered with shreds of transport— bits of bicycle, broken boats, skidoo treads, and rotten *komatiks*. It was as if hundreds of fugitives had come this far, and had then taken their chances in the sea. Across the inlet, looming above the town, was a wall of cliffs named after missionary wives: *Maria und Sophie*. They'd always disliked Nain, and now, every afternoon and all winter, their shadows hung over it like anger.

Nain shuddered. It was in the grip of its extremes—more social workers, more crime, more drink than anywhere else of its size. Eighty per cent of people were unemployed, and there were still Inuit living twenty to a house. "SMASHIN BUMPKINS," as the graffiti said. The ferry crew called it "Viet-Nain" but this was hyperbole: Nain bore its trauma in silence. From the moment I stepped ashore, I felt as if I had the town to myself.

Just me and the dogs and the dried fish.

· · ·

The Moravians had long gone, but they'd left a straggler: John Murphy.

It was hard to make sense of the composite Murphys. John was married to an Inuk called Tabea, and lived in a cabin behind the mission. Like their town, their lives seemed to lie in components. It was easy enough to ascertain the different parts but I could never assemble the whole. Tabea, barely a generation out of sorcery, had become a chapel servant, wore an avocado suit and was angry that she no longer felt Inuit. John was angry that he still felt Christian, painted Labrador as if it was China, and had become a Buddhist. None of this slotted together, and was at odds with an earlier life—the boy from Illinois who'd arrived with the Grenfell Association in 1963, defected and run off to teach for the Moravians.

"There was even less of Nain then than there is now," said Tabea, and laughed.

"No phones, no airfield," said John. "Just dogs."

"And no liquor then," added Tabea, "and our people ate more seal."

Tabea thought the rot had started with the arrival of biscuits and democracy.

Prismatic and disjointed, these were the best moments of my time in Nain. I spent hours with the Murphys, grilling char or clambering up into the wilderness with John. In his own complicated way, he was thoughtful and wise. But, like everything with John, his wisdom was fragmentary and sometimes we stood too close to the mosaic to know what we were seeing. He was happiest rootling around in botany, zoology and sorcery, and I imagined that collecting scraps of knowledge was a natural reaction to living in the wreckage of Nain. But on the bigger questions, we lost the sense of picture, and John was adrift in a void of his own, with his poems and facts, and the horror.

Where did it all go wrong? he'd say. How did the killing begin?

When I asked what he meant by this, he said I'd find out, soon enough.

115

I stayed on the other side of the brook, amongst the settlers.

"This is a place of complexity," warned John. "Nothing's what it seems."

Tabea was more forthright.

"They look down on us, the other side of the brook."

Surely she didn't include my landlady in this broad geographical swipe? Christine Ford seemed so emotionally weary, too exhausted for contempt. Nain was dismantling her; a husband had long ago fled for Ontario, the money was gone, her cabin was rotting away and now the wolves had eaten her cats. Even her face, still handsome, seemed almost uninhabited. Perhaps Christine Ford lived somewhere else, partly in the past and partly in fantasy. Her living-room was decorated with pictures of her ancestors, two Elvis clocks and a large photograph of Princess Diana on the day of her wedding.

Amongst the portraits, there was grandeur and surprise. I spotted Wilfred Grenfell ("a family friend"), and little Julius Ford, circa 1910, in black boots and Eton collar. My father, said Christine Ford, and this is my mother, Rosie. *Black Island,* read the caption, *1939.* Rosie Pamak is an Inuk, a woman of dark, rich strength and Mandarin beauty. In her hands, she held the fox she'd just killed. It was a haunting image, not least for the look in Rosie's eyes. They were beautiful and yet indelibly sad, as if she'd seen the beginning of the end, as I now know she had.

Only food invaded the dreams of Christine Ford. She was a cook and, every day, she shrugged into a survival suit, and took a boat out to the mines where she worked. She'd leave me a dish of wild berries and crab-cakes, and then be back at her stove at night. In her cooking, she seemed to rediscover all the colours and flavour that had leached from her life—hot, buttery fillets of arctic char, succulent wedges of caribou pie and flutes of bakeapple fool. In the mind of Christine Ford, taste had replaced all other sensations, including unhappiness and sound. It was only the presence of a stranger that made her conscious of the silence, and so we listened to the radio, in Inuktitut.

It was broadcast from the shed next door, the OKalaKatiget Society. "You should go see them," said Christine Ford suddenly.

I said I would, and my interview was broadcast all along the coast. What's the difference, they asked, between Labrador and London?

After a while, I realised I wasn't the only tenant at Christine Ford's. There was another man, living in the cellar, a deaf-mute called Jeremiah. He also worked in the mine and preferred the dark. I hardly ever saw him. His grandmother was called Sarah Ittulak, and she scavenged at the tip.

I met her there once, whilst I was out on a walk. It was an unearthly place, a city of fridges and Arctic junk, dead huskies, bits of bear, skidoos and oil drums. I was surprised how prosperous it looked, so fat and mountainous compared to Nain. Perhaps one day it would engulf the town that fed it, and at last Nain would become truly Nothing. Only the scavengers saw any sense of urgency, as they reclaimed their town. Old Sarah was trying on a pair of skates.

She spoke little English but thanked me for stopping.

She then told me something I now realise is probably the key to this disaster.

"Hebron," she said. "We came from Hebron."

116

Hebron is where the dying began, a plague that turned to slaughter.

Sarah was only two when the *Harmony* returned from England, with a horrible surprise. Within days, Spanish flu had brought down half the Inuit, and a foul stench settled on the town. By the end of 1918, so many had died they'd had to be carried out to sea and dumped. Hebron would never recover from this tragedy, and nor would the Moravians. After that, they said, they felt a door had closed in the Inuit conscience.

But what had been merely tragic for Hebron, proved apocalyptic further south. OKak simply ceased to exist. I looked for it on my map: it had gone. Of the original population of 270, only 39 survived. The first wave of sickness killed all the men, leaving only women and children to face what was coming. Among them were two sisters, the only members of their family to survive. One of them was barely ten, but already a creature of Mandarin beauty. It was Rosie Pamak, about to witness the end of her world.

First, the dogs went mad, and fought amongst themselves. Then they broke loose and started eating the dead and killing the weak. Some of the survivors tried running for the bush, where they died and were eaten in their tilts. One of Rosie's friends, a girl of seven, held out for five weeks, alone against a siege of dogs. Others survived on whatever came to hand: starfish, flour mould, puppies, anything. By the end, the dead were stacked so high the Moravians had no choice but to douse them in fuel. Rosie watched as almost everyone she'd ever known melted into flames. Then, as the pyres burned, the fire was carried to the houses, and OKak disappeared.

Of the survivors, some went on to Hebron, until that too folded.

Others headed straight for Nain. They'd never be happy, never accepted and never united. The Inuit of the far north had been among the most finely adapted people on the planet, and now they felt themselves adrift and pointless. All brought with them their indelible despair.

Back on the other side of the brook, it was said that Inuit art was thriving.

I often tried to reach the artists. Out here, Nain was at its most elemental: dried fish, doors bashed with rocks, dirt-bikes and odd words appearing, like "PAINKILLER" and a picture of a ghost. I had a vague idea that the artists might have made sense of it all, because no one else had. The Inuit said the police still talked to them in jargon, and made rules without their elders. The schools had managed exactly the opposite, and had swamped the Inuit in kayak-building and Inuktitut. The result, said John, was a form of apartheid.

I was wrong about the artists. The first one I visited had drunk so much shine he couldn't make sense of anything. "Art for art's sake," he kept saying, until even this was incoherent. All morning, I sat in his shack listening to the art-babble he'd borrowed, distorted and reassembled. Next to us, a woman slept under a greasy quilt, and a child ate crisps off the stove. The sculptor's art was beautiful—bears, whales and hunters—but merely affirmative. It reassured the world that, despite everything, a "primitive" people had survived. Hotels loved it, and so did governments. There was an invitation from the Queen nailed to the wall, and every week the sculptor earned—and drank—several hundred dollars' worth of shine. Art was now, quite literally, killing him. *"ArFfra Sake,"* as he would say.

My visits to another artist were even more disconcerting. I'd often seen John Terriak down on the beach, hacking out whales with a drill, but he was always out when I called. His wife showed me in, and then went back to her puzzle-book. Their cabin was light and airy, and a kitten played among the cushions.

"Our dogs eat richer than the welfare people," said Mrs. Terriak proudly.

I asked who the boy was in the photograph, a dust-mask round his neck.

"That's our son, Charlie," said Mrs. Terriak, and somewhere deep within a dam burst, dragging her along in a torrent of grief. I felt suddenly ashamed. What had I unleashed and how could I calm it? I watched helplessly as the howls of pain subsided, and as the tears splashed across the puzzles.

Eventually, Mrs. Terriak found her breath again.

The boys who beat Charlie to death, she told me, were only fifteen. "So drunk they'd remember nothing."

That was 1997, only the beginning of the forgettable, unforgotten killings.

117

There was hardly anyone not affected by this carnage.

Mrs. Terriak said never a day went by when she didn't think of Charlie.

Soon afterwards, the Murphys' daughter was killed by her boyfriend, Simeon.

People lost count of the number that died. The police said it was worse in spring, as the long winters turned to murder. Death became casual, almost frivolous, delivered with guns or picks and drunken fists. Across Canada, Nain became synonymous with pointless, motiveless slaughter. Viet-Nain.

Then, at the moment when the killing might have eased, it became simply introspective. Grenfell once wrote that suicide was almost unknown among the Inuit: jumping off cliffs, he said, was the "harikari of Eskimo-land." Not any more. Suicide was now exuberant and infectious, no longer a mark of personal collapse but an expression of collective failure. Death had never snapped up the young so easily, not since being bubonic. By 2000, said John Murphy, it felt as if we were losing a pupil almost every other day. Nearly everyone lost kinsmen in this unbiblical plague. Jeremiah, down in the cellar, lost both his brothers, a catastrophe that would leave him permanently speechless.

Nain had had a communal nervous breakdown. Even the adults began to wonder why they were still alive. Many withdrew into their own world, from which they'd yet to emerge. Others just drank, and Nain began to feel uneasily spectral. The government reacted with panic, lavishing its policies with money and confusion. More social workers appeared, and missionaries, but the answers eluded them. "Having come to Nain to understand why so many people are committing suicide," ran the Mennonites' report, "the greater lesson has been to understand why so many chose life." Nain, said its author, was "a festering sore full of gory beauty."

This plague never really ended, it just ran out of victims. There were still those who blamed the Moravians; it was said they'd protracted the agony, by making a spectacle of suicide. In the old days, said Tabea, suicides were refused Christian rites, and were buried on the paths. The funerals had only encouraged others, she said, to seek their moment of glory.

"And now our cemetery's full of kids! Go and see for yourself."

I did as she suggested, but there was little encouragement. The *Friedhof* had always been a field of plagues. At least twenty-nine of the plots dated from the Spanish flu. In one corner was a shack called The Dead House, where those who'd perished in winter were once stored until the thaw. The suicides were buried in rows: Renatus, Paulus, Julius, Gustav . . . Even though few of them were churchgoers, the Moravians had decided not to punish their families, and had taken the children in. They'd been buried, I noticed, in the manner of their ancestors, with offerings and grave goods: coins, dog-leads, knives and toys. Perhaps one day, long after Nain has ceased to exist, the Curwen of a future generation will come along and find these things. He will wonder, as people do today, what powerful forces had been at work, to effect such a virulent disaster.

Meanwhile, I wondered if all this meant the end for the Moravians in Labrador.

It hadn't been a period of unqualified adoration. At the very start, Captain Cartwright had said the Esquimaux despised them (although what he may have been seeing was just a conflict of loyalties). Rink blamed the Christians for undermining Esquimau authority, and collapsing 10,000 years of discipline. But that was 1875, when it was still just possible to believe that the Inuit might escape participation in the world. At the very least, the Moravians had prepared them for a future that was inevitable.

Others say it wasn't a preparation at all but the creation of dependence.

This was Grenfell's line (until he decided they'd been neglectful over syphilis).

John Murphy thought he remembered colonialism, back in 1963— palaces, gardens and promenades. Whenever the pastor went shooting, he said, the chapel servants used to carry his guns. Even Tabea sometimes felt her loyalties in turmoil.

"We were puppets," she'd say. "It was their little world."

But was this true? Hadn't the Labrador Inuit survived, along with their language? It wasn't hard to recall the fate of another race, the Beothuks. Hadn't they struggled on, without any friendly Germans?

118

Curwen sailed back to Newfoundland through the blades of a storm.

For such a dangerous voyage, the expedition had separated. Dr. Bobardt and the nurses took the steamer, and were lavishly seasick. Only Curwen sailed on the *Albert,* together with the crew and little Lorenzo Rumbolt. It was a vicious ordeal; the mainsail was ragged, the keel split, and the boom was ripped away.

Grenfell, meanwhile, was still out in his launch, on a side-trip of his own. No one knew where he was going, and, says Curwen, "I do not think he knew himself." One moment he was in Nain and then he'd pop up in Zoar. Captain Trezise didn't care where he was, as long as it was somewhere else. Grenfell's tendency to hurl himself overboard, after tennis balls or ducks, had alarmed everyone. He was still an appalling sailor, and in the next few years, he'd wreck several boats, and at least one crewman would rip up his contract and flee for dry land. It wasn't that Grenfell couldn't see the danger ("In Heaven, there'll be no more sea," he joshed) but he saw it all as a challenge. "Whenever two courses are open," he'd say, "take the most venturesome." Whilst, to most people, this might have sounded pleasantly meaningless, to his sailors it was terrifying. "He is a great anxiety to us," wrote Curwen, as Grenfell got lost for the umpteenth time.

Perhaps all they were seeing was the beginning of greatness. Grenfell was about to make Labrador one of the greatest "causes" of his generation, a feat that wasn't achieved by compromise. What others saw as impulsive, Grenfell regarded as quick-thinking. They may have distrusted his over-embellished stories, and the affectations of his dress (odd socks for Buckingham Palace or a yellow suit for Harvard), but it was all publicity and character. Even his heartiness—all that icy water and snorting at danger—was turned to good effect; Grenfell was tough, exemplary and—in the days before the Great War—heroic. From the people that mattered most—the general public—there was adoration.

It was always harder for those in his immediate circle, whether on the *Albert* or on land. Grenfell had no particular requirement for friendship, and often he took a rather lofty view of it (he once said, of his rugby team-mates at Oxford, "I loved them but resented their self-sufficiency . . ."). At other times he was simply priggish, and would attribute the flaws in his relationships to his own virtuosity. Of one of the 1893 nurses, he wrote: "I fear greatly Nurse Cawardine is not a Christian. Oh it will be a pity. We must make it a matter of earnest prayer that she may become one or she will be a terrible hindrance." Nor was he interested in courting popularity among his patients. If he saw a fisherman spitting, he'd swipe the man's hat off and use it to mop up the slick. Individual human frailty appalled him, as if it were a distraction from the bigger picture. Despite the malnutrition and exhaustion, he'd insist on sermons like "Sleep as the Urging of the Devil."

As always, Curwen's feelings about Grenfell have to be salvaged from the footnotes. Their relationship was never more than professional, and they didn't stay in touch. Grenfell never acknowledged Curwen's contribution in any of his autobiographies, and when he does mention him he spells his name wrong. Curwen also damns by omission; he's never sorry to be parted from Grenfell, and never pleased to be reunited; he's never unduly worried when his superintendent goes missing, and never there for the triumphant returns. The two men were fundamentally at odds, Curwen reserved, discreet, and contemplative, and Grenfell everything but. He even resented Curwen his moments of reflection, and reacted with self-righteousness. "It's all very well for Curwen to write long letters," he told his mother. "I haven't nearly the time he has."

About his departure from Labrador, Curwen was equally equivocal. Although, on his return, he'd give lectures about the Esquimaux, my mother and my aunt say he hardly mentioned Labrador in later years. Amongst his papers, I found few clues; a promise to his family that he'd consult them before returning; regret that his medical work was done. In 109 days in Labrador, he'd seen 1,052 patients, visited ten outports and held meetings for over 6,000 people. He added no further comment to this, other than to express surprise that he'd put on eight pounds.

There'd been a plan to visit the French Shore en route south, but the weather wouldn't allow it. Instead, it picked up the *Albert* and hurled it at St. John's.

119

My last day, I came across a bear, undecided whether to run for it or eat me.

After my walks with John, I often clambered out of the fjord, up into the bog laurel and poppies. The taiga gave way to tundra, and from up here I could look down on inlets, islands, a forest smoothed flat by the wind, and the millions of shiny dents that cover the plains of northern Labrador. I'd scrabble on, through arctic bramble and liverwort, and then the mountain would open out onto a carpet of moss that probably still bears my footprints. Once, I picked up a caribou skull, nibbled away by lemmings and mice. Another time, I stumbled into the aftermath of a wild, geomorphic party, vast erratics dumped across the pavement as the last glaciers rolled away.

It was brutally beautiful—or was it beautifully brutal? The thought had occurred to me, more than once, that there was something wrong in the way I felt about all this. Here I was in one of the most depressing towns imaginable, and yet unable to feel depression, merely curiosity. It was almost as if my journey had turned into fiction, and I was no longer able to absorb the detail without a sense of detachment, as if I wasn't really there at all. How could I be so callous? I was horrified by my own reaction, and yet at the same time exhilarated. Perhaps this was a perverted characteristic of my own, or perhaps all travel ends up like this? Perhaps the voyager is no more than the voyeur, seeking pain and beauty that's always someone else's?

These questions were easier up in the hills, standing back from Nain. But nothing was decided. Which is the best part of a journey: the culture shock of the beginning or the theatre that it becomes? I couldn't even decide if I'd fallen for Labrador, like Grenfell had, or if I'd merely acknowledged it, like Curwen. All I could be sure of was that I now found myself among superlatives: best, worst, maddest, most beautiful and last.

It was at a moment like this, of deep indecision, that I was found by the bear.

We were on the edge of the dump, and the bear was eating some skin or dog. It was an immature American Black Bear, about five feet long and the weight of a sofa. As it caught my scent, its head swivelled myopically from side to side, trying to place the intruder. People have often compared bears to humans but I couldn't see it. It was like comparing an excavator with the family saloon. This great, gleaming rust-black truck of a creature was perfectly adapted for a life in the taiga—a life spent digging and dozing, fuelling on berries and ants, ripping open tree-trunks, and shovelling up mice and eggs and bits of dogs.

I could see Sarah Ittulak just below me, still scavenging. The ancient Esquimaux had believed the bear was sacred, and never referred to it by name. Sarah hardly gave it a glance. Black bears were now merely rivals. Nothing was sacred any more, just parasitic.

But for the bear there were still simple, instinctive choices—meat, flight, kill. I watched for a while as its light snout probed the air, undecided just like me.

Then, with no decision made, I slipped away.

A curtain call for the cod? By 1968, the Newfoundland catch would have stretched nose-to-tail three times round the world. Now, the ocean is all but empty.

The Narrows and the most easterly rocks of the Americas.
New York is still twelve hundred miles to the west.

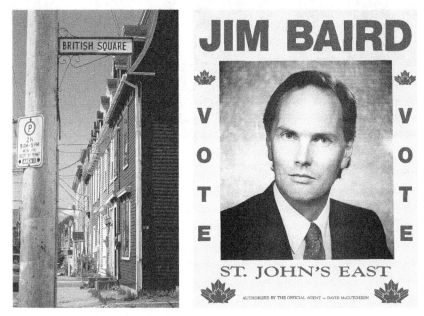

JIM BAIRD

V O T E   V O T E

ST. JOHN'S EAST

AUTHORIZED BY THE OFFICIAL AGENT — DAVID McCUTCHEON

Left St. John's today. Neither British nor truly North American, the city is like an
old fishing fleet nailed to the hill. *Right* Jim Baird, book wizard, merchant and Johnsman.
He once stood for office but fell in the early brawling.

The author on the old stage, Hermitage. Since the cod moratorium of 1992, over fifty thousand people have left the island.

Left Joey Smallwood. Anti-fish and anti-sea, he urged the islanders to burn their boats.

The hardy outporter. Recently, Job Andersen fought a polar bear with just a poker and his pet goat.

Above The MV *Northern Ranger* enters iceberg alley. Every year some three thousand bergs come groaning down from Greenland.
Left In 1772, the *Esquimau* Attuiock thrilled London with his sealskin and dogs. Even the king stopped to salute him.

Grenfell's House, St. Anthony. In 1981, his medical empire was finally sold to the state, for one dollar.

Above An iceberg in Battle Harbour, Labrador. The ice was forever disembowelling government ferries. *Below* Battle today. In Victorian times it was the capital of fish, "the most lawless and disorderly place on the whole coast."

The Spearing brothers, who for nearly sixty years fished off Labrador.
They were often out for days in open boats.

Left Albert Andersen and a
sledge-dog. Labradoreans still talk
of grog, "native territory," settlers
and bruins (bears).

A murderous Labradorean sledge-dog.
If need be, these half-wolves will kill and
eat their human masters.

Chamber Cove,
where in February 1942,
USS *Truxtun* was wrecked.
The debris still washes up
on the shore.

Below left Outporters like
John Kelly rescued 46
sailors. Another 110 were
drowned in freezing
bunker oil.

Below right Charlotte Kelly,
now eighty-eight, helped
clean the survivors.
The Americans would not
forget their debt.

The road from here? Outports established four hundred years ago
are now being "resettled." Petites was abandoned in 2003.

Act V: Back via Old New France

"Fish" s'applique à tous les produits de la mer.
—France's view of its treaty rights,
December 1888

Lord Knutsford is of the opinion that Her Majesty's government could not admit that crustacea are fish.
—British Colonial Office response, February 1889

They are essentially good people. I know that, but what sickens me is their simple failure to resist the impulse of savagery.
—Farley Mowat, *A Whale for the Killing*

120

Back in Newfoundland, the sensation of being edible soon began to fade.

At first, it was replaced by the cold seep of anticlimax, more to do with leaving Labrador than returning to The Rock. But then, gradually, I began to warm to a new wilderness: lower, smoother, dimpled with ponds and tufted in waist-high forest. Almost every feature had been planed away by the blasts that crashed across the straits from Labrador, and the tip of this great thumb of rock had been so ruthlessly roasted that it was now known as Burnt Cape, and had spawned its own mutants like dwarf hawksbeard and the Burnt Cape cinquefoil.

But the inhabitants of the Great Northern Peninsula didn't seem to think anything of this ferocity. They expected nature to be boisterous, and were always rebuilding their homes. In St. Juliens I talked to a woman whose only complaint was that she was woken each morning by the whales. Another time, I met a couple carrying buckets of dirt and gravel to the graveyard, off to re-bury their forebears after the winter.

Roads had only been scraped into the interior in the last five years. Instead of traffic they'd brought vegetables. Long queues of carrots and cabbages now marched along the verges into the barrens. I hired a car and followed a long slash of radishes for about twenty miles, until it ended in a gardener.

"By jammy, it's warm in here," he said, as if he'd never been inland before, until being carried here on a wave of mutant radishes.

What about the moose, I wondered? Moose were now the gargoyles leering from every corner of my day—luggage-faced, ugly, skinny-arsed, bog-squelching oafs. They loved the road, not just for the car-wrecking, but for the vegetables it brought. Now every other moose in Canada lived in Newfoundland, and on the Great Northern Peninsula they were eight to the acre. Once, said the gardener, the Mounties used to try and stop us poaching them.

"But now it's moose pie every night," he said. "With radishes."

"Are they dangerous?" I asked.

"Oh my jumpin', my son, dey'd give yous a good butt in de ruttin' season! And dey rolls around in deir own piss till dey's proper hummy."

That night, a moose came over to investigate my anxiety. I was sleeping on the edge of Pistolet Bay, and woke to a powerful stench. Peering upwards through the tent fabric, I could make out a huge shaggy silhouette looking down at me. I was being evaluated again, by a couple of pounds of brain set in seven hundred pounds of muscle and girder. The decision seemed to take ages but eventually I was assessed as inedible or not worth the fight, and the moose farted and lurched off down the beach.

Until less than a century ago, this was the outer margin of an unofficial country, a land in limbo; *La Petite République,* the French Shore.

121

I had a vague plan to complete that part of Curwen's journey smashed by the weather.

In his day, the French Shore was neither truly French nor wholly British. It was still Britain's prize to France for losing three wars (the spoils of defeat?), and was still a legal desert. Ever since its creation in 1713, the powers had been picking away at each other's rights, leaving nothing but an outline. No one was allowed to settle there; the French, because their rights were limited to fishing; the British, because the French rights were exclusive. The French Shore remained like this—legally empty—for almost two centuries, ungoverned, unrepresented, unowned and politically fallow. Such diplomatic petulance would have been curious anywhere, but in Newfoundland it was stupefying; a quarter of the island lay inert—over 1,500 miles of coastline, including the entire Great Northern Peninsula, and the best, most fertile, lands to the south.

The law was assiduous in enforcing this absurdity, and was energetically ignored. The Newfoundland Assembly declared it illegal to sell bait to the French but the *Terre-Neuvas* (as they called themselves) were always able to tempt a little fish-smuggling with liquor. Even the rules against settlement were highly permeable, until they were finally abolished in 1881. By then, there were already over 8,600 souls squatting on the shore, and not a doctor among them. Curwen would have been busy.

He'd have found himself among a peculiar people. For a start, only half of them were French, the rest forming part of a rag-tag fish militia. The French considered their rights far too valuable to be abandoned every winter (their enterprise was twice the size of Britain's, and fed France through 153 fish-only days a year), and so, to protect their gear, the *armateurs* employed a tatty rabble—the *gardiens*. Some were Micmac Indians from the mainland, businesslike in killing, but most were just drifters carried here by the currents, by debts, desertion, potato famines, assizes, clearances and ignorance. Wild and ungoverned, they were perfectly adapted to this wild, ungoverned land. By the 1880s, travellers were telling tales of a delirious anarchy of feasts and ecstatic gunfire. One report lists the food at a wedding: "twenty-seven enormous puddings, seven beavers, several hares and ptarmigan, a corresponding supply of vegetables, some rum . . . and cake ad infinitum."

But French authority was light and, unlike the cake and beavers, wouldn't last forever. There'd been an indulgent fishocracy: foremen, captains, *lignotiers* (who baited the lines) and—most important of all— *les élangeurs,* those who'd cut out and counted the tongues. But, by 1904, the rule of the Tonguemen was at an end. France had lost interest in Newfoundland, and no longer squabbled with Britain over fish. Africa was now the prize, and so Paris gave up all its rights to the French Shore in return for part of Lake Chad and a snippet of Gambia. Newfoundland was whole at last.

I often wondered if anything of *La Petite République* had survived the island's celebrations. The map of the peninsula was still determinedly French, with names like Grandois, Griquet and St. Lunaire, but the patois now was Waterford and seal. People showed me old French ovens and fancy graves, and in Croque I found the names of the old French schooners carved in the cliffs: *Bisson, Pomone 1868, Roland 1862* and *Chateau.* But *les élangeurs* were nowhere to be found, or perhaps their genes had simply been swamped in Noseworthys, Besseys and Tuckers.

"We's all a bit French," they'd say unconvincingly.

The gardener had said there were still Frenchmen—somewhere— down the shore. But that was all, and, in the meantime, there were rumours of another incursion.

The Vikings had landed, out at L'Anse aux Meadows.

122

I can't enjoy this Viking episode because I can't contain my disbelief.

That's not to say I didn't like L'Anse aux Meadows. Teetering at the very tip of the peninsula, it was as preposterous as anywhere can be, before slithering into myth. I was amazed at so much matchwood in the face of so much liquid violence. Labrador was only seventeen miles away across the straits, and was always bombarding the village with storms and bits of ice the size of supertankers. There were only thirty-two inhabitants left and almost all of them were Deckers. No roads had ventured out here until 1960, and every winter there was an invasion of polar bears.

L'Anse had no natural harbour, and the bay was scattered with catastrophes. Most obvious of all was the SS *Langlecrag,* now slobbed across Big Sacred Island, which is where it had landed the day it jumped out of the sea in 1947. Beyond it was another cake of rock, Belle Isle, so pale and blue it had almost faded into fantasy.

Even in the name, L'Anse aux Meadows, there's more than a hint of fantasy and a smack of the wild *république.* There wasn't a meadow in the entire peninsula—unless they meant that gush of salty knots and weeds that was pouring off the hills. I spent the entire morning in hand-to-hand combat with the flora before opting for the saner explanation; "Meadows" was just the Decker way of saying *méduses.* To *les élangeurs,* this was Jellyfish Creek. These days, the streak of whisky that babbles across the heath is known as Black Duck Brook.

Out on the battered ocean edge of L'Anse, I met an old sheep-farmer, who'd been cleared out by the bears. At first, he threatened me with flu, and said he was still handy with an axe, but then we discovered that we'd sort of met before; he was Job Andersen, the grandson of Curwen's "splendid" Norwegian from Makkovic. He told me that—as well as the sheep—he'd once had a dog-team and a cow. Now, all that was left was his plywood farm, two ducks, Fluff the cat and a magnificent fighting goat.

"She's not for milk, just fightin' polar bears! Bought her in Griquet for a pittance. Feller said she's good for fightin' but he had three, and gave me him for nothin'. Bawls at bears he does, could wake the *fuckin' dead*!"

Job's stories always erupted like this, like a fight with Popeye. His face swelled and scowled, fists flew and the animals ran for cover. Plots were in a constant state of flux, and characters changed sex mid-story, or were dead in the evening version, and resurrected in the morning. But the bear attacks had really happened. Job and Goat showed me the window, ripped by massive claws. The greatest land-based man-eater in the world had tried to prise Job out of his bathroom.

"I was inside beatin' it with the poker. Goat was out here buttin' it up the arse . . ." Job swam a huge 30.30 bullet before my eyes. "Next time, we blast the bitch . . ."

Goat came over to have her beard stroked.

"Wouldn't sell her," said Job, "not for money."

I asked him about the strange mounds, out on the heath.

"The old Indian Camps? We used to play on them as kids!"

Then, one day, his cousin, George Decker, had brought someone to look at them.

"Spoke the Devil's language—*Norwegian!* Said he was lookin' for Vikings."

Helge Ingstad was the only man wistful enough for such a task.

He was sure that being a Viking would assist in the search, besides being intellectually nomadic. It had been an odd life, spent either surviving the uninhabitable or chasing the unattainable. He'd started as a lawyer, spent four years trapping in the Canadian Arctic, galloped across New Mexico in search of the Lost Tribe of Geronimo and— in 1933—had ended up governor of Northern Greenland at the age of thirty-three. Then, after a spell on Spitzbergen, he decided that the Vikings had settled in Newfoundland, and started knocking up the evidence to prove it.

Ingstad wasn't the first to place the Vikings in the Americas, but he was the most persistent. Torfæus had stirred up the idea in 1705, but others soon followed. Fifty years later, Paul Mallet, in his *Histoire de Dannemarc*, located the Norse in Newfoundland for the first time, but provoked nothing more than alternative suggestions. Over the next two centuries, Vikings would spring up everywhere from Greenland to Nantucket. Grenfell was determined to have them in Labrador but by 1934 there were already 340 books scattering the Vikings all along the eastern seaboard.

The problem for everyone was the same; the only evidence of any Atlantic adventures were two rather lanky tales from Iceland, *The Greenlanders' Saga* and that of Erik the Red. I remembered these yarns from childhood, and have always thought them better left there. It's not that there's anything wrong with the stories (three Eriksson brothers take up the unfinished voyages of Bjarni Herjolfsson, find some grapes and fight the *skraelings*), it's just that—the moment it all sounds credible—out come the Unipeds, or the *skraelings* try out a bit of new technology (a Norse axe) and cut their own heads off. To me, it always seemed that these tales had been round the campfire once too often. The two sagas didn't even match. Like a pantomime horse, they could be quite convincing in step, but whenever they took off separately, it all fell apart.

Ingstad was undeterred, although his problem was always the grapes. According to the sagas, Leif Ericsson loses one of his men, a fabulously ugly German (bulging forehead, shifty eyes, short and puny) called Tyrkir. After a few days, Tyrkir rolls out of the grass, splendidly drunk and announces the discovery of vines. Leif fills a whole skiff with grapes, and calls the place *Vinland*. This might have presented Ingstad with something of an obstacle; grapes won't grow anywhere near Newfoundland, and the nearest are fourteen days' sailing to the south. But Ingstad didn't let this stop him; he applied an archaic translation to the word *vin* and came up with "grass." Imagine his delight, therefore, when, in 1960—after tearing up the American coast—he arrived at a place called L'Anse aux Meadows.

"George took him out to the lumps," chuckled Job, "and they decides it's Viking."

Job's cousin was every bit Ingstad's equal when it came to dreaming up the unlikely. He'd knocked off the end of his house because it was haunted, and told stories of ferocious women, more ghosts and a butcher who dug up his meat in the graveyard. George also had a huge muzzle-loader and convinced Ingstad that he could shoot twenty birds with one shot. Ingstad was rather in awe of him, and assumed he was the village leader, a curious idea to those of the old *république* ("No fuckin' leaders here," said Job). It was a joke George enjoyed for the next three years, until the excitement overcame him, and Ingstad had him buried, down by the brook.

Meanwhile, the archaeology began, under Ingstad's wife, Anne Stine. "I loved her," said Job fiercely. "She was an angel, always lightsome." Job and the others were employed as scrapers for the next five years.

"She thought the world of me. I was her little helper."

"And Helge Ingstad?"

Job scowled. "Crusty as the devil. He'd go for ye just like that!"

I clambered back across the heath, where Job, his angel and the diabolical Ingstad had rolled back the peat. They'd found eight lumpy rings (which were said to be houses), but surprisingly little else; a cloakpin, a nail, a chunk of European pine, a fragment of bone needle, a spindle-whorl and a few pounds of slag. It was enough, said the Ingstads, to prove the site was Norse. Ten years after the scraping began, L'Anse became the first-ever UN Heritage Site.

"Did *you* find anything?" I'd asked Job.

Two things, he'd told me, but he didn't know what they were.

"And I didn't give a fuck, long as I was paid."

Elsewhere, Viking fever erupted and L'Anse was no longer alone. There were visits from sea-planes, warships, Dr. Junius Bird (with bottles of brandy for his fellow-archaeologists) and several heads of state. Then a blacktop found its way across the bog, followed by a concrete museum, lawns, boardwalks, coach parties, and of course all the camp followers with their Viking Pizzas and Odin's Boat Tours.

I set off down the beach. Half way along, a brand new longhouse had sprouted out of the tussocks. Inside, a couple of well-shampooed Vikings were roasting wienies on their swords. They were arguing about the best fish and chips in St. Anthony, and so I crept away. For their predecessors, life's choices hadn't been quite so bewildering. According to the sagas, it was all brutally simple; the young squires are constantly straining for a taste of married women, and the *skraelings* keep up their war; some days, the bay is black with war-kayaks, and at least one Viking loses his head to a mysterious missile, a sheep-belly bomb; only one child survives—the first white American—and he's called Snorri. Within a few years, say the sagas, everybody's packing up and going home.

That night I camped on the shore where Job's sheep were eaten.

The wind groaned, and snapped at the tent and I was gravelled in rain. I suppose I slept: it was a night of bloody claws, deep-pan Valhalla Pizzas and exploding bellies. But I was also awake, tormented by the sound of thousands of feet marching through the moss, and by the thought that this was all some big Norwegian joke. In the confusion of the storm, nothing made much sense. Why in forty years of excavations had no one found any bodies or tombs? Was it *really* because the Vikings feared being left in unconsecrated ground? Thorstein Ericsson had expressed no such concerns when an arrow landed among his fatty entrails in 1002. And why had a piece of medieval European pine survived but none from Newfoundland? As for the other artefacts, there was conspicuously little. Was it simply the least necessary to prove it all Norse? Ingstad had spent the rest of his life navigating through the accusations.

Dawn was gentler, and was wafted ashore in banks of sparkling fog.

The storm had replenished Job's ferocity. "There was never Vikins here!"

"Why not?" I asked.

"Was they so stunned they'd settle down in this wind? I ain't hugger-muggered, boy. There was no fuckin' Vikins here, and that's that."

Even the elfin Anne Stine hadn't won Job over, although he still loved her. "I always meant to go see her, but a few years back they wrote to say she died."

Helge Ingstad had survived her, and—like one of his legends—he'd enjoyed a life spanning three different centuries. Best of all, his fellow-Vikings had never doubted him. He must be one of the most eccentric men ever to have had a Norwegian state funeral.

He died in March 2001, at the age of a hundred and one.

123

At St. Anthony, the old *république* had taken a large dose of Grenfell.

There were Grenfell houses and Grenfell hospitals, Grenfell streets and old sunken Grenfell wharves. One side of the inlet was for Grenfell's people, and the other side was for the Grenfell patients and fishermen. Some say this made Grenfell an imperialist, but to me it all looked so much more train-layout than empire. Between the two sides of the town were all the accessories the Grenfellists would need for their little world: radio masts, gleaming tanks of fuel, truck shops and miniature warehouses. I even saw Grenfell ambulances tinkling through this scene, and a clock-tower in Grenfell green.

It all reminded me of my old school. This is how Mostyn House would have looked if it had been dragged across the Atlantic and re-assembled in an inlet of dark-blue forest. It was the enterprise of a single determined man with an unstoppable urge for livery and pageant. Whilst Algie was making a purse out of his sow's ear, the old Mostyn Arms, his brother Wilfred was conjuring order from the stink of St. Anthony. In the years following the 1893 expedition, there hadn't been much to build on, except starvation. The population had eaten every mussel and every winkle on the beach, and were so nauseated by the constant herring they could hardly keep it down. Grenfell moved into the old courthouse, and furnished it with flour barrels and newspaper stuck to the walls. To begin with, there were surgeries and competitions for prizes of meat—greasy-pole fights and running races. But, by 1900, he'd blasted the beginnings of a hospital out of the rock, re-introduced Christmas and started a co-operative. Mostyn House contributed first a bed and six footballs, and then cases of old shot-guns and muskets.

Once again, I had the sensation of Grenfells off on their own campaign. In the early 1900s, this was a worrying thought for the Fish-ermen's Mission. At first, they tried to clip Grenfell back, withdrawing him to the chilly boredom of Gorleston. But he wouldn't be restrained. Grenfell was now incapable of working within an organisation, and wanted to march at the head of his own ideas. Even his old mentor, Sir Frederick Treves, was concerned ("His work now seems to have little to do with deep sea fishermen"). In 1907, Grenfell set up a new body in his own image, and five years later the IGA, or International Grenfell Association, had eased the mission out of Newfoundland.

Down on the waterfront, I found myself at the heart of this great ambition. These were the old wooden Grenfell Premises. They were supposed to be the beginning of industry, an end to the slavery of fish. But—as with so much of Grenfell—the result seemed rather less grandiose than his intentions. The workshops were now a museum to the things they'd produced—sealskin dolls, jigsaws, hook-mats reading *Do Not Spit*, Christmas cards and carvings (Grenfell's fishermen had carved so many walrus chessmen that eventually they'd had to import elephant ivory). Although it didn't look much like industry, these handicrafts were much appreciated in America, and the funds began to flow. "Grenfell Cloth" became known for its obstinacy, flew round the track with Stirling Moss and was taken up Everest by Sir John Hunt. Nowadays, the only knicknacks still sold were scented candles and embroidered parkas. The embroiders had even effected a small improvement to Sir Wilfred's appearance with the mysterious removal of his moustache.

The old Doctors' Mess had long given way to concrete. Grenfell had cut a curious figure amongst his volunteers. Many of them would remember how he'd turned up in Newfoundland with a silk top hat, his doctoral gowns and some sealskin boots (which he'd wear all at once, as his party piece). Almost everyone described him as "tireless" when what they often meant was tiring. "No day was long enough," wrote one, "and nights were wasted unless you spent them in stren-uous tasks." For a man of such extraordinary extremes, he was peculiarly exacting about the conduct of others, particularly in relation to the Sabbath, smoking or women in trousers. He made few friends, and couldn't expect to rely on his doctors' loyalty forever. Of the two most prominent volunteers, one resigned in exasperation, and the other provided much of the ammunition for the rather-less-than-hagiographic biography which the mission fired off in 1957. At least in their work the doctors were spared more time in the Mess. The entertainment consisted of banjo soirees, Kipling readings, haircutting and dressing-up. Whenever Grenfell was out in the wilderness, he left a statue of the Three Wise Monkeys on the table, a reminder to his colleagues that there was no show without him.

In such a vacant spot, Grenfell became law as well as order. Alcohol was banned in St. Anthony, and remained so until recently. Grenfell acquired magisterial powers and fought a war on drink, with Marconi radios and American volunteers (who'd sworn a cranky oath to the King). "Dr. Grenfell was a very good man," wrote H. G. Wells in *Marriage,* "but he made brandy dear, dear beyond the reach of the common man altogether on this coast." The Rule of the Doctors saw Sundays reclaimed, and stills smashed and dumped in the sea. Newfoundland hadn't known such justice since the Rule of the Fish. Grenfell even invented laws quite unknown to the island—like divorce—and held colourful trials on his quarter-deck. For these occasions, he wore his gowns, and the miscreants were sometimes tied to the mast and beaten. "For lack of other entertainment," wrote Grenfell, "our court trials were often exceedingly popular occasions."

Magisterial powers also gave Grenfell the chance to experiment with some Poor Laws of his own. In the matter of children and neglect, he was at his most haphazard and quixotic. At least once, he "confiscated" a child as a penalty for her mother's neglect, and he was always collecting children in Labrador, along with bear cubs, dogs and rotting whale-meat. Back at St. Anthony, he'd forget where he'd picked them up and so—as always—it would be left to others to untangle the detail. His orphanages meanwhile reflected the best of his own childhood: bracing cold, freedom from shoes and never a moment of idleness. Children had to be tough, he argued, to live in this hard world.

I wasn't sorry not to be staying in St. Anthony. It wasn't that I disliked it particularly. I just felt that such abundant Grenfellism belonged to my past, some thirty years before. Instead, I carried on out to the lighthouse, and slept between Haul Up Cove and Mad Mall

Point. It was exhilarating to feel so unrestrained, nothing about me but the crackling darkness, and the moon reflected in a liquefied night.

The next morning I was woken by the swish and puff of whales, and by cars.

We're always here watching, people told me; there's not much else to do now.

124

Around the headland was the icy killing-ground of my childhood.

The next morning, I climbed Teahouse Hill, and peered out across a yellowy bog.

The scene that ends with Grenfell killing his dogs begins with him sliding over this bog. It's April 1908, and the bog is still crusted in ice. Bide here, they tell him, there's more weather coming. Can't wait, says Grenfell, got a patient out on Hare Bay. Osteomyelitis, they say. And so he sets out, almost killing everyone in this story. He's not even dressed for heroism but is wearing his Oxford rugby shorts, a jacket, some long red, yellow and black-striped Richmond RFC socks and sealskin boots.

I remembered Hare Bay from my search for *les élangeurs*. It was like the sky mounted between two sprigs of rock, a hundred square miles of colourless wash and vapours. In April, they say, it's still frozen, and the vapours groan and grind together.

Grenfell urges his dogs in among the sish and clumpers, and is lost from view. For two days there's nothing, and then he's spotted, ten miles out on a shard of bloody ice. He's lost his sledge, and he's dressed in dead dogs.

A crew of seal-hunters sets out, dragging their boat on slob haulers through the ice. They can be killed at any moment but they find the doctor, and soothe him with morphine. Strangely, he insists on being rescued with his matted dog-coat and his flagstaff made of bones.

But, back on Teahouse Hill, he has himself photographed in a snowdrift, wearing his dogs, and the story is rushed round the world. "DOGS TRY TO EAT MAN," runs the *New York Tribune,* "FORTY-EIGHT HOUR BATTLE WITH HUNGER-MADDENED DOGS." The public like this story however it's told, and Grenfell's version, *Adrift on the Ice,* is a best-seller and runs to eighteen editions in no time at all. Grenfell has discovered publicity, and has salvaged myth from folly. Americans in particular are aroused by his brand of heroism, and by the belief that technology and good will triumph over the wastes. The bone-handled knife will become a museum piece, and there'll be more money, more clinics and even more of Grenfell.

Meanwhile, there were gold watches for the rescuers, and a brass plaque for St. Anthony. It was identical to the brass oddity of my childhood. "To the Memory of Three Noble Dogs, Moody, Watch and Spy, whose lives were given for mine on the Ice."

125

At the bottom of Teahouse Hill was a house built at the moment of fame and marriage. It was known locally as The Castle, not because it was grand but because it was foreign and startlingly weird. No one had ever seen verandas (or coloured glass, steam-heating, plumbing and electricity) until Grenfell introduced them. He'd promised his mother the house would be "Grenfellian," and he'd promised his bride it would remind her of home. It achieved both—a cottage in the New England style, painted Grenfell green.

Earlier, I'd met an old man who remembered the house as a child.

"Proper people. And a proper house. No one got in without an invitation."

The young Mrs. Grenfell hadn't thought it a proper house at all, and was horrified by Newfoundland. She was American, "almost beautiful" (according to her friends), and had only known Grenfell for six months. This made her the perfect choice of wife. Grenfell assumed that, being American, she was naturally idealist, and she assumed that he, being British, was naturally aristocratic. With such lofty views of their fellow mankind, they were destined either to ignore each other or get married. After a fabulously pearly ceremony in Chicago, Grenfell brought Anne back to his estate, set against all the slub and ice of Teahouse Hill.

The inside of The Castle had done nothing to cheer Mrs. Grenfell—nor, for that matter, me. Of course, I'd been here before, living with *Grenfell chic*—scorched black furniture, stuffed heads, skins, lumpy armchairs, and oaty burlap on the walls. I remembered how things accumulated, not as a matter of design but as a matter of triumph; trophies, velvet rowing caps, spears and boxing gloves. I wasn't at all surprised to find a prospectus for Mostyn House School amongst this well-wormed treasure, although there was nothing prospective about it: I was already back there. Poor Anne, she was about to discover that there's more mildew than ermine to the aristocracy. She told the society newspapers of her sacrifice, and was pictured "at home" outside a herder's shack.

A guide took me up through parlours, pantries, sculleries, dressing rooms and nurseries. There seemed to be so many rooms that we don't have any more. Anne had enjoyed the superfluity, and had even worked up a little grandeur ("My husband does not allow strong drink in his colonies," she told her friends). She ordered a Steinway, employed a seamstress, and held tea parties amongst all the trophies and bits of moose. It wasn't gentility exactly, but it wasn't despair either. Anne had found a new role, hounding out funds. She paraded Grenfell up and down the East Coast, and they developed a healthy reputation for being infuriating—commandeering houses, servants and telephones. Americans responded with applause, lavish donations and more volunteers.

Back at The Castle, Anne sat at her desk, reworking the myth. She dismantled her husband's memoirs and rebuilt them, with a flourish of her own. Grenfell re-emerges almost as an abstract, sublimely altruistic, absurdly durable and medically implausible. Anne has him stitching his own skin into wounded fishermen, and pulling out Captain Bartlett's tonsils as he pins him against the door. There was no end to the demand for such adventure, and by 1918 story-telling had begun to re-define the Grenfells. After eight years at The Castle, they abandoned their gloomy garret and set off like minstrels, hawking their story through the western world. By the end, they'd been everywhere, and had written some thirty-eight books.

The guide was speaking: "This was the nursery."

I'd almost forgotten about the Grenfells' children. Cynics would say so had Grenfell. But this is to misunderstand him; as with all his relationships, he loved idealistically, but had no time for emotional clutter. Far from being neglected, the three children were lavished with morality for the rest of their father's life, epistles covering everything from "beastly movies" to "fuzzy dances." In St. Anthony, they'd been forbidden from mixing with the fishermen's children, and were dressed formally every day. They were reared by a governess and—here in the nursery—they spoke French as a mark of their sophistication. They would never recover from being the children of a saintly man. At

Oxford, the oldest boy "Wilf" embraced his Uncle Algie's agnosti-
cism, joined the communists and denounced all religion as hypocrisy.

I was presented to Wilf once, at Mostyn House, when I was ten
and he was sixty-three. The whole school had just sung *The Battle Hymn
of the Republic* in his honour. He had an American head, I decided,
trimmed into a cube of silver bristles.

Despite his polygon head, I struck up a strong rapport with him,
quite unlike that with other adults of the time. He seemed so informal,
and talked to me as if what I said actually mattered. Perhaps this
encounter explains my lifelong affection for Americans.

We discussed the temperature in Maine.

And corn (although what he meant, of course, was maize).

Downtown, there was a statue of Grenfell, dressed as an Esquimau.

He'd worked hard to cultivate the image of Arctic champion,
although in many ways he was more than this. If the truth be told,
he'd never actually spent a winter in Labrador, and was always at his
worst when bumping round the islands. Grenfell is perhaps better
appreciated as an entrepreneur, a man who'd crash through the detail
in pursuit of his vision. He was the only man with *any* vision for
Labrador in 1893, and the only man prepared to steer it through. It
was more than thirty-five years before his grip began to weaken. By
the time the IGA had prised him from the reins, in 1928, he'd built
up six hospitals, seven nursing stations, two hospital ships, four schools,
fourteen industrial centres and a supply schooner. His organisation
continued, and remained the only medical service on the Labrador
coast until 1981. It was then handed over to the federal "Grenfell
Regional Health Service," for $1.

There were plenty of people to enjoy his failures. His ambitious
ideas for social reform had never taken off. Perhaps by continually
working against the grain, he'd been unable to re-shape the system.
The Truck and starvation lingered on in Labrador until deep into the
fifties, and Grenfell had enough enemies brassy enough to blame it
all on him. Others found amusement in his disastrous schemes, like
his plan to introduce Finnish reindeer in 1907 (each met a peculiarly
Newfoundland end: drowned, poached, eaten by dogs or retired to
Canada).

St. John's had always been at the vanguard of this contempt. For
some, the animosity was purely personal. One academic told me he'd
once started a Ph.D. on Grenfell but had had to give it up.

"I couldn't live with the subject. I simply couldn't stand him."

For others, the animosity was historical. Grenfell's work had been a constant reminder to Newfoundlanders of their inability—or unwillingness—to look after their own. He seemed devoted to the islanders but in a way that was oddly disparaging. They didn't mind being "British outcasts" but drew the line at being like "the slaves of the Deep South." The mission's use of foreign volunteers and money had only added to their humiliation, and had created the impression of a colony within a colony. As for the powers in St. John's, Grenfell had long since upset the churches and the merchants, and soon had the government braying. We have no need, snorted one politician, for "itinerant, self-dubbed philanthropists."

The criticism was at its most shrill in the 1960s. Newfoundland had emerged from the humiliation of the pre-war years, and the socialists—men like the writer Harold Horwood—envisaged a new future wafted along by the State. In this brave perspective, there was no place for entrepreneurs, do-gooders and foreigners. Grenfell was revisited with particular scorn. ("Few other men," declared Horwood, "have been so loved and so hated.") From now on, announced the revisionists, we're in the hands of the State, and things can only get better.

From where I stand—at the end of this story—such a promise sounds like hubris. Some way off yet, the New Newfoundlanders were in for a nasty surprise.

126

The next day, I took a bus seven hours south along the French Shore.

Although the bus was called the Viking Express, I was the only person in this mini-saga. This was a shame; the re-emergence of Newfoundland, from spittle and khaki bog to purple alps, seemed almost too much for me alone. The day was in a constant state of evolution. The land swelled, and the greens changed from moss to potato to hayrick and, finally, forest. Sometimes, the transformations came so quickly that they became jumbled and confused. Once, I spotted a gift shop adrift in a blast of pre-Cambrian shrapnel, and two men struggling with a prehistoric fish. It was a halibut, beginning its culinary adventures the size of a mylodon.

The driver called the road the Devil's Highway, especially when it turned to puffs of dust, and bumps. At some point, I was battered to sleep, and woke to find myself in Savage Cove, surrounded by a mob. Their placards said "We've eat enough dirt," and I imagined this was the obstinate rump of the old French *gardien* militia. They refused to let the bus pass until I'd signed their petition. I did so, although I wasn't sure what they wanted. To go home? Fresh victuals and grog? Or just some asphalt?

Eventually, we found ourselves deep in the inlets, the sky no more than a crack above us. In the darkness, this place had often been confused for New Zealand, mostly because—there—Captain Cook had used the same name all over again: Bay of Islands. Others thought it looked like Galway, and so it did in a way: Ireland built with axes. In the deepest and darkest of the clefts, we found Corner Brook, where I decided to stop for the night.

Corner Brook didn't seem to belong to the French Shore. It was a clanking, steamy beast for eating trees, and had been followed here by suburbs. The town had grown so fat on pulp that it was now the second-largest in Newfoundland (although it was said there were still more Newfoundlanders in Fort McMurray, Alberta). The whole place lived and, literally, breathed pulp. Twice a day, the whistle went for shift change, and the workers filed down to the mill with their dinner in wicker baskets. Bowater had built everything, even the church, and the local rag was called *The Humber Log*. But, as well as people, mushing up forests had brought prosperity, and the town tottered uphill in a haze of Tiffany lamps and fuchsias. My Bed and Breakfast shared a street with Nicole's Doggie Doos Grooming Service, and was painted "eau de nil" and grape. Even the cloud of pulp that floated over the town was the colour of lilac tissues.

Near the cemetery, I met a gravedigger with a peculiar insight into all of this. "People here's too busy to bury the dead in winter; they waits for the thaw," he said, and then added wolfishly, "It's dog eat dog in Corner Brook."

Intriguing though this detail was, it wasn't what I was looking for.

If it's the French you're after, people said, keep going south, to Port au Port.

I 27

The Port au Port peninsula leaps off the coast like a fish. Only a thin spray of shingle known as "The Gravels" links it to the shore. There were once ports on either side of the Gravels (and hence the name) but these were splintered by an earthquake in 1927, and then washed away altogether in 1951. After that, the peninsula returned to what it's always been: a tiny French fish, leaping clear of Newfoundland.

At first, I hardly noticed the Frenchness. It was an exquisite freshly laundered day, of the type Newfoundland saves up for months. St. George's Bay was so full of light and air that it kept bursting into emeralds, and would blaze like that for a moment before the clouds re-formed and quenched it in blue. "A more beautiful and ample basin cannot easily be found," declared the artist John James Audubon. He was bewitched, and spent five days here in 1833, killing and painting for his greatest work, *Birds of America*.

I drove along the cliffs, from adventure to adventure: Jerry's Nose, Piccadilly and Man of War Cove. Mostly, the heroes of these pieces had already moved on, leaving only oddities—a herd of alpacas, a burnt-out Chevy, a pagoda or a rocket made of fish-boxes. Once, I stopped at a vast wooden cathedral called Aguathuna built for a thousand Catholics who never came. Nothing ever happened there, it seemed, except miracles with roses.

But out through the woods, on the other side of the fish, I found myself amongst the *ancien régime*. The villages had names like Lourdes and L'Anse à Canard, and a home wasn't a saltbox but *une maison à deux étages,* cobbled from planks and slapped in limewash. Out here, people ate *la gauche aux bleuets*—or blueberry pie—and took their news from *La Gaboteur*. There's no Lent, they told me, just *la Chandeleur* (when they crowned *le Roi et la Reine* in ribbons), and Halloween was still *les Flambeaux,* a time of burning tyres. Even the fences were different, lattices of hazel and alder as if every farm was a basket of sheep. Whenever I asked people where they were from, most still said Saint-Malo. Others thought they were *Acadiens*, who'd been here since their expulsion from the British Maritimes in 1755 *("le Grand Dérangement")*. At least they were better off than the Acadians in Louisiana, who'd ended up as "Cajuns."

But we're all runaways, they agreed, or deserters.

Among the congenitally fugitive, I met an old Breton called Leo Dubé. He'd embedded his *camp* in the shingle at Mainland, where he held out with a rifle in the parlour and Jesus dying on every wall. His head was scarred and raw after his life working in the forest, and all around him were skiffs and lobster pots, and slipways of logs. A little way off shore was his old home, a hunk of scarlet rock. In June 1767,

James Cook had named it Red Island, but it was already the greatest fish-slab in the French Empire: Île Rouge. Leo told me his mother threw away the best years of her life out there. She was curing and stacking until the day the world stopped eating *morue sèche*.

"A lot of people ran away," he said. "Landed here at *La Grande Terre* (or Mainland, if ye like). Some tried to climb over the cliffs to the cape, and a few was killed. Once, they found a body, up in the rocks. Not a hair out of place! We're always getting miracles here . . ."

That afternoon, Leo asked me in for tea, *la pâte*—or "dough"—and rhubarb jam. "Mother died twenty years ago. We never had nothing."

It was a childhood without miracles: flour, begging and clothes dyed in onions. "At *chandeleur,* they cooked up any spare food, and people drank *du moonshine.*"

Leo eased along the memories with songs in Breton. It sounded like seagull. I asked him what it meant but he smiled secretively—"Just washing the sea."

Fragments of the past tumbled free all afternoon.

"At the age of thirteen, I had a brain fever, and the gadrings which is like rotten milk in your stomach. I was smashing things and saw people walking upside down and burnt up. *Alors, un miracle!* I was cured by a song . . ."

Leo cut two more slices of dough, and slathered them with jam.

"My mother's still here," he said. "She wakes me from my nightmares."

"And what does she say?"

"*Priez plus! Priez plus!* Ye must pray more."

128

It was no longer necessary to scramble over the cliffs to Cap St. Georges. There was now a road slithering through the rocks and spruce, and—said Leo—once a year, on the day of St. Jean le Baptiste, the people of Mainland marched over the hills to see their neighbours. People often talked about this feat, as if it were a journey back to France.

"It's a big click," said one, "a proper long way. Ye gotta take supplies—bread, *soupe aux pois* . . ."

"And a drop of corn-squeezings," said another.

"My *grand-père* once did it with a boat on his back," said a third.

Most agreed that they were up to no good in Cap St. Georges, and vice versa.

"They've always got plenty of moose..."

"...Must be money-laundering..."

"And they's always stealing timber..."

Half-way over the mountain was an improbably luxurious hotel which bore the brunt of all these improbable accusations, and was called The Crosswinds. As there was no one around, I took a seat amongst the very latest Louis XV, and watched the sunset. Eventually there was a galloping sound three dining-rooms away, and the owner appeared in cowboy boots. He found me two roast partridges and a bottle of claret, and told me that, tonight, the whole place was mine for nothing. "It's so unfair," he said, "I made my money in oil," and then he galloped off. I helped myself to Room 103, with pewter finials and sixty-two channels on the box.

"And if ye want some comics," said the night-watchman, "I got plenty."

Blue Benoit couldn't read but all night he snuffled around among his fungal stash of pictures. I've seldom met anyone quite so self-contained, happy and nocturnal. He even looked like something from the dead of night, with a head of stiff black bristle, and his eyeballs huge, in two thick lamps of glass. The Benoits, he told me, have been living up in these hills—secretly—for centuries.

"I'll take ye out there tomorrow, and we'll slew down to Cap St. Georges."

It was months since I'd walked under trees or been sloshed with dew. Blue ensured I'd not forget it. He shouted at the squirrels for eating all the hazel nuts, and took me on a tour of the fruit—squashberries, wild raspberries, snotberries ("They makes you sick"), and crackerberries that snapped in the mouth like a shot of cold pond. Then a bull moose erupted out of the grass in front of us, and rumbled away like a tank.

"*Holy Sweet Mother of Jesus!*" sputtered Blue.

After that, a golden eagle paddled along above us, lazily hopeful of carnage.

Up on Loreto Hill, we found the Benoits' first homes, shallow divots in the hay. "We wasn't allowed to build houses so we lived in these bunkers, called *les murs*."

Blue said there were still Benoits on the hill. Grand-père Benoit had built a lobster cannery here, and Cousin Cornelius now had a ranch (with six sheep and a cow). Uncle Bernard was a thief, and Octavius still fished, although Cousin René had drowned, going after his oar.

"They hauled him out next day," said Blue absently, "caught his pants on a jig."

We carried on through the woods, and eventually came to an unfinished cabin on the shore. Inside, it smelt of bottled clams and sleep. Anything of any value was kept in a large glass jar on the kitchen table: coins, keys, addresses, bullets and pills. There was a cat called Boutons, and I could see Madame Benoit asleep amongst all the chipboard.

"Hope you're not snipey about what ye eats, John?" asked Blue.

I said I wasn't, and he fried up eight eggs and a moose's liver.

As he cooked, I asked Blue about Cap St. Georges.

"Youse goin' find people kinda shy," he said. "Like they shouldn't be here."

129

Cap St. Georges was even more elusive than I'd imagined. It was supposedly home to a thousand people, but they were so scattered along the shore and through the woods that it seldom seemed like a dozen. Until the 1940s, they'd lived by barter, and paid the tooth-puller in fish. Now, there was a diner, like a great yellow barge that had ploughed its way inland, and a bar called "The Silverado." It was always the same three people in the bar—one of them steadying himself on White Russians, the other two in camouflage—and all they ever talked about was poaching. Every night the landlord advertised *"Une Danse de Quattres,"* but no one ever came.

"People here's kinda shy," he said. "Ye never knows when they'll be out."

Even their French had become a little foresty. Some words had simply got lost. Thus it wasn't normal "to dress" *(se habiller),* instead one trimmed oneself like sails *(gréer).* Other words were renegades, like their turnips, which were *choux-raves* (instead of *navets*), or great-grandfather, who'd dumped *arrière* to become an extra *"grand"* grand-père. It was a dialect only ever spoken or sung, and never written. For a few, it was the only language they knew. Once, I came across an old lady in the store who couldn't read the English on the packets, and Blue said he often thought in French.

"Which is queer," he said, "because it was *banned* at school. Even in 1972!"

The mayor wanted to round up all the words and lead them out of the forest. I met him one day as he was painting his shed Acadian blue. He too was a Benoit, and wore a t-shirt that said *"Au bord d'un Rêve."* I wondered if his Gallic revival wasn't also tottering on the edge of a dream.

"The young are all leaving," he said. "Off to Québec."

"Will they feel at home there?" I asked.

Not at all, said *le maire*, the Benoits were from Languedoc.

"We speak the same language we spoke the day we left in 1604. We're the *Terre-Neuviens Français.*"

Mayor Benoit was also a playwright, although even his drama was elusive.

"We go out at night, on *les veillées*," he said. "The visits."

"And what do you do?"

"Skits in people's houses, *concerts* in the kitchen, that sort of thing."

Everyone here plays an instrument, he said, and at Christmas they had *des mummers*. This was as good as janneying ever got, because there wasn't a single policeman on the entire peninsula.

I was curious to see a crowd, and so I went to the French Mass on Sunday. The surprise was not the Norman yellows and the Celtic reds, but the Micmac. Amongst women particularly, I began to notice the same recurrent features—a lightness of touch, the colour of autumn, russet across the cheekbone. There's Indian in all of us, the Mayor told me.

"The Benoits arrived without women," he'd said. "So they took Micmac wives."

Ever since then, people had been developing their own version of the Micmac.

We was brought here to kill off the Beothuks, they told me in the bar.

Confusion was rife. James Cook had merely noted they were still on the peninsula in 1767, now paid as *gardiens*. The next century saw them scrambling their genes with the French, and emerging as the "Jack-o-tars." In the eyes of the rest of Newfoundland, they were revolting creatures, of "almost lawless habits." Audubon, on the other hand, found other passions aroused. In 1833, he came upon "the belles of the village . . . flourishing in their rosy fatness":

> Around their necks, brilliant beads mingled with ebony tresses, and their naked arms might have inspired apprehension had they not been constantly employed in arranging flowing ribbons . . .

Even that hoary nationalist, Harwood, found himself a little pinker amongst the "Jakitars." His 1969 tourist guide credits them with "a tendency toward sexual freedom (and sexual hospitality even at tender ages)." Over-inspired apprehension, perhaps.

I asked the others what it was to be a Jakitar.

The mayor said they weren't Jakitars any more, unless you wanted a fight.

Blue thought it was all about boiling up a can of sea-snails, as kids. *"Burgles!"* he smacked. "Burgles with butter!"

Leo, on the other hand, still thought the idea of being Indian was repulsive.

"It's typical of them," he said, "over in Cap St. Georges."

130

Each night, I slept at the very tip of the cape, on the ruins of a soldier's lighthouse.

The soldier's son was now the owner of the yellow diner. Leonard Cornect was an unhappy man, who'd lost part of his leg in a car-wreck and part of his fortune in the diner. He only brightened slightly when I told him I was sleeping on the Boutte de Cap.

"My father loved it there," said Leonard. "Called it *le pays de bon Dieu.*"

I could understand his contentment. It was oddly calm on the cape. The headland glowed with willowherb, rue and eyebright, and ended in sky and the priestly clink of cormorants. But for Eugene Cornect, this wasn't merely the end of the peninsula, but the end of his madness; the talking mud, the whistle and crunch of angels, the roar of blood and the clouds raining arms and ears.

Eugene's war brings the past to an end and, with it, almost the future.

He's only twenty-one when he breaks with centuries of tradition, and signs up for the British. Until a decade before he was a Frenchman, but now he's off to fight for his new country in his old one (which he's never seen). Many will join him. By the end of 1914, over 3,400 will have rallied to the flag, including Inuit, floaters, mummers, Leo's father and his Uncle Tiofél. The response is so overwhelming that there's not enough khaki for the troops, and their nickname will be a constant reminder of the shortages at home: The Blue Puttees.

Eugene is not certain of the cause, but nor is anyone. Back at Mostyn House School, the headmaster, Algie, says it will be a "tonic" to wake up his failing nation. Over two hundred of his old pupils will join up, and over half of them will find eternal glory. The Grenfells can't resist a good war. Algie's cousin wins the Victoria Cross, and even Wilfred—now aged fifty—returns, parks Anne at Mostyn House and joins the army.

Eugene signs up for the duration of the war (a year maximum), on a dollar a day.

"It was an adventure," says his son. "There's nothing here."

Two months after war's declared, and Eugene's on his way with "The First Five Hundred." This is an honour his family will carry for generations (and they'll even know his number). He and his comrades sail aboard the sealer *Florizel*, and are met in England by a band playing *O Canada*, even though it's another thirty years before they'll be Canadians. Eugene now finds himself in a strange land of roads and electric light, and the Newfoundlanders are shunted up to Edinburgh and back to Aldershot. Then, a year after their departure, they're shipped to a place of flies, called Gallipoli, and watch in astonishment as the first of them is vaporised in a flash of earth and sparks. *"On entendit un grand boum,"* recalls Eugene and the slaughter begins. Thirty-one are killed by snipers, and the another ten are rotted down in dysentery. The Newfoundlanders think things can't possibly get worse, until 1916, when they're shipped to France.

Eugene had not imagined the old country like this. There's no sea and the forest is splintery and dead. The villages are sick with broken drains and putrid horses, and there are outrageous creatures living in the ruins: Pathans, Congolese and mutineers. The Newfoundlanders are billeted with the colonial troops, and there's surprise that they're white. Then they're given their own trench called "St. John's Road," near Beaumont Hamel, and Eugene is promoted to corporal. Any day, they're told, the Great Push.

The Newfoundlanders are elated by the order to go.
"Bloody decks!" they shout, as they clear the top. "And safe return!"

The First of July is still a day of mourning in the province.

Instead of harmlessly copying through the drifts into German lines, the Newfoundlanders found themselves in a storm of burning metal and fire. Some had barely got out of the trench before they were ripped apart and ragged. Others made it as far as a stump called the Danger Tree, before they too perished. Of the 801 men who took part in this attack, 710 were killed. One Water Street merchant lost all four grandsons on the same morning. As the British commander later told Newfoundland's prime minister, "It was a magnificent display of trained and disciplined valour, and its assault only failed because dead men can advance no further." Grenfell hadn't been far away, and had seen the carnage of the Somme. He recommended armour for the troops, and was censored and withdrawn.

Eugene was not at Last Parade but he'd been lucky. Although a bullet had smashed through his thigh, he'd survive, lame like his son. Whilst he was evacuated to London, the Newfoundland Regiment was resurrected. They fought the rest of the war with almost indecent courage. English newspapers called them "the Young Daredevils," and Tommy Ricketts would be the youngest soldier of the war to win the Victoria Cross. After Menin Road, Hellfire Corner and Passchendaele, the regiment was honoured with the title "Royal." Of all the overseas units, it was the only one to be accorded this epithet, though it might easily have been an epitaph; one in seven young Newfoundland men had died.

Eugene spent a year in Wandsworth, in a hospital close to my home. He'd eventually return but found few of his comrades alive. Looking back through my own travels, they're strewn with the dead and injured. In Newtown, Job Barbour lost not only his brother at Passchendaele but also his cousin. Both of Captain Bartlett's brothers perished (one took a bullet in the chest, and the other died of anthrax in the Middle East). Curwen's friends too were diminished; the railway Reids had a grandson killed, and Sir Michael Cashin's son sustained appalling injuries. The writer David Macfarlane was deprived of three great-uncles, and the only good to come of this was his luminous account of the tragedy, *Come from Away*.

Newfoundland had not forgotten its sacrifice. Every town had built a Legion Club, and a social life had developed around the concept of memorial. "Please Remove Your Cap When Entering," it says above the door, "No Profane Language to be Used." Every outport got an obelisk, and dogberries and juniper were shipped out to Flanders, and planted round the Danger Tree. Veterans became heroic in a place that—until then—had never agreed on its heroes. Homes and jobs were found for the mutilated, and Eugene Cornect was given the lighthouse on the Boutte de Cap.

I often thought of Eugene as I lay listening to the breathing of the sea. His lighthouse must have seemed like the future of the island, a brilliant flash of light along the darkened coast. But the old Newfoundland was ruined, another $40 million in debt. It would stagger through the twenties and then collapse, taking with it democracy, independence and self-esteem. At about the same time, in 1931, Eugene's lighthouse caught fire, and crumbled into the bog.

There was nothing left of Eugene now except a patch of rust and grit. He spent the rest of his life hobbling around amongst his sheep and chickens, and died in 1977, at the age of eighty-four. He's buried in a hero's grave, in the heart of Cap St. Georges.

131

I hitched a lift to the end of the French Shore, on a fish truck.

It was an exorbitant machine, twenty-four wheels, a television, a fridge and about 30,000 fins and tails. The driver had been doing the Nova Scotia run for twenty years, and was an ardent monarchist, call-sign "Corgi."

"The Queen's after bein' more friendly since Diana died," he'd noticed.

I learnt many new things about her, in a hundred miles.

She always wears gloves for eating, said Corgi, and her secretary wears a sword.

"Like to meet her," he said, "but she ain't often this way."

We were sitting alongside each other in Club Class seats. It was like flying around the island, at an altitude of thirteen feet. I felt a surge of pleasure as the coastline whizzed along beneath us; sand dunes, eel grass, table mountains, ponds (with Micmac names like Mummichog and Mollichignic), more beaches, Glencoe and an abandoned train. We'd now merged with the old railway, twenty-eight hours from St. John's.

"Trains was always blowin' over here," said Corgi. "And trucks."

And in winter there was ice. He'd often found himself upside down. "Or slidin' backwards," he said, "and then I'm sweatin' bullets."

Further on, he called over the CB for news of the sea.

The replies were often tantalisingly ambiguous: "Kinda airsome. Over."

Or biblical: "Looks like the Devil's been beatin' up his wife out here."

Then we were in Port aux Basques, among the ferries and tiny painted coves. From the cab, it looked like a rock garden inhabited by toys. I could see green and purple villages huddled together in the sea, and cemeteries just big enough for three.

"Most beautiful people in the world," said Corgi. "Scots, Micmacs, Basques . . ."

"*Scottish?*"

"Yes, boy, and I heard there's a group still holdin' out in the Codroy."

And with that, we parted, in a blast of chrome good-byes.

I then hired an Oldsmobile Intrigue, and set out, my curiosity aroused.

132

I drove west, almost as far as an Intrigue will go before plunging into the Gulf of St. Lawrence. The landscape softened, and the names became ever more delicately Scottish: McDougall Gulch, Na-Creige golf course, Loch Lomond and St. Andrews. Then I rounded a little hat of spruce and alder, and found myself above a long green glen and a sliver of loch. Beyond, I could see the ocean, swinging around as usual, but—inside—it was a different picture. Here were people cutting hay and picking apples, cows grazing and a tractor dragging its plough through the sticky black soil. I'd now been away long enough to realise that this is what I'd been missing: scenery with verbs. Up until then, Newfoundland had often seemed a place of overwhelming nouns.

But this feeling wasn't homesickness, because the Codroy Valley wasn't quite like anywhere I'd ever known. The barns were made of shingles and bark, and there were pieces of meadow out on the loch, each with its own crew of sheep. It was almost as if things had been hand-picked for their decorative effect, like the ruby-throated hummingbirds or Indian Hill, which was a perfect cone of turf and slender asters. They called me "my darling love" at the café, and said that on the river they even had their own beluga, called Echo.

I imagined that Paradise was probably a bit like this, except busier. The English had overlooked Codroy in the rush for fish, and the French had been denied it. That left only a group of crofters who'd been cleared out of the Hebrides. In 1844, the MacDonalds arrived, followed by the MacArthurs, and the MacIsaacs (who'd chosen the losing side in The '45). They weren't interested in fish, just a place without landlords, tax and Protestants. They called Codroy "God's Little Acre," and started feeding Newfoundland with greens.

"Are there any Scots left?" I asked the waitress.

"Yes, my sweet. Go see Sears," she said. "Didn't speak English till he was ten."

Sears MacArthur lived in a cabin by the estuary, lace doilies on the shelves and a plate of *bonnachs* on the stove. He said he no longer worked on the trucks, but his head was full of music. He was always playing the pipes at weddings and ceilidhs, and was one of the last people who could tap out a step-dance with just "mouth-music," or *puirt luath*. He knew "The Tobacco Song" and *Buain a' Rainich* ("Cutting Bracken"), and a clatter of heels called *Calum Crùbach*. Such volubility surprised me because Sears was painfully shy, always looking for words around his feet and up in the sky.

"Some nice place," he'd murmur, when all else failed.

I asked him if it was true, about the Gaelic.

"Sixty odd years ago, we spoke nothing else."

He said his father spoke *Gaerlach* all his life, although he never wrote it.

"But my grandmother, Jenny MacIsaac, taught him all the stories: Bannockburn, Bonnie Prince Charlie, Culloden and the Clearances."

"Do people still speak Gaelic?"

"No, my grandchildren don't know any, except their names, Caila and Kyle."

Nor did his wife. Mrs. MacArthur was half-*Terre-Neuviene*, born Marie Campbell.

"You didn't hear it much after the seventies," she said.

"Bho'n chaill mi Ghàidhlig na b'fhearr cha D'fhuair mi," said Sears.

(After the Gaelic was gone, there'd be nothing better.)

He asked me if I'd like to see their old house, and we set off through the corn.

"It was built by my great-grandfather, Angus, in a Cape Breton style . . ."

Angus MacArthur was born in 1798, on the Isle of Canna, and escaped to Nova Scotia at the age of twenty-two. After thirty years on Cape Breton, his landlords marched in one day and told him that what was his was theirs. He loaded his family into a boat and came to Codroy, rebuilding his home as if nothing had happened.

"The MacIsaacs came after them, so poor they lived under a tree."

It was a pretty house, like lace knitted from wood. At some stage, the MacArthurs had snipped off the Cape Breton mansards, and squared it up like a saltbox, but around the windows the frills and frets survived. There was a barn at the back, where (said Sears) they'd stored barrels of frozen berries through the winter, and where mother had churned curds into *gruth*.

Sears said his father's first wife had died in 1921, just over twenty. "He married Mother two years later, and they had eight chits including me."

Life had been a cycle of work and song. Children only went to school whilst they couldn't work, in winter and to age fifteen. The MacArthurs had milled their own cloth, and woven drugget until the sixties. Sometimes, there were even feasts of work called *taigh ceilidhs*, when the neighbours called with their carding, knitting, cobbling and poems. At Christmas, there were eggs saved from the autumn, mummers and Saint-Pierre Rum. Then, at *Oidhche Challuinn*, the old year was beaten out with switches of alder, and then it was back to work.

Cha bhi toradh gun saothair, as Father said: there's nothing without graft.

The old house was empty now, the curtains drawn. "The highway came," explained Sears, "and cheaper food from Canada."

His older brother had inherited an empty farm, and drank himself to death in 1999.

There'll be nothing better, as Father would say, once the Gaelic's gone.

The Micmacs too had gone, abandoning Indian Hill.

People said they'd got TB, or drifted away in the Depression. The Scots had never felt easy about the Indians, suspecting their "squaws" of magic, and of colluding with the "the wee folk," the *Sidhichean*. The only Indian left was Ally, they said, whose grandmother was a Micmac. He lived in a cabin at the bottom of the perfect cone.

"Come in, boy," said Ally. "I'm seventy-six today, and there's apple pie."

Ally's Micmac genes had triumphed over the Scottish; beaked, and smooth as nut. "The Indians came after me a few years ago, wanted me to join them."

He cut up the pie, and poured out tiny glasses of whisky. "Of course, I said no. I don't feel Indian. I'm Scottish!"

He grinned, handed me a slice of pie, and we drank to ancestors. *Deoch-slàinte a´ chuairtear a ghluais bho Albainn!*

A toast to the man who'd ventured from Scotland!

133

The long straight stretch from Port aux Basques to Burin was known simply as the South Coast. It hadn't been French since 1713, but most of the time it hadn't been much else either. Soon after the treaty, Captain Taverner RN had sailed along here seeking oaths of allegiance from its knobbly inhabitants. They'd agreed to whatever he wanted, and then government had sailed out of their lives, seemingly forever.

"We didn't even get electric until the seventies," people told me.

I bought a chart of the coast, and searched it for some sign of order. It was like a map of life before the invention of the wheel. In the next hundred and eighty miles, there were some 365 islands, sixty coves and not a single road running east to west. There were no railways, airstrips, bridges or reservoirs, and the only way to move was by sea. Until the last stages of the twentieth century, storekeepers here had found it just as easy to get their freight in Boston as anywhere else. But then the outporters had turned their aquatic thoughts inland, and a single road had set off north through the rocks and ponds. The reports that came back were discouraging. There's nothing out there, just mish, mish and bog. The road only seemed to confirm what people had always suspected: that in this world they were alone.

Even the names that dangled off the coast had been unaffected by the changes of 1713. Most places were still the butt of Norman jokes, like Isle aux Morts, Petites and Grand Bruit. Occasionally, this French had been crossbred with English, producing some delightful absurdities, like *Fosse Rouge*, which had ended up as Fox Roost. However,

many of these places—like Cul de Sac, Rencontre and Cape Le Hune—
were now marked in grey, which meant they'd been abandoned.

But, for those left, life was still pared down to the basic. In each
of the outlying communities I visited, everybody built their own
house, did their own plumbing and buried their own dead. Few knew
how to drive a car, and fresh water was still pumped from the pond
(until electricity arrived, it was carried home in pails). The arrival of
a new fridge was a village event, particularly if it came by skiff, and
the departure of old ones was summary; I often found myself peering
down from the stage, a huddle of old fridges gaping back at me. There
was never anywhere to stay, and so I usually camped on the mish. It
says everything for the sparsity of these places that when, one night,
a moose tripped over my guy-ropes, news of the incident preceded
me all the way along the coast.

From the beginning, I had the feeling that—on this last voyage—
I'd find myself in an older version of Newfoundland. Given the South
Coast's remoteness, this was no startling deduction but it brought
home to me just how quickly things were changing. A way of life that
had remained broadly unchanged for nearly four hundred years was
now crumbling into extinction.

I took a taxi out as far as roads would go, and waited for the steamer.
I spent four days waiting in Rose Blanche. These were some of my
best days in Newfoundland, partly because the town had been designed
by impressionists. They'd been typically light with the structures—
stilts and sticks and sky-walks through the rocks—but had been outrageous with the colours. Great amphitheatres of pigment burst from
every cove: copper green, boat red, bird's-eye orange and flighty pink.
Up close, there were crude splashes of cormorant, or dabs of fish
hanging out to dry, but—standing back—a masterpiece emerged. For
the people who lived here, it was enough just to inhabit this painting.
I don't remember much activity, except whittling sticks and chewing
tobacco, but the old sea-captains said it was even better in the days
of the fish.

"Always ten or fifteen scunners anchored in the coves . . ."

"And the Portuguese was callin' in," said another, "to graze their
pigs."

The other reason for my contentment was that I'd been adopted
by the Parsons. Clarence and his son Jamie were hunters, shepherds,
fishermen and builders, and in winter they worked the Arctic pipelines.

They lived on the edge of the town, in an alluring fug of smoke and sheep and boiled dog-meal, and in the evenings the whole family gathered there, round a barrel of tobacco. The conversation was like the town, brazen and pointillistic.

". . . Down here, see John, we was all criminals once . . ."

How's your moose in England?

". . . Never use banks. Who wants people know what you got?"

No moose. What about bears?

"Heard Perry's now deaf as a haddock . . ."

". . . Gotta get me a fish tomorrow . . ."

Draggers?

"Who's for chaw . . . ?"

Cockroaches?

". . . Or a slice o' glutch . . . ?"

The Parsons also owned the last house on the Neck, which is where I rented a room. They'd lived out here for generations, growing things in gravel and plucking sailors off the rocks. The only other building was a lighthouse erected by Robert Louis Stevenson's family, in 1873. It's possible the author himself had had a hand in the design because it was poetically Scottish, in that almost-forgot-the-windows sort of way. It had scattered light for nearly seventy years, under a succession of quacks, sculptors and war heroes, but then in 1940 it was struck by lightning, and the promontory was returned to darkness and the Parsons. At night, I had their old house to myself, and it creaked and snored with the swells.

From the Neck, I could see the first of the roadless outports—Petites—four miles away across the water. When I asked people if I could walk there, they looked at me as if I'd already been too long in the mish. It's thirty miles round, they said, through bog, swamp, alder, fjords and fog, and there's no trail and no map. At first, I didn't believe them and set out on an exploratory ramble. It was like wading though mattresses, except these were mattresses with claws. About fifty yards outside town, I stopped, bloody and exhausted. I felt an almost overwhelming urge to lie down and sleep, but then I noticed I was surrounded by pitcher plants all eating tiny frogs. I staggered back, clear only about one thing: the South Coast was imprisoned by its bogs.

"We doesn't walk much," said Jamie. "But I can take ye out on the quad."

This aroused other survival instincts. Jamie drove so fast that the tuckamores suddenly changed into streaks of black and pine. The only thing I could see clearly were a pair of cranes that were flapping across the sky at about the same speed. Jamie didn't seem to notice that, behind him, I was upside-down, or trailing along like a banner. Instead, he kept up a grisly commentary: this is Ugly Brook, this is where we have fry-ups, and this is where Calvin went over the edge and bust his head. Jamie only ever stopped when he saw something edible, like a beaver or a couple of nice sweet gulls.

"Beautiful," he'd say. "With a few beers, and a pan of wrinkles."

Two days later, we rode out to Petites on his skiff.

"There's only eight people left," he warned. "Used to be hundreds."

The last of Petites was pegged out over a slab of orange rock, with ring-bolts and cables. There were gantries and wobbly lanes across the harbour, a Methodist chapel and a fire hall like a potting shed. It was almost a miniature of Rose Blanche, except the colour was flaking away.

"The school closed three years ago," said Jamie, "and then the store."

Only two men still fished. They made all their own gears, "sunkers" from old socks and cobbles, and *killicks*, or anchors, from lumps of driftwood and granite. The older generation had had the advantage of a troopship, which had smashed itself across Petites in the First World War. For years afterwards, it was sawn up and bent into anchors, and everyone had dined on the silver of the White Star Line.

Now there were barely enough people to justify the electricity.

"We won't last," said a man knitting nets. "They'll just turn us off."

Jamie took me to the post office for a plate of caribou pie. The post-master was a friend, and his post office merely a hatch in the door. The community's gone, he said, and them's the facts. Within a fortnight, Petites would petition for its own demise.

After lunch, we walked out to the mish, and found a grave in the sorrel.

"Ces Major," said Jamie. "The Mounties shot him, a few years back."

This was a popular story. The police said he'd killed a girl from Port aux Basques. If this was true, it put Petites amongst the most statistically lethal places in the world. But no one believed it. They said it was another girl. "Didn't stop the cops comin' after Ces. Chased him out here, and nailed him."

For most, this had been a spectacle more than they could bear.
Government men pouring over the tucks, hunting one of their own.

134

Whilst I waited for the ferry, I was taken jigging by some poachers.

I met them at The H&B Bar. This was a dark, unappealing lair that survived on four customers and a ruthless one-armed bandit. Most of the conversation was completely lost on me, as it all sounded like West Country strained through a gale. But one afternoon I caught an unmistakable invitation to fish.

"Whattya planningup? Wanna go diddlin outinna bay?"

The preparations for this trip were simple—a skiff, some ice, and a pork barrel full of beers. The two poachers were amongst the most generous and nefarious of all the outporters I'd ever met. They knew that if they were nipped, they'd lose their boat and all their gear. Both were already on poaching charges, yet they were barely out of their teens. One was yellow and squeaky like an elf, and the other was roaring and red. I shall call them Charlie and Jug.

To begin with, there was pride, a tour of the harbour and a beer bottle in every cove. *Plop!* Big Bottom and Misery Point. *Plop!* Little Bottom. Friends came down to the edge to bellow at us like hurricanes, and once a huge dog jumped aboard and almost turned us over. "Get yer smatchy dog outta my fuckin' boat," thundered Jug, and the Newfoundland took to the ocean, and threw us back to upright.

Then—*plop!*—we were out in Bay Le Moine, and untangling lines.

"Keep yer eye out for the DFO boat . . ." said Charlie.

The fisheries officer was feared even more than the police; he was armed, uniformed and evangelical. The boys thought his laws were pettifogging and foreign, dreamed up thousands of miles from the sea. Fifteen fish per man per year. This was barely a day's catch. Many people, including the old Minister of Fish, said these rules were making Newfoundlanders criminals again.

"They're all poachers," he'd told me. "Everyone thinks he's entitled to fish."

To make matters worse, the boys were jigging. The jig is a lead fish with a moustache of lethal steel barbs. A variant of this device was used on the North Sea over two thousand years ago. It's yanked up and down through the water, sometimes stabbing the fish (which is why it's illegal), and sometimes exciting their appetite.

"They bites *anything*. Boots, keys, gear-boxes wipers . . ."

". . . ciggies, tins o' wienies . . ." *Plop!* "Bottles . . ."

Grenfell even had a story of a book in three volumes that was found inside a cod, and presented to the University of Cambridge.

Six bottles later, we were still thrashing the sea.

Jigging's the only way to fish, said the boys. They despised nets.

"Drowned fish gotta drowned taste," said Jug.

And anyway, they said, there's no traps here. The ocean goes down like a wall.

Eventually, somewhere in the chasm below, a small fish threw itself on our spike. We hauled it in, and for a while it clapped around like a silver glove. Charlie inspected it ruefully.

"Once," he said, "these fish was six feet long."

On the way back, we stopped at Caine's Island, and cooked our fish amongst the driftwood tombs. Jug said his mother was born on this waterless rock, and went to school in the kelp. Now the shingle was tangled up in filigrees of blue. Jug tore at a tuft of nylon, and held it up with horror.

"*This* is what should be banned," he snarled, "not jigging!"

He said gill nets were always breaking free, and drifting through the ocean. They'd never perish and never be found. Once full of fish, they'd sink to the bottom, and stay there until the fish had rotted away. Then they were off again, drifting and killing.

"They'll go on long after we's all dead," said Jug.

"*Ghost* nets," said Charlie. "They'll be fishin' forever."

135

The South Coast Steamer meant different things to different people.

For most, it was just a way of getting milk and letters along the coast. They didn't see the point in actually going anywhere, and were appalled at the thought of St. John's. A few of them went to Burgeo for groceries, and spent an hour a fortnight in the modern world. But most just gave their orders to the captain, or bought from the store. Although the outporters often talked of "getting away," all this meant was heading inland with a week's biscuit and a box of wienies. They thought my journey—all 180 miles—was a novel idea but rather pointless, and a waste of $12.

Others had a more exotic purpose to their journey. There were wedding guests and midwives, caribou hunters, mourners, messengers, dozens of salesmen, and an airman who'd not been home since the war. Best of all was a man with a missing finger, and gold rings on all the rest. He refused to tell anyone his name ("Need-to-know basis only"), and desperately wanted us to think he was running rum but, when he got off, I noticed that all he had with him was a tin roof and a poodle.

The lives of these people were always written in their freight. Apart from anything, it was all so conspicuous, whether it was guns or a month's incontinence pads. Usually, it told the story of a siege: salt beef by the hundredweight, ketchup in gallons and crates of hard tack. This often made it difficult for me to shop at the store (unless I wanted a torpedo of pork, or a fortnight of cheddar) but, for the outporters, it was the end of secrecy. Nothing ever happened—whether it was an affair or a new kitchen—without an extravagant preview, in raw materials.

Naturally, the freight wasn't long on the wharf. Within twenty minutes, it had all been cleared by a swarm of quads, and we were ready to go. But sometimes, this wasn't enough, and so I disembarked and followed the quads.

I enjoyed my time in these outports even though I often felt I wasn't really there at all. This was partly because people seemed to be looking straight through me, preferring to see fresh air and rocks instead of strangers. At first, only the children said anything—usually "Hello, Mister!," which made me feel like Mr. Pickwick. That was the other problem; it was all so Dickensian and implausible. The streets were only five feet wide, and everything was painted up like Christmas. La Poile smelt of gingerbread, and Grand Bruit had sprouted out of a waterfall, just a splash of inhabited rapids. There were schools for three and bars for one, and dogs living underground. Even the wilderness seemed to be playing along, with names like Scratch-Arse Hill and Johnny Fell Over The Cliff.

The only thing anyone was taking seriously was vegetables. Wherever there was dirt there were turnips. Rhubarb grew in boats, and peas in boots. I met a man who told me the best place to grow tomatoes was in a satellite-dish. He fertilised everything with rotten fish and kelp, and grew potatoes as big as babies. Every speck of mud, he said, he'd shipped across the bay, and carried up in barrels. There were always fights about earth. In the 1800s, all the big cases from the South Coast were about the theft of topsoil.

I asked the gardener what went best with turnips.

"Chislin," he said. "Cod's sperm, or sheep's head broth."

Despite their natural wariness, people did ask me in. Inside, it was a different story. Here was a world conjured from catalogues, Princess Diana plates, bound sets of leatherette and gilt and pictures of famous ferries. Often, the furniture was still in its wrapper, as if this was merely the added beauty of mail order. People too were transformed by the intimacy of home. A mug-up soon became a bottle of screech and a plate of clams, and the shyness ebbed away. One man told me he'd spent the Blitz on Trafalgar Square, pillow-fighting at the Newfoundland Club. Another said he'd lost his virginity in a lifeboat off Tripoli. In Francois, I was up all night with Ken Benoit, who'd raised ten brothers and sisters when his parents died.

"And every one of them became a graduate."

There was only one town amongst these scattered outports. Burgeo had been disappointing people ever since 1521, when the Portuguese declared it "The Islands of the Eleven Thousand Virgins." St. Ursula and the *Onze Mil Virgems* had disappeared some years earlier on a crusade of innocence, and there were many ideas as to where they'd gone (including the catteries of Cairo). But wherever it was, it wasn't Burgeo, which had never been so much virginal as barren. The consistency of failure was admirable; the church had blown down three times; the first fish plant had opened in 1961, and closed a week later when a union formed; nowadays over half the "Virgins" were unemployed. Most of them were hopefuls who'd drifted in from the outports, bought a television on the never-never, and then never got reception. All they had to show for their optimism were cars, which didn't even make good compost.

I stayed for two days, and thought I saw the shape of things to come. At the heart of Burgeo was Muddy Hole, and the rest was scattered through the rocks and sunkers. On one of these islands, a scrawny department store had appeared, with a stock of abrasive clothes and soviet colours. Everyone hated it, and few could afford it. In the absence of work, status was a matter of zebra-fur dashboards and alloy wheels. Even eating had become perfunctory and bland. "Bollapop," bleated the children, *"baggachips ana bar."* I ate at the diner, and chose "Fin and Feather," which more or less describes the taste. Burgeo, I decided, had lost the will to thrive—although dying wasn't easy either: there was no topsoil for the hopefuls, and they were buried under heaps of gravel and sod.

I can think of no better place to come and fall out of love. Burgeo just seemed to strip people of hope, whether they were looking for virgins or televisions or just a little future. That's all it'd ever done for Farley Mowat, who'd lived here in 1961. The author's last book on Newfoundland, *A Whale for the Killing,* describes a 90-foot finner that swims into Burgeo, and is spattered with bullets, and dies of gangrene in the cove. Mowat's book is an allegory of disgust, and bought him eternal exile. But what was the object of his revulsion, the old Newfoundland or the new? Sometimes, it wasn't easy to draw a line between the two.

The last stages of this voyage were the most spectacular.

The coast, which until then had been a mere utterance of land, now rose up and engulfed the sky. It was like being at the jagged edge of a continent ripped in half. There was nothing behind and nothing in front but pig-iron black and rusted night. Had anything survived this planetary forge, I wondered? Then I noticed little scratches in the breeze, doodles of flight, swoops and spirals. It was the jaegers and shearwaters, enjoying a moment of magnificence.

The ocean too was alive, like downs of cold blue corn.

"Puff pigs!" people shouted, as porpoises bounced across the bows.

And after them came dolphins and fulmars, and a pod of whales.

Then, just when it seemed this journey couldn't get any more unlikely, the steamer headed straight for the cliffs, and sailed through a crack. For a moment, there was nothing but darkness and the sound of our engines, but then we found ourselves in a vast crater, the rim six hundred feet above. All around the walls were tiny houses and gangways, a church like a nesting-box, and a vertical cemetery. There were no views—just a disc of sky above—nowhere to walk and no trees. If they wanted wood in Francois, people said, tree-trunks were hauled to the rim, and dropped on the town below. It was like living in a teacup, but—like all teacups—it had its storms.

"About every twenty year," they told me, "the wind gets in and churns us to bits."

I'd like to have stayed longer but the ferry left at dawn. Perhaps I'd have gone mad in Francois, unhinged by claustrophobia and cheese. Even bath-water here was a public spectacle. But the locals weren't mad, just Durnfords and Fudges. Not much choice for youngsters, said the teacher, and we got a bit of deafness now.

There were only two other passengers on the ferry, a couple in their seventies. Although we never fully understood each other, we became friends of sorts, and decided to travel together. Joshua was "the best twine man on the coast," and Lucy suffered from The Sugar, and had glued all her words into one.

"*Bornonanisland,*" she rumbled. "*Marriedfortyfouryear.*"

We stopped overnight in Hermitage, with an old fisherman who brought us bottled rabbit, and water from the well. Then we were on the Burin Peninsula, flying along in a blur of rust and twine. Joshua's car didn't have a floor and so I had to put my feet on a plank. I could just hear them up front, a low chirruping of glue, but my eyes were on the peninsula, speeding away between my legs. Occasionally I found the courage to look up and out, across the bog and surf. There, way off to the south, was a lone tooth.

It was the last outpost of a great empire.

136

Curwen's great, unfinished French Shore ends with a real piece of France.

It was only twelve miles from America to this last crumb of Europe.

Naturally, it was a voyage replete with drama. At first, we rolled around among the humpbacks, and then the clocks went forward and everything burst into blue. Soon, we were in an archipelago of tiny rocks, and, across one of them, I spotted a town of pastels and spires. There was stone too, cut by convicts. The crew raised the tricolour, and we were grunted ashore by the *douaniers*. France now folded in around us; *anis*, nonchalance and *gendarmes*. Saint-Pierre had been French since 1536, and was now not merely a colony but a fully fledged *département* of the whole. It had even developed an appetite for Euros, and a contempt for Saturdays.

"*Pas de change,*" they shrugged. "*C'est le weekend.*"

Eventually, I found lodgings up the hill, with a lady who wore silk pyjamas, and had a swallow tattooed on her heel. Her husband was paid for not working in a fish-plant that was often shut. France, of course, was behind it. *But why?*

"We got 6,700 square kilometres of fishing," he said. "It was the best."

"And boats still come here?"

"Some. They fish, we bag it up and send it off—and they fish again!"

France, it seemed, was fond of her last North American possession. It was still home to seven thousand Frenchmen, *les Pierrais*. Paris had kept them going through the codless years, and had let them make hoops of the European rules, and then run round them. Animals could be quarantined here for the EC, and customs cleared on the cheap. France paid for the islanders' Renaults and roads, a good time at university, and all their officials. There was even a free airport (with real aeroplanes dangling from the ceiling), and plenty of outré grandeur, a museum like a concrete melon and a town hall like a hat. New old New France, you might say.

Les Pierrais were grateful to *la Patrie* and noisily loyal. They were always marching home to defend her, and trying to forget Canada, even though it was all around. Most people told me they took their holidays on the Côte d'Azur, and few spoke English. Missing Persons posters carried pictures of children lost in the Alps or Lyons, or 4,204 km away in Paris. Everywhere I went, I found the Atlantic being ignored. Here were Fido Dido and *Paris Match*, men in tweed jackets and ox-blood shoes, *glaciers*, *chocolatiers* and deliciously subsidised bread. At times, Saint-Pierre had the air of an old ski-resort that had lost its mountains. It was all so doggedly French, despite the whales and the ice and the British. I even caught *les Pierrais* having a fashion show up a side-street, and found a courtyard where they still played petanque.

Saint-Pierre followed France in everything, even cheese. Suddenly, I was back among cartwheels of brie and salade périgourdine. It was hard to believe that, just across the water, the Newfoundlanders were still chewing their way through hard tack and peas. *Les Pierrais* ignored them (bait-men and servants), and charged me at "international" rates for a call across the bay. This was France, after all, and was even France in its history. Saint-Pierre had had its own French Revolution, its own Terror, its own Jacobin Club and its own guillotine, up on Place Néel. It was even run by the Vichy French for a while but in this it got ahead of *la Patrie*; it was liberated in December 1941 by the biggest submarine in the world, *Surcouf*.

Down on the waterfront, I found myself in a nest of fat-bellied guns, a reminder that, most of the time, the threat had been British. Between 1713 and 1814, the archipelago had changed hands eight times, once in exchange for Madras. By an odd coincidence, the only other person inspecting the guns was a Canadian—from Madras. We ended up having a drink together, at the Bar Joinville. It was a brassy place, no one there but some sailors and a Vietnamese hooker. She clacked at us for a while, until the *patron* chased her out with a stick. We drank a strange pink beer, called *La Fin du Monde.*

I asked Santosh if the British had got the better deal, with Madras. "This place is a fake," he answered, "just copying Europe."

I thought about all I'd seen, the Vietnamese girl, and the pink beer. "But, Santosh," I said, "this *is* Europe."

We decided to see if it was different on the other island, Miquelon, and met the next day on the pier. At first, we couldn't see anything, and our boat seemed to be floating along in steam and disembodied rocks. Then Miquelon appeared. It was ten times the size of Saint-Pierre, but was really two islands, seven miles apart, linked by a drool of sand. The sand had only appeared in the last two hundred years and was constantly tripping up ships. Miquelon had a population of 700, and over 800 shipwrecks. We landed at the only town, which had a church made of debris, and a museum of flotsam. *Les Miquelonnais* were quite unlike *les Pierrais*, descended from Acadians and loyal to no one but God. I will remember them best for their beards, elaborate lace curtains and cabins without foundations. In 1874 they'd rescued the crew of HMS *Niobe*, and as a reward Queen Victoria had given them £47, for which they were still mysteriously grateful.

We drove back along the isthmus. The sand had long ago digested its ships. We saw nothing except wild horses, curled up like puppies in the dunes.

In the end, I decided that Santosh was probably right, and that Saint-Pierre was in an advanced state of deceit. It took me some time to reach this point. As with any travel, one can be happy for a while on mango flan and *morue à la biscayenne,* but then the curiosity gets hungry. Although Saint-Pierre was alluring and pretty, I was troubled by the patterns emerging. The rest of the world, it seemed, was always playing dupe to the islands' schemes, whether fish scams or cargo deals, duty-free or European grants. The place had become an archipelago of chancers and *vendeuses* (with Parisian manners to match). Newfoundland detested its parasitic semi-colony, and was always seeking allies overseas—and finding only Cuba. The islands, said Fidel Castro, were "little pimples."

Being cute, it seemed, had long since replaced hard work. During Prohibition, *les Pierrais* had abandoned fishing to smuggle whisky into Maine. By 1930 they were trans-shipping 300,000 cases a month, and there were so many old boxes that Saint-Pierre became a source of fuel for passing yachts. I even found a house that was panelled in old *Cutty Sark*. The gangsters, they say, met at the Hotel Robert, and I went there once and found a boater labelled "Al Capone." I was surprised at his carelessness with hats, and made a note. I was spotted by the *hôtelière*.

"If you're a writer, you're not welcome," she said, and showed me out.

I didn't blame her particularly. Others took it out on Jehovah's Witnesses (*"PAS DE TÉMOIN JEHOVAH,"* said the signs) but the contempt was general, and diffidence part of the service. Perhaps it was because Saint-Pierre had so much to hide. After Prohibition, *les Pierrais* had lost their appetite for fishing, and were still peddling booze. Several streets sold nothing but whisky and spivvy clothes. One place even offered handbags made out of cod, fish now an accessory not a staple. I bought some Scotch from a Basque, and an intriguing pot of *aza-xukua*. This, as it turned out, was merely a fancy name for cabbage paste.

That evening, I got the ferry out, grateful to be heading back to Newfoundland.

Act VI: Baby Bonus

It's a hard, hard life with nothing to show at the end but broken health and poverty.
—E. Annie Proulx, *The Shipping News*

The moment will inevitably come to most of the children of the sou'west coast when they must board the coastal steamers, carrying their pathetic cardboard suitcases, and disappear into the maelstrom of a life they never knew, a life they have no training for and never wanted...
—Farley Mowat, *This Rock Within the Sea*

Everyone knows that Newfoundland is bankrupt and a pauper and has no power except from us.
—Winston Churchill, 1944

The poverty is appalling and I wonder that they did not have a revolution long ago.
—John Hope Simpson (British Commissioner), 1934

Greatness Newfoundland deserves; greatness she shall have.
—Joey Smallwood, Premier 1949–1971,
The Book of Newfoundland

137

I met someone once who'd known this peninsula in the days before disaster.

Dr. Grace Sparkes was born in 1908, and had nursery-blue eyes and porcelain vowels. She lived in a small wooden house, out amongst the maples and caterpillars of St. John's. On the day I visited her, there were scones for tea, and Dr. Sparkes was already at the door. "I thought you'd forgotten," she said, "you're late."

I apologised. I'd thought five minutes might be polite.

There was a girlish smile. "I'm old. I can say what I like."

She settled us in ancient armchairs, looking tiny and alert amongst all the floral chatter. All around us were paintings and photographs: her father's schooners, the bays and a husband who'd died over fifty years before.

"We left the Burin in 1935," she said. "Came up here on a slide."

She poured the tea, and a life unfolded like the story of Newfoundland.

"Father's three brothers drowned, and mine was killed on the Somme."

There'd been moments of prosperity, back at the beginning.

"I often sailed to Italy and Spain with my father, selling fish."

In Devon, they'd stayed with relatives, left behind in 1740.

"I'm proud to be English. We were raised on Dickens and Trollope."

But then came ruin, and the schooners were sold.

"I was thirteen," said Dr. Sparkes, "when the market just *collapsed*."

Then, there were the Dirty Thirties, she said. Headlice and lassy mogs.

At confederation, she was the first woman to run for the Assembly.

"We were about to lose everything," she said, "without knowing it."

I asked her what she meant.

"Newfoundland sold out," she said, "for Baby Bonus."

138

I stopped a while in Grand Bank, Gracie's old town, where she'd known refinement.

Along the waterfront, they were restoring the old merchants' houses.

The difference between the rich and poor had only ever been a matter of joinery. Success, it seems, had been measured in balustrades, spindles, leaded lights and porticoes. Everyone had had a cast-iron gantry up in the curls and tiles—called the *widow's walk*—where it was fondly believed the ladies spent their days, pining for boats. But the anxiety had been real enough. Gracie remembered one of her father's schooners that had disappeared.

"Then it sailed in," she said. "After two *months* of mourning!"

She smiled at the thought; the captain dirt-black and thinner than Lent.

Now, Grand Bank was trying to revive the old glory with colour: creams, pea-green and lemon-pie, salmon mousse, avocado and raspberry ripple. It looked like the courses of a dinner, all arriving at once. Painting their town in puddings was about all that was left to those who'd stayed on. Not a single fish had flopped through the fish plant in over ten years. At least there was money—or benefits. When the fishery collapsed in 1921, there'd been nothing but the inedible joinery.

These were the worst years, said Gracie, for Grand Bank. Two out of every three people were dependent on cod, and had never had cash. Now they were reduced to growing roots and smuggling liquor, and to some furious religion. There was only one doctor for the entire Burin Peninsula—and this at a time when consumption and beriberi were settling down among the poor. It seemed that everything Grenfell had worked to eradicate in Labrador had now merely flared up in the south. In the stale fetor of the saltbox, tuberculosis multiplied. It bounced around the population in pats of gob and rattly coughs, on cigarettes rolled from newspaper and moss, and in shared beds and rooms for ten. Some tried to scour the air with burning sulphur but it only made them sicker.

"Only the quacks did well," said Gracie, "with their patent cures and coloured water."

The rot in the outports was, however, almost nothing compared to the disease in government. All concept of nobility and service seemed to have left with the troops, and died on the Somme. In 1917, the prime minister accepted a peerage whilst on a visit to England and didn't bother to go home (he sent his resignation back by telegram). The only good thing his successor ever did was to second a vote of no confidence in his own administration, and then resign. That left the way open for Sir Richard Squires, with no nose for government but an eye for the extras.

Meanwhile, around Newfoundland, the decay got worse.

If St. John's ever responded at all, it was usually no more than a spasm of surrealism. During the Spanish Flu, the only aid it ever sent was coffins. All the public money had been committed to a wobbly array of steamers and trains, and Newfoundland was $60 million in the red. Grenfell declared "a famine," and said Squires was "a villain." He had a vision of the island's future, which was oddly prophetic: the railway would be abandoned, roads built and—more controversially— there'd be union with Canada.

Squires called it blackmail, and the two fought a vicious debate.

This was "the bloody trail of a man named Grenfell," said Squires. But it was he who fell first. Two years later, in 1923, he was charged with corruption, tax evasion and stealing from the Poor Relief. Silently, he slid away.

In St. John's, the mud had been busy but, way out at sea, there was something else stirring in the ooze. Then, on 18 November 1929, it erupted, and came roaring ashore.

139

Down the coast, at Lamaline, the houses were still askew.

I drove to the end of the peninsula, where the bogs turned to surf. The attenuation of land was almost imperceptible here, the ocean simply gathering itself into waves of lambkill and sorrel. The air crackled and snapped with salt, and great boulders of wind thundered through the weed. There were no contours, no trees, nothing to stop the Atlantic from plunging inland, which is what happened in 1929. A hundred and sixty miles offshore the seabed suddenly collapsed, and for several hours, Lamaline felt nothing but a ghostly rumble (which was also felt in New York). Then the shock waves struck.

I met a woman whose father had survived the parting of the sea.

"First thing that happened," said Mrs. King, "was the harbour emptied."

Supper and cards were abandoned, and the sheep fled inland.

"People thought maybe a cargo ship had exploded . . ."

Then the ocean returned, in a wall twenty-five feet high. As it reclaimed the seabed it ripped up cables and schooners, and millions of tons of gravel and shell. It hit Lamaline at 90 mph, gathering salt-boxes and wharves in its freezing coils, and rolling them into the bog.

Mrs. King said her neighbour's house was lost at sea, and then reappeared up the coast. Most never saw their homes again. Others found them floating round the harbour.

"Lanterns still burning," said Mrs. King. "And supper on the table!"

She took me to the family's old house, now a museum.

"They found it near where they'd left it, and dragged it inland."

It didn't look like a house that had ridden a *tsunami*, with its varnished staircase and its coronation cups. Mrs. King showed me a section of turf, with a thick seam of shell. "The whole coast was covered in this," she said. "It killed off the fishery for years."

Miraculously, only one person was killed in Lamaline but it was a different story up the coast. Twenty-nine died altogether, sixteen in one village. In Lord's Cove, I found the houses much as the sea had left them, scattered through the mish. In the cemetery was a wooden cross for Sarah Rennie, who'd died at her sewing-machine, and three more for her children, who'd drowned in their cots.

It took two-and-a-half days for news of the disaster to reach St. John's.

It made little difference. Whatever the seismic catastrophes out on the Burin, Newfoundland was in a state of terminal paralysis. It was wandering into the Depression with its debt doubled, and one in four on the dole. Outporters were surviving on a third of the income now needed to ward off starvation. The government kept them busy with relief roads, and they fed themselves on seabirds. Relief was paid at a withering 6¢ a day.

"The country is nearing the breakers," said the Speaker of the Assembly. "If it has to be revolution, let it be revolution."

But political life too had simply seized. There'd been five changes of command since 1923, and soon there'd be only one person left on the wreckage. It was Squires. He was prime minister again, looting the stores whilst Newfoundland went down. He even tried to sell Labrador to Canada, and then started begging off Grenfell. But it was Curwen's old friends, the Cashins, who nailed him. They discovered he'd set aside 200 cases of whisky to bribe the electorate. Now the mood changed, St. John's taut with violence. On 5 April 1932, a mob formed outside Colonial Building, and the windows were smashed. Squires left this piece backstage, lucky to escape with his life. He was last seen running over Bannerman Park and jumping on a Number 66 bus, which carried him off to obscurity.

Now Whitehall reacted, to end the embarrassment. Newfoundland was making a spectacle of itself, and threatening the Empire's credit. The solution was devised by a Scottish barrister, to give Newfoundland "a rest from party politics," and "to let a whole generation of vipers die out from atrophy." It was a bold proposal—not unlike receivership, both ingenious and shameful: Britain would take over the debts in return for control. The House of Assembly had no choice. In November 1933, it declared itself defunct, and signed away the democratic rights of nearly half a million people indefinitely. For the next sixteen years, the island was ruled by civil servants and men in breeches and Sam Brownes, called the Newfoundland Rangers. The outporters have never forgotten the shame, as if they'd surrendered to the Scouts. Gracie Sparkes remembered the forms and the jabs and the endless Cocomalt.

"We got what was good for us alright, but not much of what we wanted."

It was small comfort to those on the Burin, still shovelling gravel. There was no work and the sea was dead. Then news came through of new mines up the coast. Among those that went was the last surviving child of the woman who'd drowned at her Singer.

"Here's salvation," they thought, and I set off after them, over the mish.

They were right. There was salvation, but not as they'd expected.

140

After Lamaline, the coast rose up, and set into great black cliffs.

The old mine was still there, almost throttled in alder. I drove out to Iron Springs one day, and peered through the wire. It was like a giant machine hatching from the rock, conveyors and gantries all rusted solid at the moment of life. All around, the earth was scattered with fluorspar, like chips of green chalk. From 1933 onwards, Iron Springs had been the greatest producer of fluorspar in the world, belching up the green necessary for smelting and atomic bombs and glass. For a whole generation, the miners had worked the drifts with slushers and skips, grateful to be out of poverty and in the dust. One of them still lived in St. Lawrence, six miles back through the thicket.

"I started in 1940," he told me, "soon as I was eighteen."

John Kelly lived on the harbour, behind my boxy hotel. The Kellys' old Red Farm was still there but had started to crumble, and so they'd moved off, into the ragwort. They now had a new cabin of sparkling laminate and horse brasses. We kept ponies, said Mr. Kelly, and I was always Santa at Christmas. Now he was sitting in his braces, rubbing the damp from his joints.

"My brother, Michael Turpin, was also a miner," said Mrs. Kelly.

It was his shift the day a scrunker appeared, tarred and half-dead. We're American, he'd panted. Hundreds dying.

"Michael sent word back," said Mrs. Kelly, "and then set off by slide."

He'd ridden through the snow, out to the headland.

"We were behind him," said Mr. Kelly. "Off to save those we could."

"How do I get there?" I asked.

He showed me, and I drove out to the end of the track. There, I abandoned the car, and continued on foot, across the mish.

Until then, it had been a peculiar war. It had begun with Churchill's pageant on the other side of Placentia Bay, and then came the submarines. The enemy was all around but never seen. By the end, the U-boats would claim some 400 ships in Newfoundland waters (and had even taken pot-shots through The Narrows). The island had never felt so lonely—until the Americans appeared in the winter of 1941. They were extraordinary people, who turned up with whole towns in their boats, even runways and concrete homes.

One of the ships doing the gauntlet was the USS *Truxtun,* an old four-stacker with a thirst like a whale. On 18 February 1942, she tried to zig-zag through the U-boats into Placentia Bay. Dizzy, lost and blind, she missed the mouth by thirty miles, and dropped into a deep chasm of froth and freezing smoke, called Chamber Cove. It was still four in the morning, and at first the captain thought he'd hit an iceberg and threw *Truxtun* into reverse. Now she was wedged between two lethal snags of rock. With her belly ripped open, she began to bleed bunker oil which, as it mixed with the icy water, thickened into tar. Then the storm began to pick the *Truxtun* apart, peeling off the davits and bulkheads and guns. As the ship screamed itself to pieces, men were swept into the frozen sludge and were smothered in black. Only two made it to the scree at the far end of the cove. From there, they cut their way up the cliffs with a knife, and were at the top by dawn. Here they found an old hay-shack, and stopped to get warm. The youngest agreed to go on alone, in search of help.

He then set off across the barrens, in the direction of the mine.

The old hay-shack was still there, on the edge of the mish.

Beyond it was the chasm, and I peered over the rim.

Mr. Kelly had told me he'd never forget that sight. "It was the worst I ever saw . . . Sailors clinging to the hull, bodies in pieces everywhere."

Although it was calm now, the cove was still black with oil. It was hard to imagine the violence of that night. Now the sea was blue and compliant, and there was barely a sound but the chickadees and the wheeze of shingle. From where I stood, at the top of the scree, the cove curled round, and rose to a redoubt, called "the Pinnacle," some six hundred feet above the sea. It was a sheer drop but, at the bottom, was a narrow ledge. Somehow the last survivors had managed to scramble onto this ledge, and there they'd waited for rescue.

"We knew these cliffs," said Mr. Kelly, "from playing here as chits."

I walked round, and climbed the Pinnacle, lashed by tiny whips of spruce. On the north wall was a gully dropping several hundred feet to the sea. I looked over the edge and felt myself floundering in vertigo. That's where we lowered ourselves, said Mr. Kelly, down to the ledge. One by one, they'd hauled the sailors up.

"Some of them were only in shorts, and were there till the afternoon. They were blinded with oil too, and a few were swept out by the tide. We wanted to get a dory and go after them but the Americans said *No, enough have died . . .*"

The last man wasn't hauled clear until dark. Forty-six had been rescued, and another hundred and ten had died. At least one of them was under age, thought Mr. Kelly.

"I often think of him on the cliffs," he'd said. "Getting the last rites from Father Thorne. He said if he'd listened to his mother, he'd not be there . . ."

From the Pinnacle, it was possible to see out across the crags and tufts of granite, down the coast to Lawn Head. Somewhere, way below, I could hear a waterfall, and behind me I could see the mine, like a pin in the horizon. After the miners had hauled the last survivor off the Pinnacle, they'd been told that *Truxtun*'s sister-ship, the USS *Pollux*, was on Lawn Head, and had broken open. The men of Lawn were already there, and had rescued another hundred and forty men. Ninety-three had drowned.

I climbed down off the Pinnacle, and left the empty cove.

The survivors had been taken back, through the snow, to the mine.

"I took the first of the dead," said Mr. Kelly. "The ship's captain."

Back in St. Lawrence, the sailors were taken to the Red Farm, and to the diner that was now my hotel. They were still clogged with oil, in their hair and ears and eyes. The town was barely equipped for such a disaster, with no electricity, no hot water and not much else. But there was no lapse of courage amongst the miners' wives, who appeared with old clothes and sheets. Amongst them was a young woman called Charlotte Kelly.

"Aunt Lot" still lived up behind the church, now eighty-eight.

"It was two of us to each man," she said, "with just water and rags."

She smiled despite her frozen bones. Although it was warm, the stove was high. Grass grew up to the windows, and the parlour smelt of cloves.

"Violet and I had a teenager called Lanier Philips. Said he was from Georgia. Can't get him clean, said Violet. No, my dear, I'm *black*, he says, you can't get me white! He was a wonderful man, sure. Very special to me, and we never lost touch."

The Americans stayed on until a corvette came.

"Some were suspicious at first. Wouldn't eat our food."

Lanier Philips later said he'd expected to be jailed, like home.

Two days later the *Pollux* had sunk, and still lies off Lawn Head.

"I rode out there with my husband," said Aunt Lot. "It was a horrible sight. All we saw was bodies, and legs and arms."

The dead were still being washed up the following summer. Even now, reminders of this catastrophe appear in the cove from time to time: boots, canteens, ammunition, or—in 1997—a cap fossilised in oil. Originally, the dead were buried in the town cemetery but they were not there now. Mr. Kelly told me that, two years later, the Navy had collected them and taken them home.

"Perhaps they should have stayed here," he said, "with their ship."

But America hadn't forgotten St. Lawrence. There were statues and memorials and a proposal from Hollywood. Lanier Philips said the experience of white hospitality had changed his life, and given him the confidence to fight the bigots from within. He became the Navy's first black sonar instructor, and donated a playground to St. Lawrence.

"He's near eighty now," said Aunt Lot, "but he still comes to see us."

The Navy gave each of the rescuers a flag boxed in mahogany, and a letter from the commandant. John Kelly was proud of these things, even though they'd made him "an Honorary Yank." "I'm a Newfoundlander," he said, "and that's that."

Strangely, there'd been no honours for the women.

"We never made nothing of it," said Aunt Lot. "That's how we are."

141

After the *Truxtun,* Newfoundland had a beautiful war.

"It was," said Grace Sparkes, "the best time we'd ever had."

We discovered the Americans, she said, and they found us. They arrived in their thousands, built the biggest airports in the world and turned the island into a fortress. Britain gave them three vast bases in exchange for fifty destroyers, and suddenly Newfoundland was strategic. It was no longer on the edge but in the middle of a huge military migration; over 25,000 planes would pass through Goose Bay alone, and 10,000 ships through "Newfie John." It didn't matter that Newfoundlanders had never been consulted, that there was no democracy, or that what was being defended was not Newfoundland but America. If there was ever an attack, they say, the port of St. John's was to be flooded with burning oil, and the city set ablaze.

"We didn't care," said the Kellys. "We all had work."

One in five men got building jobs, putting up the concrete that's at last turning green. There were new roads and harbours and twenty-five new libraries. Household income doubled and the colony eased itself out of the red. After 1942, not a single cent was paid in able-bodied relief for the rest of the war. Money also brought new, twentieth-century rules; the truck system was outlawed, and going to school became compulsory. There'd be more changes in these few years than there'd been in the last four hundred. At last, Newfoundlanders began to move around on their own land, looking not just modern but strangely amphibious.

Almost better than their money, were the Americans themselves. Newfoundlanders, observed the governor, were dazzled by their "hygiene and efficiency." Here were people with Lucky Strikes, and with their own cars and their own teeth. In the outports, they began to copy them with brilliantine and checks. They also developed a taste for America, for Coca-Cola and processed cheese, flavours they'd not forget. They already knew about Sinatra, but now he was crooning round the island, along with the other stars: Marlene Dietrich, Bob Hope and Phil Silvers. Newfoundlanders now loved the Americans, sometimes too much.

"They carried off 20,000 of our girls," said Grace Sparkes.

Some laughed at this. If you can't get a man, they said, get a Yank.

Others discerned a note of shame, that feeling of inadequacy that dogs every islander. Our men were emasculated, wrote Christopher Pratt, by the presence of Americans. But for the girls, the sex was novel and rewarding. The Minister of Fish said this had been one of the strongest images of his adolescence, watching them losing their innocence in Bannerman Park.

I asked Dr. Sparkes what she'd thought of America coming to town. "Wonderful," she said, "but the Canadians were zombies."

It was a party almost too good to end. At its height, there were over 25,000 Americans in Newfoundland, amongst them Johnny Weissmuller, Steve Lawrence and John F. Kennedy. But the war did end, though with fewer tears than last time (some 900 had been killed). One of the worst casualties had been the Grenfell mission, whose fortunes always stumbled when Newfoundland prospered. It had lost its funds and its volunteers, and two schools had closed. But for the government there was triumph; it was $30 million in profit.

The Minister of Fish told me that, with money like that, there was no going back. "It was natural," he said, "that the Commission of Government should lose its legitimacy."

But who'd replace the British lawyers? Surely not the fish-men again?

The answer was a pig-breeder from Gambo, called Joey Smallwood.

142

Dr. Sparkes had known Joey all her political life.

Her verdict was succinct: "He stank."

Like Newfoundland, Joey'd had a good war, but the whiff of slurry never quite left him. Pigginess would be the mark of his rule, the end of the great fishocracy. But, although he was short and astute and hairless, he'd made an incongruous hog. He wasn't fat exactly but improbably fleet, and the hard, shiny eyes were framed in enormous rims like a raptor's. Looking back, he was a truly Orwellian creation: unsentimental, stark and Klaxonic. His life had even taken an Orwellian course up until then; born at the beginning of the century, educated with the best, and then ideologically restless. He'd walked through the Great Depression, started an encyclopaedia, stirred up the labour movement, bred pigs and become selectively socialist, and affectedly grimy. It was Squires who taught him the tricks of Liberal politics (always an ominous sign) but it was on radio that Joey had found himself. For six years, until 1943, he was "The Barrelman," a tireless chatterer, patriot, sage and pundit. He became the best-known voice in Newfoundland, a man with a deadly weapon: he could talk without pause.

"He could go on all day," said Gracie Sparkes, "and all night."

The sheer quantity of talk was devastating. Some were mesmerised and others were driven to surrender. It was relentless, repetitive, messianic and insistent. Opponents found themselves drained of willpower, and everyone else was transfixed. These were extraordinary displays of rhetoric, like watching an onion getting dressed layer by layer:

> What a week! In nearly 500 years, there has never been *anything* like it! There has never been anything even *remotely* like it! There may never be anything like it again . . . Newfoundland's dream has come true! Answers to our prayers. Newfoundland has hungered and thirsted for the Third Mill. *Hungered and thirsted!* Ached and yearned and *prayed* . . . !

Speeches like this could last whole meetings with no one else saying a word. The only difficulty with this was that—until 1946—there was nothing for it to attach to, no cause.

Then Joey discovered confederation. If he was to be the island's prophet, this was his best hope. It wasn't a new idea; the concept of union with Canada had been in the cross-fire for years. The merchants hated it and so did the Catholics. Once again, it was Curwen's old friends, the Cashins, who tried to rein things back. They fronted the Responsible Government League, a return to devolved rule. Joey's response was typically savage; he said he'd wipe the Cashins out (along with all the other merchants).

"Cashin was a brave man," said Gracie, who'd supported him.

But, in Britain, the new socialist government backed Joey. The opportunity to shed Newfoundland was almost too good to be true. For years, Whitehall had suffered the embarrassment of this dead democracy. Now, it saw only dole queues ahead, and had visions of an Imperial slum caked across America's doorstep. The Prime Minister, Clement Attlee, had once likened Newfoundland to a reformed drunk, tempted to have a nip once more, but unable to trust itself. But he had no intention of funding the Commission indefinitely, and nor did he fancy Responsible Government (and the spectre of Squires). As if to convince the Newfoundlanders that they didn't want to remain British, he sent them a new governor they were sure to detest: Sir Gordon MacDonald.

"He was an old Welsh miner," said Gracie. "Didn't drink, didn't smoke and didn't play cards. He wasn't going to like it here."

He was offered a gong, say The Monarchist League, to get rid of us.

The end for old Newfoundland was surprisingly quick, and still reeks of swill. Responsible Government won the first referendum—but only just (with 69,400 votes, against 64,066 for the confederates). After that, all the old wounds opened—Catholic fears and merchant envy—and Joey rushed around, rubbing in salt and snuffling out support. MacDonald was cantankerously British, and the anti-confederates divided themselves between those who wanted to go it alone and the little Americans. Everyone cried foul. The Monarchists said Joey got voters' names off graves, and the merchants said the issue was far too complex to be left to "such simple people." Even now, there were still plenty who considered the second referendum a sham. Not Gracie. She thought Newfoundlanders had simply voted to survive and fill the trough.

"Ottawa paid out benefits we'd never dreamt of—like Mother's Allowance—and we'd need that, after the war."

With confederation, they'd receive $7 million a year in Baby Bonus.

It wasn't hard to vote for the money. In the next round, Joey swung the vote 78,323 in his favour, 71,334 against. A bare majority was enough and so, on April Fool's Day 1949, Britain's oldest colony became Canada's newest province.

"In town, flags flew at half-mast," said Gracie, "and the nuns cried."

On the day MacDonald became a foreigner and headed home, a poem appeared in the *Evening Telegraph*. It was called "A Farewell!" and praised the old governor's wisdom. It was only once copies were all over the city that the editors noticed the acrostic; the first letter of each line spelt out THE BASTARD. The author never came forward to claim the laughter.

But it was only a flicker of levity. Ever since then, the generation of 1949 have argued about the wisdom of union. Some saw it as salvation, and at least one outporter has been buried with a picture of Joey clutched to her chest. Others saw it as a humiliation, and resented the Canadians with their dull politics, accents as flat as wheat, and all that French.

"We're more part of Europe than America," the Irish told me.

Joey was a Black, they grumbled, a raving Protestant.

"Union cost us the seal hunt," said the north-coast English.

"And our cod," said the fishermen.

"That's bullshit!" said the Minister of Fish. "We'd lost it anyway."

Some dreamed of going it alone, like Iceland.

"That's just talk," said the Minister. "Eighty per cent are pro-Union."

Fifty years on, that was still vociferous dissent.

But in 1949, there'd been even worse news for the die-hards: Joey had won the election and was now in power. He'd remain there for the next twenty-five years.

Gracie became a journalist, so she could fight him better.

A thought suddenly occurred to me.

Did she know who wrote the acrostic?

"They'll hang me and burn my clothes," she grinned, "but it was me."

143

If there'd ever been a funny side to the years after union, St. Lawrence missed out. The mine, that had saved so many, was now beginning to kill.

One evening, I went to the town bar, the Trophy Lounge.

Although no one could remember where the soccer had come from, the Laurentians were champions. They'd won the football eight years on the trot, and called their town "the soccer capital of Canada." There were pitches by the fish-plant, and more by the hospital. Whole families played football, and dreamed of spotlights and Manchester United. One man told me he'd had twenty siblings, and that three went professional and four died in infancy.

"... and my poor father was one of the 1952 champions."

The day Bob Kelly died was a day of mourning for all.

"He was only 53," said the footballer. "A giant of a man."

Father had worked in the mine, he said. It was a real hard death.

"He didn't die, he *perished*."

I asked what had happened.

"Go and ask my mother," he said. "She'll want to tell you."

Eileen Kelly lived in a plastic house over the harbour.

"Come in," she said, without expression.

The experience of life had left Eileen blank, a person used-up and empty. It was an odd effect, making it hard to remember anything about her. Perhaps she wanted it that way, willing herself not there. She was only seventy-one, just old enough to remember the optimism, the first wages and the corporation concerts. In those days, the miners had had a song, never suspecting that the mine would kill them all:

> Oh, so merry, so merry are we!
> We go down at seven and come up at three.
> Hi derry, hi derry, hi derry, ding dong!
> Give the miners good pay, and there's nothing goes wrong!

Bob was a driller, she said, dust gushing in his face all day. Some of the boys wore scrim or a cheese-cloth over their mouths but it didn't do much. You still had to hook your nose out, and haul away the dirt. The air was never checked and there were no medicals or regulations or even ventilation. The union tried to get something done, but no one listened.

"So Bob breathed dirt," said Eileen, "and was happy just bein' paid."

But it was more than dirt in the air. There were radon and silica, gas and tiny particles attacking the lungs. The silica nested among the bronchi, causing them to thicken with scabs and sludge. The radon was more vicious, scorching the cells, making them bubble and mutate. It wasn't long before lung cancer was ablaze among the miners, but little was done. When the men started to cough, they were sent to St. John's with "Miner's TB," and that was it.

"A cover-up," said Eileen, "from the very start."

Many blamed Joey for the inertia that followed. Joey loved mines, production, things that were assembled, factories, industry, exports in packets and workers in mills. He detested fish. He hated the way fish had left Newfoundland with nothing to show for the last five hundred years. He despised the sea, and wore bow-ties and fedoras as a statement of urbanity. Nor had the Smallwoods ever fished (they'd always been what the name suggests: little people, working in timber). Now Joey had a chance to rebuild Newfoundland in his own image. He told his subjects they didn't know what was good for them, that he'd drag them "kicking and screaming into the twentieth century," and that they must "develop or perish." "Haul up your boats!" he said. "Burn your fishing gear!" From now on, he'd rule to a single precept: "Industrialise at all costs!" He wasn't going to let a little coughing upset his plans.

So it was that Bob Kelly died, for Joey's progress.

I didn't ask Eileen about his last years. As her son said, silicosis is a real hard death. First, the breath shortens, and there's no more football. Then there's a note for the specialist, and fears for the worst. The news is incomprehensible, and some go to pieces, beating their fists or roaming the dark. There's no help and the other men are silently relieved it's not them. Now the lungs begin to saw for breath, and a man loses his "nature" and will never bother a woman again. His powerful stride becomes a shuffle, and he can no longer row his dory, and so it's sold. He's vomiting now, and his old friends don't know him, with his leathery sockets and fingers like clubs. The nights are the worst, feeling that he'll smother in his own scaly carcass. I'm still young, he tells himself, as he drowns in old age. Soon he won't need a bed, but will be kneeling over the chair, grasping at the air, trying to haul it inside. In the last months, all he ever asks himself is: which breath will be my last? When will the pump stop, and the cold come in?

"We watched him die," sobbed Eileen, and that was all she said.

Some two hundred men died like this. No reliable figures exist.

"St. Lawrence was wiped out," Aunt Lot had said.

She'd lost four brothers, her brother-in-law and her husband.

"Louis was only fifty-six when he died, in 1961."

Even the heroes of the *Truxtun* weren't spared the industrial death. Silicosis killed the best of them, including their leader, Rennie Sleaney, and Eileen's brother, Michael Turpin (who'd raised the alarm). I found them all, up at the cemetery, in their early graves. John Kelly was spared but only because—after *Truxtun*—he was caught in an underground crusher, and never went down again.

Even Joey's old socialist friends reeled at the horror.

A whole generation, wrote Horwood, was sacrificed for profit.

But compensation was no part of the plan. Louis got nothing for his six years' agony, and died on relief. The corporation resisted all redress until the seventies, and still wouldn't give up his records. Only the Americans behaved with dignity, remembered their old friends and built them a hospital. But it was too late. All that was left were the humiliating wrangles, lawyers squabbling over the different grades of dying. Eventually, Eileen and Aunt Lot settled for a widow's cap: no lump sum, no funeral expenses, $621 a month. It was enough to survive on but hardly recompense. In terms of my own travel, it would have bought a week's car hire, fifteen fish suppers, or a fortnight of dreary motels.

Unsurprisingly, the mine survived this blow, and thrived under Joey. It carried on, billowing fluorspar, until 1991, when a cheaper source was found in Mexico. Everyone was fired—except two guards—and Iron Springs was flooded. Then the corporations moved out, and St. Lawrence reverted to what it had always been: a cluster of shanties by the sea, with nothing left but football. The only difference was that now, one in every three families were bereaved by dust.

But memories were short. Now people were talking of the mine opening again. I asked Eileen about this, and she was more translucent than ever.

"Over my dead body," she said emptily. *"Over my dead body."*

144

Parts of the Burin were as bare now as at any time since Shakespeare.

As I drove around the peninsula, I often came upon abandoned names: Point Rosie, Wandsworth, Molliers, Famine and Grouse. Nowadays there was nothing there but stumps and rust and splinters of glass. There were more of these places, I'd heard, out on the islands—Jacobean hideaways and fantasies (like Great Paradise, Toslow and Haystack). They were all now abandoned. They'd been built to enable men to live among the fish, never further away than a few hours' rowing. But they couldn't compete in the age of the engine, freezers and trawlers, and the young began to drift away. By the end of the war, Newfoundland had over 1,300 outports, most of them merely quaint.

I headed west again, over the barrens. From up there, I could look back over the voyage I'd done, along the South Coast. Below me, like wisps of smoky blue, I could see the little islands of Sagona and Brunette. My old travelling companion, Joshua the Twine Man, had been born on Brunette. We had brooks and woods, he'd said, our own church and a one-room school.

"Gad's own place," he'd say. "Though we'd neither meat nor malt."

"Asgoodas ever waterwet," said his wife.

Joey thought differently, and declared a War on Isolation.

"It's a deadening thing!" he sneered. "A paralysing thing! A *cruel* thing!"

No one one can blame Joey for wanting to sweep up the pieces, but the war he fought was mean. It was a cunning offensive, more carrot than stick, luring the fishermen off the rocks. There was a purse for those who'd move ($2,000 a house, plus $200 per head), and wilderness for those who wouldn't. Gradually, the services began to shrivel; the coastal steamers were withdrawn, Brunette lost its teacher and the doctor stopped calling. Joey only needed eighty per cent approval to close a place down, and he usually got it. Between 1954 and 1975, over 250 outports were abandoned or—in the Doublethink of the time—"re-settled." Over 30,000 people were uprooted and moved. It was, wrote Farley Mowat, "a sadistic scheme."

Joshua had remembered the day they left, in 1955. "We burned down the church, and put the school on floats. We dug up the taties, and pulled down the sheds. Everything was going—every pot and porringer rolled up in coats, and packed in barrels. Even the cat was put in a box. Then we sold our gear, gave away the dogs, and put the house in the water . . ."

I looked out across the blue. It must've been twenty miles to Brunette.

"Yes, boy," said Joshua. "T'was a fair hike."

Mowat had once watched a village floating away like this. At his side was a government official. "These people are scum," she said. "They're descended from scum, and they're still scum."

Joey got away with it because Newfoundland was his.

There was no democracy left, and only sparse dissent. The British were barely home before their High Commissioner was warning of a "democratic dictatorship." Joey had wooed the people with Baby Bonus, and then he enslaved them with patronage. This was now Canada, and here to be flourished and abused. Joey had control of everything in his own, perfect Orwellian state: licenses, permissions, careers, regulations, monopolies, and—of course—the benefits. Over fifty per cent of the island's gross product was in the hands of the government, or in Joey's gift. What's more, any man opposing him could be neutered with executive action—or inaction (unable to fish perhaps, or brew, sell bait, build, lend money or catch a rabbit). In the most closely governed country in the world, Joey found himself rolling in power.

He didn't even need to worry about his own party. The Liberals had become Joey, unable to move or think without his assent. There was no ideology, and the budgets were dreamed up by Joey as he went along. His minions called him "King Joey" and he never objected. He just assumed they were infantile, and repeated everything twice. Eventually, he moved his court out of St. John's, to a royal sty set in 1,400 hectares of Crown land. There, at "Russwood Ranch," Joey enjoyed the constant attention of sycophants and callers, messengers, informers, fools, fops and helicopters. Nothing was ever paid for. It was all gifts from contractors, including the avenue and the swimming pool, and all the swanky furniture. It was a place befitting the leader of what he called "one of the great small nations of the world." He was often ringing Nixon and Khrushchev to give the bigger ones advice.

I asked Gracie Sparkes about the new king.

"I never trusted him further than I could throw a fish truck."

But he was vicious with his critics, and they seldom survived. Joey often lambasted Gracie in the House (under the cover of privilege), and even came round and screamed through her door. But the most spectacular blasts were saved for the Minister of Fish. Crosbie was only a new boy when Joey sensed dissension, and called him up.

"I'm dismissing you," he said.

"Like fuck you are," said the Minister of Fish, and resigned.

Joey ignited. He was never more vile than in his avenging address, which was broadcast live. It was a warning to those who'd defy him:

Everybody in the Assembly knows we are faced by a hate-filled man, a man whose political reason is tottering! A man who is just a bagful of hate! *A skinful of hate!* He can't conceal it . . . Sometimes I'm afraid. Maybe I should have a bodyguard? While I am alive on this earth, that man will hate me to my grave. Now *that* is a diseased mind! That's political reason that is tottering! It's undermined. The man is a sad case . . .

There weren't many who could stomach vitriol like that, and so resistance withered.

And what about the outporters, floating their homes across the bay?

"He promised us a new start," said Joshua, "in a *growth centre.*"

But, as they'd discover, that too was merely Doublethink.

145

Nowhere had suffered disillusion more than Fortune.

"I don't know why anyone ever came here," said the garage-owner.

The Lakes had been merchants in Fortune since Napoleonic times, and still sold groceries, and hired out cars. As I handed my keys back, Mr. Lake asked me where I was from, and I told him: England.

"Don't know why we ever left," he said.

I could understand his despondency. Fortune was one of the few places in Newfoundland where I felt I could trudge along for ages, getting nowhere. It was just an endless repetition of plastic hutches, humans in storage, lodged in the shale. In 1896, the whole coast had caught fire, and the trees had never returned. The population had doubled in the fifties, to nearly two thousand, and—to the new arrivals—it was supposed to have been a Growth Centre. But it was the centre of nothing, and nothing ever grew here. I knew that Lucy and Joshua lived out there somewhere, among the hutches, but I didn't visit them. I'd sensed they didn't want me to.

"Some didn't adjust too well," they'd said, "leaving Brunette."

"Olderfolks," said Lucy, "just curledupand died."

Everyone had their stories of men going mad (or whose madness was noticed). There was Jimmy D who wore his boots in bed, or Uncle Nat with a mind like a gull. I often wondered if people envied the insane, as if they'd never left the islands. A whole generation still dreamed of the rocks.

From the shore, we could just see Sagona and Brunette.

"We still go once a year," people said, "to clean the graves."

No one had ever lived there again, except buffalo.

"That was one of Joey's ideas," said Joshua. "Buffalo from Alberta."

But the animals had known only the flat, and fell over the cliffs.

"The last of them fell in 1998," said Joshua.

"Probably suicide," said Mr. Lake.

That night I wandered aimlessly around the town. It didn't seem to have a heart, and so I drifted from bar to bar, into the Legion, and back to the bars. In one place, they were selling mugs of *Sex on the Beach*, and another was full of old ladies, waltzing like cattle. I felt lonely and purposeless, and decided that I'd been tainted by Fortune. The fish-plant had closed for the season, and so only one in seven had work. The rest looked like me, itinerant and spare.

I talked to several people, but found them oddly disconnected. They didn't seem to think of Fortune as home, but as a passing phase. There was a past, and an escape, but no present. Even those around them were temporary and abstract, relationships severable at will. Some had lost their neighbours and friends during resettlement, and had never replaced them. One man said he'd been separated from his sister, some forty years before. She'd ended up 166 miles away, on the other side of the bay, and I realised I'd met her, the previous Easter; she was Freeman Upshall's wife, out in Placentia.

The disruption of ties had, it seemed, left people bitter and fractious. I remembered how St. John's had been criss-crossed with fissures, but Fortune had splintered. Everyone suspected each other of having money, running rum and cheating the benefits. We can't keep staff, said one of the landlords, because they're always fighting. Even more disconcerting was the gab. People just heaped me with gossip.

"That feller in your hotel's a fuckin' *wino* . . ."

"And they never change the sheets . . ."

In one place, I sat with a couple discussing the barmaid.

"She's got the clap," said the wife.

Her husband disagreed.

"It weren't clap!" he said. "It were *cancer*."

And how did *he* know?

"Cos I seen the scars!"

The police had learnt to exploit these divisions, and had turned the grapevine into a coastguard. Running rum from Saint-Pierre was still the best way of picking up a few extras in Fortune. A man could make $20 a crock. But now the Mounties were offering rewards for every tip-off, worth a third of the haul. They didn't need fast boats any more. Avarice policed avarice.

The community's gone, people said, fallen apart.

"And what about the informers," I asked, "if they're found out?"

"Heaven help them," they said.

On the way back, I was caught by someone I assumed was a ghost. He had an Elizabethan beard, and strong thin fingers that snapped round my arm.

"I am a man of letters, and have read widely on topics various . . ."

Although firmly attached, he was harmless, so I let him babble along.

"I'm a Cooper—that's English—but I'm also a Simms, and that's Russian in my learning . . . This place is Fortune, the best there was. Verily, a place of damnéd pirates. Tsk! Tsk! We called our ships *Golden Fortune, Fortune Hind . . .*"

I was now on the shore road, and could hear a dog barking out at sea.

Was he mad or drunk? I wondered. *Or was I?*

"A pirate am I, by my troth," said the bony face. "A fuckin' pirate!"

I felt tired, unable to make sense of it all. The hot night, the sea barking and the slapstick pirate. Soon everything would be back at the beginning, and I'd meet myself at the start. A full circle, I mused, a circumnavigation of the time of fish. That was fine for me, but what about Newfoundland? Even the pirate must have sensed my unease because he ungrappled and lurched away.

I last heard him as he disappeared into the shadows.

"It's all yours, stranger!" he howled. "Just douse the lights when you leave!"

146

I took the bus back to St. John's, through the last of Joey's schemes.

"We gotta bit of a lop on," said the driver. "Nice bit of rain ahead."

The nice bit of rain turned out to be Hurricane Gustav, scything its way through the province. I had no idea violence could be so grey. The windows pinged and rattled under watery gunfire, and we rolled around like a bottle. Outside, I could just see the barrens, roots tearing and ashen with rage, every pond an explosion of froth. They looked like little gasps of ocean, bursting in the mish. I hardly noticed Marystown and Arnold's Cove—more of Joey's "growth centres"—the cement fading into the fury.

Then we were out on the Trans-Canada, the road he'd coaxed off the mainland to eat up his railway. "Out with the old," he'd say, "and in with new." There were glimpses too of his more expansive self;

chimneys, saw-toothed roofs, water-tanks and crumbling glass. "I'll dot Conception Bay with factories," he'd promised, but with no clue how. Instead of feasibility studies and consultation, he'd hired a mysterious Eastern European who'd said that, but for the Nazis, he'd have been president of Latvia. Then they'd toured Germany, Joey beaming uncomprehendingly as Valdmanis helped himself to ten per cent. People will never forget the bargains they'd come back with.

"A chocolate factory, for Crissake! And no freckin' chocolate!"

"And a place for making gloves outta antelopes!"

Conception Bay had been dotted with absurdities. There'd also been factories making leaky rubber boots (which were an eyesore for a while, until they were burnt), and hockey-sticks. The eye-glass factory hadn't sold anything either because the equipment turned out to be worthless scrap, and its vendor had bolted. Happily, other schemes didn't even get a roof—like the plan to extract magnesium from seawater, or the "Custard Swept-Wing Aeroplane." By 1953, Joey had spent $26 million dollars on the industrialisation of Newfoundland, with not a Walnut Whip to show. He'd had Valdmanis jailed, and begun again.

He was now gambling, doubling the stakes to recoup his losses. But he'd learnt nothing about odds, or tipsters. Joey still had a weakness for long-shots and chancers. He couldn't resist people who talked in possibilities, and he assumed that their girls and cigars made them big hitters. He didn't seem to notice that it was Newfoundland's money being thrown around, or that the advisers were share-washers and corporate bandits. The next one was John Doyle.

"An evil genius," said the Minister of Fish, "a seductive slug."

Doyle would have stripped Newfoundland down to the bedrock if he'd had the chance. He spent ten times as much as Valdmanis had, with little more to show. He managed to sell the provinces' mines at a very reasonable price—to himself—and then started looting the mills. In the end, he was charged with over four hundred counts of fraud, but he didn't wait for the outcome: he jumped bail, and made for Panama where, in 2000, he died like a sultan, at Newfoundland's expense.

But there was one more fast-talker, and one more scheme. No sooner was Doyle back on the run than he was replaced by John Shaheen, whose roots were muddied together with Nixon and the CIA. He dreamed up the most fanciful project ever, at a cost of $86 million. It was a refinery, and would produce 100,000 barrels of oil a day, finally putting Newfoundland amongst the "great small nations of the world" (along with Brobdingnag and Ruritania). Joey was ecstatic, well beyond the reach of reason. In his dream of pipes, he'd lost his sense of irony, and overlooked the warnings; the new refinery was to be built in a fathomless cove, called Come By Chance.

We passed the pipes as we splashed up the highway. I could just make out a few oily threads rising out of the spruce, and the cold chimneys like old clarinets. If Joey had had his way, the sky would have been black with money, and the road cluttered with business. Instead, we had it all to ourselves. The refinery had never been as good as the day it opened in 1973. Shaheen had taken over the New York Waldorf-Astoria, and then chartered the *QEII* to bring everyone back to Come By Chance. Aboard this "ship of fools" was the Minister of Fish, enjoying a sumptuous catastrophe. By the time they got to the refinery, it was pouring, and the tented reception had been raided by the locals. The Come-By-Chancers had ransacked the marquees, and made off with anything portable—hams, roasts of pork and even the lobsters.

"It was a shambles," said the minister.

It was also Joey's swan song. Within three years the refinery had collapsed, owing over $500 million (even Cunard never got paid for the *QEII*). Joey had already lost power in the preceding election, and he'd never regain it. At one point, he'd flooded the island with 3-D pictures of himself, all paid for with graft. They hadn't done any good, although they still turned up from time to time. I have one on my study wall. In it, Joey is wearing a turquoise suit and silver leaping-cod cufflinks, a reminder of the uncertain splendour of office.

We passed the turning for Joey's ranch. He'd done well to escape the sea but there was no escaping what Newfoundland was. In time, both the Russwood Ranch and Joey became forgotten and neglected. The paint crumbled off the ranch and Joey shuffled into bankruptcy (saved only by a whip-round in the outports). Some think he should have been prosecuted for his corruption but there was no enthusiasm for such a spectacle. Many Newfoundlanders saw too much of themselves in Joey: dogged, persistent and bloody. Besides, by the end of the eighties, a series of strokes had dismantled his tyranny, and left him speechless. He died alone, aged ninety-one, on 17 December 1991.

Then he was on this road again, heading back for his fishing-port capital, always a place of dubious loyalty. In a final twist, Joey's funeral was held at the Basilica, the only building big enough for all. The Catholics had never liked Joey as much as now.

147

As we rounded Mount Pearl, the hurricane lifted and blew away.

Spread out below, I could see places I'd been to in the winter. It all looked different now, green and bright blue, like a map. I could make out draggers on Conception Bay, the Bog of Avalon and the thin, diaphanous slash of Trinity Bay. Then, it had all seemed so archaic and raw. Now, it all seemed oddly familiar, which almost certainly meant it was time to go home.

From up here, St. John's looked different too. It was Joey's city, not merely a harbour on the edge of a great ocean but a capital on the flanks of a great island. He'd ignored the harbour, and had blocked off the view with a multi-storey car-park and a great orange lump, called Atlantic Place. Attention had turned inland. Roads, carriage-ways, avenues and highways now surged out of the woodwork, in search of industry and progress. On the edge of the bog was a university in Joey's own image, chunked in concrete and Doublethink. "Shaping the Minds," ran the hoardings, "that Shape our Province."

But Joey was never more Orwellian than with his Ministry of Love. From here, Confederation Building looked like a stake, blankly marking the end of the past. But, up close, it was a tower of Babelian ambition and Stalinist sensibility. From his eyrie near the top, Joey had ranted at the world from 1960 onwards, at Canada and God, and all his ministers. He'd even had megaphones wired to all their rooms so he could bully them electronically. I visited the building once, and was surprised to find it as grey inside as it was on the outside. I got lost in all the concrete and cabbagey vapours, and thought I caught a whiff of Victory Gin. Then I was rescued by a pale, androgynous creature in a singlet.

"Some height," I said feebly, as we caught sight of the city again.

Ariel smiled colourlessly, and almost vanished.

"Our Mr. Smallwood always wanted to look down on the merchants."

I was back where I'd begun, in the greatest outport of them all, the city of sweet revenge.

Epilogue

We love thee, frozen land!
—Newfoundland national anthem

After all the bludgeonings of fate, Newfoundland's head may be bloody but it is still unbowed.
—Joey Smallwood, *The Book of Newfoundland*

Newfoundland presented me with things to paint—the fish, the cruelty, but also an understanding of the basic . . . everything stripped down; true joy, real hate, no apologies. Nobody apologises for hating anybody here.
—Mary Pratt, Canadian painter

Someone once asked how you can tell which ones are the Newfoundlanders when you visit heaven. The answer is you can always tell the Newfoundlanders because they're the ones who want to go home.
—John Crosbie, *No Holds Barred*

I love it here. If I ever have to leave, I will go sobbing and screaming.
—Elliott Leyton, anthropologist

148

The storm had moved on, and with it the plague of caterpillars.

It surprised me how excited I was to be back in St. John's. Suddenly, the reserve and propriety of the bays seemed to fall away. It was almost as if, until then, I'd been seeing everything through veils of mist, and now it was ablaze with fresh paint and footlights. I walked everywhere, re-absorbing the pantomime. I'd forgotten how Johnsmen shouted at each other as if they were audiences, how they strutted and flounced, and how they even managed to get swagger down a mobile phone. ("Hello fellah!" they'd roar. "Whaddya at?") Downtown looked as if it was at the end of a line-dance festival, and then I realised it always looked like this. Whole streets smelt of beer, and throbbed with drums. Every surface was crusted in invitations; concerts, plays, rock, feminists, swingers, swappers and weirdos (the Broken Hearts Club had a do going, at a pub called "Bitters"). The Johnsmen, it seemed, hated silence and blank space, and had devoted themselves to filling it. Even a patch of wasteland wasn't without words. "Thank-you," said a sign, "for admiring our potatoes."

I could now see why the Baymen detested their capital. The Johnsmen seemed to be talking for the whole island, doing all the dancing, making all the decisions and yet in a state of perpetual revelry. I realised that, by liking them as much as I did, I was being somewhat perverse. After all, what was there to like? The Johnsmen were boisterous, irreverent, congenitally angry and liked nothing more than a laugh at the Baywops. Even the Johnsmen weren't sure what made their city so endearing.

If we knew why it was so special, they'd say, it wouldn't be special.

As before, I stayed with the Bairds. The storm had back-combed the cats, and ripped up the garden furniture and heaped it into a pyre. I found Angie, crumpled up in the kitchen, not so much a victim of the weather as of a merciless party. She was undecided whether to have a headache or a hairdo, and so I wandered off to the bookshop in search of Jim. He looked strained and anxious.

"People are dropping dead all around me," he said.

He wondered if he was having a mid-life crisis.

"I've got to *do* something," he said. "Go to Morocco . . ."

Eventually, we decided his anxiety wasn't simply middle age.

There was a easier explanation: winter was on its way.

149

Curwen arrived back from Labrador later in the season, after his bruising voyage. Winter was already snapping at the *Albert,* cracking the superstructure and shredding the sails. In the last spasms of the voyage, the boat's launch was tossed in the air and splintered itself across the decks. I know this journey would have terrified me but—infuriatingly—my great-grandfather reports it all with his usual detachment. He even manages to name the birds as they're blasted round the sky, and notes that, though the *Albert* was almost a wreck, "this did not disturb my sleep." He makes little comment about his salvation, or St. John's, except "Trousers & black coat—ugh! Necessary I suppose."

There was no sign of Grenfell. Curwen didn't worry. The last time he'd seen him, Grenfell had been off on a whim of his own, and Curwen knew he'd reappear all in good time. After a week of hanging around, he went shooting. Grenfell was still missing when he got back, a week later. All the ports had been alerted, a search launched and London notified. "Worst of all," noted Curwen wearily, "I found a report of his being missing had been wired home." The papers had announced the death of a hero.

But Grenfell wasn't dead, of course, and a few days later came bouncing through the Narrows, guns blazing and flags aloft. He seemed oblivious to the distress he'd caused. "I simply put into the next harbour," he told his mother airily, "and had a great time among the people." His colleagues weren't there to share the celebrations. When Bobardt and Curwen heard he was on his way, they took off into the interior, on the pretext of sport. Friendship—if it had ever been that—had run its course.

The city's great fires had made it hard to reconstruct the days Curwen spent waiting. In October 1893, most of St. John's was still just a sludge of mud and ash. When I came across "The Star of the Sea," I thought for a moment I'd found the old hall where Curwen had lectured to the frozen, homeless Johnsmen. It was a hollow, wooden building like an upturned boat, the inside as blue as an egg. Curwen's talk had been a memorable occasion, with magic lanterns and a speech by his new friend, Governor O'Brien. But this wasn't the same "Star of the Sea."

"No, boy," said the curator, "the old hall burnt down in 1925."

He invited me to stay all the same, and have a drink at the Benefit.

"What's it in aid of?" I asked.

"Two families just got burned outta Casey Street."

Fire, it seemed, was still the scourge of St. John's.

I wondered if the fires had consumed Curwen's Esquimau arte-facts. He and Dr. Moses Harvey, patron of the giant squid, were regular visitors to the Museum—but so were the fires. Had Curwen left his finds in St. John's, the knives and *ulus* and the polar bear necklace? Dr. Moses had written a rapturous article for the London *Daily Chronicle,* listing the pieces and adding a few intriguing embellishments of his own (such as "a number of skulls and skeletons"). Perhaps Curwen had donated his collection to the Newfoundland Museum? If so, there wasn't much hope for it. In the Dirty Thirties the museum was plundered by its curators and then swept by fire. Almost everything was lost, and even the giant squid was grilled to a crisp.

The present-day museum was unable to help. It was a sooty-looking place that had arisen from the ashes of the old Athenaeum. No one had ever heard of the collection or Curwen, or even the giant squid.

"And there's no way of knowing," they said, "who gave us what."

My archaeologist friend was unsurprised.

"This is St. John's," he said. "We don't really do culture."

The mystery of the artefacts remained unresolved for some months. After my return to England, I rang a few collections but came up with nothing. My mother and my aunt—Curwen's only grandchildren— had no memory of ever having seen the Esquimau pieces. They weren't listed in his probate papers, and I began to assume they'd been burnt. Then—out of the blue—I got a message from a St. John's historian, who knew I was looking. Your great-grandfather's pieces, she wrote, are in the British Museum.

It was true, and a few weeks later the curator sent me a copy of the register for 1933. There were the thirty-four pieces—weapons, figures, bears' teeth and *ulus*—all minutely drawn. They'd been entered between a Fijian war club and some tree-bark from Pitcairn Island, thought to be Fletcher Christian's trousers.

150

It troubled me that I was leaving almost empty-handed. I'd obviously inherited Curwen's urge to collect but was unable to think of anything magnificent. Not only had he got his collection of antiquities, but there were also a vast array of mosses and stuffed birds and a trunk full of sealskin outfits. Grenfell had managed to fill a whole school with oddities like this. I tried not to think about the travellers before them. Corte Real had returned to Lisbon with fifty-seven slaves, and even James Audubon had managed seven enormous Newfoundland dogs. At what point, I wondered, had travel become so pitifully light-weight? All I had was a pair of child's boots, a jig, a portrait of Joey Smallwood and a caribou's head.

In desperation, I took a look around the shops on Water Street. Joey was right to say his Newfoundlanders had never made anything, and wrong to imagine that they ever would. Almost everything for tourists was imported, made elsewhere to feed the myths. There were fluffy seals, plastic "Newfies" (grinning rubber-booted runts, either fishing or drunk), chocolate moose-droppings, Newfie jokes, some suspiciously Taiwanese tartans and a whole repertoire of lift-music for goblins. These were almost anti-souvenirs, everything for which the Newfoundlanders didn't want to be remembered. Whoever had thought of the baseball caps, printed "Newfoundland Republic"? *Republic.* It was a cruel jibe: in a century of dispersal, Newfoundland had been one of the few countries to willingly vote itself part of its neighbour. Politics once bloody and fierce were now sleepily parochial.

Most people seemed to bear these taunts with their usual phlegm. Many seemed to think that being caricatured placed them way above other Canadians, whose traits were drearily amorphous. Newfoundlanders had at least got a clear image of themselves, and it didn't worry them if others thought them chirpy, elfin and cunning. These things, after all, had kept them alive through the coming and going of fish.

"Just don't call us *Newfies*," said one of the shopkeepers cheerily, "or we'll kick your feckin' arse."

151

I climbed up, above the Narrows, for the last time.

It was a perfect afternoon, the light silvery and fresh. I could hardly believe that the ice was only a few weeks off. Way below, an old schooner was taking trippers out, in the hope of one last whale. I imagined that it was on a morning like this that Curwen sailed, for his prose is light and yet lined with regret. As he passed, all the ships in the harbour dipped their flags, and there were rocket-guns, and then he was gone. Grenfell was not with him. He and Bobardt had set off for Canada, in search of funds. Bobardt's sense of vocation didn't survive this excursion. On his return, he resigned from the Mission, joined the Navy and never went back.

As he sailed away through the curtains of rock, Curwen was unsure if he'd ever return. The next year, however, events were decided for him when his mother died. There was now nothing to stop him leaving for China. He set out that autumn, and was away for the next six years. He worked first as a missionary-surgeon at the Peking Hospital, and then as acting-physician to the Imperial Customs, the British Legation and the Guard of the Marines.

Nothing in his Labrador adventures prepared him for the savagery of China. In the years leading up to the Boxer Rebellion, Peking crackled and fizzed with suspicion. No one knew if there was a war on, or how it was going (except when admirals and generals were beheaded outside the gates). There was the constant threat of Russian intrigue and Japanese invasion. Curwen wrote home of a city of spies, plotters, poisoners, executioners, a weakling emperor and a "vixen empress dowager" (she had no patience for European sympathisers amongst her eunuchs, and had them swiftly chunked and dumped). Reform, even under the guns of the legations, was spasmodic. One moment the Emperor would be ordering the forcible removal of pigtails, the next it was the pro-Europeans losing their heads. The Christians were "devils" and could expect no loyalty. Curwen discovered that his servant had poisoned his last foreign master, and prudently considered this grounds for dismissal.

Once again, his photographs tell of a peculiar life. There is a house, like an English villa but with paper windows. A tinker calls to mend the plates with rivets, and the dead lie in the streets. There are wounded soldiers in outlandish costumes (they refused to undress), and a man dying from an overdose of opium. This form of suicide was not unusual, noted Curwen, for the victim hopes his enemies will be blamed for his demise and executed. A sentence of death, however, could be bought off for around £70.

Then a handsome woman appears amongst the prints. She's a gutsy

Irish nurse and herself a veteran of China. Curwen had met Annie Pearson on the ship out, and they were married soon after landing. Annie then rushed off after the Chinese Army, to serve in the next campaign. Then she's home, and in the portraits of 1895, there's a blur between them: my grandfather, Eliot Cecil.

Curwen still made occasional comparisons with Labrador (an impenetrable language and contraptions like sledges) but conditions now were worse. That year, 67,000 died of cholera in Peking, and attacks on foreigners increased. Then there were floods and famine and more insurrection. Eventually, in 1900, the Boxers burst into the city, and the slaughter began. Now there are trenches in the photographs, and howitzers in the cathedral. A group of U.S. Marines hurries across the compound, and the Curwens' house is burnt to the ground. The family is evacuated, and sails for home.

Only an armchair survived the Curwens' fire. It's always been part of my family's life. I think I learnt to read in it, and it's where our cat had her kittens. After Peking, it had never been anywhere again. Curwen had done with travel.

152

I scrambled on, upwards onto Signal Hill. At times, the rock was so steep that I had to haul myself up on knots of hemlock and rowan. At the top was a plateau of shingle, and a peculiar purple tower. It was built for showing-off, a memorial to four hundred years of Cabot's Newfoundland. No one seemed to mind that he'd taken one look at the place, and fled.

Signal Hill has always been a place of display and performance. To begin with it was merely the criminals, swinging from gibbets. But then came semaphore and flags, and military pageants—and the purple knob. The place was like a stage-within-a-stage, a *deus ex machina* visiting ever more drama upon the city. Some of this drama still survives, and that afternoon I spotted a pipe-band marching through the straw, in their Napoleonic reds. I'd only ever been up here once before, with friends, at night. We took the road up the west side, and I was surprised to find the plateau blocked with cars, windows steamed, hands and feet pressed against the glass. Anywhere else, I'd have assumed that such love-making was simply an energetic way of enjoying the view but, here, above St. John's, it seemed like performance.

I clambered up onto the plateau. It was quiet now and I could almost feel the sun splitting the rocks. These days, not much happened here, except the pipers and rutting and the rusting of cannon. The only other person I met was a man gathering cans.

This little bald hill was never busier, it seems, than in the years after Curwen. First came an Italian, in December 1901, with a cart-load of balloons and kites. Guglielmo Marconi was used to being disbelieved; his mother's family were Irish and made Scotch, and he was hopeless at school. No one was much concerned when he set up his "electrical coherer" on the plateau. But when it captured a brace of radio-waves as they came bouncing in from Cornwall, the response was different. Thomas Edison declared it an amusing electrical hoax, but the local telegraph company were less sure. In Marconi's invention, they saw the end of wires and profit, and harried him off the island. Even his fiancée was unimpressed by his wizardry and broke off their engagement. Whatever it was Marconi had found crackling over Signal Hill, it wasn't love. After that, he was married for a while into the family of the island's old governor, O'Brien, but that too was a failure. The triumph and squalls of Newfoundland seemed to follow him everywhere, or at least until 1920. That was when he took up with a *contessa* and had the child of his dreams. Naturally, he called her Elettra.

After Marconi came the aviators, buzzing round the hill. In the Newfoundland of 1919, the idea of trying to fly across the ocean was still faintly heretical. Crowds gathered on the plateau to watch this madness. A non-stop Atlantic crossing had never been done before. Commander Morgan was the first to try, and pancaked on take-off. Captain Grieves did better, and managed 1,100 miles before toppling into the drink. That left only Alcock and Brown, and their Vickers-Vimy bomber. A team of thirty labourers cleared away a patch of mish, and then the Vimy was off, grinding over the hill. This flight which, probably more than any other, presaged the new age, was a comedy of almost "Newfie" invention. At one stage, the Vimy plummets to within a hundred feet of the ocean, and Brown is seen scrabbling over the fuselage trying to chip off the ice. But it all ends in triumph, face down in an Irish bog.

This, however, wasn't quite the end of aviation up here. Eight years later, Charles Lindbergh flew by in *The Spirit of St. Louis*. He was attempting the first solo flight across the Atlantic, from New York to Paris. For some reason, he'd added an extra loop to this journey and flown through the Narrows. This is no longer considered the most practical route.

But perhaps of all these spectacles, there was one in particular I'd have missed for nothing. It was the inauguration of the purple tower, in June 1897. Almost the entire cast of my great-grandfather's adventures had gathered up on the plateau. I can almost see them now; sealers, floaters, jowlers, hunters, poachers, Rumbolts, gunboat commanders, steamer captains, fish-boys, fishermen, fishwives and the great Fishocracy. Curwen's old friends are all there, Sir Edgar Bowring, the Railway Reids and the fighting Cashins. And there's Dr. Moses Harvey, the squid scientist. He looks frail now, with his niece beside him, in a gown of heliotrope moiré. The only person missing is Governor O'Brien (two years earlier, he'd steered Newfoundland into a financial hurricane, and had resigned with the greatest of pleasure).

To my surprise, the prayers are led by Grenfell's old enemy, Bishop Howley. It's a rare moment of calm and unity. Better still, Mademoiselle Toulinguet sings the Jubilee Hymn, her exquisite, accursed voice drifting down over the Narrows. It's too much for some, as they dab the cold from the eyes. This is a pageant of great hope and expectation. It's an invocation that will recur, ever more shrilly, time and time again in the century to come.

I scrambled down, leaving these spectres behind, like a curtain-call on the hill.

153

Before I left, I met Grenfell's biographer and we discussed the end.

Professor Rompkey was, quite unlike his subject, a man of exacting precision. He picked me up on the dot of eight, and drove very thoughtfully through the nibbled maples down to the harbour. We ate at his usual restaurant, at his usual table, in a room full of people he'd known all his life.

"Is the fish fresh?" he asked the waiter.

I had a feeling this was part of the ritual.

"Yes, sir," said the waiter. "Straight out de h'Ocean."

"*Really* fresh? Never frozen?"

Grenfell wouldn't even have cared if it was fish. How could the professor have spent so much of his precious time dabbling in a life so blunt? Weren't biographers supposed to love their subjects? Loving—or even liking—was irrelevant it seemed. The professor talked about the socio-economic climate, the political currents and the groundswell of change. These weren't concepts easy to picture, except as the sea. But, amongst it all, I could just make out Grenfell, the visionary and entrepreneur. He was now someone to be admired, and Horwood's liberals were but distant chatter. Grenfell was great again, and it didn't seem to matter that no one much liked him.

"And, of course, by the end he went a bit mad."

Rompkey had charted his way through the madness with clinical vigour. He'd found himself amongst heart-attacks and aneurisms, great clouds of depression and some violent squalls. By the early thirties, Sir Wilfred was in poor shape, the pumps gone and the logic failing. At times, the blood to his brain slowed to a trickle, but then it came rushing back in tsunamis. One moment, he might be listless and dreamy, and then he'd be everything he ever was—except more so. He was now chronically restless, unhappy in Georgia and lost in Vermont. He wrote so much that he'd become incoherent, and his speech had lost the gift of pause. Occasionally, he caught glimpses of himself as his life began to spiral. "I am become a garrulous old man," he scrawled. "It is very hard to conquer the desire to talk."

Most of his unsought advice washed harmlessly into the old foundation. The IGA was now run by doctors and suits. It no longer had a role for Grenfell, and the potterer he'd become. His chivalry and paternalism had lost their resonance as the century wore on, but he refused to resign. He was, after all, still The Founder, and his association was still the Court of Labrador. The only difference was that, without knowing it, he'd become its Polonius.

But, for those closer to home, he'd become their King Lear. Sir Wilfred was now habitually furious. He re-invented chequers, to ensure he'd win, and fought all his neighbours over boundaries and hedges. He was obsessed by his own loss of power, and found some comfort in the rise of new Germany. "Even in the New World," he wrote, "doubts are arising as to whether autocratic power may not have some advantages." It was usually his wife who bore the brunt of these outbursts. Lady Grenfell posted only a few of the letters he wrote, and edited the rest. "He was always a man of touch-and-go temperament," she told the children, "but his control now is practically nil . . ."

The effort of protecting her husband was exhausting. Then in 1938,

Lady Grenfell was diagnosed as having cancer, and was removed to Boston. Sir Wilfred was spared the diagnosis and forbidden from seeing her. He waited outside her room, sending her cartoons and notes, begging her to remember the day they'd met and their lives together. She dictated her replies: "I shall never be far from you. Love like ours can never be parted." She died on 9 December 1938, at a stroke depriving Grenfell of his best friend and his strongest ally.

Strangely, he seemed to regain his dignity in the final years. The religion that had so inflamed his early years now seemed to calm him. He offered to give everything away, denounced the Nazis and pleaded with Canada to rescue the Finns. There was also one last voyage to St. Anthony, in July 1939, to deposit Anne's ashes on Teahouse Hill. Although he arrived with the tourists, he was feted as royalty. There were tears and gunfire, and a tour of Hare Bay, where the dogs had died. Then, when it was time to go, everyone gathered on the wharf and sang *Auld Lang Syne*. The old superintendent remained on deck until Newfoundland had almost vanished, and then went below. No one saw him for the next two days. He was already muttering of "a door that had closed forever."

Sir Wilfred died the following year, after losing at croquet. It was an infuriating end for a life so rich in sport. Even in death Grenfell was unnaturally restless. He'd had funerals in New York, Boston, St. John's and St. Anthony.

"Never," said Professor Rompkey, "was a man so thoroughly buried."

Eventually, Sir Wilfred came to a halt on Teahouse Hill. I remembered his grave well, between a Union Jack and the Stars and Stripes. This, I suppose, was much as he'd lived his life, caught between countries, trapped between eras. His epitaph, on the other hand, was doggedly Grenfell. I might easily have seen it before, in my school reports.

"Life," it said, "is a Field of Honour."

154

Unsurprisingly, Curwen's last years were of a subtler complexion.

After Peking, he and Annie settled in Hove. Their life in Sussex became almost the antithesis of their travels; sedentary, bloodless and calm. There were no more icebergs or Chinese armies and eunuchs, nor were they ever mentioned again. The Curwens had moved into their crystal age, a time of refinement. They bought a house on the front and the practice grew. Curwen became a man of roots and foundations, sat on trusts and chaired committees. In his photographs, there is now a symmetry, as if life had found its pattern. Even changes in the family household are barely perceptible as the decades roll by. I can still find Tinsley the cook, and Nellie the maid and Mayhew the chauffeur as surly as ever.

Cecil, my grandfather, was the only child. He made up for his singularity by being everything to his father. He was Curwen's best friend, his partner in practice, his fellow-archaeologist, his co-author and, least of all, his junior. Together they shared a passion for the Neolithic Downs, and were up there every weekend, peeling back the turf and arousing the past. Cecil wrote his first archaeological paper at the age of seventeen, and became an authority on prehistoric farming. Between them, he and his father steered Ancient Sussex into the limelight, together writing dozens of papers and books. Even now, it's impossible to get through a south-coast bookshop without stumbling over their work.

After their Boxer experience, the Curwens had hoped they'd seen the last of war. But the new century would disappoint them. My great-grandfather was too old for the Great War but Cecil found himself before a tribunal, pleading Nonconformity, and earning his feathers. The Second World War was not so easily resisted. This time, the Downs were ploughed up into ranges, and the town was bombed and then overrun by foreign troops, ironically Canadians. Whether they liked it or not, the Curwens were back in the fight. The surgery was fortified, Mayhew joined up and Cecil signed on as a fire-watcher. But the worst was yet to come. In the spring of 1943, Nazi planes swooped onto Hove, and spattered it with cannon-fire. In this pointless raid, my mother, aged ten, was hit in the thumb by a sliver of classroom. She's probably the only one of my forebears ever to have been wounded in battle.

The war saw the end of the Curwens' good fortune. Annie never even got to see peace restored; she died as the last vapours of the Battle of Britain were drifting away. Nor would the practice survive. Mayhew had gone, Tinsley had died and Nellie's nerves were shot. It was the end too for Dr. Curwen Senior. On 17 June 1949, he wrote a valedictory to Cecil, a letter as informal as ever he got:

> I thank God from the bottom of my heart for your love and patience all these 54 years. You have given your mother and I nothing but pleasure and comfort, and I thank you for your companionship and co-operation in later years ... I have enjoyed a long, abundant and satisfying life, surrounded by the love of dear ones and friends ...

He died nine months later, at the age of eighty-four.

155

At the start of these travels, I'd often wondered if I'd turn out to be Curwen.

This wasn't an unwelcome thought. I'd had a happy vision of us wandering around together, wading through bogs and gathering curios. But now, as I sit here, surrounded by a hillock of diaries and pictures, I realise that I'm not Curwen, nor would he wish to be me. Perhaps it's simply that there's too much history between us, and that we're products more of our time than our genes. Or perhaps, it's just that, in the genetic currents that lie between us, there are too many confluences, too much of others. As much as I feel his influence, I also feel that of the Gimlettes: a ready temper, a tendency to scepticism and a love of travels without necessarily purpose or vocation. Curwen would have seen such traits as wasteful.

I hope too that there's something of the Annie Pearson about me. She was always less inhibited than her husband, more given to frivolity, and often tempted by instinct. Although she loved Curwen deeply, she sometimes had to remind him of the world about them. In 1917, she sent him a letter, which he'd preserved as if sacred. "The ripples on the surface," she wrote, "which to you seem disorderly, are in reality but signs of life—life urgent and restless."

That's it, I suppose, a respect for disorder. Curwen had travelled in the hope of change. He'd wanted to cure Labrador and to soothe Peking. Although he was under no illusions as to the scale of his task, the unfinished work overwhelmed him. He became, in a sense, preoccupied with what these places weren't, rather than what they were. My own travels were different, happily aimless. It was the unruly Newfoundland that I'd admired most, with its smashed coasts and crackery people. It was here, as Annie would say, that life was at its most urgent and restless.

156

I spent my last day in a state of half-departure, my room half-cleared, my bags half-packed. Part of me wanted to be home, most of me wanted to stay. I had, I suppose, contracted a mild case of the Johnsman's disease, or chronic ambivalence.

Jim took me on a long walk to Quidi Vidi, a village squeezed in a crack. I shan't easily forget that morning, the sea ablaze with blues, and the hillside fizzing with eyebright and rattle. Jim talked brilliantly and endlessly, as if he had only a few hours left to tell all the best stories in the world. I listened, and tripped and slithered along behind him. It didn't seem to matter that there was so much I didn't understand. St. John's is a city of private jokes. An enormous new billboard on the edge of town seemed to express this precisely: "BLACK HORSE," it said, "IS A NEWFOUNDLAND THING."

Back at the house, we found that Angie had cooked pork for sixteen, which the three of us ate. "I wanted to give you a good shipwreck," she said, "to see you home."

Just more Black Horse, I suppose.

Replete with pig, I wandered downtown to see Bernardette, my journalist friend. She was at her office, submerged in words and styrofoam cups. We discussed the news.

"Someone's pinched all the drain-covers on Mount Pearl."

I had a sudden vision of Johnsmen disappearing down holes, stories half-told.

"And they're closin' another outport," said Bernardette.

Great Harbour Deep would cease to exist before the next winter.

"On 31 October, they'll just turn out the lights."

"It sounds as if there are tough years ahead?" I ventured.

Bernardette shook her head. "No, boy, we got our *Newfie Tea*."

I'd often heard people dreaming of their off-shore oil.

"So Newfoundland's about to boom?"

Bernardette winced. "No one's buyin' their stetsons just yet."

. . .

There was one more farewell, a call to Dr. Gracie Sparkes.

"What will you call your book?" she asked.

I told her, and there were murmurs of interest.

"Sure," she said, "there's been plenty of drama."

"But has it been a tragedy or a comedy?"

At the other end of the line, I could hear her tutting.

"Now that's the sort of question we've been fighting over for years."

Afterword

The tiny outport of PETITES was re-settled in 2003, and has now been abandoned.

Dr. GRACE SPARKES died in spring 2003.

I finally caught up with CURWEN'S ESQUIMAUX ARTIFACTS at the British Museum. They are exactly as he described.

The scandal of MOUNT CASHEL remains unresolved. Many victims have yet to be compensated by the Christian Brothers.

The controversy over the SEAL HUNT also continues. The government now authorises the harvesting of some 975,000 head a year. Animal rights groups say that around 40 per cent of the seals are still alive when they're skinned. The seal-hunters meanwhile deride the involvement of celebrities, like Paris Hilton, accusing them of using the issue to publicise themselves.

JIM BAIRD got his European tour. After travelling through Spain, Morocco and France, he returned to Newfoundland ready to face another winter.

As predicted, the new Innu settlement at SANGO BAY is already floundering. "Natuashish" is still not finished, completion having been delayed by vandalism, and many accuse its Chief of encouraging drug and alcohol abuse. He denies the allegations but admits to "heavy drinking" on the Innu council.

Too late for the Innu perhaps, peace comes to GOOSE BAY. As the imaginary war draws to a close, the town faces an uncertain future. By the end of 2005, both the Dutch and the Luftwaffe will have flown home.

It's the end too for PREMIER GRIMES. He was brought down in October 2003, ending thirteen years of Liberal rule. The Tories inherit a province "drowning in debt" and all public sector pay is frozen.

The FISH meanwhile show no sign of recovering.

Further Reading

Folklore and Idiom

Devine, P. K. *Devine's Folklore of Newfoundland.* St. John's: Robinson, 1937.
Story, Kirwin, and Widdowson. *The Dictionary of Newfoundland English.* 2nd ed. Toronto, 1990.

Labrador's History

Boileau, Lambert de. *Recollections of Labrador Life.* London: Saunders Otley and Co., 1861.
Gosling, W. G. *Labrador, Its Discovery, Exploration and Development.* London: Alston Rivers, 1910.
Poole, George. *A Lifetime Listening to the Waves.* St. John's: Cuff, 1987.
Whiteley, George. *Northern Seas, Hardy Sailors.* New York: W. W. Norton, 1982.

Newfoundland's History

Andrieux, J. P. *St. Pierre and Miquelon.* Ottawa: OTC Press, 1986.
Cell, Gillian. *Newfoundland Discovered, English Attempts at Colonisation 1610–1630.* Hakluyt Society, 1982.
Chadwick, St. John. *Newfoundland: Island into Province.* Cambridge University Press, 1967.
Crosbie, John. *No Holds Barred.* Toronto: McClelland & Stewart, 1997.
Harvey, Rev. Moses. *Newfoundland As It Is in 1894: A Handbook and Tourist's Guide.* St. John's: Queen's Printer, 1894.
Horwood, Harold. *Newfoundland.* Toronto: Macmillan, 1969.
Macfarlane, David. *Come from Away.* Abacus, 1992.
Major, Kevin. *As Near to Heaven by the Sea.* Toronto: Viking, 2001.
Morton, H. V. *Atlantic Meeting.* London: Methuen, 1943.
Perlin, A. B. *The Story of Newfoundland.* St. John's, 1959.
Peyton, Amy. *Nightingale of the North.* St. John's: Jesperson, 1983.
Prowse, D. W. *A History of Newfoundland from the English, Colonial and Foreign Records.* London: Macmillan, 1895.

Smallwood, J. R. *The Encyclopaedia of Newfoundland and Labrador.* St. John's, 1981.

———. *I Chose Canada.* Toronto: Macmillan, 1973.

Stacey, Jean. *Government House.* St. John's: Queen's Printer, n.d.

Tarrant, D. R. *Marconi's Miracle.* St. John's: Flanker Press, 2001.

Tuck, Dr. James. *Newfoundland and Labrador Pre-history.* National Museum of Man, 1976.

Wilson, Beckles. *The Tenth Island: Being Some Account of Newfoundland, Its People, Its Politics, Its Problems, and Its Peculiarities.* London: Grant Richards, 1897.

Outport Life

Momatiuk and Eastcott. *This Marvellous Terrible Place.* Ontario: Camden House, 1988.

Mowat, Farley. *This Rock Within the Sea.* Toronto: McClelland & Stewart, 1968.

———. *A Whale for the Killing.* Toronto: McClelland & Stewart, 1972.

Patey, Francis. *The Jolly Poker.* St. John's: Cuff, 1992.

Poole, Cyril. *In Search of the Newfoundland Soul.* St. John's: Cuff, 1982.

Literature

Innes, Hammond. *The Land God Gave to Cain.* Fontana, 1961.

Johnston, Wayne. *The Colony of Unrequited Dreams.* Ontario: Vintage, 1998.

Proulx, E. Annie. *The Shipping News.* London: Fourth Estate, 1993.

The Vikings

Ericson, Leif. *The Vinland Sagas.* Trans. Magnus Magnusson and Hermann Palsson. London: Penguin, 1965.

Ingstad, Helge. *Westward to Vinland.* London: Jonathan Cape, 1969.

Swanton, John. *The Wineland Voyages.* Washington: Smithsonian, 1937.

Munn, W. A. *The Wineland Voyages.* St. John's: The Labour Group, 1930.

Discovery

Banks, Joseph. *The Journal of Joseph Banks.* Sydney, 1962.

Beaglehole, J. C. *The Life of Captain James Cook.* Stanford University Press, 1974.

Cook, Captain James. *Voyages Round the World.* Edinburgh: Nimmo, Hay and Mitchell, n.d.

Milton, Giles. *Big Chief Elizabeth.* Sceptre, 2000.

Quinn, D. B., and N. M. Cheshire. *The Newfoundland of Stephen Parmenius.* University of Toronto Press, 1972.

Anglo-French Wars

Baudoin, L'Abbé Jean. *The Winter War of 1696-7.* Trans. by H. Bedford-Jones.

Wilfred Grenfell

Duncan, Norman. *A Great Lottery of Hope and Fortune, Dr. Grenfell's Parish.* New York, 1905.

Grenfell, W. T. *The Romance of Labrador.* New York: Macmillan, 1934.

FURTHER READING

————. *Tales of the Labrador*. Nisbet, 1916.

————. *Vikings of Today, or, Life and Work Among the Fishermen of Labrador*. London: Marshall Bros, 1895.

Hall, Captain Charles F. *Life with the Labrador Doctor*. Hodder and Stoughton, 1920.

Kerr, J. Lennox. *Wilfred Grenfell, His Life and Work*. New York: Dodd Mead, 1959.

Pilgrim, Earl. *The Captain and the Girl*. St. John's: Flanker, 2001.

————. *The Price Paid for Charley*. Roddickton: Troius, 1989.

Rompkey, Ronald. *Grenfell of Labrador: A Biography*. Toronto: University of Toronto Press, 1991.

————. *Labrador Odyssey: The Journal and Photographs of Eliot Curwen on the Second Voyage of Wilfred Grenfell, 1893*. McGill-Queen's University Press, 1996.

Exploration, Shipping and Adventure

Audubon, John James. *Birds of America*.

Barbour, Job. *Forty-Eight Days Adrift*. Breakwater, 1932.

Barrow, John. *A Chronological History of Voyages into the Arctic Regions*. London: John Murray, 1818.

Brown, Cassie. *The Caribou Disaster*. St. John's: Flanker, 1996.

Buchan, David. *Narrative of Lieut. Buchan's Journey up the Exploits River in Search of the Red Indians*. PRO London, CO 194/50, f.153–88.

Cartwright, Captain George. *Transactions and Events During a Residence of Nearly Sixteen Years on the Labrador*. Newark, England, Allin & Ridge, 1792.

Cartwright, Major John. *Life and Correspondence of Major John Cartwright*. 1826.

Graham, R. D. *Rough Passage*. London: William Blackwood, 1936.

Horwood, Harold. *Bartlett the Great Explorer*. Toronto: Doubleday, 1987.

Hubbard, Mina. *A Woman's Way Through Unknown Labrador*. New York: McClure, 1908.

Jukes, J. B. *Excursions In and About Newfoundland*. London: John Murray, 1842; repr. Canadiana House, 1969.

Kean, Abram. *Old and Young Ahead*. St. John's: Flanker, 2000.

Low, A. P. *Report on Explorations in the Labrador Peninsula along the East Main, Koksoak, Hamilton, Menicuagan and Portions of Other Rivers in 1892–93–94–95*. Ottawa: Queen's Printer, 1896.

Millman, Lawrence. *Last Places*. Abacus, 1992.

Packard, Alpheus Spring. *The Labrador Coast: A Journal of Two Summer Cruises to That Region*. London: Kegan, Paul Trench and Trübner, 1891.

Peary, Robert. *Northwards over the Great Ice: A Narrative of Life and Work along the Shores and upon the Interior Ice-cap of Northern Greenland in the Years 1886 and 1891–1897*. London: Methuen, 1898.

Wallace, Dillon. *The Lure of the Labrador Wild*. New York: Revell, 1905.

Aboriginal People

Cartwright, John. *Remarks on the Situation of the Red Indians, Natives of Newfoundland*. Resource Library, St. Johns.

Further Reading

Forbush, William. *Pomiuk, A Prince of Labrador.* London: Marshall Brothers, 1903.

Hall, Captain Charles Francis. *Life with the Esquimaux; a narrative of Arctic Experience in search of survivors of Sir John Franklin's Expedition.* Franklin, Low, Son and Marston, 1864.

Henrikson, Georg. *Hunters in the Barrens.* St. John's: ISER, 1997.

Howley, James. *The Beothuks or Red Indians.* Cambridge University Press, 1915.

Marshall, Ingeborg. *The Beothuk.* Newfoundland Historical Society, 2001.

Nansen, Fridtjof. *Eskimo Life.* London: Longmans, Green, 1893.

Rink, Hinrich. *Tales and Traditions of the Eskimo.* New York: Dover, 1997.

Turner, Geoffrey. *Indians of North America.* Sterling, 1992.

Wadden, Marie. *Nitassinan, The Innu Struggle to Reclaim Their Homeland.* Vancouver: Douglas & MacIntyre, 1991.

Wilson, William. *An Account of the Capture of Shanawdithit, Newfoundland and its Missionaries.* Cambridge, 1866.

Tuberculosis and Industrial Disease

Cuff, Harry. *Take a Deep Breath.* St. John's: Cuff, 2002.

Grygier, Pat. *A Long Way from Home.* St. John's: McGill-Queen's UP, 1994.

Leyton, Elliot. *Dying Hard; The Ravages of Industrial Carnage.* Toronto: OUP, 1997.

The Mount Cashel Scandal

Harris, Michael. *The Unholy Orders.* Ontario: Penguin, 1990.

Flora and Fauna

Radclyffe Dugmore, A. A. *The Romance of the Newfoundland Caribou.* London: William Heinemann, 1913.

Russell, Franklin. *The Island of Auks, The Secret Islands.* New York, 1965.

Fishing and Hunting

Candow, James. *Of Men and Seals.* Ottawa: Ministry of Supply, 1981.

Hopwood, Francis J. S. *Newfoundland Fisheries and Fishermen.* London: Mission to Deep Sea Fishermen, 1891.

Kurlansky, Mark. *Cod.* Vintage, 1999.

Mowat, Farley. *Sea of Slaughter.* Boston: Atlantic Monthly Press, 1985.